The Reality of Aid 1997/8

An Independent Review of Development Cooperation

EUROSTEP ICVA (An International Working Group of ICVA Members for the Reality of Aid Project)
Edited by Judith Randel and Tony German, Development Initiatives

EARTHSCAN

First published in 1997 by
Earthscan Publications Limited

Copyright © Reality of Aid Management Group (ICVA, An International Working Group of ICVA Members for the Reality of Aid Project and EUROSTEP) 1997

All rights reserved

Citation: Reality of Aid
Eurostep and ICVA
Eds: Randel, J and German, T

A catalogue record for this book is available from the British Library

ISBN: 1 85383 479 3

Design by Paul Sands Design
Additional design, typesetting and figures by Oxford Publishing Services, Oxford
Cover design by Andrew Corbett
Cover photo by members of the Ndikiri Kunda women's group,
Bansang, the Gambia. © Liba Taylor/ACTIONAID
Printed and bound in Great Britain by Biddles Ltd, Guildford and King's Lynn

For a full list of publications please contact:

Earthscan Publications Ltd
120 Pentonville Road
London N1 9JN
Tel: 0171 2780433
Fax: 0171 2781142
Email: earthinfo@earthscan.co.uk

Earthscan Publications Limited is an editorially independent subsidiary of Kogan Page Limited and publishes in association with WWF-UK and the International Institute for Environment and Development.

Contents

List of boxes and tables	v
The Reality of Aid Project	vii
Acknowledgements	viii
ICVA and Eurostep member organisations	ix
Participating agencies	x

Part I Current Issues and Key Themes

Introduction	3
Development cooperation in a changing world	4

Part II OECD country profiles

Australia	21
Austria*	29
Belgium*	35
Canada	42
Denmark*	49
Finland*	56
France*	62
Germany*	68
Ireland*	77
Italy*	84
Japan	92
Netherlands*	98
New Zealand	105
Norway	113
Portugal*	119
Spain*	124
Sweden*	131
Switzerland	137
United Kingdom*	144
United States	153
European Union	160
The EU and Africa	179

* EU Member States

Contents

Part III Perspectives from the South

International cooperation in Argentina	193
Western assistance to post-communist countries in Central and Eastern Europe	197
A comment on NGOs, ownership and participation in Ghana	205
Guatemala	208
Haiti	212
Breaking new ground in donor coordination in India	217
International cooperation with Latin America	222
Internal management in relation to Uganda's external debt	225
Gender equity in education in Zimbabwe	232

Part IV Aid Trends, Facts and Figures

World aid at a glance	243
World aid in 1995 and 1996	244
Trends in aid and development cooperation	247
The outlook for aid	258
Leadership on public and political opinion	261
Spending on public information and development education	266
Measuring and mainstreaming aid for poverty eradication	267
Approaches to gender in development cooperation	278
Humanitarian relief, conflict and emergencies	286
Trends in ODA through NGOs	293
Political responsibility and management of development cooperation	297
Glossary	303
Exchange rates	305
Notes on data	306

Boxes and tables

Boxes
1. Summary of main messages — 5
2. The real extent of poverty — 6
3. The growing role of Northern citizens in development cooperation — 7
4. Removing barriers to self-empowerment — 10
5. Gender, participation, access, and representation — 11
6. One clear objective: Review of Australia's overseas aid programme — 24
7. Australia's 1997/8 overseas aid budget at a glance — 25
8. Examples of effective Australian aid — 27
9. Effective aid from Denmark to Nepal Nari Bikash Sangh: MS-Nepal in partnership with a Nepali women's organisation — 55
10. Examples of effective poverty reduction aid from Italy — 90
11. Decentralised cooperation in Italy — 91
12. What New Zealand's ODA is used for . . . — 109
13. What Swiss ODA is used for . . . — 143
14. Does UK give enough? — 144
15. Tied aid (UK) — 145
16. Clare Short on globalisation — 149
17. Conclusions of the Court of Auditors' Evaluation of the Med Programme — 167
18. Evaluation of ECHO by the European Court of Auditors — 169
19. Reconciling data on CEE and NIS — 198
20. Analogies with the Marshall Plan — 198
21. Assistance to Bulgaria — 199
22. Belarus — 200
23. Bosnia and Hercegovina reconstruction plan — 201
24. Soros's funding — 203
25. The eradication of the creole pig: aid – in whose interests? — 214
26. Debt swaps — 223

Tables
1. Growth rates and aid levels in selected countries — 26
2. Chosen sectors where country-strategies are completed — 53
3. Regional distribution of German ODA 1996 and 1997 — 73
4. Bilateral technical and financial assistance (TZ and FZ) to basic education and health — 73
5. Sector priorities, 1987 and 1995 compared — 84
6. Italy's ODA allocations — 85
7. Percentage distribution of bilateral and multilateral ODA for 1994–7 — 125
8. Three scenarios for the UK — 150
9. Timetable to renegotiate EU–ACP relations — 161
10. Lomé preferences versus the Generalised System of Preferences — 163
11. Financial perspectives until 1999 of external action (EC budget) and estimates of appropriations for the European Development Fund — 165
12. General budget: expenditure under the title of external actions — 167
13. EU Member State aid agencies and European Commission Staff 1991–4 — 168
14. Origin of funding in Member States — 171
15. EDF budget underutilisation — 172
16. Policy and trends on multilateral allocations — 173
17. Council Resolutions applying to the EC and Member States — 174
18. Policy to implement Council resolutions — 176

Boxes and Tables

19. Priorities and sources of international technical cooperation	193–4
20. Official net disbursements to the CEE countries and more advanced NIS	200
21. Official net development aid disbursements to CEE and more advanced NIS as percentage of GNP	202
22. Priorities for major donors	213
23. Total donor assistance to Haiti 1995–7, by sector	214
24. Debt service and interest payments	227
25. Loan balances by economic sector as at 30 June 1995	229
26. Completion rates: Grade 1 to Form VI, 1992	233
27. Inventory of donor funded projects with the Ministry of Higher Education	237
28. Real terms changes in ODA 1995 and 1996	248
29. Bilateral ODA commitments by sector, 1995	250
30. Official aid spending on public information and development education per head of population	253
31. The outlook for aid	258
32. Leadership on public and political opinion	261
33. Spending on public information and development education in US$ millions	266
34. Current measures of aid for basic needs or direct poverty reduction as a percentage of total ODA	267
35. At a glance on mainstreaming attention to poverty reduction	273
36. Approaches to gender in development cooperation	278
37. Humanitarian relief, conflict and emergencies	286
38. Trends in ODA through NGOs	293
39. The political responsibility for OECD aid	297

The Reality of Aid project

The Reality of Aid is a collaborative, not-for-profit project of EUROSTEP and ICVA (the International Working Group of ICVA Members for the Reality of Aid Project). It aims to improve the quality of development cooperation and increase the quantity of development assistance in the interests of eradicating poverty.

Its objectives are:

- to produce reliable and well informed reports on the development cooperation performance of OECD DAC donors. This is based on reports written from the perspective of NGOs based in donor countries as well as perspectives on OECD development cooperation from recipient country NGOs;
- to increase knowledge and scrutiny of development cooperation; and
- to influence policy makers at national and international level to gear their policy and practice to reducing world poverty.

EUROSTEP

Established in 1990, European Solidarity Towards Equal Participation of People (Eurostep), is an international association of European non-governmental organisations working for justice and equal opportunities for people North and South. Eurostep seeks to improve the development cooperation policies and practices of the European Union and its Member States. It draws on the experiences of its members and its partners in the South in establishing its positions and messages and provides coordination in the approaches of its member organisations on policy at the European level.

EUROSTEP
115 rue Stevin
1000 Brussels
Belgium
Tel + 322 231 1659
Fax + 322 230 3780
e-mail: eurostep@agoranet.be

ICVA

Established in 1962, the International Council of Voluntary Agencies (ICVA) has been an independent, international association of non-governmental and not-for-profit organisations active in humanitarian assistance and sustainable development.

ICVA has provided a means for voluntary agency consultation and cooperation and has undertaken advocacy work on issues of common concern to its members. Without the collaboration and pivotal efforts of the ICVA Secretariat and its members since its inception, the Reality of Aid Project and the 1997/8 Reality of Aid Report would not have been possible. At the time of writing the 1997/8 Reality of Aid, ICVA's organisational structure and status were undergoing a fundamental review by its membership. An International Working Group of ICVA members will continue to collaborate with the Reality of Aid Project. These members of ICVA are identified in the full list of ICVA agencies overleaf.

ICVA Agencies International Working Group
c/o Canadian Council for International Cooperation
I Nicholas Street
Suite 300
Ottawa
Ontario K1N 7B7
Canada
Tel + 1 613 241 7007
Fax + 1 613 241 5302
e-mail: ccicdpu1@web.net

ACTIONAID

In 1997 ACTIONAID was the lead agency for ICVA and EUROSTEP on The Reality of Aid Project. ACTIONAID is an international development agency which works with some of the poorest communities to overcome poverty and secure lasting improvements in the quality of their lives. ACTIONAID's programmes reach over 3 million people in 20 countries in Africa, Asia and Latin America.

ACTIONAID
Hamlyn House
MacDonald Road
London N19 5PG
Tel + 44 171 281 4101
Fax + 44 171 263 7599

Acknowledgements

The Reality of Aid Management Group would like to acknowledge the support and guidance they have received from the breadth of the NGO community and from many thinkers and actors on development cooperation.

In particular, the management group would like to acknowledge the Chair of the Development Assistance Committee, Ambassador James Michel, for his openness and willingness to engage in serious dialogue on the issues around action for global poverty eradication. The support of the OECD Development Centre in hosting and facilitating this dialogue has been invaluable.

The Reality of Aid is funded by grants from the Ford Foundation, the Humanitarian Group for Social Development (Lebanon), UNDP and each of the participating agencies. Without their efforts and resources the report would not be possible.

Reality of Aid is an NGO publication, drawing on modest resources but every effort is made to ensure that the information used is accurate and that interpretation is fair. The views expressed are those of the individual chapter authors and do not necessarily reflect the views of EUROSTEP, ICVA, ACTIONAID, Development Initiatives, the Humanitarian Group for Social Development (Lebanon), UNDP or the Ford Foundation.

The Reality of Aid Management Committee would like to thank Judith Randel and Tony German of Development Initiatives and Nicola Crawhall, Project Manager for the Reality of Aid.

Editors' acknowledgements

Reality of Aid national chapters, trends chapter and comparative charts are edited by Development Initiatives, an independent research and information organisation specialising in aid and development cooperation policy and NGO/government relations.

The editors are very grateful indeed for the advice and guidance they have received from all those involved in the project: the participating authors and NGOs, academics and aid agency officials in many countries. Their willingness to help with information and interpretation is very much appreciated as is their interest in improving the quality and quantity of development cooperation. In particular, we would like to thank the staff of the OECD Development Cooperation Directorate and the OECD Development Centre in Paris. Since the start of Reality of Aid in 1993, they have been unfailingly helpful in providing information and assisting our understanding of the process of aid and development cooperation.

ICVA and Eurostep member organisations

Eurostep

Belgium NCOS, CNCD; *Denmark* Mellemfolkeligt Samvirke, IBIS; *Finland* KEPA; *France* Frères des Hommes; *Germany* Deutsche Welthungerhilfe, terre des hommes BRD; *Greece* Helinas; *Ireland* Concern; *Italy* Manitese '76, Movimondo; *The Netherlands* HIVOS, NOVIB; *Norway* Norwegian People's Aid; *Portugal* OIKOS; *Spain* Intermón; *Sweden* Radda Barnen, Forum Syd; *Switzerland* Swiss Coalition of Development Organisations; *United Kingdom* ActionAid, Oxfam UK-I

ICVA

Adventist Development and Relief Agency International, Afghan NGOs Coordination Bureau, Africa Humanitarian Action, African Association for Literacy and Adult Education, African Development Programme, All Africa Conference of Churches, American Joint Distribution Committee, Anatolian Development Foundation, Arnel Association, Asian Institute for Rural Development, *Asian NGO Coalition for Agrarian Reform and Rural Development, *Asociación Latinoamericana de Organizaciones de Promoción, Asociación Latinoamericana para los Derechos Humanos, Asociación Nacional de Centros de Investigación, Promoción Social y Desarrollo, Asociación Regional para las Migraciones Forzadas, Association beninoise de lutte contre la faim et la misère du peuple, Association of Development Agencies in Bangladesh, Association for Sarva Seva Farms, Association for Social Advancement, Association of Voluntary Agencies for Rural Development, Austcare, *Australian Council for Overseas Aid, Bina Swadaya, British Refugee Council, *Canadian Council for International Cooperation, Canadian Council for Refugees, Care International, *Centre de Recherche et d'information pour le Développement, Centro Dominicano de Organizaciones de Internes Social, Chinese Refugees Relief Association, Christian Children's Fund Inc, Christian Relief and Development Association, Church World Service, Conseil des Organisations non-gouvermentales d'appui au Développement, Consejo de Educacionde Adultos de America Latina, Consejo de Instituciones de Desarrollo, Convergencia des Organismos Civiles por la Democracia, Coordinación de ONG y Cooperativas para el Acompanamiento de la Población Damificada por el Conflicto Armado Interno, Danish Refugee Council, Diakonia, Emo-Baraka–Union pour la Promotion du Paysan, Encuentro de Entidades no Gubernamentales para el Desarrollo, Episcopal Church Center of the USA, Euronaid, Federación de Organismos no Gubermentales de Nicaragua, Feed the Children International, Forum of African Voluntary Development Organisations, Freedom from Debt Coalition, Fundación Augustino Cesar Sandino, General Union of Voluntary Societies, Gonoshahaijo Sangstha, Hebrew Immigrant Aid Society, Human Appeal International, Indian Institute of Youth and Development, Individuell Maniskohjalp, Institute of Cultural Affairs International, *Interaction, Interaid International, International Islamic Relief Organisation, International Rescue Committee, International Save the Children Alliance, International Social Service, Islamic Relief Agency, *Japanese NGO Center for International Cooperation, Jesuit Refugee Service, Lebanese NGO Forum, LINK NGO Forum, Lutheran Immigration and Refugee Service, Lutheran World Federation, Mauritius Council of Social Service, Médecins du Monde, National NGO Council of Sri Lanka, Non Governmental Organisation Coordinating Committee, Norwegian Refugee Council, NOVIB, Ockenden Venture, OISCA International, OXFAM-UK-I, PACS/PRIES/Instituto Politicas Alternatives para o Cone Sul, Philippine Development NGOs for International Concerns, Queen Alia Fund for Social Development, Radda Barnen, Refugee Studies Programme, Réseau africain pour le Développement integré, Rural Development Foundation of Pakistan, Sarvodaya, Secours populaire français, Servicio, Desarollo y Paz, Solidarios: Council of American Development Foundations, The Association of Non-Governmental Organisations, Voluntary Health Association of India, World Alliance of Young Men's Christian Associations, World Council of Churches, World Ort Union, World University Service, World Vision International, Yayasan Indonesia Sejahtera.

Permanent observers

Caritas Internationalis, International Committee of the Red Cross, International Federation of Red Cross and Red Crescent Societies, Médecins sans Frontières.

* Members of the International Working Group of ICVA Members for the Reality of Aid Project.

Participating agencies

ARGENTINA
Asociación Para el Desarrollo Social
Diagonal 79 No. 1042
1900 La Plata
Provinçia de Buenos Aires
Tel + 54 21 243 927 Fax + 54 21 890 345
e-mail: plorente@isis.unlp.edu.ar

AUSTRALIA
Australian Council for Overseas Aid (ACFOA)
Private Bag 3
Deakin Act 2600
Tel + 61 6 285 1816 Fax + 61 6 285 1720
e-mail: acfoa@peg.apc.org

AUSTRIA
Arbeitsgemeinschaft Entwicklungszusammenarbeit (AGEZ) and Österreichische Forschungsstiftung für Entwicklungshilfe (ÖFSE)
Bergasse 7
A -1090 Wien
AGEZ Tel and Fax + 43 1 317 4016
e-mail: agez@magnet.at
ÖFSE Tel + 43 1 317 4010 Fax + 43 1 317 4015
e-mail: oefse@magnet.at

BELGIUM
Nationaal Centrum voor Ontwikkelingssamenwerking (NCOS)
Vlasfabriekstraat 11
B-1060 Brussels
Tel + 322 539 2620 Fax + 322 539 1343
e-mail: mschellens@ncos.ngonet.be

CANADA
Canadian Council for International Cooperation/Conseil canadien pour la cooperation internationale (CCIC)
1 Nicholas Street, Suite 300
Ottawa, Ontario K1N 7B7
Tel + 1 613 241 7007 Fax + 1 613 241 5302
e-mail:ccicdpu1@web.apc.org

DENMARK
Mellemfolkeligt Samvirke
Borgergade 10-14
DK-1300 Copenhagen K
Tel + 45 3332 6244 Fax + 45 3315 6243

FINLAND
Kehitysyhteistyön Palvelukeskus ry, Servicecentrum för Biståndssamarbete (KePa)
Eerikinkatu 11 C
FIN-00100 Helsinki
Tel + 358 9 584 233 Fax + 358 9 584 23 200

FRANCE
Centre de Recherche et d'Information pour le Développement (CRID)
14, passage Dubail
75010 Paris
Tel + 331 4472 0771 Fax + 331 4472 0684
e-mail: crid@globenet.gn.apc.org

GERMANY
Deutsche Welthungerhilfe
Adenauerallee 134
D-53133 Bonn
Tel + 49 228 22 88 0 Fax + 49 228 22 07 10
e-mail: 100335.1346@compuserve.com

and

terre des hommes BRD
Ruppenkampstrasse 11a
D-49084 Osnabruck
Tel +49 541 71 01 0 Fax +49 541 70 72 33

GHANA
African Development Programme
PO Box 3424, Accra
Tel and Fax + 233 21 662035

GUATEMALA
Asociación Latinoamericana de Organizaciones de Promoción (ALOP)
San José
Costa Rica
Tel + 506 283 2122 Fax + 506 283 5898

HAITI
Groupe de Recherche et d'Action pour le Développement du Far West (GRAF)
PO Box 1571, Port-au-Prince
Tel + 509 455 636 Fax + 509 224 129

and

ACTIONAID Haiti
Av. Jean Paul II et Faustin I, No. 165
Port-au-Prince
Tel and Fax + 509 455 664
e-mail: brigitte@acn2.net

INDIA
ACTIONAID India
D3, Blessington Apartments
34 Serpentine Street
Richmond Town
Bangalore 560 025
Tel + 91 80 224 0399 Fax + 91 80 558 6284
e-mail: pol.unit@actionaid.sprintrpg.sprint.com

The **Reality** of Aid 1997/8

Participating agencies

IRELAND
Concern Worldwide
52–55 Lower Camden Street
Dublin 3
Tel + 353 1 4754162 Fax + 353 1 4757362
e-mail: sheila.hoare@Concern.ie

ITALY
Movimondo
Piazza Albania 10
1-00153 Rome
Tel + 39 6 573 00 33 0 Fax + 39 6 574 48 69
e-mail: molisv.movimondo@star.flashnet.it

JAPAN
Japanese NGO Center for International Cooperation (JANIC)
5F, Saito Bldg
2-9-1 Kanda Nishiki-cho
Chiyoda-ku
Tokyo 101
Tel + 81 3 3294 5370 Fax + 81 3 3294 5398

LUXEMBOURG
Action Solidarité Tiers Monde (ASTM)
39, rue due Fort Neipperg
L-2230 Luxembourg
Tel + 352 400427 Fax + 352 405849

MEKONG
NGO Forum on Cambodia
PO Box 2295
Phnom Penh
Tel + 855 23 360199 Fax + 855 23 723242
e-mail: ngoforum@pactok.peg.apc.org

NETHERLANDS
Netherlands Organisation for International Development Cooperation (NOVIB)
PO Box 30919
2500 GX The Hague
visiting address: Mauritskade 9
Tel + 31 70 342 1621 Fax:+ 31 70 361 4461
e-mail: admin@novib.nl

NEW ZEALAND
Council for International Development/Kaunihera mō te Whakapakari Ao Whānui (CID)
PO Box 12-470
Wellington
Tel + 64 4 472 6375 Fax + 64 4 472 6374
e-mail: pat@nzcid.wgtn.planet.org.nz

NORWAY
Norwegian Peoples Aid
PO Box 8844
N-0028 Oslo 1
Tel + 47 22 03 77 00 Fax + 47 22 20 08 70

PERU
Centro Peruano de Estudios Sociales (CEPES)
Av. Salaverry 818 Jesus Maria
Lima 11
Tel + 51 14 336610 Fax + 51 44 331744
e-mail: cepes@cepes.pe

POLAND
Policy Education Centre on Assistance to Transition (PECAT)
ul. Topiel 20/1
Warsaw
Tel + 48 22 826 5804 Fax + 48 22 828 4288

PORTUGAL
OIKOS Cooperação e Desenvolvimento
Rua de Santiago 9
1100 Lisbon
Tel + 351 1 886 6134 Fax + 351 1 887 8837
e-mail: oikos.sec@oikas.pt

SPAIN
INTERMÓN
Alberto Aguilera 15
28015 Madrid
Tel + 34 1 5480458 Fax + 34 1 5591667
e-mail: intermon@intermon.org

SWEDEN
Forum Syd
Box 17510
S-118 91 Stockholm
Tel + 46 8 702 7700 Fax + 46 8 702 9099
e-mail: Forum_Syd@forumsyd.se

SWITZERLAND
Swiss Coalition of Development Organisations
Monbijoustrasse 31
PO Box 6735
CH-3001 Bern
Tel + 41 31 381 1711
Fax:+ 41 31 381 1718
e-mail:scoalition@igc.apc.org

Participating agencies

UGANDA
Uganda Debt Network
c/o PO Box 11224
Kampala
Tel + 256 41 220197 Fax + 256 41 235413
e-mail: cbr@imul.com

UNITED KINGDOM
ACTIONAID
Hamlyn House
MacDonald Road
London N19 5PG
Tel + 44 171 281 4101 Fax + 44 171 281 5146
e-mail: nicolac@actionaid.org.uk

UNITED STATES
American Council for Voluntary International Action (InterAction)
1717 Massachusetts Avenue NW
Suite 801
Washington DC 20036
Tel + 1 202 667 8227 Fax + 1 202 667 8236
e-mail: la@interaction.org

ZIMBABWE
Zimbabwe Women's Resource Centre and Network
PO Box 2192
Harare
Tel + 263 4 792450 Fax + 263 4 720331
e-mail: zwrcn@mango.apc.org

Part I: Current Issues and Key Themes

Introduction

Does development cooperation still have a meaning in an era of globalisation? Will foreign direct investment replace aid in the short term?

Some political and social leaders, and even members of the NGO community, think the global market will replace development cooperation very soon. Some people believe that such a market, provided for by the Uruguay Round and by the WTO, will ensure economic growth and development to all countries.

It would be easy to be mistaken in thinking that the market could replace development cooperation. In a world where poverty is growing, unemployment increasing and where conflict and insecurity affects the lives of more people, the search for alternative solutions to the development cooperation policies of the past 40 years – policies that have often missed their aims – is natural.

Globalisation characterises our times: an ineluctable process. Those who want to oppose it look like Don Quixote tilting at windmills. But it should not be taken for granted that this process automatically brings real benefits to people. In fact the evidence collected in The Reality of Aid shows that the global market is not addressing the problems of poverty and in many cases is a process that leads to increased inequalities and undermines the lives and security of wide sectors of population.

Over 3000 million people are living in poverty, if a poverty line of just over US$ 2 a day is used. We face impoverishment in Africa, South Asia, Latin America, but also in industrialised countries: even where GNP has increased, the phenomenon of unemployment has not been halted; even where wealth has been augmented, large parts of society are excluded from its benefits.

Some time ago the New York Times, commenting on President Clinton's visit to South America, affirmed that supporting economic growth had been shown to be ineffective in improving people's standard of living. Wealth had increased but to the exclusive advantage of the elites. There was a rise in the sale of portable phones, but not in food; the gap between rich and poor had widened. It is evident that globalisation and the markets do not represent the solution.

People's future demands alternative actions. First, there is a call for the state not to withdraw, but to be enabled to take effective, coherent action for the eradication of poverty and for sustainable development both nationally and globally.

Second, there is a need for international institutions to be given responsibility for the equitable management of global processes. Rules are needed to guarantee the welfare of citizens and the fundamental rights of present and future generations.

Third, governments must stick to the commitments made at UN conferences and enshrined in international conventions. Long negotiations, involving both heads of state and civil society, have identified principles and strategies that offer solutions to some of the most fundamental challenges faced by humanity. We must not waste all this effort. We must build on the intellectual and financial resources that have already been invested.

This is why The Reality of Aid wants governments to meet existing commitments, particularly on effective development cooperation.

In 1996 resources for development cooperation fell to their lowest ever level – just ¼ of 1% of the growing wealth of donor countries. New priorities are now on the donor countries' agenda. But are those priorities really the ones people want? Public opinion in donor countries strongly supports aid and many citizens make their own individual contributions through NGOs. This should be respected by donor governments, not ignored.

People understand that aid, when properly directed and well implemented, can improve the lives of the poor, prevent conflicts, enhance the status of women, protect natural resources and defend minorities. Its effectiveness will be multiplied if other government policies are made coherent with the aims of development cooperation. Such aid is in everyone's interest.

We do not fear globalisation. In fact we dream of a globalised world, where resources are equally distributed and education, health, jobs, shelter, human rights and freedom are guaranteed to all. Development cooperation has its part to play in achieving that.

Sabina Siniscalchi
Chair Eurostep

Brian Tomlinson, International Working Group of ICVA Members for The Reality of Aid

Development cooperation in a changing world

Mark Curtis, ACTIONAID*

Overview

Improved international development cooperation to eradicate poverty and promote poor people's basic rights is one of the greatest political priorities in the run-up to the millennium. This means a much greater commitment by Northern donors to high quality aid programmes that work in the interests of poor people. It also means recognising the importance of the wider economic and political context in which aid programmes operate, in order to improve the prospects for inclusive social and economic development.

With rising poverty around the globe – in both North and South – such development cooperation is not so much an option or a political choice for Northern actors. It is, rather, an obligation both morally and for reasons of self–interest: in an increasingly interdependent world where many issues can only be resolved internationally, Northern governments should regard development cooperation as an investment in their own futures.

Economic globalisation means that development cooperation between and among Northern and Southern countries should have a much higher priority in national and international politics where 'domestic' and 'foreign' issues are increasingly blurred. The eradication of poverty should be regarded as an international public good that promotes peace, security and environmental sustainability. The onus thus falls on everyone – individuals as well as governments – to take action.

The reality, however, is that Northern states and institutions are palpably failing to give priority to development cooperation. In 1997, aid levels continued to decline (see Trends chapter), a Multilateral Agreement on Investment risks stripping developing countries of control over foreign direct investment, and a positive effort to tackle debt relief, the Highly Indebted Poor Countries Debt Initiative, is not being implemented as urgently and as thoroughly as is required.

Political will and leadership are simply lacking. At the same time, citizens' commitment to cooperation remains strong. Governments are thus not only failing to live up to their commitments, as this review demonstrates, but they are also betraying their own citizens' hopes for a future secure and prosperous world.

Introduction

In the five years since the first *Reality of Aid*, enormous changes have occurred across the globe which have affected aid and the debate on aid. The central role of the state in driving 'development' has been weakened. In the South, a number of repressive regimes have recently fallen; other states have collapsed or come near to collapse, particularly in the Great Lakes region of Africa. Donor and recipient governments and intergovernmental organisations, the main administrators of aid programmes, have come to see the state as a hindrance to development rather than a help. In the North, even parties of the left have increasingly espoused reductions in the role of the state and welfare spending.

At the same time, globalisation is transforming the international economy. Private financial flows to developing countries, smaller than total aid five years ago, have tripled and are now four times as large as aid flows. The private sector has even been seen by some as more efficient in delivering traditional state functions. But while market forces have facilitated a substantial increase in financial flows from developed to developing countries, they have also contributed to the dramatically increasing gap between the wealthy and the poor in the world.

Five years ago, many were still hoping for a large peace dividend and a benign new world order – such voices have since been muted. Despite a

The **Reality** of Aid 1997/8

Development cooperation in a changing world

> **Box 1 Summary of main messages**
>
> Aid can and does work. While developing countries and people in poverty must themselves lead the process, this requires high quality input from the donor. The international community should make high quality aid a priority. It also needs the right economic and political conditions in the recipient country, where states must give priority to the eradication of poverty and the protection of human rights, and where markets are regulated so that they contribute to these goals.
>
> - Aid and development cooperation programmes should be guided by and reoriented towards clear goals: the eradication of poverty and promotion of equity and human rights.
> - Governments must demonstrate a strategy for meeting existing commitments, including the 0.7% of GNP ODA target, the 20:20 compact, and the goals of the OECD DAC's Shaping the Twenty First Century.
> - Governments must negotiate clear standards for the participation, access and representation of the organisations of civil society in policy dialogue. They must hear and take fully into account the voice of people in poverty.
>
> Governments must show leadership in ensuring a coherent development strategy: policies in one area should not undermine those in another. All areas of government policy – not just aid – should promote sustainable development and human rights.
>
> - Governments and citizens must respond to pressures of economic globalisation by promoting inclusive social and economic development. This means macroeconomic policies and trade and investment rules must give priority to generating and preserving sustainable livelihoods, equity, and human security, for both women and men.
> - Governments must have a strong role in establishing and enforcing appropriate regulatory frameworks for private sector activity, particularly with respect to foreign direct investment.
>
> With the transformations being brought about by globalisation, the future of development increasingly lies in international cooperation. This not only involves governments and multilateral institutions, but partnerships for social development between peoples and organisations in North and South. This requires the nurture of political constituencies and alliances for development.

drop of nearly US$ 500,000 million in military spending between 1987 and 1995,[1] in the latter half of that period (1992–5) aid levels fell by 14% in real terms. The year 1996 saw aid fall by 4.2% in real terms, from $58,800 million to $55,100 million. At 0.25% of GNP in 1996, aid is at its lowest level since statistics began in 1950.[2]

Several factors explain the lack of support for aid: domestic budgets of donor countries are under pressure; factors such as private financial flows and debt relief seem more important; and economic globalisation and reductions in the role of the state appear to question the relevance of aid to development.[3]

Yet the case for aid that works to benefit poor people is very clear: poverty and inequality continue to worsen in specific regions and countries;[4] many of the world's poorest countries are unable to attract other external resources and remain dependent on aid; as shown in opinion polls across the North, the public believes their governments have a clear moral duty to reduce poverty.

This report, having reviewed the past year, recognises that the process of globalisation requires creative strategies for tackling poverty. There are few tools available that can tackle it directly. This report argues that aid remains vital to help promote precisely this end. It is one

Development cooperation in a changing world

element of a potential development cooperation strategy covering trade, investment, governance, human rights and militarisation. Aid's success or failure must be judged in that wider context.

Quality aid works

Aid can and does work. While developing countries and people in poverty must themselves lead the process, this requires high quality input from the donor. The international community should make high quality aid a priority. It also needs the right economic and political conditions in the recipient country, where states must give priority to the eradication of poverty and the protection of human rights and where markets are regulated so that they contribute to these goals.

Donors need to focus aid on the eradication of poverty and the promotion of human rights. Aid policies also need to cohere with other policies that could otherwise undermine them, such as debt repayments or unfair trade. For recipients, such aid works when the economic and political environment is geared towards promoting the same objectives: the eradication of poverty and human rights. Growth must be an equitable process that works in the interest of people living in poverty and that does not exclude whole sections of the population on the grounds that wealth will eventually 'trickle down' to the poorest.

Such aid works. Multilateral and bilateral aid have leant substantial financial and technical support to developing countries' successes in increasing access to drinking water, falling infant and child mortality through inoculations and oral rehydration therapy, the spread of immunisation programmes, which have controlled smallpox, polio, diphtheria and measles, improvements in physical infrastructure and the introduction of new agricultural inputs to increase yields.[5] The chapter for the United States this year shows, for example, that polio has been eradicated from the Western hemisphere with the help of US aid funding.

Box 2 The real extent of poverty

Most human beings at the end of the twentieth century live in poverty. The most widely-used estimate of the extent of absolute poverty is that of the World Bank. Its most recent figures state that 1300 million people live on less than US$ 365 a year,[6] or less than US$ 1 a day.[7] Even this seriously underestimates the extent of poverty. The UNDP reports that 80% of the world's population lives on about 15% of the world's total GNP. These figures suggest that about 4300 million people live on an annual average per capita income of around $750, a little over $2 a day.[8]

This has led one development academic to write that: 'In the poor countries of the world there are no administratively convenient "pockets of poverty". The poor form a majority. They are the peasants and the popular urban sectors. They are the people. The World Bank did not draw this conclusion, however. To do so would have led it to abandon its traditional approach to economic growth and "development"'.[9] The World Bank's estimates instead lead it to regard the poor as a special, minority group.

Whether or not the poverty line is drawn at $1 or $2 a day, it still fails to capture aspects of human poverty that cannot easily be reduced to a dollar figure. Rather than measure poverty by income, the UNDP has introduced a human poverty index (HPI) which uses indicators that reflect the *conditions* in which people in poverty live: life expectancy, literacy, child nutrition, and access to health services and safe drinking water. The HPI was introduced by the UNDP Human Development Report 1997 to provide a complementary measurement of poverty to those traditionally using income.

The **Reality** of Aid 1997/8

Development coperation in a changing world

The effectiveness of aid in eradicating poverty depends both on the quality of the donor aid programmes and on the capacity of recipient governments to use the aid wisely. A recent study for the US Overseas Development Council on aid to Africa concluded that the most important factor in the contribution of aid to African economies 'is the extent to which governments have the capacity to use it in the service of a coherent development strategy'. For too long, the study notes, 'donors have made inadequate efforts to build capacity within central state institutions, and they have adopted practices that actually undermine these capacities'. It adds that recipients in Africa 'have acted as if aid were a free resource and have not integrated aid into their own planning and budgeting exercises'. Recipient countries need to pursue policies that promote economic growth and poverty alleviation and donors should increase aid resources to such countries.[10]

Northern public support for development cooperation

The view that the public cares little about poverty, and that there are few votes in it, is plainly wrong. As *The Reality of Aid* reported last year, the public across the OECD is constantly supportive of the principle of helping those in need. In *Development Aid: Building for the Future with Public Support*,[11] a study of European public opinion of development aid, the European Commission demonstrated that 90% of the population viewed development issues as important. In addition, 83% of Europeans thought that the EU development budget should be increased. In countries with an ODA lower than 0.7% of GNP, more than 70% of the citizens believed that their government should increase its development aid budget.[12]

The European study also showed that the public lacks accurate information on aid – over 90% of people want to be better informed. This supports the conclusion of a 1995 Canadian report, which showed that public support for aid was considerably stronger when foreign aid is explained in terms of means and goals, rather than just as a budget item. This is also consistent with a 1995 US study, which found that both the public and some politicians were not well informed and grossly overestimated the actual levels of aid[13] (see Table 32 on Leadership on public and political opinion).

It is clear that people in donor countries attach importance both to volume and quality of aid, provided it is well spent. A much greater effort must be made by Northern donors to achieve high quality programmes that contribute to the eradication of poverty and to ensure that the public is much better informed about development cooperation.

Box 3 The growing role of Northern citizens in development cooperation

The wise politicians of the next century will be those who pay attention to the changing role of Northern citizens and their increasingly important role in development, as buyers of fair-trade goods and as ethical investors, as well as concerned voters.

In 1994, for example, consumers in Europe spent over 200 million ECU on fair-trade goods. This fair trade reached 800,000 families, or 5 million people, in developing countries.[14] In the UK alone, nearly 400,000 people now buy fair-trade goods, two chains of ethical shops have recently been established, and around 300,000 people have savings or mortgages in ethical stock market funds.[15]

Clear goals

Aid and development cooperation programmes should be guided by and reoriented towards clear goals: the eradication of poverty and promotion of equity and human rights.

Development strategies, including aid programmes, should promote greater equality among people and countries. The share of income of the poorest fifth of the world's population now

Development cooperation in a changing world

stands at a mere 1.1%, compared with 2.3% in 1960.[16] Raising people over a low income threshold does not constitute a real development strategy, especially when wealth and power are concentrated in fewer and fewer hands. Participation in society is about more than income. Gross inequalities – in opportunity, power, access to resources as well as income itself – are incompatible with a development process centred on people. Donors need to promote more equality, by showing clear political leadership and commitment to this aim.

To this end, aid programmes should be directed towards eradicating poverty and promoting human rights. This is particularly vital for women, who comprise 70% of people living in absolute poverty. Donors have made some progress towards focusing on poverty over the past few years. The World Bank's focus on poverty reduction as its 'overarching objective' over the past few years is one example. More recently, the British government has stated that the reduction of poverty is the first priority of its aid programmes. An independent commission established to review Australia's aid programme recommended strongly that poverty reduction through sustainable development become the 'one clear objective' of the Australian aid programme.[17]

But there is much more that could be done. While aid administrations devote a lot of rhetoric to poverty, most official aid simply does not reach people living in poverty. Only a small proportion is directly focused on poverty eradication and basic services (see the 'At a glance' section of this report); and there is little evidence that the rest of it reaches people living in poverty through 'trickle down' economic growth. Donors have not made substantial overall shifts in resources to the social sectors. This point is highlighted by Danish development minister Poul Nielson who notes that 'we must be better at focusing on poverty reduction when we prepare country programmes and design interventions. Our policies and guidelines must to a greater extent than today be reflected in the project documents'.[18] (See Table 35 on Mainstreaming attention to poverty reduction)

Donors need to take greater steps to target their aid programmes towards the social sectors (see Table 34 on Measuring aid to direct poverty reduction). Basic rights to health, education, food and employment continue to be denied to hundreds of millions of people. Investment in health and education is one of the most important determinants of human development, and of employment, productivity and economic competitiveness. At the same time, it is a vital determinant of welfare, income and social cohesion.

Government commitments

Governments must demonstrate a strategy for meeting existing commitments, including the 0.7% of GNP ODA target, the 20:20 compact, and the goals of the OECD DAC's Shaping the 21st Century.

Significant progress has been made at international summits in the 1990s to secure government commitments to a host of targets. Among these are the 1992 Earth Summit in Rio, the 1994 International Conference on Population and Development in Cairo, the 1995 World Conference on Women in Beijing, the 1995 Social Summit in Copenhagen, the Human Settlements Conference in Istanbul in 1996, the 1996 Food Summit in Rome, and the ill-fated Earth Summit II in New York in 1997. The tremendous effort that went into reaching agreement on commitments at each of these conferences must not be wasted. Non-governmental organisations and citizens must push governments to honour their commitments.

Shaping the 21st Century In *Shaping the 21st Century: the Contribution of Development Cooperation*, a number of specific targets agreed in UN Conferences were reconfirmed by DAC member countries. These include:

- a reduction by one-half in the proportion of people living in extreme poverty by 2015;
- universal primary education in all countries by 2015;
- demonstrated progress towards gender equality and the empowerment of women by eliminating gender disparity in primary and secondary education by 2005;
- a reduction by two-thirds in the mortality rate for infants and children under age 5 and a

The Reality of Aid 1997/8

Development cooperation in a changing world

reduction by three-fourths in maternal mortality, all by 2015;
- access through the primary health care system to reproductive health services for all individuals of appropriate ages as soon as possible and no later than the year 2015; and
- the current implementation of national strategies for sustainable development in all countries by 2000.

These are worthy goals, and OECD governments should be applauded for recommitting themselves to them. Now, citizens, non-governmental organisations, and other civic organisations must put pressure on governments to demonstrate a strategy for meeting these commitments. A critical factor here is political leadership. All donor countries should show how they are going to reform their aid and other policies to achieve these goals.

As well as making significant shifts in resources towards these targets, donors need to work with recipients on building the targets into country assistance strategies. Measuring and monitoring progress towards these objectives is imperative and there need to be mechanisms for this. Interim steps towards the 2015 targets need to be established. The targets can be achieved only if there is a framework of mutual agreement and contractuality between the donor and the recipient. The efforts of both the donor and the recipient must be monitored. The role of the DAC in developing indicators of development progress and the establishment of an International Working Group towards this end are welcomed.

The 20:20 compact Increased social services to people living in poverty can only be assured if donors and recipient governments work together to achieve this objective. This requires a mutual understanding of the priorities in the use and objectives of aid. At the 1995 World Summit for Social Development, governments committed, on a voluntary basis, to the '20:20 compact', a principle proposed precisely for this purpose. This compact calls on donors to commit 20% of aid resources and on recipient governments to commit 20% of public expenditures to the provision of basic services.

At the same summit, NGOs endorsed a proposal which increased the share of social sector spending to 50%, with a focus on:

- the basic social services identified in the 20:20 compact, such as basic education and primary health care, nutrition programmes and safe water;
- support to income-generating activities for the poor in rural areas and the urban informal sector, including small-scale credit facilities; and
- strengthening social and civil organisations.

Donors should give priority in their aid programmes to countries whose governments make a mutual commitment to achieving the objectives in basic social services set out in the 20:20 compact: aid needs to focus on countries pursuing credible poverty-reduction strategies. They should also press international financial institutions to make structural adjustment loans conditional on government action to improve universal access to basic services.

Non-governmental organisations are committed to monitoring governments' progress towards Social Summit commitments. *Social Watch*,[19] an annual digest of reports from national NGOs on their countries' human and social development initiatives was launched in 1996 to monitor such progress.

0.7% of GNP In 1969, the OECD DAC affirmed a needs-based target of 0.7% of donor countries' GNP for overseas development assistance. Since then, very few countries have met this goal. Despite declines in aid volumes over the past few years, the OECD DAC member countries, with the exception of the USA, continue to affirm their commitment to the 0.7% target for aid. The most recent reaffirmation of this commitment was made in June 1997 at the UN General Assembly Special Session (UNGASS).

Untied Aid Although there is as yet no collective commitment from donor governments to untie their aid, there is a strong case for countries to take unilateral steps to untie aid in favour of aid geared to poverty reduction. Many countries support untying in principle, but there is not yet much

Development cooperation in a changing world

evidence of progress. Currently, France is effectively blocking the prospects of reaching a multilateral agreement on untying. In the case of the UK, a recent report by the Overseas Development Administration showed that unilateral untying would be in the interests of the British economy. The British government has hitherto failed to take this step, although the new government has signalled its intent to end tied aid (see UK country chapter).

> **Box 4 Removing barriers to self-empowerment**
>
> *The poor are completely capable of changing their own lives with their own efforts, provided barriers which are put around them by the existing system are removed. ... If the bottom 50% of the world's population – the poor and the small producers – are allowed to bring out their productivity, ingenuity and creativity the world will be a better place for all. ...*
>
> *Let us all agree that we shall not accept any investment as development expenditure unless it touches the lives of that bottom 50%. I urge taxpayers in donor countries to make sure that their money directly benefits the bottom 50% in recipient countries.*
>
> *Poverty has not been created by the poor. It is created by the institutions and policies we have built around us. Unless these are redesigned, and alternative institutions and policies are made, poverty will continue to flourish.*[20]
>
> Professor Muhammad Yunus
> founder of the Grameen Bank

Participation, access, representation

Governments must negotiate clear standards for the participation, access and representation of the organisations of civil society in policy dialogue. They must hear and take into account the voice of people in poverty.

The quality of participation is crucial to the quality of development cooperation. Often, however, little provision is made to consult with the beneficiaries or potential beneficiaries of programmes or with organisations already working in a particular sector. Under the current framework of EU development cooperation, for example, the objectives and design of EU-funded national development strategies are created almost exclusively by officials of the recipient government and the EU. Many bilateral programmes suffer from similar deficiencies. Aid programmes must incorporate broader participation in their design, implementation and evaluation, and this needs to be firmly built into country assistance strategies. Particular efforts are needed to promote the equal participation of women, which has proved essential to improving the quality of aid.

To foster greater participation, accountability and transparency, steps need to be taken to strengthen local and national organisations in the South, such as farmer associations, women's organisations, cooperatives, trade unions and human rights organisations. This will help increase their influence in policy decisions and their ability to access resources and secure their basic social and economic rights.

Governments should vastly improve their disclosure of information so that national development strategies, indicative programmes and financing agreements are in the public domain. Equally, it is essential to improve the transparency and accountability of multilateral institutions, like the World Bank, the International Monetary Fund and the World Trade Organisation.

The need for coherence

Governments must show leadership in ensuring a coherent development strategy: policies in one area should not undermine those in another. All areas of government policy – not just aid – should promote sustainable development and human rights.

Aid is only one part of the relationship between developed and developing countries. International trade, investment, conflict prevention and debt

The **Reality** of Aid 1997/8

Development cooperation in a changing world

Box 5   Gender, participation, access and representation

What does 'development' mean if women, more than half the world's population, are not involved in development planning processes on equal terms with men? Equality between women and men is more than a matter of justice. It was made clear at the Beijing Women's Conference of 1995 that there can be no real development unless the realities of women as well as men are taken into account in analysis, policy, and particularly in programme delivery. Women and men must be given equal opportunity to participate and benefit from the development process.

As Ghita Sen, an Indian economist, explains,

A gender perspective means recognising that women stand at the crossroads between production and reproduction, between economic activity, and the care of human beings, and therefore between economic growth and human development.

Women's involvement and empowerment in development programmes should be an explicit goal of development cooperation.

One very neglected aspect of this concerns emergency responses, the majority of which have ignored the special needs of women, missed opportunities to strengthen their position, ignored women's own resources and characteristics and disregarded the long-term social rehabilitation needs of the communities they serve.

A second aspect concerns the negative impact on women of macro-economic policies and programmes. As women are usually concentrated in the most vulnerable and least organised industries, and they often have sole responsibility for child care, women and their children have been disproportionately affected by some structural adjustment policies which have had the effect of lowering labour standards and cutting basic social services.

---

relief are far more important for determining the opportunities for equitable human development in an era of globalisation. Arms exports, environmental policy and foreign policy generally are also critical factors. For aid to promote poverty reduction and human rights, it needs to be seen as part of a mix of policies that ensures a coherent overall development strategy.

As two Dutch writers, Max van den Berg and Bram van Ojik, note:

What is the point in, say, using aid money to support indigenous peoples in sustainable forest management if commercial operators can at the same time fell all the timber they want and export it to the hardwood-consuming rich countries?...The important thing is understanding that development cooperation has more to do with supporting rights and claims than with economic growth, modernisation and the simple transfer of resources.[21]

There are numerous examples of Northern states pursuing inconsistent policies. This is the case with trade policy, where the efforts of developing countries to increase exports have been undermined by unfair trade rules and practices of Northern governments. Such contradictions are found in the European Union's (EU) Common Agricultural Policy (CAP), which, through direct payments to farmers and food dumping, artificially reduces the world market price, while at the same time the EU is financially supporting efforts to achieve food security in developing countries. A recent example is the dumping of subsidised EU beef in southern Africa while supporting the development of communal cattle farming. Through such inconsistencies, and the intransigence of some members in removing trade barriers for Southern produce entering Europe, the EU has systematically undermined food producers in the South.

The whole area of arms exports policy of some donor governments is rife with 'incoherence' – aid cannot be used effectively in reducing

Development cooperation in a changing world

poverty in regions torn apart by conflict. An obvious case is highlighted in the chapter on Switzerland. Swiss aircraft have been used against partially Swiss-funded Burmese refugee camps. This is but one example of the way in which Northern governments fail to take responsibility for their part in undermining development efforts by fuelling conflicts in developing countries.

Similarly, some donors' espoused commitment to support human rights is often backed by little action: consistent human rights abusers such as China, Indonesia and Israel[22] have been among the largest recipients of aid from DAC members.

There has been progress in promoting more coherent policies in some countries. Foreign ministries are increasingly concerned with issues that were previously seen as narrow development questions, such as human rights, peacekeeping and environmental issues. Some Northern countries – for example, Denmark, the Netherlands and the UK – have undergone or are undergoing reforms either of development cooperation policy itself or the structure within which aid and development policy are linked to other areas of government policy. In June 1997, the EU Development Council adopted a resolution on coherence, which, among other things, calls for a yearly report by the EU Commission on the issue of coherence. NGOs will monitor closely further developments of such initiatives.

The Highly Indebted Poor Countries Debt Initiative A key area where policies have been catastrophically incoherent concerns the debt burden carried by so many developing countries. Increased and uncontrolled bilateral, multilateral, and commercial lending in the mid-1980s brought many developing countries to the point of bankruptcy. The results of the loans made available in the latter half of the 1980s and 1990s for debt servicing and structural adjustment support have been doubtful.[23] While some developing countries did indeed increase their exports of primary products, due to lower prices and increased competition, their debt burdens remain. Indeed, total debt outstanding for developing countries increased from $1132,000 million in 1986 (at the peak of the debt crisis) to $2177,000 million in 1996, a 92.2% increase.[24] Most of the Severely Indebted Low Income Countries (SILICs) are in sub-Saharan Africa (SSA). In 1995, 30 of the 48 countries in SSA were classified as 'severely indebted'.[25] For some African debtors almost all the debt service is paid to international financial institutions (IFIs), which would not, in the past, reschedule or cancel any portion of their loans. Highly indebted countries have had to take new loans, often from bilateral donors, to repay the old loans. Debt to the IFIs of 20 out of 29 SILICs exceeded 100% of exports.[26]

The international community has now recognised that a resolution of the debt problem is essential, particularly in sub-Saharan Africa. Following a commitment at the 1996 Group of Seven (G7) summit meeting in Halifax, the Highly Indebted Poor Countries (HIPC) Debt Initiative was launched at the World Bank/IMF Annual General Meeting in October. The central aim of the initiative is to enable the world's poorest countries to achieve a sustainable debt level within a period of six years and so remove the need for rescheduling. There are 41 HIPC countries, all part of the SILIC group, characterised by disproportionately large multilateral debt service payments.

In April 1997, creditors decided upon an accelerated debt relief deal for Uganda, the 'best pupil in the HIPC class' (see the chapter on Uganda). As the first beneficiary of the initiative it was originally expecting to receive US$ 338 million debt relief in 1997 in what was described as 'exceptional treatment' by the World Bank and IMF. Unfortunately, despite these promises, the member governments of the World Bank could not agree to an accelerated timetable. As a result, this debt relief payment has been postponed until April 1998.[27] Losses resulting from the delay are calculated by the Ugandan government at an estimated $35 to $40 million.

The prospects for other countries still in the pipeline are worse. Bolivia, the other textbook case for the HIPC initiative, will probably be the only other country that will receive comprehensive debt relief before the year 2000.[28]

Extensive and timely debt relief would enable HIPCs to allocate more of their scarce resources to social and human development.[29] The inflexible framework of the initiative, and the minimalist

The **Reality** of Aid 1997/8
Development coperation in a changing world

approach of some of the key G7 creditors, threatens to make ineffective what could be an effective instrument in combatting world poverty, at a total cost that is lower than current annual aid flows to SILICs.

Inclusive social development

> Governments and citizens must respond to pressures of economic globalisation by promoting inclusive social and economic development. This means macroeconomic policies and trade and investment rules must give priority to generating and preserving sustainable livelihoods, equity, and human security for all, both women and men.

There is much evidence that the global deregulation of markets and unfettered structural adjustment have, in some regions of the world, increased inequality, social exclusion and poverty levels. Rapid liberalisation has often destroyed rural livelihoods and food security. Intensified global competition, combined with moves to deregulate labour markets, is also exerting downward pressure on labour standards.

Currently, even though most governments and institutions have recognised the need for broad-based growth, the process of globalisation means that promoting economic growth through liberalisation and deregulation of markets has become the dominant model for 'development'.

However, evidence suggests that this form of economic growth does not necessarily lead to a reduction in poverty, and can increase it. Even the International Monetary Fund has recognised a growing polarisation among developing countries, noting:

> There has also been a sharp decline in upward mobility of developing countries within the international distribution of average per capita incomes and an increased tendency for countries to become polarized into high- and low-income clusters. (. . .) Simply put, over the past 30 years, the vast majority of developing countries – 84 out of 108 – have either stayed in the lower-income quintile or fallen into that quintile from a relatively higher position. Moreover, there are now fewer middle-income countries, and upward mobility of countries seems to have fallen over time. (. . .) The forces of polarization seem to have become stronger since the early 1980s.[30]

The devastating conclusion that economic growth in an era of deregulation and globalisation has created greater poverty and inequity rather than less calls for a thorough analysis of the effects of economic globalisation and the policies that have been implemented with the aim of lifting developing countries out of poverty. The UNDP notes that 'economic growth explains only about half of poverty reduction. The rest depends on good policy to harness the growth for poverty reduction.'[31]

If development cooperation is to be effective it must go beyond an approach that bolts aid and safety nets onto this flawed macro-economic framework. Instead, development cooperation needs to aim consistently to encourage more inclusive patterns of growth which put equity and poverty reduction at the core of the development process. Development cooperation must be about social and political change that promotes human-centred development.

An example of successful human-centred development is found in the Indian state of Kerala. According to analyst Govindan Parayil,

> Kerala has shown that, despite tremendous odds, it was able to eliminate acute poverty and deprivation without attaining rapid growth in per capita GNP as is 'expected' of all economic development models/theories.[32]

Kerala's success is due to a number of factors including meaningful land reforms, promoting high literacy (especially among women) through free and universal primary education and developing

Development cooperation in a changing world

social movements through the establishment of a civil society to promote environmental conservation. Promoting peoples' rights, reducing inequalities and mobilising workers and farmers all also played a role. Kerala has by no means succeeded in eradicating all poverty, and there are question marks over the degree to which it can sustain these achievements. Nevertheless, the fact is that these real gains have not been achieved by following the model currently being pushed on most countries of the South.

Private financial flows

The State must have a strong role in establishing and enforcing appropriate regulatory frameworks for private sector activity, particularly with respect to foreign direct investment.

In the past five years, there has been a tremendous surge of international private financial flows. In 1996, private financial flows to developing countries reached $234,000 million – over four times greater than aid flows of $55,000 million.[33] Only five years ago, total private financial flows were less than total aid flows. These private flows have since tripled, and are now over four times greater than total aid flows of $55,000 million.

An increase in long-term and strategically directed foreign direct investment is of course welcome by many developing countries. However, private flows continue to be heavily concentrated in a small number of countries – in 1996 the top 12 out of 108 developing countries received 73% of private capital flows in 1996, while countries in sub-Saharan Africa received only 4.8%.[34] Such concentration of financial flows is likely to exacerbate international inequalities and reinforce the marginalisation of large areas of the globe.

With declining aid levels and increasing private financial flows, agencies such as the UNDP, the World Bank, and some bilateral donors, are increasingly looking to private financial flows to act as key resources for poverty reduction and development. While private capital may be directed towards poverty eradication in limited circumstances, the increase in private flows to developing countries should not be seen as replacing declining aid flows or public budgets. As the DAC has stated, aid and private finance are 'two very different types of flows'.

Private financial flows like foreign direct investment (FDI) are not at all focused on poverty reduction or social needs. As the DAC notes, 'private resources generally do not flow directly to some key sectors of priority need, such as health and education', social infrastructure, or the protection of the environment. Poverty often remains widespread in countries that have received large amounts of FDI as investment and growth have tended to be concentrated on a few urban areas.[35]

Also, domestic policies adopted by developing countries to attract FDI can often undermine the prospects for the reduction of poverty. The DAC notes that 'an attractive business environment for investors in general is the first prerequisite' for attracting FDI.[36] But this climate may include low taxation for foreign companies, easy profit repatriations and equal treatment of foreign and domestic firms.

The DAC concludes that the continuation of the trend of increasing private flows, on the one hand, and declining aid, on the other: 'casts a shadow on the credibility of a development partnerships strategy based upon goals that will require the greatest progress among the poorest people and the poorest countries. The continuation of those trends could have grave consequences'.[37]

The Multilateral Agreement on Investment

Such a shadow has certainly been cast by the OECD/WTO negotiation of an agreement to liberalise investment rules. The OECD members are currently negotiating a multilateral agreement on investment (MAI), which would essentially prevent national governments from imposing trade-related restrictions on investment and would guarantee generally free entry into countries for foreign investors, and full national treatment for established investments and high standards of investment protection. The completed agreement, set for May 1998, will be presented to non-OECD countries for ratification, without prior consultation.

The MAI is expected to become *the* standard for investment policies in the globalising world economy, establishing a 'level playing field' for global business in all countries. However, in its present state, the MAI does not fit the development needs of developing countries, or efforts to direct investment towards supporting more

The Reality of Aid 1997/8

Development coperation in a changing world

equitable growth and human development.

The agreement's key principles of 'national treatment' and 'non-discrimination' would require governments to give the same or better benefits to foreign investors as they give to national businesses. Protection of, for instance, small and medium sized enterprises of national origin against multinational foreign investors would be prohibited, as would some government initiatives to promote skills development in the workforce. And while the MAI is clear on the rights ascribed to foreign investors, it says very little about their obligations, in terms of meeting social and environmental standards.

Such an agreement would be a step backwards for developing countries trying to direct their economies towards more equitable growth and human development. As the East Asian economies have so clearly demonstrated, some control of foreign investment is vital to nurture domestic capacity and allow local enterprises to become more competitive.

Martin Khor, of the Third World Network in Malaysia, explains:

> Malaysia has a sophisticated system of combining liberalisation with regulation in a policy mix that can be fine-tuned and altered according to the country's economic conditions and development needs. . . . From this experience, it is clear that developing countries need to maintain the right and option to regulate investments and have their own policy on foreign investment, instead of an international investment regime that would remove those rights. Giving total freedom and rights to foreign firms and foreigners will lead to the disappearance of many local enterprises, unemployment and greater profit outflows.[38]

The experience of the East Asian newly-industrialising economies has demonstrated that the state needs to play a much greater role in the development process than is currently fashionable. This is not to suggest that the East Asian model can or should be replicated by all developing countries. The reality is that development works best in different ways in different situations. This involves a different mix of the state, the market and civil society in different situations, where the balance varies according to the specific national and local development context. The need to achieve a balance has, in a welcome move, been admitted in the World Bank's latest World Development Report (1997).[39]

It is with these qualifications in mind that the international community should help to attract the necessary foreign investment to the world's poorest countries. Technical assistance should also be provided to developing countries to strengthen their capacity to negotiate investment agreements that promote emerging industries, guarantee minimum labour and environmental standards, while encouraging foreign investment in a fashion that promotes sustainable development and global competitiveness.[40] Aid used in this way is likely to work in the interests of the poor; the danger is that, otherwise, foreign investment will be used simply to promote growth that exacerbates poverty and inequity.

The need for international cooperation

With the transformations being brought about by globalisation, the future of development increasingly lies in international cooperation. This not only involves governments and multilateral institutions, but partnerships for social development between peoples and organisations in North and South. This requires the nurture of political constituencies and alliances for development.

International development cooperation will have to change in order to meet the new challenges of the next century. As the DAC has pointed out: 'we do not have the option of preserving the status quo in development cooperation in a changing world.'[41]

How should the international development cooperation community respond to the following four key trends?
- Governments and multilateral institutions are no longer playing an exclusive role in development;

15

Development cooperation in a changing world

- market-driven policies are continuing to predominate around the globe;
- citizens in North and South, often grouped in NGOs, are becoming more active participants in an increasingly vibrant civil society; and
- poverty is continuing to rise in the North (the emergence of a 'Global South'). Over 100 million people live below the income poverty line (set at half the individual median income), 5 million are homeless and 37 million unemployed, in Northern industrial countries.[42]

There is a need to develop real and equal partnerships in the international cooperation effort. Jean-Martin Tschaptchet, coordinator of SOS Grassroots in Africa, an African NGO, has noted the existence of 'poor partners' attitudes' in Africa. He argues that Africans need to cast off previous attitudes to aid and now 'should welcome technical cooperation as a supplement, not as a substitute to national efforts to achieve national prosperity'.[43]

But it is Northern actors above all who need to face the issue of partnerships squarely. Some people have been very critical of how partnerships might work in practice, and real power continues to rest with the funder.[44] Mustafa Barghouti, founder of a large medical voluntary movement in Palestine, asks 'whether it is truly possible to establish relations on an equal footing between a funder and a recipient. Can one honestly speak of partnerships in this context?'[45]

Many forward-looking analysts see the trend in development cooperation needing to move away from patronage, charity and predetermined development models towards genuinely cooperative relationships.[46] This partly involves shifting control of resources to Southern partners in a context where the latter's needs determine development priorities. Yet development is about much more than securing resources.

Indeed, some believe that increasing the overall pool of resources is not necessarily a good idea in the absence of fundamental reform of the governance structures of recipients, development cooperation institutions and of international society more generally.

Increasing global interdependence brought about by globalisation means that poverty, social exclusion and personal insecurity in both North and South are the result of the same international processes. Some argue that globalisation offers real opportunities to the poorest countries. Yet the governance gap means that the increasing influence of private capital and transnational corporations over the international and local economies is undermining democratic control over resources and political processes.

Many NGOs are increasingly working to promote sustainable human development through helping to forge an ethic of global citizenship.[47] At the heart of this is the belief that human beings are the agents of change and that people must define their own development. Global citizenship seeks to nurture collective action, linking people in the North and South, for the good of the planet. NGOs have a central role to play in this, providing resources, helping to build capacity among partners and helping to generate informed public opinion.

In the South, new social movements are challenging state and corporate power and practising and advocating people-centred development.[48] In the North, internationalist NGOs, often with a long history of working in development, are increasingly influential politically, communicating 'Southern realities' to Northern publics.

The Northern and Southern actors are linking up in networks and in joint policy and advocacy campaigns. The trend is towards what one Southern writer has called 'the establishment of a trans-geographical coalition of people who believe in social justice, equity and democracy in order to influence the [development] process'.[49] Such coalitions are likely to involve groups concerned with issues ranging from human rights to development to the environment, from the domestic to the international. They are building a real constituency for change. Key concerns about governance underpin the activities of all groups irrespective of their often 'narrow' focus. The building-blocks of this relationship between Northern and Southern partners are 'solidarity, mutual respect and a fair distribution of tasks'.[50]

Notes

* ACTIONAID, as lead agency for The Reality of Aid Project,

The **Reality** of Aid 1997/8

Development coperation in a changing world

steered a process of discussion and debate among Reality of Aid NGOs and the wider development community on the purposes and future of development cooperation. This chapter is a product of those discussions and of an international workshop hosted by ACTIONAID in London in June 1997. The chapter was written by Mark Curtis, ACTIONAID, and edited by Reality of Aid Project Manager, Nicola Crawhall.

1. US Arms Control and Disarmament Agency, *World Military Expenditure*, Washington DC, 1996.
2. OECD News Release, 18 June 1997.
3. See Roger Riddell, 'Aid in 21st Century', *Discussion Papers Series No 6*, Office of Development Studies, UNDP, New York, undated, pp 42–9.
4. Using World Bank estimates, the number of people living in absolute poverty increased from 1220 million in 1987 to 1310 million in 1993, though this represented a slight decline in percentage terms from 30.1% to 29.4%. See World Bank, *Poverty Reduction and the World Bank: Progress and Challenges in the 1990s*, Washington DC, 1996, p 4.
5. Development Assistance Committee, *Shaping the 21st Century: The Contribution of Development Cooperation*, May 1996, OECD, Paris. pp 7–8.
6. World Bank, *Poverty Reduction and the World Bank*, op cit, p 4.
7. The dollar-a-day poverty line is based on an estimate of the income needed to pay for a person's minimum living requirements.
8. United Nations Development Programme, *Human Development Report 1994*, Oxford University Press, Oxford, 1994, pp 63, 212. The figure of $750 average annual per capita income is derived from dividing 15% of world GNP ($21,550,000,000) by 80% of the world's population (4300m).
9. John Friedmann, *Empowerment: The Politics of Alternative Development*, Blackwell, Oxford, 1992, p 58.
10. Nicolas van de Walle and Timothy Johnston, *Improving Aid to Africa*, Policy essay No 21, Overseas Development Council, Washington DC, 1996, pp 117–18.
11. International Research Associates, European Coordination Office, Eurobarometer, 46.0, *Development Aid: Building for the Future with Public Support*, prepared for the European Commission, Directorate General Development, DG VIII, Version 3A, 8 January 1997.
12. With the exception of Belgium and Austria where support for an increase of national ODA is only 50%.
13. See *The Reality of Aid 1996*, Earthscan, London, 1996, p 201.
14. Information from European Fair Trade Association internet site.
15. Ed Mayo, 'Back to our Roots', *Guardian* (London) 19 March 1997.
16. UNDP, *Human Development Report 1997*, Oxford University Press, Oxford, 1997, p 9.
17. The Australian Overseas Aid Program, *One Clear Objective*, Report of the Committee of Review, Canberra, 1997.
18. See Denmark country chapter.
19. *Social Watch*, Instituto del Tercer Mundo, Montevideo, 1997.
20. United Nations Non-Governmental Liaison Service, 'Small Farmer, Producers and Microentrepreneurs Caucus', *Social Priorities of Civil Society*, pp 103–5.
21. Max van den Berg and Bram van Ojik, *Rarer than Rubies: Reflections on Development Cooperation*, Novib, The Hague, 1996, pp 61, 123.
22. Due to changes in DAC eligibility rules, Israel will no longer qualify for ODA in 1998.
23. See for instance, Summary of the World Bank Report 'Adjustment Lending, An Evaluation of Ten Years of Experience' (1988), in Importsteun, Ministry of Development Co-operation Netherlands, *Evaluation*, Inspectie Ontwikkelingssamenwerking ter Velde, 1989, bijlage II.
24. World Bank *World Bank Debt Tables 1997*, Oxford University Press, March 1997.
25. Chandra Hardy, 'The Case for Multilateral Debt Relief for Severely Indebted Countries', in *International Monetary and Financial Issues for the 1990s*, Vol VII, United Nations Conference on Trade and Development, New York 1996. p 39. These countries include Angola, Burundi, Central African Republic, Cameroon, Congo, Côte d'Ivoire, the Democratic Republic of Congo, Ethiopia, Equatorial Guinea, Ghana, Guinea-Bissau, Guinea, Kenya, Liberia, Madagascar, Malawi, Mali, Mauritania, Mozambique, Niger, Nigeria, Rwanda, São Tomé and Principe, Sierre Leone, Somalia, Sudan, Tanzania, Togo, Uganda, and Zambia.
26. Chandra Hardy, ibid.
27. Information provided by the European Network on Debt and Development (Eurodad).
28. Information provided by Eurodad.
29. Information provided by Eurodad.
30. International Monetary Fund, 'World Economic Outlook', May 1997, pp 77–8.
31. United Nations Development Programme, *Human Development Report 1997*, Oxford University Press, Oxford, 1997, p 71.
32. See Govindan Parayil, 'The "Kerala Model" of Development: Development and Sustainability in the Third World', *Third World Quarterly*, vol 12, no 5, 1996, pp 941–53.
33. OECD news release, 18 June 1997.
34. *The Globe and Mail*, Toronto, 30 June 1997.
35. Development Assistance Committee (DAC), *Development Cooperation 1996 Report*, Organisation for Economic Cooperation and Development (OECD), Paris, 1997, pp 25, 50–1.
36. DAC, op cit, p 48.
37. DAC, op cit, p iii.
38. Martin Khor, 'The WTO and Foreign Investment: Implications and Alternatives for Developing Countries', *Development in Practice*, vol 6, no 4, 1996, p 313.
39. World Bank, *World Development Report 1997: The State in a Changing World*, Oxford University Press, Oxford, 1997.
40. EUROSTEP, 'Partnership 2000', Brussels. p 11.
41. DAC, op cit, p 11.
42. UNDP, *Human Development Report 1997*, Oxford University Press, Oxford, 1997, p 3.
43. Jean-Martin Tchaptchet, 'The Poor Partners' Attitudes to Technical Cooperation in Africa', in UNNGLS, *Voices from Africa: Sustainable Development*, Issue No 6, Geneva, August 1996, pp 68, 72.
44. See, for example, Kamal Malhotra, co-director of the Focus

Development cooperation in a changing world

on the Global South in Bangkok, in 'A Southern Perspective on Partnership for Development: Some Lessons from Experience', Draft, October 1996.

45. Mustafa Barghouti, 'North–South Relations and the Question of Aid', *Development in Practice*, vol 3, no 3, October 1993, p 205.
46. A number of analyses critical of the traditional aid and development cooperation practices of NGOs have recently appeared. See Alan Fowler, *Striking a Balance: A Guide to Enhancing the Effectiveness of Non-Governmental Organisations in International Development*, Earthscan, London, 1997; Michael Edwards and David Hulme (eds) *Non-Governmental Organisations: Performance and Accountability – Beyond the Magic Bullet*, Earthscan, London, 1995; David Sogge (ed) *Compassion and Calculation: The Business of Private Foreign Aid*, Pluto, London, 1996; and Michael Edwards, 'Foundations for the Future: International Cooperation in the 21st Century', forthcoming.
47. See, for example, Canadian Council on International Cooperation, 'Global Citizenship: A New Way Forward', September 1996; see also Fowler, op cit, pp 228–34.
48. See Ponna Wignaraja (ed) *New Social Movements in the South: Empowering the People*, Zed Books, London, 1993.
49. Bargouthi, op cit, p 207.
50. Mamadou Lamine Thiam, 'The Role of African NGOs in Africa's Sustainable Development', in UNNGLS, *Voices from Africa*, op cit, p 26.

Part II: OECD Country Profiles

Australia

Penelope Lee
Australian Council for Overseas Aid (ACFOA)

Change of government – election promises

The Liberal/National government assumed office in March 1996 with election policies that promised an aid programme to assist developing countries help meet the basic needs of their people and achieve a more secure and equitable international order. Further, the programme was to emphasise humanitarian purposes and poverty reduction, the role of NGOs, community level health, programmes for women and girls in developing countries, primary education, agriculture and rural development, and resource management and environmental activities.

Basic health and education programmes have become focal, women and the environment have been mainstreamed with mixed success, and agricultural assistance has been maintained. Poverty reduction has become the key phrase, featuring in policy documents, ministerial speeches and promotional material.

The new government also kept its election promise to cut the aid programme. Australia's aid budget for 1996/7, which was presented in August 1996, was set at $1450 million, a reduction of $114.4 million over actual expenditure in 1995/6 and of $160.3 million on the 1996/7 forward estimate. This 10% real terms reduction of the aid programme represents the greatest cut in a decade, sending the ratio of ODA to GNP to an all time low of 0.29%. The reduction, according to the Minister for Foreign Affairs, directly reflects the need to address Australia's budget deficit problem.

The government confidently states that Australia is still above the 1995 weighted DAC average of 0.27%, but NGOs are quick to point out that Australia is well below the unweighted average of 0.41% for 1995 and 0.40% for 1996.[1] Australia's performance is declining in relation to other donors.

The cut was advertised well in advance, with a pre-election announcement that the DIFF, Australia's mixed credit scheme, was to be abolished, thus constituting a cut to the aid programme of $124 million or 8%. The additional 2% cut, however, was a breach of the election promise to cut only subsidies to business. The cut to the DIFF programme sparked considerable debate with criticisms emanating from companies involved in the scheme, some of which stood to lose a considerable capital outlay, and from recipient country governments, which cited the loss of highly valued infrastructure and of bilateral agreements. Some NGOs welcomed the move while seeking assurances that the funds would be redirected to other parts of the aid programme. Others guardedly point to the recent improvements to the programme (the required compliance with OECD guidelines), but stressed that the DIFF programme distorted geographical and overall humanitarian priorities for the aid programme and failed to foster local private enterprise in developing countries.

An independent review of Australia's aid objectives

By far the most significant of the election promises was to be the major independent review of the aid programme, coincidental with major cuts to the aid budget, but subsequently commissioned by the Minister for Foreign Affairs soon after taking office. The Review Team was chaired by one of Australia's foremost business leaders and included a leading economist as well as the manager of a tertiary institution.

The Review was charged with examining how the aid programme could best contribute to lasting poverty reduction, while also serving Australia's interests. This Review represents the first major public and parliamentary consideration of the Australian aid programme since the Jackson Committee Report of 1984. Since that time there

Australia

The **Reality** of Aid 1997/8

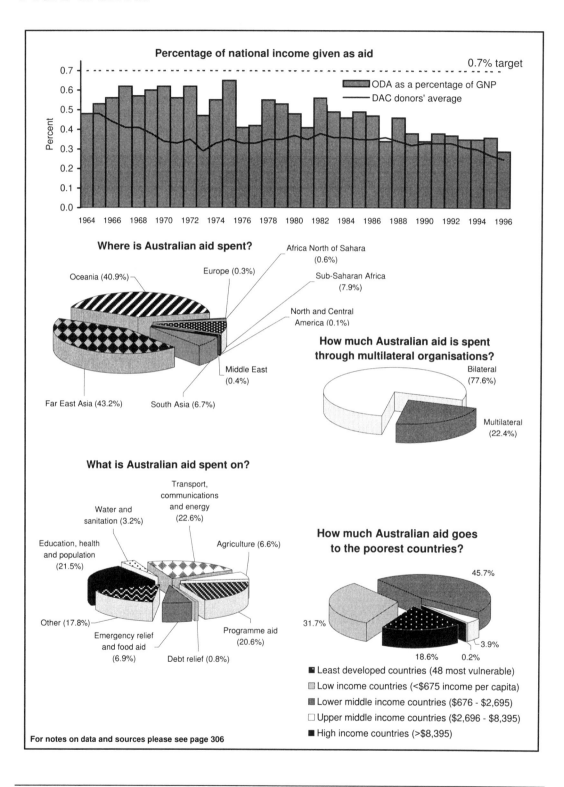

The **Reality** of Aid 1997/8

Australia

Australian aid at a glance

How much aid does Australia give?

Australia gave	US$ 1093m, A$ 1564m in 1996
that was	0.29% of GNP
and	1.96% of public administration
which meant	US$ 60.5 or A$ 87 per capita for 1996

Is it going up or down?

In 1996 aid	fell by $101m, down 15.1% in real terms over 1995
Australia was	less generous in 1996, dropping from 0.36% GNP to 0.29%
The outlook is	very poor with ODA/GNP ratio declining steadily since 1984

How does Australia compare with the other 21 donors?

Australia ranks	13 out of 21 for its volume of aid
It is	13 out of 21 in the generosity league
It gives	a lower proportion of its aid (50.3%) to Low Income Countries than 16 other donors
Private Flows	amounted to $1281m, almost identical to ODA
Total Flows	to developing countries were 0.76% of GNP and rank 10 out of 21 in the DAC

How much does Australia spend on basic health and basic education

Australia reports	4.5% of its ODA spending on basic health and 1.9% on basic education

How important are commercial interests in aid?

Australia requires	44.4% of its aid to be used to buy Australian goods

What do the public think about aid?

60% of Australians think development aid important. 60% are in favour of giving more or it remaining at same level

23

Australia

Box 6 One clear objective: Review of Australia's overseas aid programme

In April 1997, a major review of the Australian Overseas Aid Programme was presented to the government. The review, One Clear Objective: poverty reduction through sustainable development, was commissioned by the Minister for Foreign Affairs in June 1996. The Review Committee was asked to report on how the aid programme could best contribute to lasting poverty reduction, while also serving Australia's interests and to cover the overall priorities, objectives and focus for the programme.

The Review Committee found that the aid programme lacked a clear objective, and recommended that the single, clear objective should be to assist developing countries to reduce poverty through sustainable economic and social development.

They found that the focus of the programme needed to be sharpened. The review suggests a more strategic approach where unequivocal priority must be given to activities that maximise the developmental benefits and have the greatest long-term impact on poverty.

The Review suggests that in order to maximise its effectiveness, the aid programme needs to sharpen its geographic focus. Australia needs to limit the number of countries it assists and to develop a transparent and rigorous approach to graduating the more advanced developing countries out of the aid programme. East Asia and the Pacific should continue to be the primary geographic focus, although there is a need to reduce the number of countries supported, both in the region and beyond. NGOs agree that the number of countries could be reduced, and also that as countries graduate from the programme, resources could be redirected to the regions of greatest need – South Asia and Africa – where Australia currently provides little in bilateral assistance.

The Review recommends more sectoral concentration to allow for the development of greater expertise and to maximise effectiveness. It argues that properly targeted and designed activities in the fields of health, education, basic infrastructure, agriculture and rural development can directly benefit the poorest, while building a broader base for economic growth. NGOs fully support the sectoral concentration suggested by the Review.

Moves towards untying Australian aid to reduce supply-driven distortions are supported and the Review says that Australia should work in international forums to encourage other donors to untie their aid. This can be done by untying aid to the poorest countries, and partially untying aid to other countries by allowing the local procurement of goods and services. The issue of tied aid is one on which there are varied views. The business community sees advantages both ways. NGOs will normally argue for untying, particularly to the recipient countries, while the government will probably favour tying whenever possible to ensure maximum benefit to Australia.

The Review further suggests a new, untied concessional loan scheme be considered, but it must be carefully designed and managed to ensure that it contributes effectively to achieving the aid programme's objective.

It is suggested that the aid programme needs to be reoriented to focus more consistently on outcomes and should be managed by an organisation that values critical analysis and fosters an evaluative culture; that learns from past successes and failures while focusing on the future.

Finally, the Review Team has recommended that the long-held commitment to the aid volume target of 0.7% of GNP is no longer credible and that an achievable three- to five-year ODA/GNP target should be set in its place. It is likely that there will be considerable argument over withdrawing from an internationally agreed target. Many within the Government, the Opposition and the community would rather see Australia set a series of achievable interim targets, while not losing sight of the 0.7% goal.

Many within the NGO and wider community have welcomed the recommendations made in this Review and will be anxious to see how the government will facilitate their implementation. Although the Review is weak on the integration of cross cutting issues, especially human rights, the framework that has been suggested is likely to draw more public and parliamentary support for Australia's development cooperation efforts.

Australia

Box 7 Australia's 1997/8 overseas aid budget at a glance

Australia's aid budget for 1997/8, announced in May 1997, will total A$ 1430 million, A$ 16 million less than the 1996/7 figure, a reduction of 3% in real terms. This comes on top of last year's 10% real terms reduction and brings the ODA/GNP ratio down to 0.27%, its lowest level ever.

This is well below the unweighted DAC average, which in 1996 was 0.40% of GNP.

Comparisons between 1996/7 and 1997/8

To be maintained or increased:

- aid for the South Pacific maintained, but a 2% reduction in real terms;
- country programme assistance to most East Asian recipients maintained, but significant reductions in total aid flows to some countries, in particular Indonesia, China (primarily because of the abolition of the Development Import Finance Facility, the DIFF) and Laos;
- funds to the NGO matching grants scheme increased by A$ 3 million (17% in real terms), and volunteer programmes maintained (but a 2% reduction in real terms). Total flows to NGOs, however, decrease substantially from A$ 102 million in 1996/7 to A$ 88 million in 1997/8, in part due to decreases in funds available through country programmes;
- emergency and refugee assistance to decrease slightly; and
- the largest increases to be in payments to the multilateral banks to meet ongoing obligations – A$ 230.8 million in 1997/8, an 11% increase in real terms over the 1996/7 payment of A$ 204.7 million.

Australia will meet its obligations to the Montreal Protocol and the Global Environment Facility (A$ 4.5 million and A$ 8.9 million respectively).

Major reductions:

- Africa, South Asia, East Asia Regional programmes and UN development organisations suffered the greatest reductions.
- Total development assistance to Africa is expected to be A$ 87.7 million, a 13% reduction in real terms. Of the total to be spent in Africa, A$ 28.3 million will be spent on humanitarian relief. Only A$ 32.3 million will be spent on country programmes (and this includes A$ 2.1 million in scholarships).
- Total aid flows to South Asia will drop 9% in real terms from A$ 89.5 million to A$ 83 million. Pakistan has suffered a devastating 80% cut over two years.
- Contributions to UN organisations dropped 10% in real terms to A$ 67.5 million. This brings the reduction over two years to 25.5%.
- International health programmes to lose A$ 600,000.
- The East Asia Regional programme to decrease by A$ 2 million (9% in real terms).

The government, in presenting the budget, stated that it was 'a very good outcome in the prevailing budgetary circumstances' and that it is 'a considerable commitment to the reduction of global poverty in developing countries, particularly in our own region'.

NGOs have strongly criticised the budget outcome stating that it was simply 'a miserable measure' and referring to Australia's 'badly tarnished international reputation' They stated that it was hard to reconcile the government's stated commitments to poverty reduction with this budget.

Australia

have been substantial changes to the international context in which development takes place, and significant commitments made by governments to a changing international agenda at a range of United Nations conferences and other international fora.

Within a much shorter time frame than that provided to the Jackson Committee, the Review Team has drawn a total of 258 submissions and representations from a broad spectrum of interests: from government departments, the business community, NGOs, academics, and from recipient countries and international organisations. Their report, released in May 1997, will be followed by a period of public comment, public seminars, government consultations, and finally a government response by the end of the year for incorporation in next year's budget.

Given the time and resources absorbed by the review process and the expectation of a renewed focus and direction for the aid programme, there has been little in the way of new initiatives and commitments made by the government in the past year. Nevertheless, the government has already indicated a shift in the general philosophy for Australia's overseas aid.

Programme focus

The government has committed itself to ensuring that the aid programme assists developing countries to reduce poverty through sustainable development. The Minister stated in the Budget Paper that 'The achievement of lasting poverty reduction must be at the heart of Australia's aid programme.' This marks a considerable shift in the rhetoric, there being little mention of the commercial or foreign policy implications of the aid programme.

Until 1991, 60% of Australia's aid was focused on contributing to economic growth, with only 30% directed towards poverty reduction directly and indirectly. There is a growing consensus among aid policy analysts that, while growth is important, investment in social as well as economic development is required to ensure that growth translates into maximum benefits in terms of poverty reduction.

As can be seen from Table 1 many of the countries currently receiving assistance from Australia are experiencing reasonable growth rates. Growth is rarely distributed equitably so growth rates are an inadequate indicator of development. An aid programme needs to go beyond merely focusing on economic growth, rather, it should focus on those sectors or localities that are not benefiting from growth.

Table 1 Growth rates and aid levels in selected countries

Country	Average annual GDP growth 1990–4	ODA as % of GNP 1994	Aid as % of total Australian aid 1994/5
Papua New Guinea	11.5	6.5	21.5
Indonesia	7.6	1.0	9.1
Malaysia	8.4	0.1	1.3
Thailand	8.2	0.4	2.0
India	3.8	0.8	1.4
Bangladesh	4.2	6.9	1.7
China	12.9	0.6	5.7
Zimbabwe	1.1	10.1	0.5
Uganda	5.6	18.3	0.1
Zambia	-0.1	22.3	0.1

Sources: From Plan to Market, World Development Report 1996, Oxford University Press, table 11, growth of the economy, p 208, Table 3: external economic indicators, p 192. Australia's overseas aid programme: statistical summary 1990/1 to 1994/5.

Mixed motives in aid

The Parliamentary Secretary for Overseas Aid, Andrew Thomson, MP, acknowledges that 'much of our foreign aid goes to the fastest-growing region in the world – China and Southeast Asia', and in a speech given in October 1996 stated that the motives for the aid programme are mixed, including:

1. alleviating poverty;
2. helping in humanitarian crises;
3. creating a geopolitical presence for Australia;
4. contributing to security of the region by encouraging development; and
5. promoting our trading interests.

These views of the Parliamentary Secretary for Overseas Aid reflect the tension within the government on the motives and purposes of Australia's aid programme. There is a strong lobby among the business community that clearly desires the aid programme to bring mutual benefits, reflecting an Australian content and presence. Yet the government has received clear messages from the Australian community, and is now articulating that expectation, that the aid programme should address poverty. The government is very keen to

Australia

> **Box 8 Examples of effective Australian aid**
>
> **Water – an essential of life**
> Australia is a country that is familiar with drought, arid soils and fragile water systems. The sustainable management of water has been an area of constant challenge and Australia now has considerable experience and expertise in this area to offer developing countries. Expenditure on water supply and sanitation within the bilateral aid programme has increased over the past five years from A$ 10 million in 1990/1 to A$ 50 million per annum in the past two years.[3]
>
> AusAID's approach to water and sanitation provision is to involve the local communities in the design, implementation and management of projects.
>
> Local community involvement, taking into account women's and men's roles in the sector, is cost-effective, focuses on the real needs of communities and builds skills, understanding and commitment, which will assist the long-term maintenance of services.
>
> **Philippines water project** A$ 30 million project involving both the Philippine and Australian governments has attracted one of Australia's most prestigious engineering awards. The Central Visayas Water and Sanitation Project will provide over 500,000 people in the most disadvantaged areas of the central Philippines with clean, safe water, along with related improvements to their health and quality of life. The Award of Merit from the Association of Consulting Engineers, Australia, particularly acknowledges the project for its 'strengthening of community capabilities and for helping to improve the lives of hundreds of thousands of people'.
>
> The project involves the local people in identifying and solving their own water and sanitation problems. Activities include the rehabilitation of existing water and sanitation systems and the design and construction of new ones. Through the setting up of local water user associations, the communities actually have ownership of the facilities. The project is of particular benefit to women, who no longer have to cart water from distant locations. They are now able to participate in other productive activities.
>
> **Planning development in the Mekong Basin** An Australian aid project is establishing strategic links and encouraging the sharing of knowledge and experience between the Mekong River Commission (MRC) and the Murray-Darling Basin Commission (MDBC) in Australia. The project is designed to assist the Mekong states in using the natural resources of the Mekong Basin in ways that are equitable, cooperative and sustainable. According to AusAID, appropriate management of the Mekong Basin is crucial because of the competing demands between and within countries for electricity, irrigated land, drinking water and fish and forest products.
>
> The interchange between MRC and MDBC is relevant because they face similar management challenges. The Murray-Darling Basin is shared by states and is subject to the same sorts of competing resource demands and management priorities. AusAID has committed $900,000 to the project over three years.

involve the private sector more in development and is actively encouraging alliances between NGOs and business.

The Aid Review has attempted to resolve some of these tensions in the mandate for Australian overseas aid, following extensive consultations between the Australian community, government and business interests, and with some of the recipient country governments and communities. NGOs have stated clearly that development cooperation funds should be targeted to sectors that will not attract private investment and that will contribute towards building human and social capacity by enhancing the productivity of poor people using participatory approaches.

Accountability: NGOs under the microscope

Studies of the relationship between AusAID and

Australia

NGOs were conducted by the Industry Commission's Inquiry into Charitable Organisations (completed in June 1995), by the AusAID Review of the Effectiveness of NGO Programmes (completed in July 1995) – both pronounced that NGOs had made an effective contribution towards development – and by the Australian National Audit Office. The efficiency and effectiveness of volunteer programmes was also reviewed during 1996. The government announced a number of reforms aimed at simplifying systems and at reinforcing the work NGOs have been doing to improve their own professional capacities to deliver effective assistance and to manage the funding the Australian community provides.

The major element of the reform package was an improved system for accreditation of NGOs to be jointly managed by government and NGOs. This is consolidated with standardisation of administrative procedures for all NGO funding schemes, improved systems for accountability and performance measurement, changes to monitoring procedures, along with streamlined and simplified project application and reporting processes.

This reform package will not, however, apply to the funding of local NGOs in developing countries, an activity that is increasing across the bilateral programme.

A less than promising outlook for aid

Further cuts to the aid budget have taken place this year and may well continue next year. Government forward estimates indicate some small recovery movement upwards towards the year 2000, but these are not expected to reach even the levels of 1995.

Political and public support for aid is hot on the agenda and is constantly being reassessed. A study commissioned by AusAID analysing various surveys conducted since the early 1970s concludes that:

> Overseas Aid is approved of by a majority (66–75%) of Australian adults [and] this level of support has been maintained for over two decades, as has been the case in most developed countries when examined over time. There is no evidence of any decline in support. Where perturbations occur they are likely to be a reflection of different survey techniques.[2]

Yet there has been a strong parliamentary critique of the aid programme, particularly in the context of a conservative and inward looking political climate. Domestic issues are dominating parliamentary and media debate: indigenous people's rights, reconciliation issues, industrial restructuring, workers rights and unemployment, immigration and environmental issues are high on the political agenda. Global and regional relationships have, for the moment, been put to the side.

Notes
1. The weighted average is calculated by adding the GNP of all DAC donors and dividing this by their combined ODA. The weighted average is therefore heavily influenced by the larger economies, particularly Japan and the USA, whose aid performance as a percentage of GNP tends to drag down the figure. A more accurate way of comparing donors' commitment to ODA would be to use the unweighted figure – a simple average of aid levels as a percentage of GNP for all donors.
2. Elliott, B, *Review of Community Attitude Surveys on Overseas Aid*, AusAID, Canberra, 1997.
3. AusA!D, *Focus*, March 1997: 10.

Austria

Helmuth Hartmeyer, AGEZ
and Michael Obrovsky, ÖFSE

Main forces, new initiatives

In 1996, for the first time in Austrian history, a two-year overall budget was fixed by the new government. This followed a year when a newly elected coalition government split (new elections had to be held in December 1995) and when Non-Governmental Development Organisations (NGDOs) cooperating with the state faced a most difficult situation as it was unclear what budget would be available to finance their work.

The new two-year overall budget has helped to consolidate the main budget for development cooperation – the project and programme aid administered by the DDC (Department for Development Cooperation) in the Ministry of Foreign Affairs. An amount of ATS 870 million plus a further ATS 100 million budgetary supplement was negotiated with the Ministry of Finance and, after still more uncertainty, actually realised at the end of 1996. It was again made clear that anything that would decrease the budgetary uncertainty caused by planning on an annual basis, would be welcome. Following the coalition government negotiations in Spring 1996, AGEZ published a document in the following July, *For an Efficient Development Cooperation*, which demanded an annual legal provision of ATS 1000 million for project and programme aid, with a gradual increase built into it, leading to the doubling of the amount over the next ten years.

The outlook for aid and new approaches – shaping the 21st century

The OECD Development Assistance Committee (DAC) document *Shaping the 21st Century* is an important contribution to development cooperation, but it has to be seen whether it will be more than an expression of intent. No implementation in Austrian practice can be observed yet. This is partly due to the fact that there is no institutionalised discussion of development cooperation issues within the government and no open debate about the principles of aid. In particular, there is too little dialogue between the two most important actors, the Ministry of Finance and the Ministry of Foreign Affairs. Even within the Ministry of Foreign Affairs there is little dialogue between the departments (sections) responsible for multilateral and bilateral aid, or within the Section for Project and Programme Aid, or between the political and the project departments.

The rationale for aid is not explicitly made public by the government. For example, security is discussed almost exclusively in a militaristic context and therefore the question whether Austria should join NATO overrides any argument of international human and social security through increased development cooperation. Thus, the outlook for aid has a number of question marks over it. Furthermore, public support seems to be sinking in Austria and political support is traditionally low.

Regardless of its contributions to the EU development budget and its future payments into the European Development Fund, the Austrian government, specifically the Ministry of Foreign Affairs, wants to continue its own Austrian programmes and projects. Despite this wish, the official country programmes, which exist for some of the eight Austrian priority countries, have not yet been discussed in public. Although the planning of budget lines for priority countries and priority sectors has improved, putting them into practice is another matter. Staff capacities in the administration are limited and it is necessary both to monitor the various projects and to encourage staff to feel the need to develop an approach that involves intervening in matters of detail. For these reasons, and in order to be able to participate in the various OECD and EU committees, the construction of a

Austria

The **Reality** of Aid 1997/8

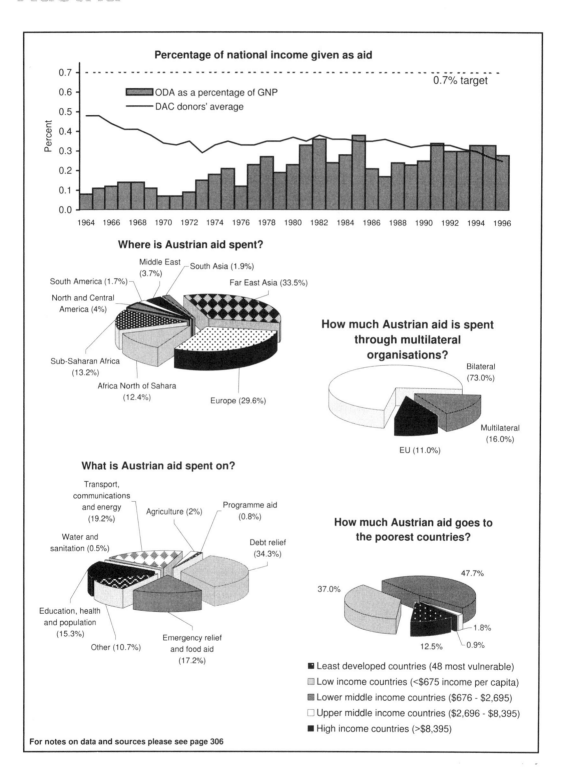

The **Reality** of Aid 1997/8

Austrian aid at a glance

How much aid does Austria give?

Austria gave	US$ 640m, 7090 million Austrian Schillings in 1996
that was	0.28% of GNP
and	1.74% of public administration
which meant	US$ 80 or 883 Austrian Schillings per capita for 1996

Is it going up or down?

In 1996 Austrian aid	fell by $147m, down 14% in real terms over 1995
Austria was	less generous in 1996, dropping from 0.33% of GNP to 0.28%
The outlook is	for a decline in 1997 to 0.27%

How does Austria compare with the other 21 donors?

Austria ranks	16 out of 21 for its volume of aid
It is	14 out of 21 in the generosity league
It gives	a lower proportion of its aid (49.5%) to Low Income Countries than 17 other donors
Private Flows	amounted to $6m, less than 1% of ODA
Total Flows	to developing countries were 0.39% of GNP and rank 15 out of 21 in the DAC

How much does Austria spend on basic health and basic education?

Austria	has not yet reported to the DAC on its basic health and basic education spending

How important are commercial interests in aid?

Austria	has not reported for 1994, but figures reported for 1993 show that 41% of ODA had to be used to buy Austrian goods

What do the public think about aid?

> **Public support exists, but political support is traditionally low**

Austria

system of advisers and contractors will be enlarged. In 1996, a contract with an adviser for gender issues was signed.

Coherence

There is no overall national budget for ODA in Austria. The Ministry of Finance administers more than 50% of ODA. Almost 10% of ODA was administered by the Ministry of the Interior in 1995 and was used to support refugees (mainly from former Yugoslavia) and a further 5% was used by regional and local authorities for the same purpose. This high proportion was criticised by the OECD Development Assistance Committee (DAC) in its 1996 Aid Review of Austria. It was also the case that Austria allocated the entire costs of supporting refugees, although according to DAC guidelines only costs in the first year can be regarded as official development assistance (ODA). The Austrian government has agreed that this money has little to do with development cooperation issues and hopes to bring these figures down, now that the war in former Yugoslavia has, hopefully, come to an end.

On top of this, almost 10% of ODA was allocated as imputed students costs in 1995. This was also criticised in the DAC Aid Review. Doubt was cast on the idea that universities' expenditure would come down by the amount of the imputed costs if these students were not in Austria. Most students involved have come from Turkey, Iran, Korea and Taiwan, not from Austrian priority countries, and the funding of their higher education contributed little to poverty alleviation. On top of this, in the small number of other countries that report such figures, the amounts were much lower – between 1% and 5% of ODA.

There was a third harsh point of criticism in the 1996 DAC Aid Review. It was made clear that only Spain and Austria had a system of subsidised export credits, which they included in their reporting system.

The Aid Review drew attention to the lack of developmental criteria in decisions on extending export credits. It noted that aid quality comments were often unsubstantiated and that export credits were not restricted to priority countries or sectors and were only loosely subject to DAC principles. While concluding that 'there remain doubts as to whether these credits are extended with the main objective being the promotion of economic development of the recipient countries' it also acknowledged that Austria was taking some steps towards improving the quality of its development assistance in line with recommendations in previous Aid Reviews.

The Austrian government has promised to respond to all the criticism, but it has to be feared that it will not change any statistical habits (especially in the Ministry of Finance) as long as these help to increase the ODA figures in general and get Austria to a better international ranking than it deserves. Yet, in an answer to Parliament on 19 June 1996 the Minister of Foreign Affairs stated that the Austrian reporting system would be rechecked and that negotiations with the OECD about the way export credits were allocated had already begun. AGEZ took up this promise in its July document *For an Efficient Development Cooperation* demanding that export credits, imputed student costs, help for refugees from European countries and costs of Austrian embassies in developing countries should be excluded from ODA figures.

In 1995, 18.72% of ODA was left to the Ministry of Foreign Affairs. This Ministry is responsible for the coordination of Austrian development policy, but handicapped by its weak financial position. It therefore comes as no surprise that there are no generally accepted common principles for an overall Austrian development cooperation policy. When NGOs talk about 'Austrian development cooperation' they are generally referring to project and programme aid based in the Ministry of Foreign Affairs. The lack of real coordination in the government can be seen from the official Austrian Three Year Programme of Development Cooperation, in which both the Ministry of Finance and the Ministry of Foreign Affairs each write what they think best.

There is little coordination between bilateral and multilateral development cooperation. There is too little transparency about Austrian IMF or World Bank policy and Austria does not take part actively enough in the international UN fora for multilateral aid.

To overcome this, the Official Advisory Committee for Development Cooperation should become a committee responsible for the totality of ODA. A special reform paper was developed in 1996, but many fear that its implementation will remain a long lasting challenge.

Can relevant reactions to the Austrian DAC Aid Review really be expected, particularly as the report was basically seen as a contribution of praise for some progress achieved? The State Secretary, who is responsible for development cooperation in the Ministry of Foreign Affairs, has spoken about

Austria

relevant development issues on only a few occasions in Parliament, in bigger conferences or to the media. AGEZ would therefore like to see the government make a detailed annual report to Parliament on development cooperation.

The new Parliament itself in 1996 reconstituted a standing subcommittee for development policy, which took up its work by looking into Austrian cooperation with Uganda. This followed a study tour by some Parliamentarians to this priority country of Austrian development cooperation.

Aid and poverty

The DAC and the EU claim the eradication of poverty as a priority. This is also the case in the Three Year Programme of Austrian Development Cooperation, but it cannot really be verified in practice. Austrian statistics do not give enough evidence of the specific content of programmes and projects. What can be observed as a new trend is a certain prioritisation of the productive sector – small scale business and trade. NGOs claim that basic social services should not be left out of consideration in this context.

There is no sectoral programme called 'poverty elimination', but it is an aim of practical sectors like agriculture or health. Statistically it is not explicitly taken into account. A special codification would certainly help. In his answer to Parliament from 19 June 1996 the Minister of Foreign Affairs claimed the elimination of poverty to be a cross-sectoral task, which would be taken into consideration in all planning. He also stated that about half of the budget for project and programme aid was realised through NGDOs.

The application of the 20:20 principle is hard to judge, because there is no definition of 'basic social services'. Gender aspects of poverty are not a central point of consideration, although also in this respect the Foreign Minister claimed that the consideration of gender aspects was a priority in Austrian development cooperation. Although no given percentage was foreseen for gender-oriented projects, activities to strengthen this area are planned.

A campaign, *Initiative 96*, with the aim of lobbying for debt reduction measures to be taken by the Austrian government, was carried out mainly by Catholic NGOs but supported by many others. It had its highlight in October, when more than 50,000 signatures were handed over to Parliament. The political results still have to be accomplished and would effectively contribute to poverty alleviation in a number of LLDCs.

Cooperation with the EU

The Austrian government has no official policy towards EC development policy, yet its importance is clearly recognised and the basic aims in the Treaty of Maastricht are accepted. However, the principles of Coordination, Coherence and Complementarity have – as in the EC itself – not yet been translated into reality. Generally speaking, any EU policy is supported more or less uncritically. NGOs demand a more active role of the government, especially when it comes to the negotiations on Lomé V in 1998.

The EU has created a certain pressure for a more explicit internationalisation of Austrian aid, which is positive, but it is not reflected by all the NGDOs that have not yet taken this internationalisation on board in the way in which they work and there is too little transparency about its effects. EU resolutions are often unknown and have only a very general influence.

AGEZ and the EU platform of Austrian NGOs staged a hearing with prospective Austrian members of the European Parliament before the European elections in October 1996. All of them promised to keep development issues high up on their agenda. Meanwhile, it has become known that only one of the 21 Austrian MEPs will be a substitute in the Committee on Development and Cooperation. A new interest in EU development policy could be evoked before and during the Austrian presidency in the second half of 1998.

The remarkable interest of a number of NGOs in the EU and possible cooperation with Brussels has been fading away somehow and has, on occasion, even turned into frustration. This is partly because the 'big Brussels funds' have proved to be far less accessible by NGOs with small funding of their own than had originally been expected. A few NGOs have left the common Austrian EU NGO platform and some fear the moment when increased co-financing of contributions to the Liaison Committee from the national platform are demanded. Others have developed successful working relations with the Commission and have already realised a number of bigger projects.

Humanitarian aid

The Chancellery is responsible for humanitarian assistance although a number of ministries are

Austria

involved. The main activities in 1996 concerned former Yugoslavia and most were carried out through a few NGOs, which also continued a successful TV and radio campaign.

Cooperation with NGOs

Austrian NGOs basically support the Austrian government in its claim to develop and run its own programmes and projects. This is partly because some have good working relations with the Ministry of Foreign Affairs and are subsidised for their programmes and projects with considerable sums.

What worries these NGOs is a trend in the administration to build up its own contacts to Southern NGOs. The administration has continued to establish its own offices in Austrian priority countries and feels encouraged in this policy by the decentralising concept of the EU. The role of Northern NGOs is thus put into question. It also causes uncertainty because this policy is not discussed publicly. The NGOs want to continue the discussion about their role in civil society and vis-à-vis the state and have themselves taken up an initiative to look into the quality of their work. They have again expressed their hope that tax relief on charitable donations will be made possible by the government in its next tax reform. Most NGOs do not get any public funding and, even in 1996, a year of common recession and increased burdens from taxation, allocated more money from private sources than in 1995.

Public support and awareness raising

In 1996 a big Africa festival, *Sura za Africa*, took place in Austria. It attracted remarkable interest from the media and hundreds of thousands of people to its various events, which included exhibitions, concerts, African markets and discussions.

AGEZ launched a campaign to adopt parliamentarians. NGOs and their members are encouraged to contact their local MPs and inform them regularly about topical development issues.

The Society for Development and Cooperation (KommEnt), having the task of coordinating, monitoring and administering NGO activities in the field of development education and public information, has become an accepted leader in the field of awareness-raising and has exercised a positive influence for more stability and coherence in this area.

The administration itself also strengthened its own efforts to inform the public about its activities and to create a positive image of development cooperation in a broad sense.

Belgium

Geert Jennes and Melanie Schellens, NCOS

Kleur Bekennen: Commitment to reform of Belgian development cooperation

For Belgian development cooperation, 1996 has been another 'intermediate' or lost year. Since the end of 1995 an atmosphere of crisis has been provoked by the continued publication in Flemish newpapers of a number of old aid money scandals – most of which predate the time of the current Secretary of State for Development Cooperation. Most dramatic, however, has been the sinking of the *Bukoba*, a Tanzanian ferry, in May 1996, in which more than 700 passengers drowned. The *Bukoba* had been delivered by a Belgian shipbuilding company to Tanzania in the early 1980s as a result of a tied government-to-government loan. The *Bukoba* lacked stability from early on. After a formal request from the government of Tanzania in 1989 to repair it, the Belgian administration in charge of development cooperation (ABOS) still had not succeeded in properly contracting out the repair.

In reaction to this and other scandals, an indignant Secretary of State made a firm commitment to the reform of Belgian development cooperation in *Kleur Bekennen* ('Showing our Colours') in October 1996, followed by an information campaign *De tijd van knikken is voorbij* ('The time for nodding yes is over') in Spring 1997. At the same time, he made an important gesture by appointing as head of ABOS a civil servant from outside (whose previous experience had been in a social security ministry but who had had some experience of development cooperation) and demonstrating a more accountable leadership style. Equally important was the Secretary of State's attempt to limit the scope of the discredited former directors.

The new head has tried to flatten the structure of ABOS, by delegating more decision-making power to the levels below director-general. In practice, the signature of approval of the three directors-general (who are political appointments, two of whom have strong ties with the (big) business lobby) is no longer needed on a number of dossiers. However, rigid Belgian civil servant regulation allows them, at least physically and financially, to stay within the administration until they retire so they still have some scope to block ABOS reform.

Volume and spending capacity

Kleur Bekennen does not seem sufficiently determined to rationalise the management of the Belgian development aid budget. ABOS, which has been traditionally politicised, is top-down and weak in terms of both its political power and spending capacity. Top civil servants rank the problem of lack of *qualified* staff even higher than that of *quantity* of staff. Respected aid administrations like UK ODA and Danida employ fewer staff in total than ABOS does. Although ABOS is expected to undergo profound reform and has slightly improved its 'spending ratio' – the amount ABOS spent (disbursements) as a proportion of its budget (commitments) – from 75% in 1995 to 78% in 1996, Belgian development cooperation is likely to remain seriously understaffed and will continue to cope with spending capacity problems. These render a spending level of 0.7% not only unlikely but also undesirable on a short-term basis, unless ABOS contracts out an even higher share of its budget to NGOs and multilateral donors.

From 1997, Belgium's contribution to IDA is to come from the ABOS budget. Belgium's IDA contribution for 1996 amounted to BEF 3200 million; for 1997 it is BEF 2100 million; and for 1998 and 1999, BEF 1700 million. For 1997, there has been an increase of only 900 million in ABOS resources to fund this and the Ministry of Finance, formerly responsible for IDA, has not released funds for other development cooperation. Expectations for a substantial increase of Belgian development aid in 1997 are, for this and other reasons, low.

This contrasts with *Kleur Bekennen*, which repeats the commitment made by the Prime Minister

The **Reality** of Aid 1997/8

Belgium

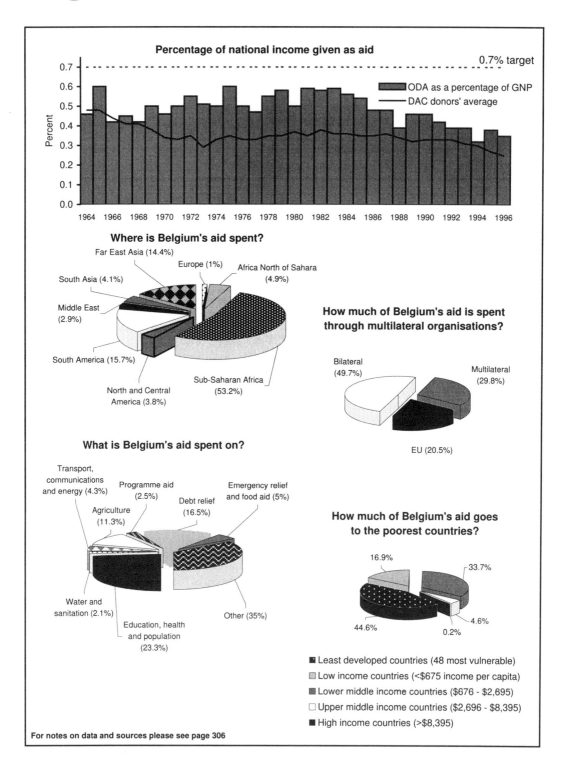

For notes on data and sources please see page 306

The **Reality** of Aid 1997/8

Belgium

Belgian aid at a glance

How much aid does Belgium give?

Belgium gave	US$ 937m, 28,252 million Belgian Francs in 1996
that was	0.35% of GNP
and	2.6% of public administration
which meant	US$ 93 or 2811 Belgian Francs per capita for 1996

Is it going up or down?

In 1996 Belgian aid	fell by US$97m, a drop of 6.4% in real terms over 1995
Belgium was	less generous in 1996, dropping from 0.38% GNP to 0.35%
The outlook is	that the current level will stabilise rather than continue to fall

How does Belgium compare with the other 21 donors?

Belgium ranks	15 out of 21 for its volume of aid
It is	7 out of 21 in the generosity league
It gives	a lower proportion of its aid (61.5%) to Low Income Countries than 11 other donors
Private Flows	returning to Belgium from developing countries exceeded flows from Belgium by US$1554m, one and a half times times ODA
Total Flows	to developing countries were just negative (that is Belgium got back more than it spent) at - 0.09% of GNP - bottom of the league in the DAC

How much did Beligum spend on basic health and basic education?

Belgium reports	1.5% of ODA spending on basic health and 0.2% on basic education. This was the first year that Belgium has reported on these figures

How important are commercial interests in aid?

1992 was	the last time tied aid from Belgium was reported to the DAC. At that time, 50.8% of ODA had to be used to buy Belgian goods

What do the public think about aid?

51% of Belgians are in favour of giving more Belgian aid
72% of Belgians think development cooperation is important

Belgium

at the Rio conference in 1992 to spend 0.7% of Belgian GNP for development cooperation 'by the year 2000 or as soon as possible thereafter and depending on budgetary imperatives'. A concrete intermediate goal is for aid spending to reach at least 0.5% of GNP by the end of the legislature in 1999. *Kleur Bekennen* states that an increase of the budget for Development Cooperation should be possible as soon as Belgium fulfils the criteria for (in the government's view primordial) access to economic and monetary union (EMU).

Aid management and coherence

The Belgian development budget is split between ministries. The major need for coherence is between ABOS and the Ministry of Finance, which together account for more than 90% of Belgian aid. Coordination between them is mostly informal.

Achieving coherence between these two ministries is made even more complex by the different responsibilities of national and regional authorities. The Flemish region is using the crisis within ABOS as an argument for a transfer of development cooperation to the regions. Flemish development cooperation is gradually gaining importance. It is mainly business oriented towards (lower) middle income countries, which are 'promising' for the plethora of Flemish small and medium sized enterprises (SMEs) but at the moment it is largely concentrated on strengthening the judiciary in South Africa.

In pursuing one of his key objectives – conflict prevention – the Secretary of State has to reckon with the competencies of more powerful government bodies. Coherence has been damaged by the Belgian official Export Credit Insurance Agency (NDD), which has guaranteed export credits for the arms trade. A particularly painful example was the NDD guarantee for the construction of an arms plant, started in 1988, by 'Fabriques nationales de Herstal' (FN) in Eldoret (Kenya). The 1991 transfer of authority for arms exports from the national level to the Flemish and Francophone regions has been particularly harmful to coherence. Mainly because arms production is, economically, more significant in Francophone Belgium than in Flanders, and because, economically, Francophone Belgium fares much worse than Flanders, 'export visas' for arms are more easily granted by the Francophone region than by the Flemish region.

The Minister of Foreign Affairs tries to monopolise diplomacy, while the Secretary of State for Development Cooperation is interested in practising 'field diplomacy' in central Africa. Also, for party-political reasons, the Secretary of State for Development Cooperation is, for the first time in Belgian history, 'attached' to the Prime Minister (who belongs to the same political party) and not to the Minister of Foreign Affairs. Both factors have led to haggling and incoherence with regard to the conflict in central Africa. Therefore, the Secretary of State for Development Cooperation has argued the case for a single 'Ministry for International Cooperation', which would imply an integration of Foreign Affairs and Development Cooperation drawing on the Dutch and the Danish models.

However, coherence in development issues has in principle been promoted by the establishment of a so-called Interdepartmental Working Group on Development Cooperation in 1994 (as a result of NGO pressure). It is chaired by the Secretary of State for Development Cooperation and consists of most government departments that have anything to do with development aid, including Agriculture and Defence. Up until now, it has been a slumbering body.

Aid tying

Belgium has an implacable tradition of (commercially) tying its bilateral aid.

ABOS 'financial cooperation' comprises 'investment, sectoral programmes and capital participation'.[1] Financial aid is heavily tied to 'Belgian' (but in some cases French-owned) companies. An example is ABOS's Debt Relief Programme. Since its start in 1991, ABOS has had to tie BEF 550 million a year to 'buying' non-performing debt claims (most of which would never have been paid back by the debtor country concerned anyway) from NDD (NDD guarantees export credits provided by 'Belgian' banks to 'Belgian' companies). In effect, this is bailing out NDD under the cloak of debt relief. Paradoxically Minister of Finance Maystadt, who can veto export credit guarantees provided by NDD, is also known for his efforts to help the Highly Indebted Poor Country (HIPC) multilateral debt reduction plan, and is even mentioned as a possible successor to Camdessus at the IMF. Therefore, the 'national' debt reduction efforts by Belgium contrast with its 'international' debt reduction efforts.

Even some multilateral contributions from ABOS are tied. Part of the Belgian contribution to the World Bank is in the form of the 'Belgian Consultant Trust Fund'.

The (albeit shrinking and in budgetary terms marginal) bilateral part of development cooperation administered by the Ministry of Finance is almost completely tied. Interest rate subsidies granted by the Ministry of Foreign Trade are tied to 'Belgian' banks giving export credits to 'Belgian' companies. Ironically, aid tying in Belgium is largely in vain, because a lot of companies in Belgium are foreign (often French) owned. Sectors benefiting from soft loans and interest subsidies are mainly infrastructure-related, often to power and transport. The development impact of the projects financed by these loans and subsidies is not formally evaluated. However, both instruments together accounted for only about BEF 1000 million in 1996; the bulk of Belgian tied aid is spent by ABOS.

Public opinion puts the blame for the scandals on ABOS, even though they largely result from these last two forms of tied aid administered by the much more powerful Ministries of Finance and of Foreign Trade. These scandals have provoked such a stir in the Belgian development community over the past two years that the current Secretary of State bravely announced his intention to abolish aid tying right away in *Kleur Bekennen*. It had been a long time since a Minister or Secretary of State for Development Cooperation had stated so clearly that development cooperation has its own, specific objectives, which differ from export promotion and foreign policy.

The Secretary of State will probably have to limit his ambitions to untying aid administered by ABOS. But even this may be difficult. As the (less visible) aid budget of the Ministry of Finance, as well as official export credit insurance are under even more budgetary pressure than ABOS, proposals by the Belgian business lobby entailing new commercial 'hold-ups' on the ABOS budget have increased during 1996.

Nevertheless, in April 1997, in reaction to the publication of the 'scandals', the Secretary of State proudly announced the cancellation of ABOS commitments amounting to BEF 2000 million and relating to projects of 'doubtful developmental value'. Apart from mentioning that these projects concern telecommunications, railways and electrification, no further justification is provided. We can, however, assume that these projects concern commercially tied aid. Nothing has been said about on what the freed funds are to be spent.

Another new feature of *Kleur Bekennen* is its 'Private Sector Development Programme' (PSOP). This aims to support joint ventures between Belgian and Southern SMEs on the basis that it is more feasible for the budget (cheaper), more redistributive and more labour intensive than contracting out large infrastructure projects to 'Belgian' big business.

Critics consider PSOP a party-politically inspired substitution of 'white mice' for 'white elephants'. The Secretary of State can probably only do away with the big business lobby by replacing it with the small business lobby. He might have been able to avoid this compromise, however, not by trying to untie Belgian aid unilaterally, but instead through coordination with other bilateral donors. Academics reject PSOP as an 'abdication' of official development cooperation and criticise it for confusing large infrastructure projects with tied aid and small-scale projects with untied aid. They think official development cooperation has adopted too much of a small-scale oriented NGO vision and should instead be complementary to an NGO approach.

This view is reinforced by *Kleur Bekennen*'s limited and patchy coverage of macro-economic issues such as debt, conditionality and trade – a weakness that will not help to foster coherence with other ministries. An illustration of the need to address these issues is provided by the tendency of the Secretary of State to earmark Belgian counterpart funds – generated by balance of payments aid and often requested by ABOS in return for debt relief – to specific Belgian social sector projects 'in the field'. Macro-economically speaking, this is a harmful practice and runs counter to the policy of spending counterpart funds through the regular recipient government budget, something that most other donors have recently adopted.

Concentration policy

Belgian development aid is not only fragmented on the donor side, but also on the recipient side. Another laudable intention of *Kleur Bekennen* is to counter the trend in the 1990s towards increasing geographical, sectoral and multilateral de-concentration, which is particularly damaging in a small donor country like Belgium. In fact, Belgian aid has always been de-concentrated, but this has been masked by the large share of the aid budget allocated to Belgium's former colonies – Burundi, Rwanda and Zaïre/Congo – before the 1990s.

Belgium

Geographical concentration

Kleur Bekennen sets out some laudable, if numerous (seven), criteria for geographical concentration. They are said to have resulted in the following countries being identified for ABOS concentration: Rwanda, Burundi, Zaire/Congo, Bolivia, the SADC region, Burkina Faso (Burkina Faso will apparently be entitled to only BEF 200 million a year but, despite its limited budget, it will be provided with nine ABOS staff, the largest local staff of all countries receiving Belgian aid) and the Philippines. The most positive feature of this list is that it is the shortest that has ever been presented. In reality, however, the list of Belgian 'concentration' countries depends on cabinet preferences, legitimised by the criterion 'affinity' (instead of objective criteria), and is ever changing and highly informal. The two newly added countries at the end of the short list are especially subject to political haggling and labelled 'Christian Democrat' countries.

Palestine has already been added to the list and, in the Spring of 1997, the Belgian government announced a series of initiatives to strengthen the Belgian commercial presence in the 'emerging markets' of Latin America, including the use of instruments of development aid where possible. In 1996, a comparable initiative was taken for Asia. Worse, pressure from some influential NGOs led the Secretary of State in April 1997 to establish a number of new local ABOS sections in a number of countries, such as Brazil, some of which do not even receive direct ABOS funding. Again, this results in further fragmentation of scarce ABOS resources. Finally, neither other ministries nor the international donor community seem to have been involved in *Kleur Bekennen*'s concentration proposals.

It is difficult to predict who will be the Secretary of State for Development Cooperation after the 1999 elections. It will depend highly on political preferences. A long-term policy is not guaranteed.

Sectoral concentration – poverty reduction

Kleur Bekennen stresses the micro level: sectoral concentration towards health, education, agriculture and 'the social economy' – local socioeconomic initiatives based on cooperation rather than on profit-seeking; for example, informal savings and health insurance groups. At the same time, the 1997 budget contains two new lines totalling BEF 500 million for 'conflict prevention' – the keynote, and personal, objective of the current Secretary of State.

Though clearly poverty-oriented, these core sectors of future Belgian development cooperation are still understood too broadly. No reference is made to international coordination. No tangible targets for poverty reduction have been set, apart from the fact that the 20:20 compact is to be included as a condition in every bilateral agreement between Belgium and a developing country.

For the present, the 'Belgian Survival Fund', established by Parliament in 1983 and financed by non-ABOS budgetary means, remains the only category of ABOS spending explicitly earmarked for poverty reduction (and to sub-Saharan Africa). In practice, however, poverty reduction is understood to mean food security, but also agricultural and health projects in general. Its reputation has long been damaged by serious underspending (see *Reality of Aid* 1994, pp 44–5), but things have changed for the better since 1993, when a competent civil servant was put in charge of close follow-up of the programme. In 1996 an all time high of BEF 667,000 million was spent within the Fund. The Fund is expected to be depleted within a few years. Belgian NGOs, through which some 20% of the Fund is channelled, will ask for a continuation of the programme. ABOS, however, thinks the Survival Fund saddles it with an extra parallel structure, which could be easily integrated into the ABOS structure itself.

Some BEF 650 million has been budgeted for 1997, to be channelled through IFAD, UNICEF, FAO and Belgian NGOs. The Fund will concentrate on countries suffering from continual food insecurity, countries in or recently emerging from a conflict situation, and poor countries that are ready to design an effective strategy for poverty alleviation. Most country examples given are not future ABOS concentration countries. The bulk of the Survival Fund is channeled through IFAD, of which ABOS is a major donor. IFAD's reputation, however, has suffered from its provision of loans (mostly) instead of grants, from its centralised structure, and from its lack of an evaluation culture.

A novelty of 1996 was the preparation of 'sectoral notes' on health, food security, education and 'society building'. ABOS had started this important policy preparation work before *Kleur Bekennen* was published, but both appear to be consistent with each other. The Secretary of State appreciates these efforts and intends to involve ABOS more in such policy preparation. In 1997, it will direct its efforts towards 'country notes'.

Belgium

Multilateral concentration

Largely as a result of former personal commitments by successive ministers and secretaries of state, Belgium now supports about 57 multilateral development institutions. A positive intention made explicit in *Kleur Bekennen* is to halve the number of multilateral development institutions supported by ABOS. The decisions will be made on the grounds of links to sectoral and geographical priorities in Belgian development cooperation – agriculture, health and SSA among others. The European Development Fund and IDA, currently almost 50% of Belgian multilateral contributions, are expected to remain at the core of Belgian multilateral aid. The multilateral concentration plan does not refer to UN reform.

Public opinion on aid

Public opinion is one of the new priorities for Belgian aid. Funding for public information and development education has gone up from BEF 57 million in 1995 to BEF 96 million in 1996. Activities are not limited to an increase in grants for NGO and school-based development education, but also involve increased education activity by ABOS itself. An example is the information campaign mentioned above, *De tijd van knikken is voorbij* ('The time for nodding yes is over') in Spring 1997, which even included big posters in Belgian railway stations. In reaction to the negative press on official development cooperation, the Secretary of State for Development Cooperation intends to broaden the public base in favour of development cooperation in Belgium. This is welcome, but is part of a pattern of occasional launches of large-scale information campaigns. What is lacking is a sustained information effort.

A survey carried out by the European Commission at the end of 1996 found out that the Belgian general public ranks North–South issues low on its 'problem scale'. 'Home issues' (such as unemployment and the judiciary) are given explicit priority by 31% of the respondents. Only 51% of the Belgian public is in favour of more Belgian development aid, compared with an EU average of 67%. Only 72% of Belgians think development aid is important, compared with an EU average of 87%. Only 41% of Belgians think investment in the poorest countries pays off more than investment in more developed countries. Suspicion of aid money fraud is stronger in Belgium than in other EU member states (15%), and one out of every two Belgians doubts the accuracy of information provided on development aid. Reportedly these are all EU extremes.

A positive evolution has been the functioning of a 'parliamentary follow-up commission on ABOS' during 1996, which investigated aid money scandals. It is hoped that it will generate more interest in Parliament for development cooperation in general. The Commission has pushed for more transparency and for 'a culture of evaluation' within Belgian development cooperation, attributing much of the cause of the scandals to aid tying and lack of evaluation.

NGO reform

The Secretary of State has presented a proposal for reform of NGO co-financing to be implemented in 1997, and operational in 1998. By aiming a shift from laboriously financing thousands of single NGO *projects* towards financing consistent five-year *programmes*, it contains laudable incentives for: more professionalism and specialisation, scaling up, cooperation between NGOs, and *ex post facto* evaluation as opposed to auditing of NGOs by ABOS; and time for this is supposed to become available thanks to the transition from project to programme financing. This is to be funded by a new budget line of BEF 50 million for planning and evaluation by external experts.

However, it is doubtful that the external planning and evaluation input will be enough to enable systematic *ex post facto* evaluation, let alone policy preparation by ABOS. There is only sufficient funding guaranteed in the near future to match the spending capacity several NGOs have now acquired within the framework of programme financing. Others fear that political pressure from NGOs will result in enabling every NGO to benefit from the programme without any significant strings being attached.

Note

1. In the latter case ABOS will buy shares in a company it thinks relevant from a developmental point of view. An example is its profitable participation in the Shanghai subsidiary of Alcatel Bell, a French owned telecommunications giant.

Canada

Brian Tomlinson
Canadian Council for International Cooperation

What future for Canadian development cooperation?

Repeated and substantial cuts to the international assistance envelope over the past five years in Canada have been leading many in government and NGOs alike to question the efficacy of current priorities and mechanisms for delivering Canadian development assistance.

The February 1997 federal budget brought no respite, with a confirmation of the 15% total cut for 1997/8 and 1998/9 announced last year.[1] Moreover, it also failed to outline any plan to stabilise or increase Canadian ODA beyond 1998/9, despite the prospect that the federal deficit will be eliminated, well ahead of target, by next year. As a percentage of GNP, by 1998/9 Canadian ODA will reach its lowest level since the mid-1960s – 0.27%. But the questioning is less and less about aid allocations *per se*, and increasingly about the rationale for aid, the changing nature of relations between Canada and developing countries, an overburdened aid agenda, and the consequent choices for Canadian foreign policy.

There are strong signals that government officials are rethinking assumptions about priorities and channels for Canadian development assistance. Some of this originates in a return to a foreign policy that seeks active roles for Canadians in shaping solutions to global problems. A long-standing debate between the Canadian International Development Agency (CIDA) and the Department of Foreign Affairs and International Trade (DFAIT) on the focus and institutional responsibility for development cooperation policy has resurfaced. But, questioning assumptions has not been confined to government. The entire development community has been weighing in with its own policy perspectives and prescriptions.[2]

Some of the parameters of this debate are starting to emerge informally in discussions with government officials and in recent policy papers. This chapter sets out some of the issues behind these new directions and their implications for development cooperation and NGOs.

A return to foreign policy activism

Foreign Minister Axworthy has fulfilled expectations that he would be a minister keen to establish a distinct and activist foreign policy, one that responds to the values set out in *Canada in the World*, the government's 1995 foreign policy statement. Through his leadership, and with encouragement from the voluntary sector, academics and other non-state policy actors, he has an ambitious agenda for Canada:

- Achieving a universal treaty for a global ban on antipersonnel landmines to be successfully negotiated by December 1997;
- Supporting human rights and democracy in Nigeria, Burma, and through the UN Commission on Human Rights;
- Taking initiatives in peacekeeping and peace-building in Haiti, the Great Lakes region of Africa, Bosnia, and Guatemala, and in multilateral fora;
- Recognising the importance of global flows of information through new communications technologies, but also the gross inequalities in access and impact in the South;[3]
- Taking leadership and action on the rights of the child (including child prostitution and child labour) as a strong priority in Canadian foreign policy.

All are important initiatives and provide opportunities for effective NGO policy interventions and for more complex (non-financial) relationships between government and some NGOs. But there is debate within government about ceding too much 'policy space' to non-state actors, and questioning of the legitimacy and capacities of NGOs in these processes.

Trade promotion versus sustainable human development

The positive qualities of these high profile initiatives are contradicted by the continued strong promotion of trade and investment linkages with countries whose governments are widely condemned for human rights violations. The policy influence of Canadian trade interests are ever present and the interests of the marketplace seem to prevail. This past Autumn, the government rescinded by edict its environmental assessment legislation to permit the sale of CANDU reactors to China. Joining some European countries, Canada refused to sponsor the annual China resolution at the UN High Commission on Human Rights.

A January 1997 Team Canada trade and investment mission to Asia, led by the Prime Minister and provincial premiers was confronted by evidence of the social and environmental costs of their narrow focus on market opportunities and 'jobs for Canadians': national strikes in South Korea; protests by NGOs against the possible sale of CANDU reactors to Indonesia; and demonstrations in the Philippines against the environmental destruction brought by Canadian mining activity (Placer Dome) in that country.

Overall policy coherence remains the key issue. How can human rights initiatives, concern for child labour, or peace-building activities be reconciled with the overwhelming priority to promote Canadian trade and investment interests abroad? How do they fit with Canada's active promotion of regional trade agreements in the Americas, or with Canada's policies for the international financial institutions?

The challenge for Canadian NGOs will be to influence government policies to make them coherent with a long-term agenda of sustainable human development. But coherence itself is not the policy goal. The danger is that NGOs' own short-term needs, for instance for funds, will drive them towards government imposed coherence, which may be at a substantial cost to the fundamental values of social justice that underlie NGO work. These long-standing dilemmas for NGOs everywhere may be sharpened in Canada over the next year as thought is given to a reorganisation of international development cooperation policy.

Public interest in global issues

Importantly, much of the current debate has taken place behind 'closed doors'. Successive governments, the media and many NGOs have largely failed to engage Canadians around the importance of global issues. Foreign policy in general has fallen off the public agenda and played no part in the June federal election campaign that brought the Liberals back to power with a reduced majority. Widespread (but soft) public support for aid is sustained by public rationales for development assistance that remain locked into a 30-year-old *donor–recipient framework*. Canadians, unfortunately, may be ill prepared to participate in setting new directions for development cooperation.

Private agencies, donor governments and multilateral institutions share much of the responsibility for the *donor–recipient framework*. It results from repeated appeals to Canadians to respond to emotionally charged images of humanitarian crises and of the desperate human faces of absolute poverty. Deliberate and purposeful leadership by government and NGOs is urgently required to break free from these images, to involve the public media and to channel an often naïve humanitarianism towards more authentic relations with developing countries that are still value-led, but are more complex and reciprocal, involving both government and society.

Whither North–South policy dialogue?

Policy tensions, but also opportunities for creating a more propitious environment for North–South dialogue, are evident in a recently completed foreign policy review by DFAIT. The conclusions stress the crucial importance of an open rules-based global economy for Canadian trade and investment competitiveness, emphasise the need for strong multilateral action to counter a plethora of post-Cold War threats to human security (crime, drugs, terrorism, environment and population growth), but also highlights the importance of non-state actors – corporations and NGOs – seeking to influence the agenda and the results of foreign policy.

The border between domestic and international issues is dissolving in areas such as basic social and labour rights, migration and population issues, aboriginal rights, or women's rights. DFAIT's rationale for Canadian international cooperation policies appears to be shifting from altruistic

Canada

The **Reality** of Aid 1997/8

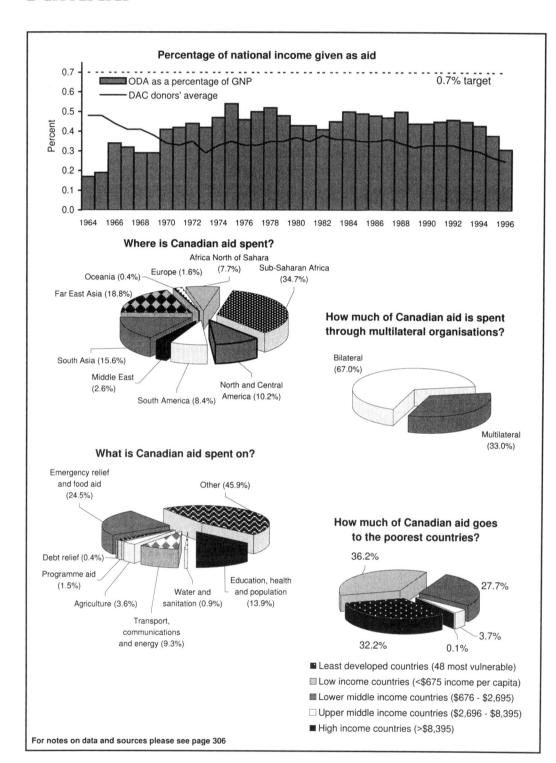

The **Reality** of Aid 1997/8

Canada

Canadian aid at a glance

How much aid does Canada give?

Canada gave	US$ 1782m, 2684 million Canadian dollars in 1996
that was	0.31% of GNP
and	1.89% of public administration
which meant	US$ 60 or C$ 90 per capita for 1996

Is it going up or down?

In 1996 aid	fell by $285m, a drop of 15.4% in real terms over 1995
Canada was	less generous in 1996, dropping from 0.38% of GNP to 0.31%
The outlook is	ODA is projected to reach 0.27% of GNP for 1998/9

How does Canada compare with the other 21 donors?

Canada ranks	9 out of 21 for its volume of aid
It is	11 out of 21 in the generosity league
It gives	a higher proportion of its aid (68.4%) to Low Income Countries than 13 other donors
Private Flows	amounted to $2074m, 100% of ODA in 1995
Total Flows	to developing countries were 0.86% of GNP and rank 7 out of 21 in the DAC

How much does Canada spend on basic health and basic education?

Canada reports	0.2% of ODA spending on basic health but has not yet reported on spending on basic education

How important are commercial interests in aid?

70 cents out of	every Canadian development dollar was used to pay for Canadian goods and services in 1995/6 – up from 65 cents in 1991/2

What do the public think about aid?

> Around 63% of Canadians support the aid programme and 53% think that official aid levels are about right or should be increased

humanitarianism, much less poverty eradication or global equity, to a 'narrower' political view of Canadian interests in human security. International intervention is seen as essential to protect Canadians from the consequences of failure to address global threats.

Seeking policy alliances Policy discussions in DFAIT stress trends in international capital flows, global trade, and domestic capital mobilisation as the key engines of development in the 1990s. In this largely market-oriented context, international assistance has a diminished role in Canada's relations with developing countries and in the strategies now available for advancing Canada's interests in human security. More and more, Canadian initiatives in environment and human security are seeking out policy-specific alliances with selected developed and developing countries. These are mainly in the multilateral arena, involve a range of relationships, including NGOs and other non-state actors and often require financial and technical resources.

For example, Malaysia, Brazil, China, Russia and Mexico are seen as crucial to the achievement of Canadian objectives for an international forestry convention. Canada has been working closely with them and has financed several pilot forestry projects. Several major environmental organisations working informally with the Canadian government have achieved status at the negotiating table with government representatives. More recently, these same organisations have become highly critical and opposed to Canadian proposals brought to the UN in February 1997.[5]

This example points to newly emerging opportunities for NGOs (mainly in the North) to have a policy impact on critical development issues. But it also raises questions. Do most (Canadian) NGOs have the capacities and the grounding in international policy coalitions, involving authentic dialogue and policy consensus with southern counterparts, to be able to manage and change the character of these emerging government-led North–South initiatives?

Clearly, some of these trends have potential for greater North–South policy reciprocity in Canada's future relations with developing countries. They are more inclusive of NGOs and others, and are characterised less by 'donor charity'. But a government oriented to politically motivated short-term objectives and to the promotion of narrow economic interests will surely skew current development cooperation policies and practices. The critical question is how might these trends affect the potential for longer-term Canadian strategies to address global imbalances in favour of people living in poverty?

How will the rationale for development cooperation affect people living in poverty?

Winners and losers
What might be the implications for the declining allocation of international cooperation resources? In Canada, replacing the more traditional debates between aid to the poorest countries and people versus aid tied to economic interests in donor countries, the DFAIT review seems to use the language of *winners* and *losers* among developing countries to discuss the allocation of aid.

There are those within Foreign Affairs who continue to argue that scarce aid resources should be concentrated upon the *winners* – those countries that have the potential to grow out of the need for assistance, or that have followed the 'right' economic policies, and that have achieved a level of political stability.[6] Ghana, Uganda and countries in Southeast Asia are given as examples.

Others argue for a more balanced approach that includes protecting Canadian interests from the consequences of deteriorating human security among the *losers*. The latter are seen as the 'failed states' of Africa that have destroyed their development capital, where aid may be buttressing forces that are resisting much needed political change, and that lack the resources ever to achieve sustainable development. Today, development interventions in many of the poorest countries are seen to be more complex and uncertain in their results. They are more political in their choice of channels and partners, and more interventionist in the degree of policy dialogue required and conditionalities attached to assistance. Increasingly, NGOs and other non-state actors are proposed as the most appropriate channels to address basic needs of people living in extreme poverty in these countries, to be accompanied by government contributions of humanitarian assistance.

The Sustainable Human Development Agenda
NGOs argue for a more comprehensive, long-term, values-led approach. Coherence in

Canadian development cooperation should be achieved through sustainable human development (SHD), implemented through policy dialogue and programming alliances involving civil society organisations, government and the private sector as appropriate, within and between countries. The priorities, the alliances and the means for promoting SHD will vary between countries and regions, but the point of departure must be the host country. At the centre of the SHD agenda are the goals of global equity and poverty eradication, both in the South and the North.

Canadian NGOs have been largely supportive of core CIDA policy statements for poverty reduction, women in development and gender equity, and (approved this past year) a policy framework for the role of the voluntary sector in development cooperation. They speak to the framework of SHD. But they have also been consistent critics regarding limited evidence of impact and the absence of transparent implementation strategies.[7] While progress is being made in identifying and coding the intent of development projects against broad policy goals, this is only a small step in advancing shared learning within CIDA and beyond about the impact of long-term development programming for poverty eradication.

Development cooperation overload Compounding the questioning of development cooperation, has been the 'loading' of the development assistance agenda. To some degree this is provoked by budgetary cuts in other departments that have been 'off-loading' administrative and programme costs for special initiatives onto the aid budget. Examples from the past year include:

- C$ 10 million dollars for DFAIT's peacebuilding fund;
- CIDA money to support training for the Haitian police force from Canada's national police force, the RCMP;
- C$5 million to preserve Radio Canada International; and
- Canadian contributions to expensive de-mining activities in Cambodia and Mozambique for the Department of Defence.

Added to this 'off-loading', are multiple and diffuse policy goals for the development cooperation regime – improved governance, private sector development, environmental security and institutional capacity-building.

Over high expectations are placed on the roles and possible impact of development cooperation, leaving it vulnerable to the perception of failure. At present, aid is very much oriented to the interests of various Canadian stakeholders, with particular sensitivity to the interests of the private sector, and less to those of NGOs. Any realistic intention to concentrate CIDA resources strategically on clear poverty eradication goals will have to be sharply focused, well thought out, and with a strong strategy to build public engagement.[8]

What are the options?

Responsibility for managing Canada's international cooperation policy is again under discussion. There has been a long-standing debate, and sometimes tension, between DFAIT and CIDA over the authority to set Canada's international cooperation policy.[9] This has been accentuated by the recent creation of the *Global Issues and Culture Branch* within DFAIT. This Branch has been developing parallel policy authority around current issues such as human rights, economic and social development and peace building, but without the budgetary resources of CIDA with which to finance initiatives.

Strengthening the voice of SHD in Canadian foreign policy should be the priority. For the *Global Issues Bureau* in DFAIT, this implies a strengthened knowledge base in SHD and a strategic policy role within DFAIT, including responsibility for economic relations with developing countries. Strengthening CIDA's ability to deliver quality long-term SHD (especially poverty reduction) programming should be an equal priority. This requires programme focus that is guided by a substantial knowledge base, enhanced by augmented policy, research and evaluation capacities. Both require opportunities for knowledgeable non-governmental actors bringing new voices in public policy dialogue, implying greater transparency and accountability.

Finally, it is incumbent upon the government, after years of continuous cuts totalling more than 40%, to restore a positive outlook for sustainable human development, beginning with a specific timetable for rebuilding the aid budget. It is impossible to conduct any coherent public foreign policy with respect to developing countries when the resources available are subject to protracted attrition, compounded by uncertainty about the future.[10]

Canada

A key challenge over the next year for Canadian NGOs, and others committed to a global strategy for sustainable human development and poverty eradication, is to rethink how best to design Canadian official and non-state contributions for these efforts, while contributing leadership to policies that will affect the achievement of a more equitable world order. One Canadian author who has looked at other donor experiences around these dilemmas concludes that bureaucratic structure may be the least of the problems; the best structure will flow from political leadership and a clear articulation of policy and purpose.[11]

Notes

1. For details on the February 1997 federal budget and the 1997/8 Expenditure Plan for CIDA see CCIC Policy Team, '1997/8 Federal Budget and CIDA's 1997/8 Expenditure Plan Estimates', February 1997 mimeo and available on CCIC's web site, www.web.net/ccic-ccci. See also the Canada chapter in the 1996 edition of *Reality of Aid*.
2. IDRC, North South Institute, IISD, 'Connecting with the World: Priorities for Canadian Internationalism in the 21st Century', A Report by the International Development Research and Policy Task Force (Maurice Strong, Chairman), November 1996; North South Institute, Canadian Development Report, NSI, 1996; Report on an Aga Khan Foundation Roundtable 'Systematic Learning: Promoting Support for Canadian International Cooperation', 22–23 June 1996, forthcoming.
3. See IDRC et al, 'Connecting with the World', op cit for an elaboration of the implications of an evolving knowledge-based global economy for international cooperation. The report suggests that Canada's strategic advantage in the twenty-first century will be as a 'knowledge-broker' and emphasises the importance of elaborating knowledge-based networks as central to Canadian foreign policy. It suggests that at least 15% of Canadian ODA be devoted to knowledge-based activities by the year 1999. NGO commentators welcomed the identification of knowledge and development as a process of change and learning. However, they have expressed concern for the rather narrow definition of knowledge and a tendency to portray knowledge as an end in itself in the report. Without articulating the kind of world we are seeking to build, even a knowledge-based strategy may lead us to squander resources. A knowledge-based strategy needs to reflect much more authentically on the sources and application of knowledge. NGOs, in the North and the South, contend that to be useful and relevant, the knowledge of the 'experts' – the researchers and evaluators – needs to be combined with that of the 'doer' – those who implement and manage and participate in programmes and projects on the ground. They suggest that ODA resources for these activities (the 15%) should be directed to all levels of these knowledge networks and not just for the research centres and the (important) role they play.
4. The following overview of the conclusions of this internal DFAIT policy review has been constructed from comments by knowledgeable DFAIT officials. To date no report has been made public.
5. 'Canada Opposed on Forestry Rules', *Globe and Mail*, 12 February 1997, B6. An environmental coalition said that 'the Canadian proposal would enshrine weak rules, undermine existing environmental agreements, bury critical problems under years of fruitless debate and do more to protect international trade than trees.'
6. These issues were first brought to light by the infamous DFAIT International Assistance Policy Update, prepared by Assistant Deputy Minister Barry Cairn in late 1993, that proposed to Cabinet that development assistance be restructured more closely to serve Canadian interests in 10 to 16 growing economies of the developing countries. See Cranford Pratt, *Canadian International Assistance Policies: An Appraisal* (McGill/Queens Publishers, 1996) for an analysis of this Update and the reactions to it as the precursor for the 1994/5 foreign policy review and its outcomes.
7. See the Canada chapter in the 1995 and 1996 editions of *Reality of Aid*.
8. See the discussion of this issue in Roger Riddell (Overseas Development Institute, London UK) 'Trends in International Cooperation', to be published as part of the report from the Aga Khan Foundation Roundtable 'Systematic Learning: Promoting Support for Canadian International Cooperation', 22-23 June 1996, forthcoming.
9. See Cranford Pratt, 'Policy Coherence and the Institutional Future for Canadian ODA', a draft background paper commissioned by the North South Institute and the CCIC, March 1997.
10. The previous two paragraphs are based on the conclusions of an April 1997 workshop sponsored by CCIC and the North South Institute to look at issues of policy coherence and the institutional framework for Canada's relations with developing countries.
11. Ian Smillie, 'Notes on the Structure and Restructuring of Official Development Assistance in Europe and Elsewhere', commissioned by the North South Institute and the CCIC, March 1997, drawing on David Gordon et al, 'What Future for Aid', The Foreign Policy Project, Overseas Development Council and the Henry L Stimson Centre, Occasional Paper number 2, November 1996.

Denmark

Susanne Pedersen, Mellemfolkeligt Samvirke

Danish aid to developing countries, not including special appropriations for environmental protection and emergency assistance, is 1% of Gross National Income,[1] which amounts to DKK 10,361 million in 1997 (at 1997 prices).

On the multilateral scene, some notable changes include an increase in appropriations for the UN population and health programmes (despite a reduction in Danish aid through the World Health Organisation) and a cut in aid through the World Bank Group.

In the five-year plan 1997–2001, it is indicated that Denmark's aid will be maintained at 1% of the country's GNI, but in the distribution of kroner there are some interesting changes.

In the debate on the 1997 state budget estimates, some politicians argued, with reference to the budgetary deficit and cuts in development aid budgets in other countries, that aid from Denmark should be reduced. The proposal was met with resistance, especially from one of the government parties and NGOs, and it was not incorporated into the state budget estimates.

Danida's strategy for poverty reduction

Over the last year, a central debate has been about the approach to poverty reduction: how to conceptualise and operationalise the objective of poverty reduction as outlined in Danish development policy?

In September 1996 – two months before an Evaluation of Poverty Reduction in Danish Development Assistance(!) – Danida published a strategy for poverty reduction. Current Danish aid efforts are based on a long-term understanding among policy makers and aid bureaucrats that a basic premise of Danish aid is the focus on alleviating poverty. But lack of a more explicit and operational poverty focus throughout the last two decades has meant important constraints on the effectiveness of past poverty reduction efforts. Prior to very recent analytical and policy work, neither the Danish aid administration nor others had tried to define more specifically how Danida's activities can and/or have contribute(d) to poverty alleviation.[2]

Danida states in the policy paper that it is strengthening its procedures and tools for the planning, implementation and evaluation of assistance. The aim is to make sure that poverty reduction is clearly understood as the pivotal point for all aid activities.

In an aid strategy document from 1994, a range of different but interconnected features related to poverty are identified: lack of access to land, lack of education, poor health conditions, limited coping capacity in situations of crisis, women being especially exposed to poverty. This is further elaborated in the 1996 policy paper, which contains a detailed presentation of the characteristics and causes of poverty. Here, there is a deliberate emphasis on moving away from perceiving poverty as primarily related to lack of income, focusing instead on an inability to cater for basic needs, lack of opportunities to exploit human resources, isolation, lack of status and power, and a high degree of vulnerability due to a very limited economic base. The paper refers to data emphasising the gender dimension of poverty and stresses the rural dimensions of poverty.

A rather long list of 'closely related causes of poverty' is presented in the policy paper emphasising *inter alia*, lack of political will, lack of economic infrastructure, lack of access to social services, degradation of natural resources, population growth, and adverse international conditions. The paper does not award any priority to the different causes of poverty – let alone identify one more 'fundamental cause'. Rather, it emphasises how the many complex causes hamper efforts to break out of poverty and argues for a mixture of efforts at the macro-level (such as policy reform, budget restructuring) and complementary interventions aimed at more focused interventions (such as organisations of poor farmers and women,

The **Reality** of Aid 1997/8

Denmark

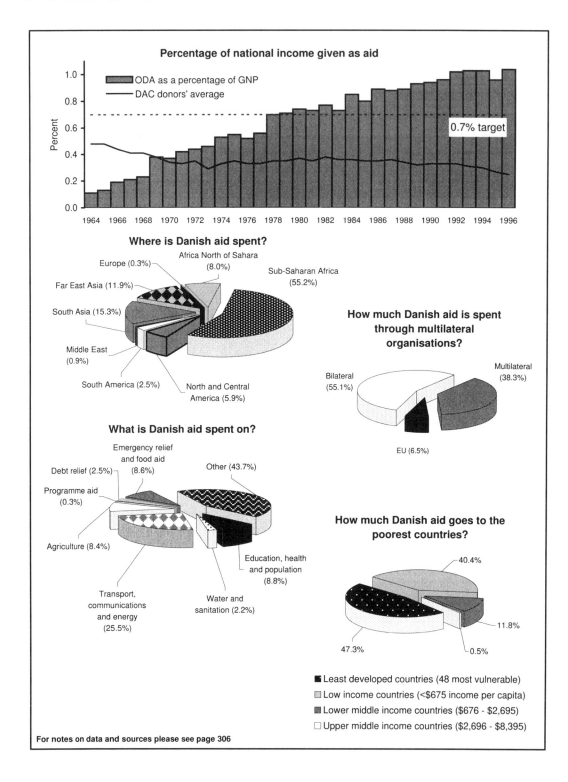

For notes on data and sources please see page 306

The **Reality** of Aid 1997/8

Denmark

Danish aid at a glance

How much aid does Denmark give?

Denmark gave	US$ 1773m, 10,454 million Krone in 1996
that was	1.04% of GNP
and	3.74% of public administration
which meant	US$ 338 or 1991 Danish Krone per capita for 1996

Is it going up or down?

In 1996 Danish aid	rose $150m, up 10.5% in real terms over 1995
Denmark was	more generous in 1996, rising from 0.96% GNP to 1.04%
The outlook is	good with ODA remaining at around 1% of GNP

How does Denmark compare with the other 21 donors?

Denmark ranks	10 out of 21 for its volume of aid
It is	first out of 21 in the generosity league
It gives	a higher proportion of its aid (87.7%) to Low Income Countries than 18 other donors
Private Flows	returning to Denmark from developing countries just exceeded flows from Denmark by US$7m, 0.43% of ODA
Total Flows	to developing countries were 1.07% of GNP and rank 3 out of 21 in the DAC

How much does Denmark spend on basic health and basic education?

Denmark reports	0.2% of its ODA spending on basic health and 1.1% on basic education

How important are commercial interests in aid?

Denmark	works on a general principle that 50% of bilateral aid should be used to procure goods and services in Denmark

What do the public think about aid?

> In 1995, 75% of the population supported aid from Denmark at 1% of GNP

targeted social sector interventions in support of marginalised groups).

The policy paper states that Danish assistance to agriculture will increase substantially over the years to come. The argument is that the economic policies and sector policies must create the foundation for growth in those sectors where poor people are concentrated and from which they derive their income. Creating a foundation for growth in the agricultural sector, through increases in productivity, is thought to give the best possibility of contributing to a broad-based growth and poverty reduction, especially in Africa.

Bearing in mind the social and humanitarian foundation of Danish assistance, Danida sees it as natural to concentrate assistance on the poorest of the poor. But, in the words of the policy paper:

> *It is, however, not the extremely poor people who are the carriers of the dynamic economic and social development, which Danida strives to support with development assistance. Aid to this group will often be composed of aid more or less in the character of relief. It does not start a development process, but only contributes to the chances of immediate survival.*

With these conflicting considerations, the strategy paper foresees problems when it comes to the aim of providing evidence of the poverty reduction effects of any Danida activity.

With the transformation from project assistance to sectoral programme support, the difficulty of designing practical poverty reducing strategies (and showing that they can have an impact) will be the responsibility not just of Danida, but also of ministries in the programme countries. And where aid is being used to support a sector – or for instance as budgetary support – it will be even more difficult to show a visible impact on poverty than it is in a traditional project with a clearly defined target group.

Evaluation of poverty reduction in Danish development assistance

In 1994 Danida initiated a major Evaluation of Poverty Reduction in Danish Development Assistance to be carried out by private consultants. The synthesis report was delivered in November 1996.

General Danida policy statements imply that the poverty reduction objective encompasses the whole aid programme, including multilateral contributions, support for Danish NGOs, the private sector programme and support for mixed credits. In practice, though, primary attention is attached to the Danida portfolio sent to the 20 programme countries, and it is also this part – around 25% – of the total Danish ODA with which the evaluation deals.

The report is permeated with a mixture of praise and criticism for not having performed well enough. Overall, the evaluation concludes that aid provided in the past gets high marks when appraised from the poverty reduction perspective. It says that nearly all the selected interventions have contributed towards positive improvements in the lives of the beneficiary groups, often through increased employment, diversified sources of income, improved quality of food, household items and medicines. However, an ambiguous or even a negative impact on some aspects of people's livelihoods was also experienced in a few cases: increased workload for women and children is one example; the deteriorating nutritional status of household members is another.

The impact seems to be most significant in relation to resources, with improved access to a range of services such as water supply and sanitation, health, rural roads, rural credit schemes, education, regional administrative structures, and markets for the sale of produce and materials.

The enhancement of people's knowledge is also reported to be a result of most development aid interventions. The impact on rights, in terms of participation in decision-making and democratic processes, is said to have been of a more limited nature.

On the more negative side, the evaluation team finds that Danida could have done better if it had been more specific in its definition of methods for reaching the poor.

In a comment, Development Minister Poul Nielson takes up the challenge:

> *We must be better at focusing on poverty reduction when we prepare country programmes and design interventions. Our policies and guidelines must to a greater extent than today be reflected in the project documents.*[3]

The relevance of the evaluation is necessarily somewhat reduced since it has taken place at a

The **Reality** of Aid 1997/8

Denmark

time when Danida is moving from project aid to sectoral programme support. As far as the new assistance is concerned, the evaluation team notes:

With sector programme support and policy-based programme assistance, Danida will not only be held responsible for the quality of the specific support, which Denmark provides, it will also be expected to ensure that Danish support fits well into a poverty-focused development framework, which is managed by the recipient government and effectively coordinated with other donors.

Danish NGOs have started to plan a study of the effect of their own development efforts. The actors/partners/receivers in the South will be actively involved in the process. The aim is to make a constructive contribution to the debate about Danish development aid, including the capacity of aid to make a better life for the poorest.

Sectoral programme assistance

Sectoral programme assistance is becoming the dominant aid form within bilateral Danish assistance. Sectoral programme assistance consists of broad support for a variety of activities within a sector. It is intended to be integrated into the recipient country's sector policy and coordinated with support from other donors.
   The Development Minister Poul Nielson thinks that sector programmes are good platforms for aid dialogue, ownership and aid coordination.

The process of preparing sector programmes forces us and the recipients to make priorities instead of the more convenient approach of jumping from project to project. During the process, we have hearings in Denmark as well as in the recipient countries. This contributes to a feeling of ownership in the recipient country when the final choice is made, and contributes to priority-setting in the recipient country.[4]

The shift in the Danish aid strategy resulted in 1995 in the underspending of DKK 405 million against the appropriation of 1% of GNI for development assistance. This was because it has taken time to adapt to the new system. (Total Danish aid amounted to DKK 9263 million in 1995). In some cases, a reserve from 1995 was carried forward into 1996, which has consequently resulted in a substantial decrease in bilateral aid from 1996 to 1997. But it has been a temporary problem, in 1996 the ODA/GNI ratio was 1.06%, of which the 0.04% (DKK 405 million) is the underspending transferred from 1995.
   Table 2 shows the sectors chosen in the 14 country strategies that had been concluded at the time of writing (out of 20 programme countries). Different forms of infrastructure are chosen in ten countries, agriculture in ten countries, health in six countries, education in six countries and water supply in five countries.

Sector priorities

Table 2 Chosen sectors where country-strategies are completed

Bangladesh	Water and sanitation, infrastructure, agriculture
Benin	Water, agriculture, transport
Bhutan	health, environment and natural resources management, development of cities
Burkina Faso	Water, energy, agriculture
Egypt	Environment, energy, water and sanitation
Eritrea	Education, agriculture
Malawi	Agriculture, telecommunication, education
Mozambique	Education, health, agriculture, fisheries, electricity
Nepal	Education, environment, use of natural resources
Tanzania	Health, transport, infrastructure, agriculture, private sector
Uganda	Health, water, agriculture, infrastructure
Vietnam	Fisheries, agriculture, natural resources management, infrastructure
Zambia	Education, health, infrastructure
Zimbabwe	Health, agriculture, industry, infrastructure

Environment and development

The Framework for Environmental Protection and Emergency Assistance (FEPEA) was established in conjunction with the agreement on the 1993 State budget. FEPEA will receive increasing finance annually until 2002, and from then on, will be fixed at the level of 0.5% of the Danish GNP. A quarter of this will be channelled to environment projects in developing countries – approximately DKK 1500 million in 2002. The FEPEA fund is divided between Danida and Danced (Danish Cooperation for Environment and Development in the Ministry of Environment and Energy). Danida is responsible for environmental assistance in so-called Danish 'programme countries', while Danced will be in charge of initiatives in countries with a GNP above the limit for bilateral development assistance.

The responsibility for administering the FEPEA will, in the remaining countries, be assigned in connection with the development of regional strategies. Denmark has developed regional strategies for environmental cooperation with Southeast Asia and southern Africa.

The resource base

A study by the Danish Technological Institute (DTI) concludes that the so-called resource base – people with interest, talent, knowledge and experience in the field – is insufficient in comparison with the projected budget increase of DKK 1500 million by 2002 for environment projects. Of this amount, DTI estimates that some DKK 500 million will be used for Danish consulting services. These increased environmental activities will double the current demand on the resource base. Most of the consulting services needed for FEPEA-financed activities will be in the field of environmental protection.

The shortage will apply in particular to people with 'soft' qualifications, defined by DTI as team-building and management skills, process-oriented and intersectoral methodology, cross-cultural understanding and communication, and participatory methodology.

Evaluation

Environment is considered to be both a crosscutting issue[5] in Danish ODA, and a sub-sector in its own right. In 1995–6 an evaluation was carried out, with the overall objective of assessing to what extent, and how, environmental considerations have been integrated into Danish ODA since 1988. Based upon this, the evaluation was to make recommendations for the future.

In the last decade, a lot of improvements have taken place regarding the integration of the environment into Danish ODA. But the evaluation also found that not all Danida's declarations of intent have been sufficiently followed up.

It is estimated that in the ten programme countries screened by the evaluation, Danida's bilateral assistance to environment as a sector and as a crosscutting issue combined constitutes about 12–14% of the annual bilateral disbursement in 1994, compared with 5–6% in 1989.

Danida claims that between 15% and 20% of bilateral assistance has environment protection as a crucial or important component. NGOs have criticised this account for being opaque and misleading, for a project that only has environmental protection as an important part of the aim is not considered as an environmental protection project.

The critics have argued that if Danida's counting method is to be used, the share of environmental activities should be higher than 15–20%, since sustainable environment is proclaimed to be a key objective of Danida's assistance.

During the evaluation's examination of many project documents, it became clear that many projects included limited economic analysis, which, if done differently, could include environmental economic evaluation. It is recommended therefore that, in future, Danida incorporate the use of economic valuation techniques in estimating the environmental costs and benefits of Danida's own proposed projects and programmes.

The evaluation also noted that no formal unit in Danida monitors the implementation of policies and strategies. So it recommends that Danida strengthen this, define baseline conditions and establish relevant indicators and/or parameters to facilitate the monitoring of interventions in terms of their impacts on the environment.

Consultancy fees for Danish aid services

Fees charged by consultants for overhead costs triggered a conflict with Danida. Development Minister Poul Nielson had demanded that not more than 90% of the fees should be charged as overheads, while various firms maintained this was unrealistic. When they refused to comply, Danida experimented by opening 16 contracts for international competition. The result was lower prices. Even Danish bids managed to drop below the 90% level. According to the Minister's review of the situation, Danida would have had to pay 10% more if the 16 projects in the market test had not been put up for international tender.

> ## Box 9
>
> ## Effective aid from Denmark to Nepal Nari Bikash Sangh: MS-Nepal in partnership with a Nepali women's organisation
>
> By Nina Ellinger
>
> Nari Bikash Sangh (NBS) is a Nepali women's NGO founded in 1980 in the south-southeastern part of Nepal. NBS has a membership of 15,000 women organised in 25 branches in 15 districts and with five regional offices. The main objective of the organisation is to alleviate poverty by focusing its activities on the socially and economically disadvantaged communities and by applying a strategy of self reliance in these communities. A gender sensitive implementation strategy encourages harmonious and participatory relationships between men and women, but women are the main focus of the programme activities. The population in the districts where NBS operates are composed of eight ethnic groups.
>
> NBS has carried out development work in the last 17 years; however, in the first ten years activities were carried out with its own and local resources. Since 1991, international development assistance has been received. As of 1996, NBS contributed 8.8 % of its own budget in kind and cash contributions. A Danish development worker was requested in 1994 and a partnership project proposal was finally signed for a five-year period of commitment by both parties in 1996.
>
> The aim of the partnership is to increase the sources of income and the self-confidence of the rural women and their capacity to participate in local development through literacy training, participatory awareness campaigns, skills training, and savings group formation in eight districts in Nepal by the year 2001. The main strength of NBS is undoubtedly its training capacity with ten long-experienced, qualified trainers as core members of the organisation. Training and service are provided for NBS members, as well as for other NGOs and for Maila Bikash Sarah, the governmental women's organisation.
>
> By gradually decentralising in a selected number of branches and by developing the staff, sustainability of the organisation will be strengthened. The central office will then improve its ability to act as an advocacy platform for destitute women and provide more efficient support to community development. Some 1170 disadvantaged men and women are direct beneficiaries of the activities being carried out, but the effects of the partnership activities are expected to spread to family members, neighbours and relatives, with a total of 6,500 community members.

Nevertheless, from now on, bidding will be closed to foreign companies, except when Danida feels local firms lack capacity, or when competition in Denmark is not sufficient. In principle, Danida still wants Danish supplies of goods and services. According to the Minister, the argument is that the popular support for maintaining development aid at 1% of GNP is possible because broad layers of Danish society, including private companies, take part in development work. Furthermore, Danida need Danish companies as a resource base and therefore has an obligation to contribute to the maintenance of their competence.[6]

The chairperson of the Danish Association of Consulting Engineers insists that Danish consultants understand Danida's policy and organisation better than their foreign competitors and, normally also, than Danish aid recipients and that this should give them a preferential position. But the organisation is satisfied with the result on the conflict with Danida and agree with the view that there should be reasonable competition.[7]

Notes

1. Broadly equivalent to GNP.
2. Lars Udsholt, *Danish Aid Policies for Poverty Reduction*, CDR Working Papers 96.7.
3. *Development Today*, 22/96.
4. *Development Today*, 16/96.
5. Inferring that it is to be systematically integrated in all sectors of aid, in all stages of the project cycle and in all aid forms.
6. *Development Today*, 23–24/96.
7. *Development Today*, 1/97.

Finland

Folke Sundman and Mark Waller, KePa

New trends and developments

The most important development of 1996 came in the autumn with the release of the government's *decision-in-principle*, or policy profile, on the strategies and objectives of development cooperation. This had been preceded by the publication in February 1996 of a wide-ranging policy review that set out a series of priorities and options for improving the funding and content of ODA. The new government decision represents a welcome shift in focus toward a firmer commitment to development, and a clear break from the low point of the early 1990s when ODA spending was cut, under the previous administration, from 0.8% of GNP to 0.3% of GNP. Reductions in ODA as a percentage of GNP have now been reversed. What increase there is in funds will, this year, be divided equally among all categories of aid.

The main points from the decision-in-principle

- The government has unfrozen ODA spending, reaffirmed its commitment to the 0.7% level of ODA as a long-term goal, and has set 0.4% as the level to be reached by the year 2000.
- Policy will target poverty by support for economic reform for growth. ODA will emphasise basic education and health services, and highlight the security of food supply.
- Sustainable development goals will emphasise environmental programmes and be integrated into agricultural and forestry activities. They will also aim further to develop the ownership of the partner in cooperation.
- Issues of human rights, equality and democracy will be dealt with openly in Finland's dialogue with partner countries. The government will regularly assess results in these areas and reconsider its support to projects and cooperation in the light of whether goals are attained. It will in all contexts promote the implementation of the action programme of the Beijing IV World Conference on Women.
- Bilateral cooperation will continue to focus on long-term development for the poorest developing countries, particularly in sub-Saharan Africa, but Finland will be prepared to react to rapid changes in developing countries. This means that Finnish policy will allow more flexibility in the choice of partner countries (although at present it is unclear exactly what that means), channel some of its aid through regional cooperation projects and develop new forms of projects alongside established ones.
- NGO support will be increased gradually to between 10% and 15% of the development cooperation budget and new forms of NGO activities will be encouraged.
- The use of aid to subsidise interest for developing countries purchasing donor country products (tied aid credits) should be ended by agreement within the OECD, and in the meantime the use of Finnish aid for interest subsidies will be decreased (by FIM 10 million for 1997).
- Humanitarian aid will remain at between 10% and 15% of overall ODA, with greater focus on crisis prevention and long-term solutions.
- Finland is prepared to examine the nature of EU development cooperation as a complement to that pursued by individual member states, and with a view to a possible division of labour. Poverty alleviation must be the main starting point, not colonial history.

The government's stand on development cooperation, and its effort to make this cooperation an integral part of policy to developing countries, has received a general welcome from within the NGO community. This welcome is qualified, though, by disappointment that the government did not go far enough on some points, and by criticism of the vague nature of others. Concerning ODA as a percentage of GNP, the government has not committed itself to reaching the midpoint 0.4% GNP level by the end of its electoral period in 1999 – as had been proposed by the policy review – but opted for the year 2000, beyond its present policy reach. And it has not set a target date for when 0.7% should or could be attained. This lack of clarity in part reflects the severe budgetary pressures the government faces in overcoming recession, keeping on track for economic and monetary union (EMU) and in the light of its problems in reducing unemployment (on average 16% in 1996).

Also open to criticism is the government's handling of tied aid interest subsidies as a form of ODA. Although it condemns the subsidies as 'unsound', it has cut them by only 5%, to nearly 7% of ODA. The policy review had suggested doing away with subsidies altogether or at least seriously reducing them. The recommendations of the policy review have therefore been taken into account but have been watered down. The same goes for other issues: the increase in funds for NGOs; ending the artificial inflation of the costs of refugee support in Finland so that more of the ODA budget is available to spend in developing countries; and giving more coherent attention overall to the situation of women in development cooperation.

Moreover, the government's position on bilateral cooperation need clarifying, as its commitment to long-term development sits uneasily with the intention to pursue speed and flexibility in choosing partners. While a rapid and flexible response suits the demands of humanitarian assistance or situations where sustained cooperation becomes impossible, it is inappropriate in development cooperation proper and could lead to such work hinging on the political ups and downs of partner countries.

In a similar vein, the government's policy profile suggests that the Cold War period until recently unduly influenced the choice of Finland's bilateral partners; however, a more global approach of mutual dependence has now opened up. It is unclear, though, whether this global view also rules out allowing development cooperation to turn into a system of sticks and carrots according to how well or badly developing countries follow the instructions of industrial countries in carrying out structural adjustments.

The new approach towards bilateral aid was the single issue which was met with the greatest scepticism both within the Advisory Board for Relations with Developing Countries (attached to the Foreign Ministry) and the NGO community in the policy debate during Autumn 1996.

In a letter to Minister Pekka Haavisto in August 1996, the Advisory Board pointed out that concentrating Finnish bilateral aid on roughly ten major recipient countries is not 'old fashioned'. Finland cannot, particularly with the heavily decreased volume of aid, engage in a vast number of developing countries and sectors in a meaningful way. According to the Advisory Board, the aim should be that in the countries and sectors where Finland is active, the knowledge of the working environment, the know-how and the quality of the work should meet standards high enough for Finland to be able to use its own experience in influencing the general trends of donor performance in development cooperation.

This position of the Advisory Board was reaffirmed later in Autumn in a statement on the allocation of financial commitments for 1996–98. The government decision on allocations included considerable reserves for new and flexible initiatives, which would also be available on the regional level, to support conflict prevention, democratisation processes, environmental cooperation and strengthening of local administration. The Advisory Board supported these priority areas in principle, but questioned how these could be implemented through rapid interventions or ad hoc type projects.

Although the government's Decision-in-Principle provides an overview of the direction development cooperation policy will take, the details of that policy are still to be worked out. Spending on ODA is on a gradual upturn but has yet to release significant funds, the use of which will markedly reflect changing priorities. More at issue is the reassertion of development cooperation as an integral part of Finland's foreign policy and international relations. A clearer idea of what this means might be given when the government elaborates a more general strategy for its relations with developing countries during 1997, covering both foreign policy, trade and development cooperation.

Eradication of poverty and coherence

One of the main, long-standing goals of government development policy has been to tackle poverty. The present administration gives the alleviation of poverty prime place in its policy profile, and outlines a number of ways in which it intends to pursue practical results in this area. They can be summarised as follows:

Finland

The **Reality** of Aid 1997/8

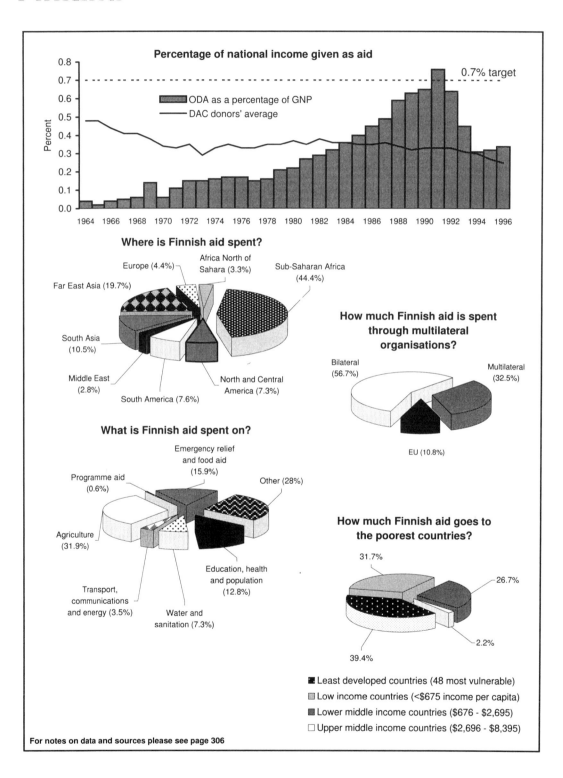

The **Reality** of Aid 1997/8

Finland

Finnish aid at a glance

How much aid does Finland give?

Finland gave	US$ 409m, 1983 million Finnish Markka in 1996
that was	0.34% of GNP
and	1.42% of public administration
which meant	US$ 80 or 387 Finnish Markka per capita for 1996

Is it going up or down?

In 1996 Finnish aid	rose by $21m, up 9.3% in real terms over 1995
Finland was	more generous in 1996, rising from 0.32% of GNP to 0.34%
The outlook is	to reach 0.4% of GNP by the year 2000

How does Finland compare with the other 21 donors?

Finland ranks	17 out of 21 for its volume of aid
It is	8 out of 21 in the generosity league
It gives	a higher proportion of its aid (71.1%) to Low Income Countries than 16 other donors
Private Flows	amounted to $51m, 13% of ODA
Total Flows	to developing countries were 0.53% of GNP and rank 12 out of 21 in the DAC

How much does Finland spend on basic health and basic education?

Finland spends	5.4% of its ODA on basic health and 1.4% on basic education

How important are commercial interests in aid?

Finland requires	17.5% of its aid to be used to buy Finnish goods

What do the public think about aid?

Of a recent sample of 1004 Finns, 1% said Finland should not give aid at all. Within development cooperation, 69% favoured a priority to health care, 58% Education, 55% Emergency aid

Finland

- supporting programmes of economic reform in developing countries, contributing the policy content of such programmes, and aiming for both economic growth and social development;
- channelling assistance expressly to the development of human resources and the independent capabilities of developing countries;
- emphasising basic education and health services, and supporting family planning and reproductive health;
- focusing more on the security of food supply and its promotion by environmentally sustainable independent food production;
- increasing efforts to strengthen the participation of women in social and economic activity, for instance by encouraging more basic education for girls and women; and
- drawing special attention to the status of disabled people in developing countries.

These pointers do not amount to a firm strategy concerning poverty alleviation, but appear more as general priorities that seek to address poverty in various contexts. The aim of the Department for Development Cooperation (DDC) of the Ministry of Foreign Affairs (formerly FINNIDA), however, is to integrate these guidelines in the different regional and country programmes with which it deals. The bulk of these programmes is, as in the past, directed to the poorest developing countries, especially sub-Saharan Africa.

At present, the DDC is evaluating its approaches to the regions and outlining integrated strategies in terms of overall foreign policy priorities, EU activity, the UN and other international organisations. At the time of writing only some information on these strategies was available. Those, for example, concerning Asia and Oceania, central Asia and the Caucasus place development cooperation in the context of promoting sound government, respect for human rights, improving the situation and education of women and children, and environmental and economic development. In the strategy outlined for Finland's relations with the countries of Asia and Oceania, the alleviation of poverty, together with environmental protection, is mentioned as a third strategic goal, after economic expansion and regional stability.

In April 1997 the government adopted a preliminary position paper on the renewal of the Lomé Convention. The paper summarises the basic position as follows:

- Finland puts poverty eradication in a central place for developing EU relations with developing countries;
- all developing countries should be treated equally, considering their different stages of development;
- the Least Developed Countries now outside the Convention should be included in the future framework;
- the EU's relations with developing countries should be reviewed in the context of EU external relations, whereby the significance of coherence between the different sectors (foreign policy, trade, agricultural policy and development cooperation) increases;
- the management of development cooperation should be based on increased division of labour between the Community and the Member States; and
- flexible trade arrangements are necessary; the aim is gradual application of WTO principles and rules.

There is a close dialogue between the Foreign Ministry and the NGDOs (mainly through KePa) on the future of Lomé. The NGDOs have been reasonably satisfied with the three first points in the Finnish position paper, but critical about the three others.

Coherence

More coherence of approach to development assistance is implicit in the government's commitment to renewing the process of ODA and seeking to integrate economic, environmental, human rights and gender issues. On the other hand, there is at present a lack of definition about what these issues mean in specific contexts. The problem is that there is a dearth of information about how development aid strategies will fit in with the government's overall regional policies towards the South. The Decision-in-Principle is the most detailed policy document on development cooperation strategies and, even there, there is a problem over coherence.

Public opinion and political support

There are no fresh polls or reviews on public support for ODA in Finland, but a fair assumption is that no dramatic changes have taken place.

When it comes to political support for ODA, the

most significant events are the Decision-in-Principle by the government in September 1996 and the decision to break the freeze on Finnish aid related to the budget proposal for 1997. Although the absolute increase of ODA is rather symbolic so far and the mid-term commitments rather vague, they still reflect a real change for the better in the position of the *present* government. Since the funding of ODA is exclusively dependent on political (and fiscal) decisions, and no legislation, it is also very vulnerable. The commitments to a re-increased ODA have to be reconfirmed by the next government and parliament, and the next elections are in Spring 1999.

The abolition of the 'freeze' decision on the aid budget, led to a 'freeze' on the Percentage Movement Campaign. The judgement of the percentage movement in Autumn 1996 was, that in the short term, there was not much political sense in continuing with an active campaign with the emphasis on quantitative issues and demands. If the present (and the next) government fail to meet their commitments, the Percentage Campaign will be reactivated. But, for the time being, priority is given to quality issues, through KePa and using the Advisory Board on Relations with Developing Countries as a forum for this advocacy work.

NGOs

Due partly to the decision of the government on increased and diversified support for NGOs, and partly to the outcome of the broad evaluation of the programme of the Service Centre for Development Cooperation (KePa) – Finland's umbrella organisation of development NGOs with 180 member organisations – a number of new initiatives and processes have emerged within the Finnish NGDO community.

Besides increasing the funding for the co-financing support programme for Finnish NGOs in 1997 and 1998, some changes are expected in the general conditions for co-financing. The self-financing share will be decreased from 25% to 20% and the share of administrative costs increased from 6% to 10%. Direct financial support to international and regional NGOs will continue to increase. Discussions within the NGDO community and with the Ministry on creating direct funding systems for Southern NGOs in the field of environment and human rights are proceeding. Special support programmes for micro credit schemes and cultural cooperation are being discussed.

NGOs' efforts to reorient their work to build partnership in the South have been reflected in the changes taking place in the Finnish volunteer programme run by KePa. The year 1996/7 was designated as a period of transition, re-examination and restructuring and the dispatch of more volunteers were put on hold. The renewal is focused on a twofold approach: a partnership programme and a strategy for strengthening the notion of global responsibility in Finland.

The partnership programme builds on experience with traditional partner countries (Mozambique, Zambia and Nicaragua) to recast relations and the work of volunteers in more diversified, participatory ways. One aim is to widen involvement in southern Africa, South and Southeast Asia and Central America and to focus on countries in which Finnish NGDOs are active or about which they need better information and contacts. Another is to develop new openings in the area of financing. This is being sought through the creation of micro-funds to support projects focused on environmental protection/sustainability and on human rights. One option being explored is to create a new structure for micro financing to be run by NGOs. To increase the flexibility of Finnish–Southern exchange, volunteers from partner countries are encouraged to come to Finland to work on cooperation projects.

Activity for global responsibility in Finland includes creating new forms of campaigning, and revamping information services and education work.

The two aspects of effective partnerships between Finland and the South and the importance of building a sense of global responsibility in Finland are deeply intertwined. This process of change mirrors a similar recognition among many NGOs in Europe who have seen the need to build partnerships and to revamp relations with the South.

France

Olivier Blamangin, CRID

The good performance of France among OECD donor countries, second to Japan in volume and first in percentage of GNP among the G7, should not hide the reality of French Public Aid for Development (ODA) in 1995: like most members of the OECD Development Assistance Committee the French government reduced its public spending and, by the same token, its development assistance.

An underdeveloping budget

French aid fell from Ff 47,000 million to Ff 42,100 million and from 0.64% of GNP to 0.55% between 1994 and 1995. In real terms this was a decrease of 12%. While not reaching the devastating scale of the decline in Italy (42% in real terms) or the USA (27%), the volume of French aid fell more than any other donor and suffered a sharper percentage decrease than all countries except Sweden and Portugal.

The figures for 1996 and estimates for 1997 show continued decline. Aid in 1996 was Ff 38,000 million, 0.48% of GNP and in 1997 will still be under 0.5% of GNP.

The decline in French aid is such that a speaker in parliament during the last budgetary discussions was able to coin the phrase, an 'underdeveloping' budget of cooperation. France is far from the commitment to reach 0.7% of GNP for the year 2000 repeated many times at the end of the 1980s and beginning of the 1990s. Today, this objective seems to have been abandoned.

Devaluation of the African financial community franc (CFA) and debt cancellation

France justifies the 1995 decrease in ODA as a 'return to normal' after two 'exceptional' years in 1993 and 1994. During these two years, aid was said to have increased 'abnormally' following a special financial undertaking to accompany the devaluation of the CFA franc.[1] In fact, it is necessary to go back as far as 1986 to find as small a share of GNP devoted to development assistance.[2]

The Reality of Aid 1995 highlighted the insufficiency of the measures to reduce the negative consequences that had accompanied devaluation. These were concentrated mainly on the cancellation of debt, which had increased to almost 23% of bilateral development assistance in 1994 (excluding debt rescheduling).[3] Beyond the fact that these cancellations often involve loans without any direct connection with development and whose inclusion as part of French development assistance could certainly be contested, the growth in the use of ODA funds for debt cancellation has not led to any proportional increase in ODA. In fact, the growth has been achieved to the detriment of other forms of aid, in particular of aid to investment. Debt cancellation decreased in 1995 but it still represented 16% of bilateral ODA and aid to investment at 21.2% of ODA is far from regaining its earlier level (32.5% in 1991).

The European Union at the cost of the United Nations

Multilateral aid still represents between 20% and 25% of French development assistance each year, following a strongly rooted tradition. Nearly half of these credits go to the European Union. In 1995, the European Fund for Development (EDF) was re-established – not least thanks to the far from negligible role of the French government. During those difficult negotiations, France, desirous of retaining its image as the spokesperson for Africa, opposed the EU member countries in favour of Eastern Europe and those countries that wanted to reduce their contributions on the grounds of lack of efficiency in European Union aid. The EDF was finally renewed at its previous level, as was France's contribution, while almost all other member states, taking advantage of the extension of the Union by three new members, contributed less than they had done before. Thus, the government has become the largest contributor to the EDF for the period 1996–2000, outranking Germany for the first time.

Unfortunately this good French performance on

The **Reality** of Aid 1997/8

France

the European stage took place in the context of budgetary restrictions and was therefore achieved at the cost of other contributions to multilateral agencies from French development assistance. An acceleration in the decrease of French contributions to UN organisations is thus noticeable in 1995. Contributions to UN bodies represented only 5.5% of multilateral aid in 1995 as opposed to 14% in 1993. Between 1994 and 1995, the credits to UNDP, WFP and UNFPA were halved and those to UNICEF reduced to a fifth of their previous level.

More grants and less financial cooperation

A detailed examination of the distribution of French development assistance reveals changes in 1995 which could be the start of positive developments. The first change is the increase of grants relative to loans. Grants represented 83.6% of bilateral aid in 1995 (debt cancellation included) against 70.1% in 1991 and 77.2% in 1994. It seems that this is a consistent trend. Unfortunately, in the context of budgetary restrictions, this increase in the share of grants does not compensate for the decrease in the total volume of ODA: the actual volume of grants declined from Ff 30,200 million in 1994 to Ff 26,800 million in 1995. It is particularly important to emphasise that the debt reduction measures absorbed more than a quarter of the grant element in 1995.

A second positive trend is the reduction in the proportion of bilateral ODA going to economic and financial cooperation, in particular to programmes in support of structural adjustment. NGOs have been worried that the increasing share of financial aid in support of SAPs and the IMF conditionality, which is attached to them, taking the view that such aid does not go to the poorest people. Support for structural adjustment programmes had reached 11% of bilateral aid in 1993. The decrease noted in 1994 has been confirmed in 1995, with a return to a more satisfactory level of 5.8%

The third promising trend is in the reduction of tied aid. In 1994/5 it was 42% of bilateral aid compared with 59% ten years ago.

Priority to strategic and economic interests

'Sustainable development and the reduction of poverty' were reaffirmed as 'priority objectives' in the French Memorandum to the DAC. But it is almost impossible to find any logic linking the distribution of French ODA with these objectives. According to the DAC examination, more than 55% of bilateral aid was concentrated on a dozen countries in 1994/5. Not one Least Developed Country could be found among them. In contrast, two French Overseas Territories (OST) – namely New Caledonia and French Polynesia, with 7.9% and 7.5% respectively of bilateral aid – fare well. The Republic of Niger, the first LLDC on the 1994/5 list, is in twelfth position with only 2% of bilateral aid. In 1995, the share of bilateral aid going to LLDCs reached barely 18.6% (scarcely Ff 6000 million)[4] and way below the average of other DAC donors. In general, France favours middle income countries with which it has important political, strategic or trade interests.

The traditional choice of sub-Saharan Africa as the region to receive the largest amount of French aid (42.1% of bilateral ODA in 1995) fully meets these objectives which do not have much to do with the fight against poverty. Certainly, Africa is the region of the world where the LLDCs are the most numerous, but the countries helped most by France are not the poorest. The government does not hide the fact that the choice of sub-Saharan Africa is explained 'by historic and cultural ties between France and these countries'.[5] But, along with the Mediterranean Basin, sub-Saharan Africa is the region of the world where France has the most important political, economic and military interests. Consequently, Pascal Chaigneau, director of the Centre for Diplomatic and Strategic Studies in Paris can say, 'For France, Africa is the last continent where it is first. . . . The only continent where, when it grants one franc of aid, it generates three francs of turnover and 1.6 francs of profit for its enterprises.'[6]

Opposed to these interests, the criteria of poverty or democracy do not weigh heavily.

Progressive redeployment

Some of these favoured countries find themselves extremely dependent on French aid. In the Côte d'Ivoire, 71% of total ODA comes from France, in Cameroon it is 76.8%, in Gabon 79% and in the Congo 83%. These countries are not protected from a strategic deployment of French aid to other regions such as the Far East or the Mediterranean basin where trade interests are equally important. In fact, the downward trend in the share of aid to sub-Saharan Africa, which started at the beginning of the 1990s, is confirmed in 1995. Small from one year to the next, this decrease becomes truly significant over a longer period: it exceeded 12 percentage points between 1990 and 1995. North Africa, with an increase of four percentage points despite a

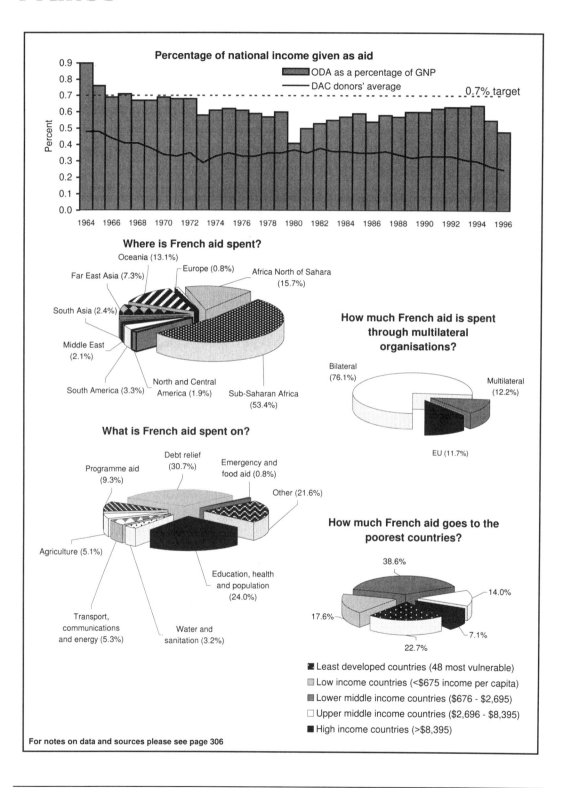

France

French aid at a glance

How much aid does France give?

France gave	US$ 7430m, 41,600 million French Francs in 1996
that was	0.45% of GNP
and	2.85% of public administration
which meant	US$ 128 or FF717 per capita for 1996

Is it going up or down?

In 1996 French aid	fell by $1013m, a drop of 11.3% in real terms over 1995
France was	less generous in 1996, dropping from 0.55% of GNP to 0.48%
The outlook is	that the government expects aid in 1997 to be below 0.5%

How does France compare with the other 21 donors?

France ranks	4 out of 21 for its volume of aid
It is	5 out of 21 in the generosity league
It gives	a lower proportion of its aid (40.3%) to Low Income Countries than 19 other donors
Private Flows	amounted to $4137m, 49% of ODA
Total Flows	to developing countries were 0.83% of GNP and rank 8 out of 21 in the DAC

How much does France spend on basic health and basic education?

France	has not yet reported to the DAC on its basic health and basic education spending

How important are commercial interests in aid?

France requires	30.5% of its aid to be used to buy French goods

What do the public think about aid?

In 1995, 63% of the population were reported to be concerned about world development – an increase on previous polls.

France

stagnation in the share of the Maghreb, the Far East and Oceania (up three percentage points) and Latin America (up two points) are the main beneficiaries of this decrease. There is therefore not a total abandonment of sub-Saharan Africa to the benefit of another region of the world, but a slow redeployment of French aid. Such diversification of the field of its aid involves managing more varied interests around the world. It should also be emphasised that an increased share of bilateral ODA is earmarked for Overseas Territories.

Fight against poverty: impossible to evaluate

It is particularly difficult to realise the real financial effort of France directed towards the reduction of poverty and the satisfaction of fundamental social needs. If some progress has finally been acknowledged by the DAC in setting up evaluation procedures, the conclusions of these studies too often remain confidential. The official figures divide public aid into large sectors, which cover up very different realities depending on individual projects. For example, although the amount of credits earmarked for education is known, it is not possible to know what part goes to primary, secondary, tertiary, or to subsidise the production of school books or to promote the study of the French language. By the same token, it is impossible to evaluate the reality, importance or impact of the commitments made by the government to reinforce its aid programmes for basic education, primary health care or to support action for women in developing countries.

Gender issues are a particularly significant gap between the good intentions proclaimed by the government and the reality. In 1995, French cooperation defined support for women as one of its priorities. However, the DAC Aid Review emphasises that little progress has been made in this domain despite the recommendations of the examining committee.

The French aid programme's emphasis on gender is certainly late compared with its partners and in fact it is content to put into place some isolated projects in favour of women, without integrating this dimension into the totality of its projects and programmes. The fact that the theme 'women and development' is proclaimed as a priority, that some actions in this domain are put forward, does not mean that a gender dimension has been truly integrated into practice.

It is necessary nonetheless to note that a ministerial directive of 1 January 1996 renews the *Special Fund for Development* (SFD), which is changing its name to the *Social Fund for Development*. This instrument, put into place in the days following the devaluation of the CFA franc, allows the financing of projects originating in civil society and destined to meet elementary social needs. Put into place by the missions of cooperation in each of the countries of the franc zone, the SFD seems to combine flexibility, proximity and dialogue, notably with *associations of international solidarity* (as NGDOs are known in France). It constitutes a promising new tool for French cooperation but unfortunately disposes of very limited means in comparison with the total volume of bilateral aid.

Aborted reform

This brief survey of public aid should end with a few words on the organisation of the French system of cooperation. Each year, NGOs, the DAC, experts mandated by the government to write reports or the Cour des Comptes[7] renew their recommendations for an overall reform of its organisation. There is no need to repeat everything that has been said about a system that astonishes all its observers, for its complexity (more than ten ministries or organisations) and lack of transparency (absence of democratic control and evaluation) have become legendary. In 1995, a wind of reform blew in the first months following the nomination of Alain Juppé as prime minister. All kinds of conservatisms opposed the early aims of reform and the government decisions of February 1996 looked more like the patching of a façade than real reform. The changes that have taken place in the organisation of French cooperation since 1995 can be summarised by the following three points:

- making a more formal link between the Ministry of Cooperation and the Ministry of Foreign Affairs by appointing a deputy minister responsible for development cooperation attached to the Ministry of Foreign Affairs;
- creating an Interministerial Committee for Aid to Development (ICAD) to define the orientations of French official development assistance and to ensure coordination among the different organisations involved; and
- Putting into place the Local Committees for Aid to Development (LCAD) in the ACP (Africa, Caribbean and Pacific) countries to harmonise and monitor programmes.

These decisions are certainly moving things in the direction of better coordination of French Public Aid for Development – finally! But for those who know the rigidities of French cooperation they appear clearly insufficient. Although there are some moves in the right direction within French public aid, the overall reform of the system to meet the objectives of sustainable development and poverty reduction, does not appear to be the order of the day.

Notes

1. On 11 January 1994, the government broke a 46-year-old status quo in its relations with Africa. France, in fact its international financial institutions, imposed a 50% devaluation of the CFA franc on the African states of the West Africa Monetary Union – Benin, Burkina Faso, Côte d'Ivoire, Mali, Niger, Senegal and Togo – and of the Central Africa Monetary Union – Cameroon, Central African Republic, Congo, Gabon, Equatorial Guinea and Chad – and a 25% devaluation on the Comoros.
2. In 1986 and 1983 ODA represented 0.54% and 0.55% of GNP respectively.
3. Memorandum from France to the DAC.
4. Ibid.
5. Ibid.
6. *Le Figaro*, 26 February 1997.
7. The Cour des Comptes is an organisation that controls the expenditure of public institutions.

Germany

Birgit Dederichs Bain
Deutsche Welthungerhilfe and terre des hommes

Overview

At the beginning of the 1990s, the rationale for German development aid shifted from preserving peace in a polarised world, to establishing and maintaining global human security. The official foci of the government coalition of Christian Democrats and Liberals since then are:

- combating poverty;
- protection of natural resources;
- education/training of people in developing countries with special emphasis on rural development; and
- the promotion of women's role in development in all three areas.

These priorities are also reflected in the latest cross-sectoral Ministry for Economic Cooperation and Development (BMZ) guidelines.[1] How has this new rationale since been reflected in the reality of German development cooperation?[2]

In recent years NGDO criticism of government performance has focused on:

- the declining level of ODA – in spite of contrary commitments;
- the lack of coherent policies towards the South;
- the inconsistent application of the five criteria for bilateral assistance established in 1991 (respect for human rights, good governance and the rule of law, participatory democracy, support for the market economy and public policies that promote development);
- the insufficient financial contributions to self-help-oriented poverty alleviation;
- the shift of available ODA resources from development cooperation to humanitarian aid;[3]
- the reduction of multilateral aid and the setting of an arbitrary limit of 30% for multilateral aid when problems become more and more global and instruments and solutions need to reflect this shift;
- the poor results in implementing the 20:20 initiative from the Copenhagen Social Summit;
- inadequate aid instruments that, among other things, allow the use of foreign aid for export promotion and the need for an administrative reform; and
- insufficient debt relief to poor countries.

The 1996 OECD Development Assistance Committee (DAC) Report still notes that the five criteria established in 1991 are applied with a degree of inconsistency.

> *where the strict application of the criteria would interfere with German political interest, the failure to fully meet the policy conditions does not seem to preclude the provision of ODA.*[4]

The BMZ as ministry in charge of up to 70% of ODA has not been given the required enlarged responsibilities, in spite of the 1995/6 OECD DAC recommendation:

> *the coherence of German development cooperation policy and programmes would be enhanced, if the policy making and field roles of the BMZ were further strengthened.*[5]

A reform and/or reduction of instruments and actors involved has not taken place although this too has been targeted as a weakness of German ODA administration in the DAC Peer Reviews: 'the complexity of the German aid system reduces the flexibility for policy change.'[6]

The same applies – in the context of aid management and coherence – to the suggestion in *The DAC Report* that:

Germany

to help strengthen the policy-planning capacity of the Ministry, the BMZ country guidelines for major aid recipients should be endorsed by the German Government as a whole.

The dividing line between bilateral financial assistance and technical aid, between policy-making and policy implementation has become increasingly blurred and administrative reforms are needed.[7] NGDOs have raised this point on a number of occasions.[8]

Aid volume

A few trends can be made out by looking at some facts and figures, among other things:

- overriding budgetary pressures;
- provision in the aid budget and the co-financing line for NGDOs to prepare for further cuts;
- the instrumentalisation of aid for trade/ increasing commercial interests; and
- the declining importance of self-help poverty reduction.

Facts and figures – NGDO comments: volume of German ODA within the DAC

Germany ranks – in absolute volume terms – third among DAC member countries in 1996 with a total ODA of US$ 7515 million.

The BMZ budget[9] amounts to DM 7651 million in 1997, which is DM 494 million or about 6% less than in the previous year (8145 million).[10]

Total planned 1996 disbursements of DM 13,521 million (which include other ministries, the Bundesländer and the German share of EU spending), are supposed to shrink by DM 852 million or 6.3% to DM 12,669 million in 1997. Experience in past years suggests that real net disbursements will be lower.

Comment The Minister for Development Cooperation has already announced that he expects budget cuts of up to DM 500 million for the next budget.[11] Other sources believe it will be even more.

Another consequence of the budgetary pressures was that the Ministry of Finance had suggested a change whereby contracts for funding between government and NGDOs would not be binding, meaning that NGDOs would carry full financial responsibility for project implementation by Southern partners in circumstances where there was a budget freeze. The consequence would have been a drastic cut in the number and scope of projects in the South and both the BMZ and the Parliamentary Development Committee supported NGDO protests on this.[12] A compromise seems to emerge now. The budget provision for NGDOs will be lifted; however, a 15% financial reserve is being established in the Ministry. In other words, NGDOs have more security for ongoing funding contracts, but less money in the end. NGDOs hope that this will not be a guide to future procedures.

German ODA as a percentage of GNP

German ODA as a percentage of GNP has been declining for the past few years: 1991 (0.4%), 1993 (0.36%), 1994 (0.34%), 1995 (0.31%). In 1996 the percentage increased to 0.32%. In 1997 it is likely to fall. Some sources talk about 0.29% or 0.28%.

Comment The political aim of 0.7% is still verbally proclaimed,[13] but the declining figures suggest that development cooperation could well fall to a 'negligible quantity'. NGDOs feel that this would be a severe mistake in a world that is increasingly interdependent, with 1000 million people in poverty and problems arising at national level such as environment, social sustainability, resource use, migration and food security, which are taking on increasingly global dimensions. Northern governments should regard development cooperation as an investment in their own future. NGDOs also feel that, because of the global nature of the challenges, the arbitrary limit of 30% (32.7% for 1997)[14] set for multilateral disbursements within the BMZ budget (see *Reality of Aid 1996*) by the Budget Committee of Parliament is counterproductive. This is especially so when the BMZ itself declares that a growing number of African countries' problems increasingly can be solved only on an international level.

Development of net disbursements[15]

While the ODA to GNP percentage has been declining, planned development budget revenues (mainly interest and repayments on capital aid credits/debt service on outstanding aid credits) have increased from 1620 million in 1996 to 1701 million in 1997, DM 81 million more. So there is a net-relief (comparing planned disbursements 1996/7) of the Federal budget totalling DM 575 million.

The **Reality** of Aid 1997/8

Germany

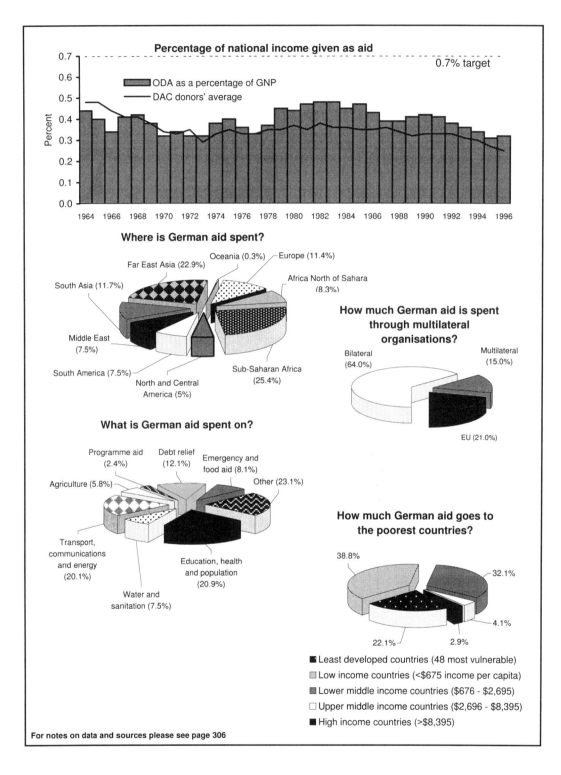

For notes on data and sources please see page 306

The **Reality** of Aid 1997/8

Germany

German aid at a glance

How much aid does Germany give?

Germany gave	US$ 7515m, in 1996 (the budget of the Ministry for Economic Cooperation, BMZ was 8145 million DM)
that was	0.32% of GNP
and	1.6% of public administration
which meant	US$ 93 or 99 Deutsch Marks per capita for 1996

Is it going up or down?

In 1996 German aid	fell by US$ 9m in cash terms although taking inflation and exchange rates into account it rose by 3.8% in real terms over 1995
Germany was	slightly more generous in 1996, rising from 0.31% of GNP to 0.32%
The outlook is	for a fall to below 0.3% for 1997

How does Germany compare with the other 21 donors?

Germany ranks	3 out of 21 for its volume of aid
It is	10 out of 21 in the generosity league
It gives	a lower proportion of its aid (60.9%) to Low Income Countries than 13 other donors
Private Flows	amounted to $11,723m, 1.6 times ODA
Total Flows	to developing countries were 0.88% of GNP and rank 6 out of 21 in the DAC

How much does Germany spend on basic health and basic education?

Germany reports	1.6% of its total ODA spending on basic health and 2.9% on basic education

How important are commercial interests in aid?

Commercial pressures	on German aid are very strong. The percentage of total ODA that is tied to the purchase of German goods (37.4%) understates the returns to Germany from the bilateral programme –estimated in the past at 50% or more

What do the public think about aid?

> **Poverty is regarded by 28% of the population as the third most important global problem, after hunger/malnutrition and environmental problems**

Germany

And, whereas recent experience shows that actual disbursements are distinctly below those planned (in 1994 about 500 million), debt service revenue stays within estimates.

Comment Through their debt and trade policies Northern governments often contribute to global poverty (which they then address in their aid policies). Even so, revenues are not fed back into the aid budget. In 1995, external debt stocks for the developing world rose to a record US$ 1940,000 million.[16] Debt servicing kept pace and rose to US$ 194,000 million – paid back by developing countries, which at the same time received a mere US$ 58,000 million in aid – its effect being more or less wiped out by paying back three times as much!

Germany has endorsed the multilateral Highly Indebted Poor Country (HIPC) debt initiative. However, in the first case (Uganda) Germany had blocked an earlier settlement and subsequent refinancing of Uganda's multilateral debt, in order to make the whole initiative less costly for the German government. It also wanted to avoid a reanimation of the discussion around the IMF gold reserves.

Meanwhile, Uganda is kept waiting, perhaps until Spring 1998 or 1999, even though it has already exceeded the requested period of economic good governance by four years. However, it seems that an agreement has finally been reached in April 1997 to start as soon as possible with the Uganda initiative.

A positive signal was the government decision to extend the instrument of debt conversion beyond the 1996 dimension (DM 200 million) to 210 million in 1997.

German NGDOs urge their government to:

- support a generous implementation of the HIPC Initiative in the first test cases; and
- grant debt relief beyond Paris Club regulations in cases where the government itself has found this to be necessary.[17]

Export promotion

Due to budgetary pressures, finance available for both financial (capital) aid and technical aid instruments is declining. But capital aid is declining faster than technical aid, which is both interesting and in principle welcome to NGDOs.

It leads to big industrial companies like Siemens, Krupp, MAN and others lobbying the Minister of Finance against further reductions in the (capital) aid budget and supporting the Minister for Development Cooperation! The industrial companies fear losing orders amounting to DM 2000 million as a result of cuts in the development budget. Fewer development projects means less export business and, so they say, fewer jobs in Germany.

Comment This latter rationale has been increasingly used by the BMZ to emphasise the importance of development cooperation. NGDOs have warned repeatedly that the new instrument of 'composite financing',[18] introduced by BMZ in 1994, needed to be treated with scepticism, since NGDOs feared that it might be used to promote domestic exports.

Export promotion clearly follows a different rationale from development cooperation.[19] Though there might be cases where both interests are compatible, it has to be quite clear that the allocation of aid resources should follow the declared priorities for German development policies. Aid has to be based on the recipient's needs and not be regarded as a mechanism to promote Northern domestic objectives.

Furthermore, with this policy, the BMZ is actually promoting the arguments of those who want it to be part of the Ministry for Foreign or Economic Affairs.

Poverty focus

The amount of bilateral ODA commitments planned for direct poverty reduction has been reduced from 18.6% in 1996 to 14.2% in 1997.[20] Basic needs, according to the German government, took up 50.7% of bilateral commitments in 1997 and 54.1% in 1996.

The share of German aid to Least Developed Countries[21] has been steadily declining from 31% in 1984/5, 25% in 1994 and 21% in 1995.

Regional distribution

The regional distribution of ODA planned for 1997 shows pretty much the same picture as last year.[22]

Comment The overall figures in the aid budget seem to suggest that political support for development cooperation is declining. There seems to be a much stronger need to legitimise spending on development cooperation, particularly in terms of job creation and job security. Recent surveys among the German population, however, show that poverty is still regarded by 28% of the public as the third most important global problem – after hunger/malnutrition and environmental problems.

Table 3 Regional distribution of German ODA 1996 and 1997[23]

Region	1996 in DM millions	1997 in DM millions
Sub-Saharan Africa	1062 (28%)	968.5 (27%)
South and Central Asia, Other Asia and Oceania	1249 (32%)	1245 (34.6%)
Central and Eastern Europe and NIS	342 (9%)	205 (5.7%)**
Mediterranean, Middle and Near East (North Africa and Southern Europe)	743 (19%)	710 (19.8%)
Latin America	463 (12%)	465 (12.9%)

** Including DM 155 million additional funds for technical aid (under separate budget lines the figure for CEEC and NIS rises to DM 360 million or 10%).

BMZ explains the high level of aid for the Near East on the basis of the high priority of the peace process and reforms and the need to fight migration. NGDOs continue to ask for a much stronger concentration of the German aid programme on self-help oriented poverty reduction.

Deutsche Welthungerhilfe and terre des hommes object to the decreasing support for Africa in bilateral aid and – in times of scarce resources – the shift to more promising markets in Asia. NGDO criticisms of the lack of specific criteria for targeting and for participation in the poverty programme, and of the striking lack of coherence with other sectors, remain valid.

Regrettably, the study commissioned by BMZ last year dealing directly with these issues has not been published. Deutsche Welthungerhilfe and terre des hommes continue to ask for a much higher share of bilateral aid to be allocated to direct poverty reduction projects. In addition, the feminisation of poverty, which is recognised by Government in all publications as a key issue for poverty alleviation, should be reflected in the reality of direct poverty reduction projects.

The 20:20 compact

Government commitment to the 20:20 compact is not reflected in the planned allocations for 1997. In fact, they show an opposite trend, particularly in basic education and health. Only the 'population' sector has increased from 3.6% in 1995 to 4.2% in 1997.

Table 4 Bilateral technical and financial assistance (TZ and FZ) to basic education and health

Basic education	95: 8.5%
	96: 6.5%
	97: 4.2%
Health	95: 4.4%
	96: 3.9%
	97: 3.4%

Planned allocations for 1995 and commitments for 1996 and 1997.[24]

Comment As pointed out in *The Reality of Aid 1996*, German NGDOs strongly support the 20:20 initiative accepted by many governments, including Germany, at the Copenhagen World Summit for Social Development. NGDOs regret therefore that a clear political signal on its implementation is still missing, despite its integration as a political goal in some BMZ agreements with Southern governments.

Basic education and health as central parts of social services are codified rights of the Social Compact to which Germany is a signatory. This implies, among other things, support for other states in the implementation of those rights – striving to secure a global future, an aim BMZ quite rightly emphasises.

NGDOs therefore ask BMZ:

- to take a lead on the 20:20 initiative (in the way The Netherlands has done);
- to make it a focus first in OECD discussions on improved donor coordination and second in expanded provision for budgetary support to the basic social sectors; and
- to direct all suitable instruments of development policy towards strengthening the capacities of interested recipients in the areas of basic social services.[25]

Deutsche Welthungerhilfe and terre des hommes call on the German government to show in next year's budget that it takes seriously the issues of improving the quality of aid for those who need it most.

Germany

The declaration of the BMZ Parliamentary Secretary of State, which indicates a reduction of support for primary education is remarkable in the circumstances (see 'New Initiatives' below).

Gender

In the existing guidelines on poverty eradication and in many declarations, the promotion of women is given high priority.[26]

One of the German government commitments at the Women's Summit in Beijing was to allocate US$ 40 million over the next five years for 'social and legal counselling of women' in developing countries. We are not talking about 'fresh money'. The funds are to be reallocated from within the BMZ budget, but from where exactly, it is difficult to tell. A list of projects for 1996 has been presented. NGDOs have been invited for a dialogue.[27]

Comment The overall implementation of Beijing is slow and disappointing. The government did produce the so-called *Strategies for Implementation* by the end of 1996. But the paper only concentrates on three areas (equal access to decision-making positions, improving the economic situation of women as well as their chances in the labour market and human rights and abolition of violence against women and girls). Reasons for these choices are not given. The paper claims, however, that in many other areas progress has already materialised and been implemented in Germany. The paper represents an agglomeration of proposals not consolidated into a concise strategic paper for implementation. The *National Strategies* do not live up to the promise their title suggests.

Furthermore, so far the German government has not taken any initiative to push the implementation of the EU Gender Resolution (the follow-up of Beijing on the European level). Deutsche Welthungerhilfe and terre des hommes ask that the implementation of the *Beijing Declaration* and *Platform of Action* should be a high priority in the political reality of all German government policies.

New initiatives, new trends

Opposition party wants to strengthen multilateral cooperation!

It is interesting to note that members of the opposition Social Democrats recently presented a new concept for development policy, that of strengthening the Ministry for Development Cooperation and development policy. Only a couple of years ago they called for the abolition of the Ministry and the placing of development policy under the auspices of the Ministry for Foreign Affairs. The campaign for the 1998 federal election seems to have started!

One important aspect of the Social Democrat proposal is the reactivation and reform of existing multilateral instruments. Reform of the EU and German cooperation with the EU are regarded as the basis for an effective answer to economic globalisation, which is more and more developing its own dynamics. In contrast – as was pointed out – the current government's policy is to reduce the level of involvement in multilateral aid as a whole and to strengthen bilateral aid.

Government party demands changes in EU development cooperation

The Christian Democratic Union Committee for Development Policy has demanded new criteria for the allocation of EU tax money to poor countries, to give priority to justice and democracy as against a policy of donor national interests.[28] Criteria should be, among other things, per capita income, respect for human rights and good governance.

The CDU paper also contains a clear call for a common arms export policy. (This has met with vehement opposition from France and Great Britain for reasons of vested interest.)

Climate protection initiative

NGDOs appreciate the positive role of BMZ in the negotiations on the Global Environment Facility (GEF). There is a clear tendency for BMZ to give more emphasis to the link between development cooperation and the initiative for the protection of the global climate (which receives DM 75 million from financial aid). This seems like a promising innovation.[29] However, its implementation should be primarily guided by efficiency criteria for CO_2 reduction. Export promotion for German companies should not become the guiding principle in spite of the economic difficulties and pressures within Germany.

More support for the future elite – less for primary education

The BMZ Parliamentary Secretary of State has recently declared[30] that a decreasing aid budget should mean priorities that reflect national interests more strongly: East European countries in transition have enjoyed a higher priority for Germany than African countries and this is likely to continue.

But new priorities, argues the Secretary of State, should also be reflected in sectoral shifts. Allocations for basic education (which should be seen more as a responsibility of national governments) should be reduced in favour of university education. University Cooperation Programmes should be initiated. This would be more profitable for Germany, since the promotion of students would enhance contacts with the future elite of the partner countries, the future decision-makers. The rationale is for Germany to remain competitive as an economic and scientific location.

Deutsche Welthungerhilfe and terre des hommes feel this shift works against the proclaimed focus on poverty eradication and the explained new rationale of German development policy. It is also diametrically opposed to the 20:20 compact.

Concluding remarks

Deutsche Welthungerhilfe and terre des hommes feel that, in general, budgetary pressure on development cooperation should lead to a reconsideration of overall objectives and a focus on addressing issues of global concern and the long-term needs of recipient countries.

Where there are conflicts with short-term German economic interests, the genuine development focus of poverty eradication and social sustainability should be given priority. In the long run, this will prove favourable for both sides, both for reasons of enlightened self-interest (markets, migration, terrorism, crime, social peace, democracy) and for fundamentally humanitarian considerations. Everybody is less secure in a world of poverty and misery.

Development policy needs to be complemented by other policies and ODA to be complemented by other development resources. Capacity building – of human development and civil society – in developing countries and so-called developed countries should be a primary goal.

The global nature of problems and solutions should be communicated to the public (environment, poverty, food security and health) and the role of state and its duties emphasised. One of them is the implementation of the Platforms of the UN Conferences and the creation of a sound and stable policy framework – good governance in the widest sense.[31]

Notes

1. BMZ-Vermerk, Zusammenfassung der übersektoralen Konzepte, 22 January 1997, which emphasises that the principles for the concepts of target groups, promotion of women in developing countries, the main elements of combating poverty, combating poverty through self-help, socio-cultural criteria – have to be considered in all programmes of development cooperation.
2. Development Cooperation Review Series, Germany 1995, No 9, OECD.
3. 'Amongst other things these strains have created unprecedented shortfalls in financing of the United Nations System and the multilateral development banks. These multilateral institutions remain a cornerstone in global efforts to foster development.' OECD, Shaping the 21st Century, Paris, May 1996.
4. OECD DAC Report 1996, p142.
5. Ibid, p143.
6. Ibid.
7. see Development Cooperation Review Series, Germany 1995, No 9, p9.
8. It is remarkable that against this background that BMZ-evaluations nowadays seem to focus more on issues of aid management efficiency than on those of effectiveness of German assistance for the recipient's development process. Ibid, p10
9. According to BMZ-EZ 23 (Einzelplan 23 = Budget of the BMZ).
10. See Saligmann, Rolf, Haushalt des BMZ-E fur 1996 and 1997, Aufsatz, Bonn, 24 February 1997.
11. BM Spranger, AWZ, 23 April 1997.
12. At the time of compiling this report, May 1997.
13. Chancellor Kohl, Social Summit, 95; Plan of Action of the World Food Summit;
14. BMZ budget only, based on government draft 1996; slight changes possible due to budgetary cuts.
15. Saligmann, op cit.
16. OECD DAC Report 1996, p82.
17. Initiativkreis Entwicklung braucht Entschuldung, April 1997.
18. A combination of funds from the financial aid budget and funds from the capital market, which are guaranteed by government – a favourable financial mix for German suppliers, since the ratio of aid:commercial credit can go up to 1:4. Yet, the credit costs for the borrower are still far below market interest rates – an important argument for competitiveness. While such aid is not necessarily tied to purchases in Germany the fear of NGDOs was that it might be used to promote domestic exports, a concern which was fully shared by the DAC in its 1995 Review of German Aid (see Reality of Aid 1995 and 1996).
19. Reality of Aid 1996.
20. Verpflichtungsermächtigungen / commitments TZ/FZ.
21. OECD DAC, op cit.
22. Informationsvermerk BMZ zu den Vertraulichen Erläuterungen 1997 für die bilaterale Finanzielle und Technische Zusammenarbeit mit Entwicklungsländern.
23. BMZ-Informationsvermerk 27/96 für AWZ/Vertrauliche Erläuterungen für TZ+FZ 97.
24. Fues, Thomas, Rahmenplanung des BMZ für 1997: Die 20:20-Initiative ist in Vergessenheit geraten, September 1996.
25. see declaration, Deutsches NRO-Forum Weltsozialgipfel, September 1996.
26. There has been a concept in existence about The promotion of women in developing countries for a number of years (since 1988, which was an elaboration of the concept paper of 1978), in which the promotion of women is declared a cross-sectoral issue (one of five) and its importance in the context of poverty

Germany

reduction is underlined. The gender aspect and the necessity of gender-specific analyses in the planning and design of projects is emphasised.
27. Ministry in charge is the Ministry for Families and Elderly People, Women and Youth.
28. *Die Welt*, 4 June 1997: CDU will Kehrtwende bei EU-Entwicklungshilfe.
29. See *Reality of Aid 1996* for a discussion about the usage of the funds set free from the lower than planned replenishment of IDA 11.
30. Hannoversche Allgemeine Zeitung, Andreas Rinke: *Welche Interesen hat Deutschland in Mali?*, 5 September 1996.
31. OECD, DAC: *Shaping the 21st Century*, May 1996.

Ireland

Sheila Hoare, Concern

Irish Aid's growth path

Irish Aid in 1996 totalled IR£ 106 million or 0.29% as a share of GNP. Estimates for 1997 indicate that aid expenditure will further increase to IR£ 122 million or 0.31% of GNP. This is moving towards the average EU performance, but behind the 1993 Aid Strategy Plan interim target of 0.4% of GNP in 1997.[1] While the government has allocated significant absolute increases in ODA since 1993, the average annual increase in terms of share of GNP is less than 0.03%. As recently as the World Food Summit, the government restated its commitment 'to increasing Ireland's ODA by 0.05% each year, so that we continue to progress towards the UN target'. The main reasons cited for not meeting this annual target are rapid GNP growth and internal capacity constraints in the Development Cooperation Division (DCD) due to the current public service recruitment embargo.

While the absolute increases in Irish Aid since 1993 are warmly welcomed by the development community, there is concern that no specific time schedule has been set for achieving the UN target. At current rates of increase the target will not be reached before 2012.

Political outlook for aid

Four main forces have contributed to framing Ireland's ODA:

- commitments in The Programme for Partnership Government and the subsequent 1996 White Paper on Foreign Policy to increase ODA;
- unprecedented GNP growth rates of 6.74% in 1994 and 7% in 1995;
- public support for aid directed towards poverty alleviation as reflected in donations to voluntary agencies; and
- NGO lobbying.

In addition to the government's stated ODA target, recent written commitments by the main opposition party to increase ODA to a minimum of 0.45% of GNP mean that for the foreseeable future there is cross-party support for the current growth path in Irish aid.[2]

Bilateral assistance

In 1996, expenditure in the six priority countries (Ethiopia, Lesotho, Mozambique, Tanzania, Uganda, Zambia) accounted for one quarter of total ODA. The largest expansions in country allocations have been to Uganda and Ethiopia, with the latter rising from IR£ 7.09 million in 1996 to IR£ 8.5 million in 1997. The allocation to Mozambique, Irish Aid's newest priority country, will double in 1997 to IR£ 2.5 million.

In 1997, programmes will begin in Malawi, which ranks in the bottom 10% of the UNDP Human Development Index. Significant increases are planned for project aid to Vietnam, which is not a LLDC and is one of East Asia's fastest growing economies. Irish Aid recently stated that 'Sudan cannot be categorised as a priority country as long as the present human rights situation continues unchanged; the future of the programme following the completion of existing projects is under close review.'

The volume of project aid to post-apartheid South Africa, which is not a priority country, is expected to increase to IR£ 3 million, a figure in excess of the amount of aid to either Lesotho or Mozambique.

Increasing demands for emergency assistance resulted in this component of the programme absorbing nearly 7% of total ODA. In 1996, emergency expenditure increased by 40% to IR£ 8 million, but is projected to fall in 1997. Rwanda and Bosnia will continue to receive most of this aid.

Rehabilitation expenditure rose in 1996 to IR£ 4 million. This rise reflects recognition of the need for simultaneous rather than sequential activities in relief and rehabilitation so as to establish a basis for effective development work. The growing

Ireland

The **Reality** of Aid 1997/8

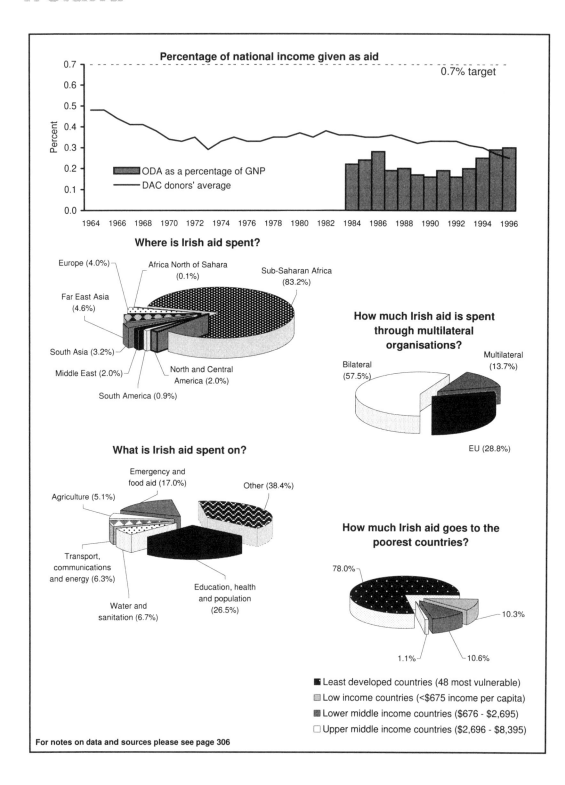

For notes on data and sources please see page 306

The **Reality** of Aid 1997/8

Ireland

Irish aid at a glance

How much aid does Ireland give?

Ireland gave	US$ 177m, IR£ 106 million in 1996
that was	0.3% of GNP
and	1.62% of public administration
which meant	US$ 49 or IR£ 29.5 per capita for 1996

Is it going up or down?

In 1996 Irish aid	rose by $ 24m, up 14.5% in real terms over 1995
Ireland was	more generous in 1996, rising from 0.29% of GNP to 0.3%
The outlook is that	Irish aid is continuing to rise in real terms

How does Ireland compare with the other 21 donors?

Ireland ranks	19 out of 21 for its volume of aid
It is	12 out of 21 in the generosity league
It gives	a higher proportion of its aid (88.3%) to Low Income Countries than 19 other donors
Private Flows	amounted to $48m, 31% of ODA
Total Flows	to developing countries were 0.46% of GNP and rank 13 out of 21 in the DAC

How much does Ireland spend on basic health and basic education?

Ireland reports	less than 1% of its ODA spending on basic health and on basic education

How important are commercial interests in aid?

Ireland	sees any commercial returns as a spin off. Irish aid is untied except for technical cooperation which is linked to Irish personnel

What do the public think about aid?

80% of the population support aid, 60% of them very strongly

79

importance of rehabilitation in the aid programme led to the appointment of a rehabilitation adviser to the DCD in 1997.

Bilateral aid programme: reorientation

The Bilateral Aid Programme has seen a reorientation in recent years, which in part has involved an expansion in area-based programmes. This is viewed as a logical approach for a relatively small aid donor (since well designed and implemented programmes, focused on a small geographical area, can more successfully address the needs of the poor directly) and a means of maintaining the poverty focus of Irish Aid. Priority sectors within area-based programmes are those deemed to be most relevant to poverty alleviation, namely, health, education, rural development and low technology water supply.

In 1997, the government will examine the feasibility of programme aid (macro support) to specific sectors of the recipient country's budget. According to the DCD, Sectoral Investment Programmes (SIPs) – particularly in the education and health sectors – provide an opportunity to move beyond 'isolated islands of excellence' to a more coherent approach to social sector support at regional and national levels. Macro support, in theory, helps to remove restraints or bottlenecks at national or regional level which may hinder activities at district or community level. Since programme aid is more distant from the individual beneficiary, Irish Aid will have to ensure that mechanisms exist for tracing the link between SIPs and poverty alleviation.

Poverty focus

In 1996, 85% of total ODA was allocated to sub-Saharan Africa and to countries with an average GNP per capita of less than US$ 300. The proportion of Irish Aid to LLDCs is approximately twice the DAC average. The poverty focus of Irish Aid was reconfirmed recently by the Minister for Development Cooperation when she stated, 'Development aid that is not dedicated to poverty reduction is a contradiction in terms.'[3]

While the government has committed itself to the 20:20 initiative agreed at the World Summit on Social Development (WSSD), no official calculation of the amount of ODA currently allocated to basic poverty alleviation is available. Thus, it is not possible to give a detailed statistical analysis of the poverty focus of Irish Aid. However, in 1996, the DCD undertook to quantify resource allocations to human development priorities, which includes items in the directly productive sector, in Ethiopia.[4] It is hoped that by the end of this year a clearer picture of the proportion of ODA allocated to human development priorities will be provided.

Country reviews in Lesotho and Zambia revealed the need for greater emphasis on the poverty focus of Irish Aid, and subsequent three-year country plans have put this in place. However, Irish Aid has noted that there is a 'need to achieve a stronger poverty focus in the initial analysis' so that it is a central aspect of implementation and can be identified in evaluation and monitoring. Some progress in this direction has been made by strengthening the Evaluation and Audit Unit through the appointment of additional sectoral experts.

While the reaffirmation of the poverty focus of bilateral aid is very positive, the real challenge will be to develop and institutionalise poverty reduction strategies, and to develop an effective monitoring and evaluation mechanism so that performance can be examined against policies.

Gender

In response to the Beijing recommendations, the DCD drafted and adopted a gender guidelines document. The guidelines cover all stages of the project cycle and the priority sectors in which Irish Aid works. Some progress has been made in implementing these guidelines in the area of gender-sensitive planning. Country programme planning exercises in Uganda and Tanzania involved a gender expert and each three-year country plan has an overall gender strategy, as well as a gender dimension to each of its components. Of the six priority countries, three have local gender experts as advisers to the programmes.

NGO funding

The 1996 review of the NGO Co-financing Scheme was broadly welcomed by the NGO community. The revision was designed to add clarity to the purpose of the funding, to give greater financial stability to NGOs and to reduce the administrative workload. The DCD has indicated that funding to NGOs will be maintained at its current level of approximately 12% of total ODA. The revised scheme has six funding mechanisms:

- Emergency Humanitarian Assistance;
- Emergency Preparedness and Post-Emergency Rehabilitation;

- Co-financing of Individual Projects;
- Block Grants to the larger NGOs;
- Democratisation and Human Rights; and
- Micro-Projects Operated by Developing Country NGOs.

In previous years NGOs could also apply to the Other Countries Fund and to a fund for Women in Development. Access to these funds has now been withdrawn, but there has been a substantial increase in block grants to compensate the larger agencies.

The reduction in the number of funding mechanisms and the substantial increase in block grants will help reduce the administrative load on government and the larger NGOs, while giving greater flexibility to the latter. However, concerns have been expressed that, should this trend continue, it will reduce access to government funds for new and smaller NGOs.

The Emergency Preparedness and Post-emergency Rehabilitation Fund is not available for work in Irish Aid priority countries. Several agencies feel this to be unfair. It gives rise to an interpretation that there is increasing competition for funding between NGOs and the priority country budget.

The DCD states that rehabilitation grants are not appropriate in priority countries, as priority status is only agreed with a country that has a stable political environment within which it is possible to develop a multi-annual approach to programming funding.

Equally, the Democratisation and Human Rights budget line cannot be accessed for work in priority countries. Some agencies feel that this line should be open to NGOs, as they are in a better position to highlight issues of human rights abuses in countries where the Irish government's activities may preclude it from becoming overtly critical.

The NGO community welcomed the DCD's proposal for regular dialogue with agencies to discuss progress in the management of the NGO co-financing scheme, to clarify aspects that may be unclear and to resolve problems.

Other initiatives

A recent study, commissioned by the Irish Aid Advisory Committee (IAAC), notes that 'agriculture is the most important sector in the Priority Countries in terms of providing employment, incomes and basic food needs'.[5] The study made a number of important recommendations. These included:

strengthening Irish Aid's role in sustainable agriculture and other income generating activities, and increasing significantly the volume of support to food security-related areas. It also recommended that Irish Aid should participate more often than it has in the past in international fora to address issues that damage the livelihood prospects of the poor, such as the debt burden, impact of SAPs, aspects of the GATT agreement and some EU subsidies.

In 1997, Irish Aid will re-examine its approach to the directly productive sector. In this regard, discussion with the International Fund for Agriculture Development took place earlier in the year with a view to possible co-financing of projects. In 1998, the government is expected to contribute for the first time to the International Food Policy Research Institute.

Ireland's presidency of the EU

During Ireland's presidency of the EU, between July and December 1996, two major issues dominated EU relations with developing countries: the ongoing crises in central Africa; and the issue of coherence between development cooperation policies and other policies of the EU.

At the outset of the presidency, there was optimism at the governments' intention to ensure that Africa was a priority issue. Although the first major conference of the presidency focused on the issue of 'Humanitarian Crises: Prevention, Consequences, Rehabilitation', there was some disappointment that it failed to deliver any firm recommendations on how the EU can enhance its response to humanitarian crises or, in particular, how it can work to prevent such crises emerging.

In November, Concern Worldwide and Oxfam in Ireland hosted a conference on Europe's evolving Common Foreign and Security Policy (CFSP). His Excellency Julius K Nyerere, former president of Tanzania, delivered the conference keynote address. This address was given 24 hours after EU foreign ministers failed to reach agreement on EU policy toward central Africa at the Stuttgart meeting.

Mr Nyerere noted 'that in the long run the real dangers to peace come from desperate poverty . . . poverty without hope of relief is like a pile of gunpowder waiting for a spark to set it off.'

The conference concluded that, without explicit commitment to poverty eradication and the protection of human rights, EU foreign policy, and in particular the CFSP, will continue to be directed by national and strategic interests. Such interests prohibited a coherent EU response emerging to events in the Great Lakes region during and since the Irish presidency.

A number of positive developments occurred in the context of Europe's relationship with the world's poorest nations. A gender and emergency resolution, adopted by the Development Council, commits the EU to ensuring that gender equality is a central issue in emergency and rehabilitation programmes. Adequate resources will be needed so that this commitment can be effectively implemented.

The Development Council adopted a resolution on anti-personnel landmines which seeks to improve EU coordination of landmine programmes such as mine clearance, victim rehabilitation and mine awareness activities. A Joint Action by the European Council put in place a common moratorium within the EU on the export of all anti-personnel mines.

A resolution on Human and Social Development (HSD) was adopted by the November 1996 Development Council. The resolution, which is in line with conclusions reached at Beijing, Cairo and Copenhagen, calls on the Commission and member states to demonstrate a renewed and strong commitment to HSD. At the end of 1998, the Commission is to report to the Council and Parliament on progress achieved in implementing this resolution. Irish NGOs have urged that the targets for social development investment in the OECD/DAC 'Shaping the 21st Century' document are equally pursued by the Commission and member states in their policies and programmes.

In general, Irish development agencies and solidarity groups welcomed the high level of consultation that took place with the government throughout Ireland's presidency of the EU.

Lack of coherence between Irish agricultural trade policies and development objectives in South Africa

EU member states, including Ireland, have publicly stated their commitment to assisting the reconstruction and economic development of South Africa and to the transition to a functioning and non-racial democracy.

Since 1994, there has been a sixfold increase in Irish aid to South Africa. In 1997, an estimated IR£ 3 million will be used to support projects in the rural development, education and capacity building sectors. This is in line with commitments made in the White Paper on Foreign Policy to support South Africa's reconstruction. As part of this, efforts to support sustainable agriculture are vital. However, the current practice of dumping heavily subsidised EU beef (including Irish beef) runs contrary to this commitment by undermining the agricultural sector and its related industries.

Since 1993, EU beef exports as a share of total supply on the South African market have risen from 1.4% to 11%. Between January and October 1996 over 30,000 tonnes of subsidised beef, predominantly Irish beef, were imported at prices lower than half the local wholesale price.[6] Thus, at a time when South Africa and its neighbouring countries are going through a period of economic transition, this imported beef is undercutting the price of locally produced meat in the region and threatening the livelihoods of those working in the farming and food sectors.

Beef dumping by the EU has contributed to a 40% reduction in incomes received by South African farmers for livestock sold to commercial feedlots. Real losses to the national economy are estimated to be equivalent to 95% of the EU's annual aid allocation to South Africa in support of reconstruction and development.[7]

The South African government has called for the removal of all EU beef export subsidies to South Africa. South African politicians argue that the 20% reduction on export subsidies, announced by the EU in 1997, does not significantly alter the impact of trade as long as the level of farmer support in the EU remains at over three times that of farmer support in South Africa.[8]

Ireland's policy in relation to beef exports to South Africa is clearly undermining agricultural development in that country. Irish NGOs therefore urge the government to ensure that the Interdepartmental Committee on Development Cooperation examines coherence issues between development cooperation on the one hand and trade and agricultural policies on the other (in line with commitments made in the White Paper).

In line with the Dutch emergency resolution to the European Parliament, Irish NGOs have further sought:

- immediate reclassification of South Africa so that beef exported to that country is no longer eligible for export refunds;

- that the EU Development Council establish immediate and ongoing dialogue with the EU Agricultural Council and the appropriate departments of DGVI to ensure that the application of the various instruments of the CAP do not undermine the promotion of the objectives of EU development cooperation policy.

Ireland's debate on ESAF

In July 1996, the Minister of Finance announced that Irish participation in ESAF would not be 'progressed in advance of a satisfactory operational implementation of a comprehensive debt relief framework'. The managing director of the IMF was informed that 'participation by Ireland in ESAF would need to follow rather than precede implementation of the Highly Indebted poor Country (HIPC) initiative'.[9]

Ireland's policy of non-participation in ESAF is advocated by the Debt and Development Coalition, Ireland – a grouping of over 70 NGOs and community bodies – which initiated the 'No to ESAF' campaign in 1995. The Coalition is highly critical of the IMF's participation in the HIP through ESAF, whose conditionalities have impacted negatively on the poorest. The government, in welcoming the HIPC initiative, identified the coordinated action by bilateral and multilateral institutions, including the active participation of the IMF, among the scheme's notable merits.

However, groups such as the Debt and Development Coalition maintain that eligibility should not be linked to narrow IMF conditionality. Nor should countries have to wait a further six years, in which they would subject their weakened economies to deflationary adjustment programmes, before qualifying for substantial debt reduction. This is particularly the case for countries such as Mozambique, endeavouring to recover from protracted civil conflict. The Minister of State at the Department of Foreign Affairs has criticised such an approach as 'extremely unsound economics'.

Speaking at a conference on Structural Adjustment in Dublin, in December 1996, the Vice President of the World Bank with responsibility for External Affairs described Ireland as 'the country in Europe with the strongest opposition to structural adjustment'. While the Irish government's policy of non-participation in ESAF would seem to confirm this view, there is little evidence that Ireland is pursuing a rigorous critical analysis of adjustment within the international financial institutions.

Notes

1. The average EU ODA/GNP percentage performance has declined from 0.42% in 1994 to 0.37% in 1996.
2. At the time of writing the government refers to the 'rainbow coalition', namely Fine Gael, Labour and Democratic Left. The 6 June general election saw the establishment of a Fianna Fail/Progressive Democrats coalition. The new government has committed itself to an interim ODA target of at least 0.45% of GNP by 2002 on the way to reaching the UN target!
3. Minister of State for Development Cooperation, *Irish Times*, November 1996.
4. Human Development Priorities as defined at the 20:20 Oslo meeting in April 1996 include the following: maintenance transfers and subsidies to the poor; agricultural extension and support for small-scale (including women) farmers; credit, marketing and technical support for small-scale production; employment opportunities; support for shelter and public transportation.
5. IAAC, *Irish Aid and Agriculture*, a report to the Minister for Foreign Affairs, September 1996.
6. European Research Office Report, *EU Beef Export Refunds and its Effects on the Livestock Industry in Southern Africa*, January 1997.
7. Ibid.
8. Christian Aid, *Out of Joint: Report on Research into EU Beef Dumping in South Africa*, February 1997.
9. Minister for Finance, Dail (parliamentary) questions, November 1996.

Italy

José Luis Rhi-Sausi, Marco Zupi and Claudio Bernabucci, Movimondo

Main outline of Italian ODA

In 1995, Italy's ODA continued its declining trend started at the beginning of the 1990s: it dropped in real terms by 46.2% over the previous year, the most significant reduction among all the OECD donors. Italy's ODA has thus passed from 0.42% of the GDP in 1989 – its highest point – to 0.14% in 1995, making Italy, in absolute terms, the ninth largest OECD donor country.

Beside the declining trend of Italian ODA volume, a number of key points have emerged during 1995:

- The damage that the actual idea of development cooperation has suffered among people and the mass media. The risk is that people might completely lose confidence in the value of development cooperation as a consequence of the corruption in the management of public affairs (the phenomenon known as *Tangentopoli*.)
- The importance of international credibility. Indirectly, the common initiatives of the Italian–UN agencies (in particular the Italy–UNDP initiative) and the expansion of the multilateral channel could help gain international consent for the Italian proposal for the reform of the UN Security Council. This proposal is based on creating ten new regional semi-permanent rotating seats allocated on a regional basis.
- The administrative reorganisation. The Ministry of Foreign Affairs (MFA) is now pursuing a more rational and effective approach to aid management – by implementing a project cycle approach, and country programmes.
- A new geopolitical approach. A deeper rethinking of ODA policies has arisen as a result of the emergence of regional crises close to Italian national borders in former Yugoslavia and the Mediterranean basin, and a number of peace-keeping and rehabilitation processes – in Mozambique, Somalia, Ethiopia and Eritrea – which have had the effect of ending the bipolar international system.

Political objectives

As a direct effect of this revision, Italian ODA aims to pursue two broad political objectives: strengthening its traditional multilateral orientation; and promoting, via bilateral channels, political, economic and social stability in those developing countries whose situations are crucial in terms of European security. This will result in a concentration of ODA on a limited number of recipients. Also linked to this change in aid policy is the emergence of poverty reduction as a priority objective (see later). This means a shift away from certain sector priorities and towards others:

Table 5 Sector Priorities, 1987 and 1995 Compared

1987	1995
Economic infrastructure	Integrated human development
Agriculture	Human rights and democracy promotion
Industry	Institution building
Education	Local entrepreneurship support
Health	Technical assistance and training
Energy and raw materials	Balance of payments support
Natural resources	Social infrastructure and debt relief
	Natural resources and cultural heritage

Another important feature is the shift from a truly worldwide aid programme, which included some 101 recipient countries in 1992, to a more concentrated approach, with 1996 ODA extended to only 32 countries. Even the priority countries have been reduced: from 37 in 1992 to 16 in 1995.

The outlook for aid

Declining ODA and the dominance of multilateral aid

The radical cut in aid since 1989 is the most outstanding feature of Italy's cooperation policy and is likely to be a continuing trend.

Table 6 Italy's ODA allocations (000m liras)

	1996	1997	1998*	1999*
Bilateral and voluntary contributions to international organisations	596	519	513	525
Compulsory contributions to international organisations	1700	2200	n.a.	n.a.
Of which: European Development Fund (FED)	450	450		
Other EU programmes	550	550		
TOTAL	2296	2719		

* Projections
Source: Camera dei Deputati, Servizio Studi

The data show that bilateral cooperation will continue its trend of decreasing in absolute terms, as a proportion of GNP and as a proportion of total ODA.

The multilateral channel carries the greatest weight in Italy's development cooperation activities. Compulsory obligations to international banks and funds represent the main component of Italian ODA: this high proportion of aid going through compulsory contributions reduces the scope for the Italian bilateral programme. It also hides the fact that the flow of purely bilateral aid is continuing to go down. If we add voluntary contributions to international organisations to the compulsory ones, multilateral cooperation now represents about 90% of total ODA. And the multilateral share is even higher if we also consider the (multi-bi) trust funds that Italy has agreed upon with a number of international institutions – particularly with UNDP – which are included in the statistics for bilateral aid.

This imbalance is in part a product of the radical cut in ODA; but it reflects government policy as well. The Italian government considers that the reduction of multilateral aid might be more damaging to its international prestige than the reduction of bilateral aid. In addition, the management problems suffered by bilateral cooperation over the last years have pushed the government to favour multilateral assistance. Finally, many government departments, namely the Treasury, seem convinced that multilateralism may somehow compensate for the lack of bilateral cooperation.

Grants versus loans

A third significant potential trend is the imbalance, in terms of resource allocation, between the main tools of bilateral cooperation: grants and soft loans. Historically, grants and loans have been allocated more or less the same amount of funding but, due to the resource reduction, soft loans could potentially receive more resources than the grants. This may be explained by the fact that loans depend on a revolving fund that is in part reimbursed by annual loan repayments. These amount to about 300,000 million liras each year: a sum that today equals total bilateral aid. The revolving fund is allowed to keep any residual amounts from previous years in contrast to grants, where any unspent funds are, after a period, withdrawn from the ODA budget.

Four main elements of italian cooperation

Italian cooperation is highly differentiated and has four main elements:

- first and foremost, multilateral cooperation, the most important share of ODA, which is mainly managed by the Treasury;
- second, the promotion of the private sector, which is a priority of bilateral cooperation, and benefits from the bias towards soft loans;
- third, the establishment of *human development programmes at local level*, as a consequence of the fruitful cooperation with UNDP (through trust funds);
- fourth and finally, non-governmental cooperation, which has been particularly badly

Italy

The **Reality** of Aid 1997/8

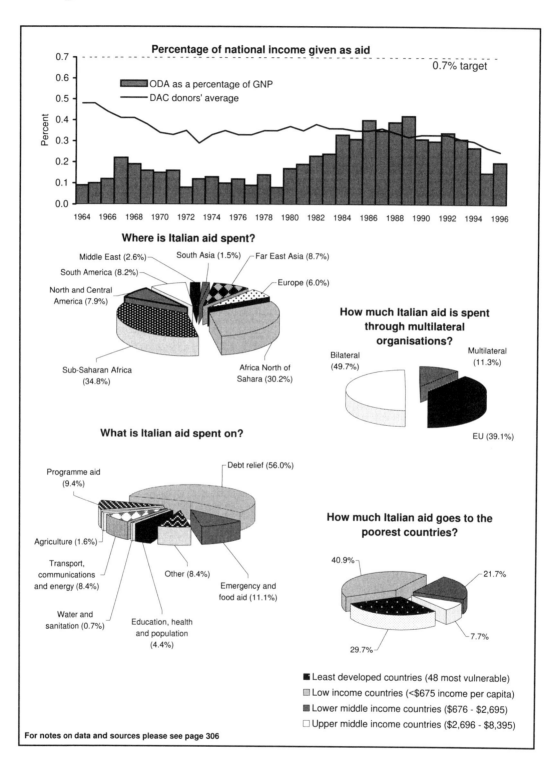

The **Reality** of Aid 1997/8

Italian aid at a glance

How much aid does Italy give?

Italy gave	US$ 2397m in 1996
that was	0.2% of GNP
and	0.92% of public administration
which meant	US$42 per capita for 1996

Is it going up or down?

In 1996 Italian aid	rose by US$ 774m, up 33.9% in real terms over 1995
Italy was	more generous in 1996, rising from 0.15% GNP to 0.2%
The outlook is	unknown

How does Italy compare with the other 21 donors?

Italy ranks	7 out of 21 for its volume of aid
It is	19 out of 21 in the generosity league
It gives	a higher proportion of its aid (70.6%) to Low Income Countries than 14 other donors
Private Flows	amounted to $120m, 7.4% of ODA
Total Flows	to developing countries were 0.26% of GNP and rank 20 out of 21 in the DAC

How much does Italy spend on basic health and basic education?

Italy reports	1% of its ODA spending on basic health and has yet to report on basic education

How important are commercial interests in aid?

Italy requires	18.2% of its aid to be used to buy Italian goods

Italy

affected by the reduction of national resources, but has nonetheless managed to establish itself as one of the main components of Italy's cooperation.

Non-governmental cooperation

Non-governmental cooperation has undergone an important process of transformation. In particular, three trends are currently underway.

In the first place, the multiplication of non-governmental actors. This is partly a consequence of Italian social and professional organisations now having access to international cooperation resources in addition to the traditional NGDOs and partly as a result of the growing role of decentralised cooperation.

In the second place, the expansion of programmes that are co-financed by the European Commission (particularly by ECHO) has meant not only reduced importance for Italian cooperation as a source of funding of NGO projects, but also a growing weight of emergency aid in the activities of Italian NGOs. The new scenarios that have emerged as a result of the crisis running through Italian ODA policy have given NGOs an opportunity to change the way they work and to intensify their relationship with the EU, where the specific weight of Italian NGOs has increased in recent years.

The third trend in non-governmental cooperation is tied to the fact that the Italian ODA reduction has affected the geographical priorities so severely that in many countries – especially in Latin America – the only surviving form of Italian cooperation is the non-governmental one. Despite this, NGOs have yet to receive any government's concrete appreciation in terms of their relevance as a national 'resource'. However, the gap between the scale of NGO operations and their modest political status in governmental policy is slowly being reduced. Up to now there has been no coherent or long-term government policy towards NGOs.

The need for reform

These trends demonstrate how important it is for Italy's cooperation to undergo a deep revision. Starting in 1995, a reform process was set in motion which involved the government, the parliament and the non-governmental world. The main outcomes of this debate are: the activity of the Parliamentary Inquiry Committee on Development Cooperation (1995/6), and a number of bills for the reform of the governing legislation, the 49/87 Law, presented by several political parties. These bills will be discussed by parliament in the near future.

Given the persistent crisis of the administrative machine, which the approval of decrees, regulations and new procedures towards the rationalisation of aid management has only mitigated, a new law could finally provide a solid base to solve the current embarrassing situation that prevents even the limited bilateral resources from being disbursed.

Eradication of poverty

A well-structured and conceptualised poverty reduction policy, which had been in the process of being developed since 1990, was established in 1995. The growing importance of poverty reduction in Italian ODA during the 1990s is linked to the crisis in the orientation of bilateral aid towards serving the interests of Italian exporters and to the international community's consensus on poverty reduction.

The current Italian approach to aid for poverty reduction is based on practical experience, particularly on programmes implemented in Latin America, such as the Programme for Health, Environment and the Struggle against Poverty (the SMALP); and, most important, the Programme for Refugees, Displaced and Repatriated Persons in Central America (PRODERE). The poverty policy owes much of its character to the new guidelines on multilateral cooperation, basically devised by UNDP.

The growing importance of poverty reduction oriented ODA is due to the wish to improve the reputation of Italian aid policy; but it is also a reaction to emergencies that have occurred in a number of countries internationally considered to be part of Italy's social, political and economic sphere of interest: in other words, those countries that rely mainly on Italy for their foreign aid, such as Albania with its migration and transition problems, Mozambique with its conflicts, Somalia, Ethiopia and Eritrea, and former Yugoslavia.

As Mr Paolo Bruni, MFA/DGCS General Director since 1995, said:

> Social development is not a new sector for Italian ODA, but it is a change of culture. Development does not mean only economic growth, but it should be qualified as human development, a sustainable, participatory, decentralised process.

The Copenhagen World Summit on Social Development, in 1995, provided an opportunity to make the new Italian ODA guidelines public.

People's participation

People's participation is probably the key concept in Italian poverty reduction oriented aid. Here the theoretical definition of UNDP has been adopted:

participation means that people are closely involved in economic, social, cultural and political process that affect their lives. The important thing is that people have constant access to decision-making and power.

Most important is fitting the idea of people's participation to the specific context, particularly to situations of post-conflict recovery, and to local cultures and traditions.

This kind of approach encompasses a wide range of activities designed to address the causes of vulnerability and of poverty. The poverty reduction oriented aid strategy cannot confine itself to building physical infrastructure and supporting the growth of productive capacities. A human development strategy must operate through policies that support the consolidation of community ties and through institutions aimed at creating the social network that is a crucial condition for development.

The people's participation approach leads to an integrated approach: ODA should take income, health, education, environment and human rights into consideration at the same time, as inseparable elements of development. These basic needs (political, economic and social) are not isolated but intimately connected and cannot be promoted through sectoral or vertical activities. Development must be balanced and durable. The process leading to local, public and private institution building is crucial as well.

The people's participation coupled with local development creates decentralised cooperation (see Box 10), which in turn creates a cooperation circuit among Northern and Southern communities. This implies not only a horizontal relationship among corresponding local authorities and professional components, but also territorial relations to which everybody can contribute – NGOs, groups of active citizens, social partners, scientific institutions.

All this represents a contribution to a new partnership process. The important origins of this approach lie in the attempt to promote both emergency and development objectives, as opposed to the old methods and techniques of emergency intervention. This results in broadening people's capabilities to participate effectively in the reintegration process without duplicating existing institutions or creating new emergency institutions through aimless institutional engineering experiments. It could be said that, as new Italian ODA guidelines were giving the first priority to international stability and security, it was necessary for Italy to show a greater activism in the regional conflicts. Not only did Italy participate in international peacekeeping and peace enforcement actions, but it could also offer a kind of strategy capable of linking emergencies, social and economic rehabilitation and development.

Examples of effective aid and the measurement of Italian ODA for poverty reduction

The idea of reducing poverty as a consequence of strengthening local capabilities must become a concrete, visible and measurable strategy in order to make an evaluation of ODA actions possible.

At present, there are calls for the administration to set targets for aid that reflect its poverty reduction policy in basic education, primary health care, family planning, gender status and the social sectors. But, when it comes to implementation, the evaluation of project commitments and expenditure in terms of meeting planned objectives (aimed at improving accountability, influencing the policy debate and assisting in the design of projects) remains a very weak spot in the Italian administrative machine.

In this context, some possible criteria for the evaluation of actions in social development have been proposed. The DGCS and UNDP have suggested an interesting subdivision into the various sectors of social development whereby actions in, for instance, education or basic health would be classified and given a value. This is being considered as a possible methodology to test all the poverty reduction and empowerment interventions.

Even if it is still too early to judge whether the poverty reduction oriented aid programmes work, some brief considerations are possible:

- Italian ODA has no preference toward a particular multilateral channel, and when Italy is working with recipient LDC governments and the World Bank to develop a country programme, it tries to involve, whenever this is

Italy

possible, other UN agencies, such as UNDP and FAO (this happened in Albania).
- Italian ODA does not plan to set up a strong coordination mechanism with the European Commission and the EU member donors in aid policies for poverty reduction. When this has happened, it has been the result of a request coming from a recipient LDC government or from the multilateral agencies. Italy seems to search for pragmatic coordination in the field and a task division suggested by the donors' geographical priorities;
- Without entering into further details, the Italian-funded World Bank Poverty Reduction initiative has generally lacked as strong an Italian contribution as was given to UNDP. In the World Bank-led Albanian initiative, the Italian contribution was focused on areas from which important migration flows originated. In this case the World Bank had a strong political authority, while the Italian contribution was relatively less important. In the Ethiopian and Eritrean cases, the Italian role has been more active in designing the objectives, methodologies and phases. In the Ethiopian case, for example, a previous Italian comprehensive rehabilitation programme, the Regional Socioeconomic Rehabilitation Programme (RESOURCE), funded with a total allocation of US$ 32 million, allowed Italian ODA to play an important role in the Economic Recovery and Reconstruction Programme (ERRP) led by the World Bank.
- Italian ODA seems to sum up the Poverty Reduction approach as based on the PRODERE and UNDP human development approach, with some more specifically economic features added (such as the promotion of local entrepreneurship) and put into the World Bank structural adjustment framework, with people's participation, poverty assessments and safety nets along with corrective policy measures.
- The MFA would like to be more involved in the policy discussions leading up to funding decisions, but the lack of flexibility, transparency or clear rationale in the mechanisms of aid management hold it back from fuller involvement. In recent years, the establishment of UNOPS (United Nations Office for Project Services) as an autonomous international agency, and the promotion of a *Trust Fund for Sustainable Social Development, Peace and Support to Countries in Special Situations*, launched during the Copenhagen Summit, have clearly presented Italy's role on development policy in the international arena. The UNOPS management structure seemed to the DGCS to be a possible solution to the Italian situation for the following reasons: the trust fund mechanism allows for continued financing of aid programmes and projects planned to last several years, as opposed to the existing Italian annual budget provisions; and because Italy has a great influence with it.

Box 10 Examples of effective poverty reduction aid from Italy

These are examples of programmes co-financed by Italy and coordinated with the World Bank that have been aimed at achieving human development and poverty reduction.

Albania *Rural Poverty Alleviation*, a co-financed World Bank–Italian ODA programme, covering 1993–5. Other supporters: EU, UNDP, IDA. Italian support: US$ 3 million.

Ethiopia The Social Rehabilitation Fund (SRF), specific component of the Economic Recovery and Reconstruction Programme (ERRP), launched under the coordination of the World Bank in 1992.

Eritrea The Eritrean Community Rehabilitation Fund (ECRF), the social fund of the Recovery and Rehabilitation Project for Eritrea (RRPE, an initiative that amounted to $26 million).

In 1996, four human development programmes will be implemented in Mozambique, Tunisia, Bosnia and Central America (Belize, Costa Rica, El Salvador, Guatemala, Honduras and Nicaragua), as economic, social and political reconstruction programmes.

Box 11 Decentralised cooperation in Italy

Mid-way through the 1990s, decentralised cooperation is undergoing a period of strong growth and substantial experimentation, formed in workshops of new experience, it is capable of having a significant impact on the reform of Italian policy on cooperation for development.

Diverse factors, from both inside and outside the field of cooperation, have contributed to the endorsement of the decentralised approach. The need for a change in the structure of the state towards an increase in local autonomy; ample and profound redefinition of the identity and organisation of social forces – signalled by the recent strengthening of the private social sector; and the crisis in cooperation for development policy, have all opened fresh spaces for the search for new methods in the field of international solidarity and cooperation.

The singular characteristic of Italian experience in carrying out that search is to employ the special methods of decentralised cooperation – based on cooperation between communities. Within the framework of new and complex partnership agreements between communities in developing and developed countries, decentralised cooperation brings together and synthesises the Italian and international experiences of the struggle against poverty which matured in the 1970s and 1980s. Central to the concept is the idea of co-development, an idea that led to new strategies being devised which were designed to join a commitment to development in poor countries with the struggle against social exclusion in rich ones, and in the process establish new links between development policies and development cooperation policies. In this context NGOs are beginning to play a specific role, particularly in creating relations with communities in poor countries, in training operators from, for instance, local authorities, and in providing technical support.

These partnership agreements between communities first took form in PRODERE (Programa de desarrolo para desplazados, refugiados y repatriados en Centro America), a US human development programme for which Italy was the principal backer. The format of this programme was later to spread to other programmes and other geographic areas. The foundation of the Foro delle città per la cooperazione decentrata (Forum of Cities for Decentralised Cooperation) in 1995 proved to be one of the principal events in the process of innovation. As of mid-1997, 26 cities are taking part in the Forum – including the major Italian cities of Venice, Rome, Milan, Genoa, Turin and Naples – while another 40 or so are about to join.

Although the fundamental contribution of the decentralised approach is given by its capacity to mobilise know-how, to value social capital and put it to use, one of the indicators of the interest and consensus mentioned above is the significant financial commitment shown by numerous local authorities. In 1997 Bergamo reserved 1000 million lira (approximately 500,000 ecus) for cooperation, Milan gave 800 million lira, and even a small city of roughly 66,000 inhabitants like Viareggio allocated 180 million lira. These commitments were made possible by the approval of a law (*Legge* 68) in 1993, which allows municipalities to earmark 0.8% of their first three budget items for cooperation for development activities. This law and its regional counterparts – currently 16 out of the 20 Italian regions and the two autonomous provinces have passed regional laws on cooperation – have contributed greatly to going beyond the phase of generic twinning and one-off responsive actions of solidarity. In addition, they have introduced, from within, strong stimuli for a global reordering of the old legislative framework as characterised by the *legge* 49 of 1987. The various proposals for reform tabled in 1997, of diverse political colours, represent an eloquent expression of just how much consensus has been reached on the need to allocate more resources to decentralised cooperation in the second half of the 1990s.

Japan

Akio Takayanagi, Japanese NGO Center for International Cooperation (JANIC)

Overview

Japan has been the world's largest aid donor since 1991. But 1996 became the year that Japan's ODA was cut dramatically. Net disbursement was 1.04 trillion (thousand, thousand million) yen, a 24.8% decrease in yen terms compared with financial year (FY) 1995. In dollars, at US$ 9600 million, Japanese aid has fallen by 35%. Aid represents only 0.21% of GNP, compared with 0.28% in 1995.

The decrease was largely due to cuts in multilateral aid and increased loan repayment.[1] Commitments for bilateral loans were in fact increased by 17%. Another factor that led to the decrease in dollar terms was the depreciating yen rate. According to the FY 1997 budget, multilateral aid is to return to the level in FY 1995, and bilateral aid is also to be slightly increased.

But from FY 1998 there is going to be a large decrease in the amount of aid. With the worst budget deficit among OECD members, the government is reviewing all its spending, including foreign aid. This has brought about an increasing pressure to tighten the ODA volume. In early June 1997 the government decided to cut ODA by 10% in FY 1998, and also in FYs 1999 and 2000, although the decrease rate has not been decided for the latter two years.

The government's goal of providing US$ 70,000–75,000 million in FYs 1993–7 now looks difficult if not impossible to meet. The government decided not to set a new medium-term target for foreign aid after FY 1998 – apparently abandoning the idea of medium-term plans for ODA, which it started in 1977. But, despite the rapid cut of the amount, foreign aid is still considered to be a major component of foreign policy, especially since the constitution restricts overseas Japanese military commitments.

Public attitudes toward foreign aid are mixed. According to the government poll carried out in October 1996, there is still public support for aid. Some 47% of the public favour maintaining the present level and 33% favour an increase. But in another survey in March 1997 by a major national newspaper, *Asahi Shinbun*, while 41% said Japanese official and private (meaning NGO) assistance should be further promoted, 47% considered that priority should be given to solving domestic, rather than international problems.

The government now emphasises both humanitarian concerns and the long-term benefit of aid to the Japanese people. This approach probably reflects the need to maintain support for ODA programmes in an age of recession and tightened budgets.

On the one hand, the government underlines the significance of working on poverty alleviation, improvement of education and health, environmental protection, peaceful resolution of conflicts and so on. It states that Japan should take a leadership role in the global initiative for 'people-centred development' and the achievement of the goals outlined in the OECD DAC's *Shaping the 21st Century* document.

But, on the other hand, the government also puts emphasis on the possible long-term benefit to the Japanese people of economic development in the South. It stresses the role aid could play in terms of national security; especially because Japan depends on imports for natural resources and food. No major changes can be found in Japanese aid decision-making procedures or the actual distribution of ODA for FY 1995 (details on distribution for FY 1996 were not available at the time of writing this chapter). The majority of bilateral aid is provided in the form of loans. Geographically 54% is allocated to Asia, and sectorally 45% to economic infrastructure.

Eradication of poverty

The government says poverty is the fundamental issue for the South. Poverty is described as the cause of problems like lack of education, environmental destruction, population growth, terrorism and regional conflicts. Commitment to achieving the goals outlined in *Shaping the 21st Century* is clearly stated by the government. Within the DAC, Japan is reported to have played a key role in the preparation of this document and in setting the specific goals. (But at this moment it is difficult to find any change in the actual policy and distribution of ODA.)

The discussion going on in the 'development community' – ODA administration people, NGOs, academics and other experts – is on how to work on poverty eradication. The view maintained by the government and 'traditional' economists (they are still in the mainstream in the academic community) is that, based on the experience of Japan and the Asian 'tigers', growth is a prerequisite for and is indispensable to any efforts at poverty eradication. The major role of aid should be to promote growth through industrialisation and expanding exports of industrial goods, while allocating some aid for basic human needs (BHN) projects and programmes as a 'safety net' for the poor.

The alternative view articulated by NGOs and critical academics is that the growth-centred model, the basis of the Japanese ODA programme, is the cause of the marginalisation of the majority of the people and that efforts to tackle poverty directly should be mainstreamed.

In Japan's ODA 1996 Annual Report, emphasis is put on 'people-centred' development. But the report says that 'a major concern inherent in the idea of people-centred development is whether or not the benefits of an enlarged economic pie brought about by economic growth will filter down to individuals in the form of increased employment and incomes'. By saying this, the Japanese government seems to be sticking to classical trickle-down theory and maintaining that promoting growth and export-oriented industrialisation is the only way to alleviate poverty. But it is true that there is increased mention of more direct measures dealing with poverty.

With 26.7% of ODA allocated to social infrastructure – education, health, water, population – in FY 1995 (3.5% higher than in 1994) the government asserts that Japan has already met the 20:20 Compact proposed at the World Summit on Social Development. According to government statistics, 36.3% of ODA is distributed to BHN sectors, namely social infrastructure and agriculture. But the definition itself is too broad, for it even includes university equipment and the placement of Japanese language teachers. So the amount spent on what is really for meeting basic human needs must be smaller.[2]

Despite the problems of the enduring domination of the growth-centred vision and questions on the definition of basic human needs sectors, it is possible to find some positive developments in the Japanese government's efforts towards the eradication of poverty. Distribution to the BHN sectors under the government's definition is increasing. Earlier this decade the figure once went down to 22%.[3]

Among yen loan projects, which have traditionally supported the build-up of economic infrastructure, we can now find some examples in the basic human needs sectors, including the two-step loan[4] to the Grameen Bank in Bangladesh, forestry in India, and financial support for agrarian reform in the Philippines. Allocations to NGOs are also increasing rapidly, more than doubling in the past three years.

Gender

The Japanese government announced its 'WID Initiative' at the Beijing conference and set some goals, which include:

- by 2010 giving all women access to basic education; and
- by 2010 bringing the maternal mortality rate down to below 200 per 100,000.

However, in government publications and documents there is little mention of the feminisation of poverty. Concrete measures so far taken by the government are setting up sections on WID in the Overseas Economic Cooperation Fund (OECF, the implementing agency of loans) and the Japanese International Cooperation Agency (ICA, the implementing agency of technical cooperation) and making some guidelines.

Coherence

The government has recently put more emphasis on coherence between different types or aspects of aid. However, probably because of the limited emphasis on direct measures of poverty eradication, Japan seems to lack the commitment to take a coherent approach to poverty alleviation.

Recently, the government has started to pursue coherence in promoting growth by emphasising the

Japan

The **Reality** of Aid 1997/8

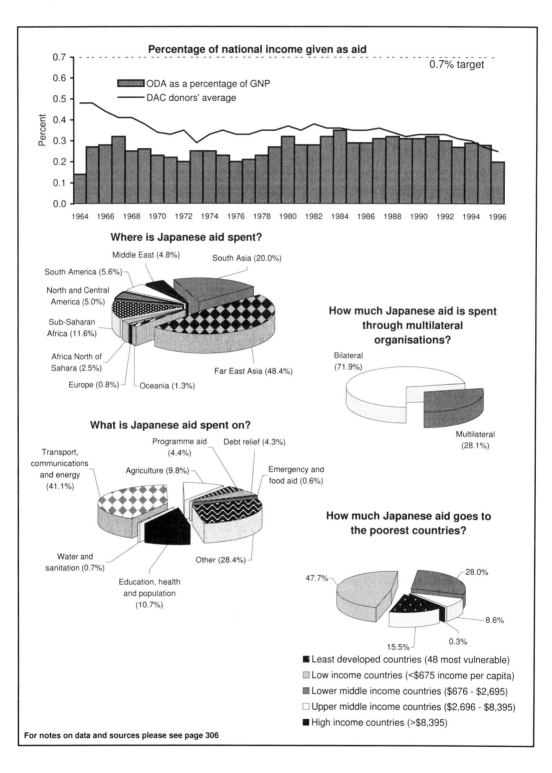

The **Reality** of Aid 1997/8

Japan

Japanese aid at a glance

How much aid does Japan give?

Japan gave	US$ 9437m, 1043 billion Yen in 1996
that was	0.2% of GNP
and	2.91% of public administration
which meant	US$ 75 or 8306 Yen per capita for 1996

Is it going up or down?

In 1996 Japanese aid	fell by $ 5052m, a drop of 24.7% in real terms over 1995
Japan was	less generous in 1996, dropping from 0.28% of GNP to 0.2%
The outlook is that	Japan will cut its ODA by 10% in 1998 with further cuts in 1999 and 2001

How does Japan compare with the other 21 donors?

Japan ranks	1 out of 21 for its volume of aid
It is	19 out of 21 in the generosity league
It gives	a lower proportion of its aid (63.2%) to Low Income Countries than ten other donors
Private Flows in 1995	amounted to $22,046m, 1.5 times ODA
Total Flows	to developing countries were 0.82% of GNP and rank 9 out of 21 in the DAC

How much does Japan spend on basic health and basic education?

Japan	has not yet reported to the DAC on its basic health and basic education spending

How important are commercial interests in aid?

Japan requires	13.9% of its aid to be used to buy Japanese goods

What do the public think about aid?

32.9% of Japanese are in favour of giving more aid

Japan

importance of collaboration with the private sector in infrastructure development. Also, according to the government, aid, investment and trade are a 'trinity' in promoting development in the South.

The government has emphasised the role of development aid in its foreign policy, especially in maintaining friendly relations with countries in Asia. Strategic concerns are emphasised at times of international tension (like in the early 1980s and at the time of the Gulf War when Japan increased aid to or prepared special aid programmes for pro-US countries).

Specific issues

NGOs

Over the past year, there have been increasing opportunities for NGO-government dialogue and cooperation. Dialogue meetings between NGOs and the Ministry of Foreign Affairs (MoFA) are now held regularly four times a year. The dialogue, which was initiated by JANIC, involved JANIC and its members and NGO networks in the Kansai and Nagoya regions. Among other things, the dialogue agreed to examine the possibility of 'mutual learning and evaluation' of development cooperation projects.

Meanwhile, the Japan International Volunteer Centre (JVC) sponsored a workshop on NGOs and Government Dialogue on ODA in Indochina, in which the government (MoFA, OECF and JICA) and NGOs participated and exchanged views on sustainable development and participatory methodology (with case studies from both sides) and discussed the future of Japanese cooperation in the Indochina region. There are increased numbers of cases of NGO participation in the implementation and evaluation of bilateral aid projects in the health sector and income generation for women.

Government funding to NGOs has increased dramatically. In the NGOs–MoFA dialogue, NGOs said that in both NGO Project Subsidies (for Japanese NGOs, handled by the MoFA) and the Grassroots Grant Programme (handled by local embassies, for Southern and international NGOs and local governments), the criteria are too narrow. They include only 'hardware' – provision of equipment, construction of buildings, and so on – and not 'software' – human resource development and support for civil society. But the ministry now covers administrative costs and overheads directly related to the projects.

This increased dialogue, NGO participation in ODA projects and increased funding, all mark progress in NGO–government relations. But the other side of the coin is the danger of some NGOs being co-opted or becoming too dependent on government, which NGOs themselves must realise and avoid by empowering themselves and strengthening their own constituency.

The 'Citizens Organisations Bill' was passed by the House of Representatives in late May 1997 and will be discussed at the House of Councillors during the next session of the Diet (Japanese parliament), expected to start in September. Although the bill will increase the possibility of Japanese NGOs getting legal status, NGOs are critical of the absence of articles on tax-exempt status or tax relief for NGOs and other organisations, and tax exemptions for those who donate to these organisations. NGOs are also critical of the screening process proposed by the government for granting legal status, saying that it is too complex and also that the proposed bill could open up the possibility of the government investigating and even depriving groups that are considered to be operating outside the terms of the bill of their legal status.

Commercialisation of aid

Because of the prolonged recession, there is increased pressure from the business community for ODA to bring more benefit to Japanese businesses. Currently, loans are for the most part (97.7% in 1995) untied and, according to the government, only 27% of loans are procured by Japanese companies (60% by companies of the developing countries, and 13% by those of other OECD members). Grants are basically tied. OECF is now considering examining the technical capacity of companies, thereby giving Japanese companies more opportunities for procurement in loans projects.

It is difficult to describe an optimistic scenario in terms of aid volume. (The heavy government budget deficit and the pessimistic outlook on the Japanese economy have driven the government to decide on a sharp decrease in the ODA budget, at least in the coming few years.) But aid is important in foreign policy terms, and the government needs to continue using it to win the support of the South in achieving foreign policy goals. The government will find it difficult to strike a balance between the importance of aid as a foreign policy tool and domestic pressure to tighten the aid budget.

The future scenario in terms of poverty

eradication is mixed. The 'positive' side is Japan's commitment to the *Shaping the 21st Century*. The 'negative' side is the strong proliferation of the growth-centred vision, based on the experience of Japan itself and other 'East Asian' countries. One agenda for the NGO community is both to monitor and to seek more active critical involvement in the government's efforts on poverty eradication, particularly achieving the goals in the *Shaping the 21st Century*.

Notes

1. Japanese loans are financed from the Fiscal Investment and Loans Programme. When ODA loans are repaid, the repayment returns to that fund and does not automatically contribute to ODA. For Japan, the figure for net disbursements of ODA is gross disbursements minus repayments. Sometimes, when a new disbursement to a country is small and a repayment is large, net disbursements could be a minus figure.
2. According to the UNDP's *Human Development Report 1994*, only 3.4% of Japanese ODA was distributed to human priority areas. However, UNDP has not included statistics on aid to human priority areas since 1995.
3. The government first showed the proportion of ODA going to the BHN sectors for FY 1988 when the figure was 24.3%. It reached its lowest reported level in FY 1991 when it went down to 22%, but has steadily increased since then.
4. The two-step loan is a scheme whereby the Japanese government supports credit programmes for small enterprises, farmers and so forth in recipient countries. It is called a *two-step loan* because the Japanese government first provides loans to the Southern government agencies, which, as a second step, provide loans to the beneficiaries.

The Netherlands

Caroline Wildeman, Novib

Dutch aid policy: looking for a new form but how about the content?

A lot has changed in Dutch development cooperation over the last year. The policy aims, the budget structure and the staff have been reshaped in order to deliver a more effective and cohesive policy. But to what extent will this new shape be noticed by the receivers of aid, the people living in poverty?

The review of Dutch foreign policy was formally concluded in September 1996. At the time of writing it was still too early to draw any conclusions about the practice of the new aid policy in the field. Nevertheless, the new policy direction offers plenty of challenges to react to.

The effectiveness of aid

The new Dutch aid policy is aimed at achieving greater aid effectiveness through new policy objectives and different policy instruments. The policy objectives are concentrated around a bigger effort to contribute to human development. The choice of sustainable development as a major priority has raised a lot of media interest. Dutch aid policy, reflected in the explanatory memorandum of the Foreign Ministry, shows a remarkable shift towards a policy for basic social services.

The allocation of development funds in 1997 will be based on five concrete, measurable aims agreed at international level:

- the 20:20 compact which sets the target of allocating 20% of the development budget of donor countries to provide universal access to basic social services, matched by 20% of the national budget of developing countries;
- the target that 4% of the development budget should be allocated to reproductive health care;
- the target that 0.1% of GNP should go to improve the environment in poor countries;
- the agreement to spend a minimum of 50 million guilders a year on preservation of the tropical forests; and
- the agreement to spend at least 0.25% of GNP on aid to the Least Developed Countries (LLDCs).

Another example of the orientation towards social development is the recognition of the targets in the OECD document *Shaping the 21st Century*, on the reduction by one-half in the proportion of people living in extreme poverty by 2015; universal access to primary education by 2015; reduction by two-thirds in the mortality rates for children under five and access through primary health care to reproductive health services for all by the year 2015.

The 20:20 initiative

The 20:20 initiative has been incorporated into the budget. In 1995, The Netherlands spent 18.4% of ODA on basic social services; in 1996 it rose to 19.45% of ODA; and in 1997 it is estimated to be 20.31% of ODA. Unfortunately, only 55 million guilders are reserved for basic education in 1997, 1% of the ODA budget. Questions have been raised in the annual budget debate in Parliament stressing the fact that basic education should be a key priority in poverty eradication policy and therefore needs a higher input. The Minister did not make any new promises on this point. He explained that basic education elements were incorporated into other spending categories, like agriculture or health programmes and were not visible in the budget. NGOs put forward the importance of basic education and made a plea for higher expenditure. Apart from the quantity, they also stressed the need to improve the quality of development policy in delivering support for basic education. Too often girls drop out of school before they reach the fifth grade of primary education. Development policy should incorporate concrete measures to reach the girl child.

A problematic issue is the way the 20:20

initiative has been calculated in the new budget. Preparing for the budget, the financial officials at the ministry examined all items of expenditure and calculated what percentage of each could count towards the 20:20 target. Both bilateral and multilateral expenditures would be considered eligible to be counted towards the 20:20 target. Some 100% of country programmes addressing social and institutional development or child related programmes could count towards the target along with 100% of contributions to UN agencies such as the World Food Programme, the UN Population Fund, the UN Aids programme and UNICEF. This compares with 10% of the Dutch contribution to the European Development Fund, 20% of funds aimed at improving the position of women and 40% of funds for emergency relief programmes. The emergency relief element amounted to 180 million guilders in 1995 and there are serious doubts about its inclusion in the 20:20 definition.

Emergency relief programmes can be a prerequisite for progress towards social goals in countries affected by natural or man-made emergencies. However, such assistance is temporary in nature and should not, therefore, be seen as providing support to the achievement of universal access to basic social services in a sustainable fashion. Moreover, adequate provision of basic social services might serve as a powerful and effective preventive factor against future emergencies and crises. The original 20:20 initiative was based on the assumption that humanitarian assistance should be considered separately.

The aid budget envisages the start of the 20:20 initiative in five countries: Bolivia, Burkina Faso, Guinea, Tanzania and Vietnam. If these countries make a national plan to spend 20% of their national budget for basic social services they will get more aid from the Dutch government in support of this. The fora to discuss the implementation on a country basis are the donor meetings; these are the Consultative Group meetings organised by the World Bank and the Round Table Conferences, organised by the UNDP. Up to now, the 20:20 initiative has not been discussed in any of these fora. Novib has called upon the Dutch government to take a more active role in promoting the 20:20 initiative in the donor meetings. A further task for the Dutch government lies in convincing the other members of the EU to take the adoption of the 20:20 compact seriously in their development cooperation. It is noble and progressive to put social goals into development policy, but if The Netherlands is acting alone not much benefit will be felt by the receivers. For the proper implementation of the 20:20 initiative governments should look for allies in civil society and go beyond the traditional intergovernmental relationships. The strengthening of civil society and the importance of participation has been fully recognised at all possible policy levels. But the practical implementation lags far behind. As a first step, NGOs should be consulted on the design of social policy measures and invited to give their views on social development spending.

Instruments for effective aid

One of the major policy instruments designed to deliver more effective aid is the orientation towards themes instead of countries. According to Minister Pronk, the core of development cooperation is to address questions such as how to reduce infant mortality, how to improve food security and how to guarantee safety. 'Such issues are far more important than whether Nicaragua, or any other country, should get more or less money.'

In the new budget there will be no predictions about how much money will be spent in each country or region. The scale of aid to a particular country depends on the extent to which it is believed possible to achieve Dutch policy aims in that country. Consequently, the country list, which was always included in the Explanatory memorandum, has been discarded. Pronk states:

> We can now in effect operate in all developing countries. We no longer have to restrict ourselves to a list drawn up beforehand. If, for example, aid is requested for Liberia or Sierra Leone – two countries in conflict – you can hardly say 'Sorry, but you are not on my list!'.

The policy is oriented on ten themes:

- Economy and employment;
- Agricultural and regional development;
- Environment;
- Social development;
- Education;
- Research and culture;
- Human rights, conflict management;
- Democratisation and good governance;
- Humanitarian aid;
- Macro economic support and debt relief.

The Netherlands

The **Reality** of Aid 1997/8

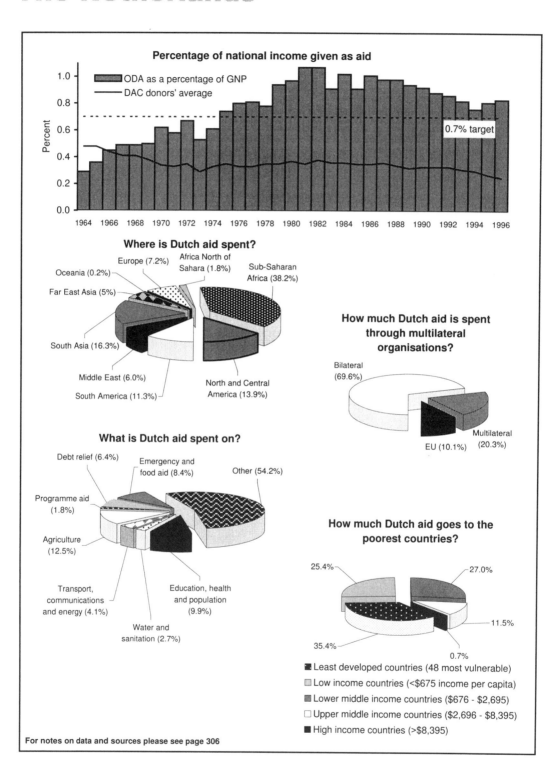

The **Reality** of Aid 1997/8

The Netherlands

Dutch aid at a glance

How much aid does The Netherlands give?

The Netherlands gave	US$ 3303m, 5770 million guilders in 1996
that was	0.83% of GNP
and	5.7% of public administration
which meant	US$ 213 or 372 guilders per capita for 1996

Is it going up or down?

In 1996 Dutch aid	rose by $77m, up 6.2% in real terms over 1995
The Netherlands was	more generous in 1996, rising from 0.81% of GNP to 0.83%
The outlook is	that a new norm of 0.8% of GNP has been reaffirmed for development cooperation for 1997

How does The Netherlands compare with the other 21 donors?

The Netherlands ranks	5 out of 21 for its volume of aid
It is	3 out of 21 in the generosity league
It gives	a lower proportion of its aid (60.8%) to Low Income Countries than 14 other donors
Private Flows	amounted to $3123m, 97% of ODA
Total Flows	to developing countries were 1.71% of GNP and rank first out of 21 in the DAC

How much does The Netherlands spend on basic health and basic education?

The Netherlands reports	0.7% of its ODA spending on basic health and 1.5% on basic education

How important are commercial interests in aid?

The Netherlands requires	2.2% of its aid to be used to buy Dutch goods

What do the public think about aid?

About 50% of the Dutch public donate money to some development related activity

The Netherlands

While it looks like a very sensible direction with regard to a greater effectiveness, it also raises questions about the management of the policy. One of the major critiques is that intervention in a lot of countries will result in a very fragmented policy. The new policy also results in a very complicated matrix of countries and themes and requires many consultation bodies and complex procedures. Women's groups have questioned the lack of a specific theme devoted to the position of women. The programme for women is integrated in the theme on social development. Gender issues should be integrated in the overall policy, but the improvement of the position of women should also be an autonomous policy goal. Leaving these questions aside, the choice of the new themes and the more consistent policy approach should be considered as a positive development.

Another significant change is the shift of the responsibility for the bilateral programme from the Ministry in The Hague to the various embassies in the developing countries. The money, the people and the decision-making process are decentralised and about a hundred people have moved from The Hague to the embassies. The country programme to be executed by the embassies accounted for 1396 million guilders in 1995. Although the embassies have to be accountable to the central policy decisions made in The Hague, it is not yet clear to what extent they can take decisions unilaterally or when they have to channel funds back to The Netherlands. For instance, if money for a project on the promotion of primary health care is not spent in country X it is not clear whether the embassy can make the decision to spend it on another project in the same country or whether they have to channel it back to The Netherlands. This question is raised because according to the new budget, the priority is the thematic approach, not allocations to countries.

To bring the implementation of official development cooperation from the donor governments closer to the recipient countries will mean a quicker disbursement of the funds and a better understanding of the projects. On the other side, NGOs from North and South do not yet know to what extent the direct funding will affect their work. They do fear that direct funding will lead to a greater control by developing country governments over the way that Southern NGOs are operating.

This year the Ministry will develop country policy plans. The embassies have prime responsibility for these policy documents, which contain the concrete plans and programmes to be implemented in each country. During the annual budget debate in Parliament, NGOs asked that these country plans should be drawn up in cooperation with local NGOs and organisations of civil society, especially women's groups. It remains to be seen how seriously this suggestion will be taken.

About 10% of the ODA budget is channelled through NGOs. There are four categories in the NGO programme; the largest is the co-financing programme, with 529 million guilders in 1997. There are four co-financing organisations: Bilance, Hivos, Icco and Novib. In addition, there is a small programme for Food Security and Nutritional Improvement. Thirty million guilders was allocated to this programme in 1997 and it is run by Novib, the Committee for Inter-Church Aid, Service to Refugees and Mensen in Nood/Caritas. There is a trade Union Co-financing programme of 22 million guilders for 1997, which works for stronger labour rights and a fairer distribution of power and income. And there is the Programme for Personnel Cooperation (PSO), which received 34 million guilders for 1997.

As a result of the shift to policy themes, the budget no longer contains any detail of the scale of aid to individual countries or regions. Under the old system, the main distinction was who provided the aid – the Dutch government itself, international agencies or non governmental organisations. Now, it will be easier to see the sectors to which aid is channelled and the big advantage, according to the civil servants, is that the policy is much more flexible.

For aid watchers, the new system is very hard to follow; policy is much more complicated and decentralised. This, combined with the mixed channels in the different themes makes it more difficult to work out how much money is spent through the multilateral channel. Traditionally, the Netherlands has spent about 30% of its aid through multilateral channels. It is very difficult to judge the use of this money and there is very little political control over the functioning of the multilateral agencies, especially with regard to the effectiveness of aid. Since an explicit choice has been made to stress aid effectiveness, Parliament should demand a policy for improved monitoring of the spending through the multilateral channel.

The Netherlands

Coherence

Europe is too often concerned only with itself

It was in the early Spring of 1997 that the Dutch prime minister, Wim Kok, at a huge rally of his Labour Party indicated the question he saw as one of the main challenges of the 1997 Dutch EU presidency: 'Europe too often is concerned only with itself', he said. In its external relations, Europe, said the Prime Minister, is narrow minded and incoherent. He gave the EU–South Africa relationship as an example:

> We've supported the Anti Apartheid struggle for so long. Now Apartheid is over, we should support South Africa as much as we can to expand their production and exports to the EU. That seems to be very difficult.

In its preparations for the EU chairmanship during 1996, the government of The Netherlands put a lot of weight on the promotion of coherence. Article 130 V of the Maastricht Treaty and Article C of the Treaty of Rome give coherence a firm legal foundation. In theory, EU policies that are against the interests of developing countries should be modified. In practice though, it often happens that the trading or political interests of EU member states dominate decision-making and policies to the exclusion of developing countries' interests. While chairing the EU in the first half of 1997, The Netherlands government intended to make some progress on this complicated issue, where big economic interests are at stake. In the June Development Council, a resolution was adopted to provide for more coherent external policies. Specific instruments for implementation, however, are lacking. Nor is it clear to what extent ministers in other policy areas – finance, agriculture, trade – are obliged to adhere to this resolution. There are no substantive new measures to strengthen coherence in EU policies in the revised treaty, adopted in the Dutch capital at the end of June.

Beef

The gap between principle and practice is demonstrated by the EU subsidies on the export of meat. Some years ago European NGOs campaigned against the dumping of EU meat on West African markets. Hundreds of thousands of West African cattle farmers – many of them directly supported out of EU and/or bilateral development funds – were directly affected. They were not able to compete with the subsidised EU imports. The NGO campaign was successful. Subsidies were lowered by 30%. The CFA, the main West African currency, was devalued in the same period and the combined effect was to reduce EU exports to the region by 80%. Local farmers can now use development money to make themselves a decent living. But the principle of coherence in beef exports to Africa is being violated again. Now it is the South African farmer who has become the victim of this policy. Since the West African market has lost significance for the EU cattle farmers, subsidised EU beef exports to South Africa are growing fast. From a mere 7000 tonnes in 1993, beef imports from the EU reached an estimated 47,000 tonnes in 1996. The prices of meat on the local market have gone down by 30%. Not only local farmers are affected. Cattle farmers in the neighbouring countries of Botswana and Namibia are losing their share of the South African meat market as a result of unfair EU competition.

Fisheries

Fisheries Agreements between the EU and African states also demonstrate incoherence between EU policies. These agreements allow for European trawlers to explore and exploit the African waters for fish, which provides the basic livelihood for small-scale African fishermen. A recent case in point is the March 1997 Agreement between the EU and Senegal. Despite campaigns by Novib and Eurostep and some support for the demands of the Senegalese fisheries organisations within the Dutch government, an agreement was reached which is far from sufficient to guarantee the local fishing people their fishing rights. There are some improvements compared with the previous agreement. But European boats are still allowed to fish within the Senegalese 12-mile zone. They were also given the right to catch fish species that are vital for the Senegalese fisheries sector in the 200-mile zone. Several of these species are already over fished, affecting not only the fishermen and women who process the fish, but also threatening the diet of the West African poor. As long as European trawlers are allowed to search for fish within the Senegalese 12-mile zone, this agreement runs the risk of making these fishing people unemployed. Moreover, as the fish catch is taken away to Europe, it will affect the

The Netherlands

availability of high protein food for the Senegalese poor. The European Union should take its own development policy objectives seriously and not hamper the development potential of the local fisheries sector in developing countries. A thorough assessment of the available fish stocks and the exploitation potential of the local fisheries sector should be done before any agreement is concluded. For the case of Senegal, the available research indicates that many species are already over fished and that the room created for foreign fleets in Senegalese waters is directly detrimental to local fishermen and women. The current fisheries policy means a subsidy to EU fishing companies, paid for by European taxpayers, which also limits the possibilities for the local sector to do the work that they have been doing for generations.

Cocoa

Cocoa is another case where the economic interests of EU industries and developing countries are in conflict. The EU is considering reducing the amount of cocoa that is required to be in chocolate. If this share declines, it will result in a huge loss of income for cocoa exporting countries. In the Dutch government this has led to a big, and so far undecided, debate between the interests of chocolate processing companies and the interests of developing countries.

Arms

All these examples make it clear that there is a long way to go before coherence will guide EU policies in practice. Looking to the arms trade, time and again European politicians are asking for peaceful solutions for Third World conflicts; conflicts which are fuelled by arms sold by the West. Big profits are made in Europe and elsewhere, while the price is paid in Africa, where people die every day because of these arms. The EU is not willing to stop the trade in arms. Even in the case of the Great Lakes Region, where arms have been used for genocide, it seems impossible to implement an arms embargo. The most far reaching compromise that appears to be feasible is a weak and non-binding code of conduct which tries to curtail the trade in illicit arms only. Many NGOs campaign for the extension of these restrictions. In The Netherlands, arms exports to developing countries – such as Egypt, Pakistan and Indonesia in 1996 – were criticised. In the view of NGOs like Novib, these countries are already too heavily armed and not sufficiently stable to be allowed to buy weapons from the West.

It was not just the EU chairmanship, but also the 1996 reformulation of Dutch development policy, that brought the issue of coherence to the forefront of Dutch foreign policy debates. Labour Party foreign policy spokesmen, with the support of NGOs, criticised the lack of commitment to human rights. Especially in relations with economically powerful countries – like the ones in the Far East – the government seems to be too worried that human rights issues will interfere with trade and investment. In efforts to achieve a more integrated and coherent foreign policy, there is always a danger that economic interests will dominate the 'softer' parts of policy like development cooperation and human rights. NGOs will have to be alert to seeking coherence that puts the interests of the weaker parties in first place.

New Zealand

Pat Webster and Michelle Auld, Council for International Development (Kaunihera mõ te Whakapakari Ao Whãnui)

During 1996 New Zealand's Overseas Development Assistance Programme (NZODA) continued on a course of cautious growth despite a change in government. A new policy framework was produced, which clarified the rationale, purpose and focus of NZODA and laid out a set of guiding principles and strategies to govern its operation.

New Zealand experienced the changeover to a new political system in 1996. It has gone from a Westminster 'first past the post' system to a mixed member proportional (MMP) representation system. The change caused a long period of hiatus within government departments while those parties successfully returned to Parliament worked out a governing coalition. The outcome was a coalition between the centre right National Party and the populist, centrist, New Zealand First Party.

The result for NZODA has been the substantial retention of the policies of the previous government, with the previous Minister of Foreign Affairs returning to that role. Other National Party MPs were appointed to the portfolios of Associate Minister of Foreign Affairs and Minister of Overseas Trade. The Ministry of Foreign Affairs and Trade encompasses the Development Cooperation Division, which oversees NZODA and the Associate Minister has responsibility for this area. The Minister of Foreign Affairs retains control over major policy direction and an overview of Pacific Islands issues in NZODA.

The Associate Minister is new to the area of development assistance. He is also the Minister for the Environment and will take a strong interest in environmental issues within NZODA. He has also expressed an interest in making NZODA more relevant to small local communities within New Zealand.

Coalition policy

The Coalition policy is committed to continuing increases in NZODA and states that the greater proportion will be directed to the South Pacific. The policy supports an effective role for New Zealand in international organisations, particularly in the peacekeeping and humanitarian activities of the United Nations.

The policy's only departure from general statements is a specific reference to a plan to refund debts incurred by Pacific Island nationals to New Zealand hospitals, from the bilateral grant to their country. This policy has been strongly opposed by NGOs, the main opposition parties, and the Pacific Island countries themselves. NGOs do not believe that aid money should be spent on uncontrollable *ad hoc* services that benefit only those who can travel to, or have relatives in, New Zealand. Rather, funds should be used to develop in-country systems or, where this is not possible, access to New Zealand health services should be negotiated between governments to ensure that those in need have access.

The Minister has confirmed his intention to maintain growth beyond the commitment to the NZ$ 20 million (approximately 10%) increase for 1997/8. Past statements indicate a desire to bring New Zealand more into line with the OECD average but, if the average continues to fall, New Zealand may achieve this goal within a short time. NGOs believe that years of lower than average spending require New Zealand to lift its performance above the average in the future.

NGOs support the primary focus on the South Pacific within NZODA, for many of the same reasons as the government. The Pacific Islands are the closest developing countries to New Zealand. There are strong historic and cultural links between the countries. Many Pacific Island people have migrated to New Zealand and strong family ties exist. However, without a clear rationale, NGOs cannot support a readjustment of the current

New Zealand

The **Reality** of Aid 1997/8

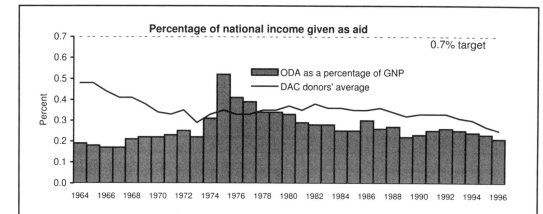

Percentage of national income given as aid

0.7% target

ODA as a percentage of GNP
DAC donors' average

Where is New Zealand's aid spent?

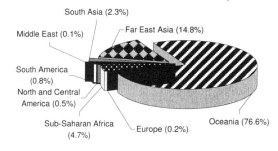

- South Asia (2.3%)
- Far East Asia (14.8%)
- Middle East (0.1%)
- South America (0.8%)
- North and Central America (0.5%)
- Sub-Saharan Africa (4.7%)
- Europe (0.2%)
- Oceania (76.6%)

What is New Zealand's aid spent on?

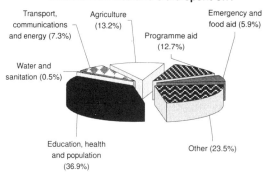

- Transport, communications and energy (7.3%)
- Agriculture (13.2%)
- Emergency and food aid (5.9%)
- Programme aid (12.7%)
- Water and sanitation (0.5%)
- Education, health and population (36.9%)
- Other (23.5%)

How much of New Zealand's aid is spent through multilateral organisations?

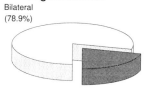

- Bilateral (78.9%)
- Multilateral (21.1%)

How much of New Zealand's aid goes to the poorest countries?

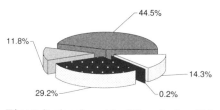

- 44.5%
- 11.8%
- 29.2%
- 14.3%
- 0.2%

■ Least developed countries (48 most vulnerable)
▨ Low income countries (<$675 income per capita)
▨ Lower middle income countries ($676 - $2,695)
□ Upper middle income countries ($2,696 - $8,395)
■ High income countries (>$8,395)

For notes on data and sources please see page 306

The **Reality** of Aid 1997/8

New Zealand

New Zealand aid at a glance

How much aid does New Zealand give?

New Zealand gave	US$ 122m, 165 million New Zealand dollars in 1996
that was	0.21% of GNP
and	1.44% of public administration
which meant	US$ 34 or 46 New Zealand dollars per capita for 1996

Is it going up or down?

In 1996 New Zealand aid	fell by $1m, a drop of 7.3% in real terms over 1995
New Zealand was	less generous in 1996, dropping from 0.23% of GNP to 0.21%. This has not been caused by a cut in funding but by anomalies caused by variations in calendar year and fiscal year spending patterns between the latter part of 1996 and early part of 1997
The outlook is	that New Zealand continues to support the 0.7% target and is making increases of approximately 0.01% per year

How does New Zealand compare with the other 21 donors?

New Zealand ranks	20 out of 21 for its volume of aid
It is	17 out of 21 in the generosity league
It gives	a lower proportion of its aid (41%) to Low Income Countries than 18 other donors
Private Flows	amounted to $26m, 21% of ODA
Total Flows	to developing countries were 0.31% of GNP and rank 17 out of 21 in the DAC

How much does New Zealand spend on basic health and basic education?

New Zealand reports	0.7% of its ODA spending on basic health and 0.1% on basic education

How important are commercial interests in aid?

New Zealand's aid is completely untied

New Zealand

regional balance toward increased funding for the Pacific, which currently receives between 50 and 55% of NZODA. Some Pacific countries are among the highest, per capita, recipients of aid in the world. NGOs suspect that this policy has more to do with New Zealand First's concerns about reducing immigration into New Zealand than with the particular needs of the Pacific.

Despite criticisms suggesting a strong trade motivation, NGOs support the recent increases in funding to Southeast Asian programmes, which have focused on some of the poorest countries in the region. NZODA programmes in South Asia and Africa are small but expanding. NGOs view the commitment to the latter regions as an important recognition of the international effort required to assist some of the world's poorest communities.

When government departments were asked this year to identify spending cutbacks, NZODA was not affected by this request. The Development Cooperation Division received a small increase in funding for administrative purposes, following concerns expressed in the 1996 OECD Development Assistance Committee (DAC) Aid Review. With ongoing increases in the budget expected, this will remain an issue.[1] NGOs would be concerned to see the availability of administrative support becoming too large a factor in the allocation of funding in the future. There is a danger that if there is expansion of programmes without corresponding administrative resources, then the increases will go into activities that are easier to administer, not necessarily where the funding can be most effective.

The stability of the coalition government with its small majority, has yet to be tested. Assurances of support for the government have been given by a new party, the Association of Consumers and Taxpayers (ACT), which supports reduction of the state, reward for hard work and thrift and individual responsibility. An ACT MP, a former National Party minister, has been elected to the chair of the Select Committee on Foreign Affairs and Defence to bolster this support.

New framework for NZODA

In early 1996 NZODA produced a new framework in which the rationale for aid is given as the investment in a peaceful and more equitable common future in an interconnected world; the principal purpose of NZODA is sustainable inter-generational improvements in the living conditions especially for the poor; and the focus of NZODA is the Pacific, expanding to parts of Asia and encompassing a range of sectoral activities.

The framework contains guiding principles, which include the responsibility of partner governments for their own development; capacity building; sustainable improvement of conditions through equitable economic development; a primary focus on reducing poverty; participation; and the involvement of the New Zealand community.

Key strategies supported by NZODA include policy and regulatory reform; good governance; private sector development; a civil society strategy; enhancement of the role and position of women; greater attention to social development and protection of the environment.

The framework is complemented by policy statements on *Development and the Environment*, *Implementing NZODA to the Private Sector in Developing Countries in the South Pacific*, *Women in Development*, *Recurrent Cost Finance in the South Pacific* (with Australia) and *Education and Training*.

Key features of the framework

Economic and social development form the two major strands of the framework. The inclusion of poverty in the purpose of aid and in the guiding principles has been welcomed by NGOs, as have the strategies that focus on civil society, the role of women, social development and the environment.

NGOs are more cautious about endorsing macro-economic reforms and some strategies that aim to improve the operation of the public sector. Many of these strategies have an alarmingly familiar ring to those who have experienced the domestic impact of public sector reforms that are designed to reduce costs and generate profits; and macro-economic strategies that give absolute primacy to the needs of business.

Domestically, 'New Zealand style' reforms have brought about economic growth at the expense of the social cohesion NZODA aims to achieve in other countries. The result at home has been increased poverty and social inequality. NGOs do not believe that these policies, unless heavily adjusted, will achieve better results in countries less well resourced to cope with their impact.

NZODA's policy framework acknowledges the complexity of aid and recognises that it cannot be implemented outside the political, economic and social realities of the countries, regions and

New Zealand

> ### Box 12 What New Zealand's ODA is used for ...
>
> **Kiribati seaweed commercialisation project** Growing and selling seaweed in Kiribati is a good example of an environmentally appropriate project that is producing social and economic benefits for the intended beneficiaries. The production of seaweed is well suited to the specific lagoon conditions prevalent on Tabuaeran and Kiritimati and on some other islands in Kiribati. NZODA has set up a project which aims to improve the well being of outer island communities in Kiribati through the sustainable development of seaweed farming.
>
> NZODA is helping the existing seaweed industry to become more productive and to established new farms while encouraging households to share in the economic and social benefits.
>
> NZODA supports a seaweed specialist, an agronomist who is based in the Line Islands, and various capital items for local seaweed storage and processing. NZODA works closely with the local Atoll Seaweed Company, a public corporation responsible for seaweed purchasing and export. It has managed to obtain an exclusive long-term contract with a Danish company which guarantees the purchase of all Kiribati products at world market prices.
>
> Latest reports from Kiribati reveal substantial increases in production and further quality improvements. Kiribati production in 1996 was the highest since commercial farming began in 1985, and further increases are anticipated. Annual incomes of between AS$ 500 and AS$ 2000 per supplier are now common, with the larger suppliers generally earning between AS$ 2000 and AS$ 5000 per annum. These earnings represent substantial amounts for most outer island dwellers and a considerable improvement on the earnings from the traditional copra industry. Seaweed revenues are contributing to a range of purposes such as settlers' payments for land, local council revenues, school fees and as a boost to an expanding commercial retail sector. It also appears that the project is having a positive impact on women, with women making up 50% of the suppliers on Kiritimati.

communities involved. Given this, the task of assisting partner countries to adapt to current global conditions has obvious challenges for a country so strongly supportive of one particular version of economic reform.

Poverty

Poverty reduction was only implicit in the 1992 to 1995 guiding principles for NZODA. It is now an explicit aspect of NZODA policy and has been accompanied by the creation of a new position for a social impact specialist in the Development Cooperation Division.

In the guiding principles, social cohesion is identified as the goal of poverty reduction. Poverty reduction is therefore seen as a means to an end – social cohesion – rather than an end goal in its own right. This is the only government statement that addresses poverty overseas. NGOs would see social justice and basic rights as more useful goals but recognise that, in a government with a strong ethos of individual responsibility, social cohesion may be the only agreed basis for action.

It is not yet possible to identify the aspects of NZODA programmes that address basic needs but a new information system (FMIS) is being installed, which will improve statistical reporting capabilities. In the current system, only 1.03% of bilateral commitments can be attributed to basic needs, although NGOs acknowledge that many bilateral programmes address this issue. Part of the social impact specialist's work in the coming year will be to develop criteria and indicators for identifying and evaluating aspects of programmes that tackle poverty. New Zealand did not sign up to the 20:20 compact as it did not believe that it was relevant to the largest area of its work – the Pacific.

Over 40% of bilateral NZODA is spent on the basic needs of health, education, water and sanitation but, as noted by the OECD, much of this is spending on education, a large part of which is devoted to higher school and tertiary scholarships. There has been a move from tertiary to basic education programmes in some parts of NZODA, for instance in the African bilateral programmes and in parts of the Pacific. The size of some Pacific Island populations means that national governments

New Zealand

cannot meet educational needs and that NZODA will continue to have a significant responsibility for funding higher education and training. NZODA has been trying to ensure that students study in areas relevant to in-country needs to give a better developmental focus to this part of the programme.

Women in development

Women remain a strategic focus for NZODA. In 1996 there was further progress in the implementation of a WID action plan. Some 30% of NZODA programme components were able to be measured against WID criteria in 1995/6, a 6% improvement on the previous year. Some 33% of programmes were classified as partly WID integrated, according to DAC criteria. Participation rates for women in NZODA study and training award schemes is now over 40% and in some schemes is close to 50%. There is now a more consistent and adequate integration of gender issues into all consultancy terms of reference and a model has been produced to guide programme managers.

An independent review of WID was conducted by the Minister's Advisory Committee on External Aid and Development (ACEAD) in 1996 and, while they noted significant progress in this area, they also made recommendations within the context of the outcomes of three recent UN conferences: International Conference on Population and Development; World Summit on Social Development and the Fourth World Conference on Women. In particular they seek increased effort in areas of women's general and reproductive health, basic education, women's NGOs, legal issues and the better integration of gender issues in macro-economic programmes, all of which are being acted upon.

Community involvement in NZODA

In the past, NZODA guidelines have identified NGOs as a group with a special contribution to make to NZODA. The new framework includes suppliers of goods and services in the private sector, educational institutions, NGOs, ethnic communities and government agencies as groups representing community involvement. It also states that the indigenous people of New Zealand, the Maoris, have a special contribution to make.

The private sector
New Zealand does not tie its aid, but:

> encourages the use of New Zealand and Australian goods where these are cost effective and compatible with the principal purpose of NZODA.

Despite this, New Zealand businesses get good returns from NZODA (see *The Reality of Aid 1996*). They are specifically encouraged through the Asia Development Assistance Fund, the IFC Consultants Trust Fund, the World Bank Consultants Trust Fund and through the contracting out of aspects of programme management. A South Pacific Development Assistance Facility was reviewed in 1993/4 and completely revised in 1995/6 to utilise private sector skills more effectively in the delivery of NZODA to the South Pacific. It has now been merged with a *Pacific Islands Industrial Development Scheme*.

In contrast to this, *The Asian Development Assistance Fund*, which provides funding for businesses to identify and implement development opportunities in Asia, has received a further increase in the last year. Started in 1993/4, this is now one of the larger individual funds in NZODA accounting for 3.4% of the total programme. Reviews of the operation of this fund were conducted in 1995 and 1996, but NGOs have not yet had access to the reports. A summary, in the 1996 OECD DAC Aid Review of NZODA, says that, in four years of operation of the fund and its predecessor, 124 contracts totalling NZ$ 10.4 million had been signed. Some 52% of the projects had been in Vietnam, and 14% in China; 71% of the contracts were feasibility studies and 29% training studies. Many of the studies lead consultants on to work with the World Bank and the Asian Development Bank. NGOs are sceptical of the benefits of this type of fund to developing countries, regarding it rather as a subsidy for domestic business, and are keen to see the results of the most recent review, which was designed to measure the development impact.

NGOs
NGO participation in NZODA continues to expand, but remains at a low level by world standards. The non-operational nature of New Zealand's NGOs may account for this, as well as the higher proportion of

their income, which comes from child sponsorship and cannot be used to match grants from government. NZODA support for NGOs increased by 14% in the 1996/97 budget, which included two new NGO funds.

The key NGO fund, the Voluntary Agency Support Scheme (VASS), accounts for 2.1% of NZODA. It provides matching grants for projects, which are allocated by a panel elected from among the NGO users. NGOs range from church and community groups to international NGOs, with most money going to the latter through block grants. VASS increased by only 1% in 1996/7 because NGOs were having difficulties with the application process and with the interpretation of criteria. These issues have been addressed by training and the current year's demand on the programme has prompted NGOs to push to have the ratios increased and ceilings raised. The rigorous block grant review process continues to produce a range of project management issues, which are also being addressed by training programmes and by clarification of criteria. NGOs have helped define boundaries on religious activity in development programmes and are currently working on welfare, education and health issues.

An Alternative Trade Organisations Support Facility was introduced to fund project activity which no longer qualified for support from VASS.

NGO involvement in bilateral programmes

NZNGOs have not had significant involvement in bilateral programmes other than in Indo-China and Papua New Guinea. A recent revamp of the southern Africa and South Africa bilateral programmes has provided an opportunity for greater participation. It also acknowledges NZNGO experience and involvement in the region. It is expected that the first funds will be allocated in the current year.

Development education

Funding for development education was cut from NZODA in 1991, an action criticised by both NGOs and the 1993 OECD DAC Aid Review. Since then, all but one of the three development education NGOs has closed. Development agencies continued to carry out their own small programmes, but both they and the remaining agency, the Development Resource Centre (DRC), lacked funding. In 1995, the Minister's Advisory Committee produced a report, *Preparing New Zealand for International Cooperation in the 21st Century*, which recommended an ongoing programme of public awareness and development education in partnership with NGOs and NZ$ 500,000 a year from NZODA for this purpose. The report gave priority to school-based development education, public awareness and education through NGOs, and the upgrading of the DRC. NGOs welcomed and supported the overall recommendations. In 1996 a feasibility study of the DRC was conducted by the Development Cooperation Division and a business plan was drawn up. The Minister agreed to allocate NZ$ 140,000 as the first part of a three-year funding programme, in which funding is reduced each year, and during which time the DRC is expected to find supplementary income from commercial activity.

The Minister believes that a gradual strengthening of non-government organisations will be, in the long run, more effective than committing substantial resources to public campaigns. NGOs have begun discussions with the Ministry to explore further avenues for development education funding.

Summary

The 1996 OECD DAC Aid Review of NZODA commented favourably on the improvement in the quality of its aid programme in recent years. Particular mention was made of the creation of the evaluation unit, the operation of country programmes and the policy basis for the programmes.

NGOs, at this stage, lack the resources to undertake comprehensive research into the quality of NZODA. They support the role of the evaluation unit and welcome the policy framework. The main concerns for NGOs continue to be the impact of economic reform programmes and the need to evaluate the poverty impact of NZODA as a whole. The continuing growth of the programme, albeit more slowly than NGOs would like to see, is welcomed as is the growing involvement of NGOs.

Note

1. OECD figures for 1996 indicate a fall in NZODA to 0.21% of GNP. This has not been caused by a cut in funding but by anomalies caused by variations in calendar year and fiscal year spending patterns between the latter part of 1996 and the early part of 1997.

Bibliography

ACEAD (1995) *Preparing New Zealand for International Cooperation in the 21st Century*, Discussion Paper, Wellington: ACEAD
— (1996) *Report on the Activities of the ACEAD*, Wellington: ACEAD
DAC (1996) 'New Zealand', *Development Cooperation Review Series*, No 17, Paris: OECD
OECD DAC (1996) *Development Cooperation 1996 Report*, Paris: OECD

New Zealand

DEV (1995) *NZODA Programme Profiles 1995/96*, Wellington: MFAT
— (1996) *NZODA Programme Profiles 1996/97*, Wellington: MFAT
MFAT (1995) *NZODA: Annual Review 1995*, Wellington: MFAT
— (1996) *Investing in a Common Future: Policy Framework for New Zealand Official Development Assistance (NZODA)*, Wellington: MFAT

Eurostep and ICVA (1993) *The Reality of Aid 1993*, edited by J Randel and T German, London: ACTIONAID
— (1996) *The Reality of Aid 1996*, edited by J Randel and T German, London, Earthscan Publications

Norway

Gunnar Garbo, Norwegian People's Aid

Parliament's handling last year of the government's White Paper on Norwegian policies on developing countries (see *The Reality of Aid 1996*) was encouraging. Again it turned out that elected Members of Parliament, sensible to the attitudes of youth and solidarity movements, tend to be more responsive to the claims of the South than are ministers and bureaucrats. The parliamentary group of the governing Labour Party formed an ad hoc alliance with the Center Party, the Christian People's Party and the Socialist People's Party – all progressive on North–South issues. A solid parliamentary majority told the minority government to improve its aid policies. If the intentions of the parliamentary majority are followed up through practical policies, it will mean a definite strengthening of the poverty focus and the solidarity character of Norwegian development aid.

In its comments on the White Paper, the majority of the Parliament's Foreign Affairs Committee pointed out that globalisation may cement injustices and benefit countries with a stronger economy to the detriment of the less favoured ones. It called not only for better international economic governance but even for the introduction of rules and frameworks for the best possible national governance of own economies. 'Globalisation of the economy, lopsided power distribution, capital flows outside the control of national states and scarcity of non-renewable resources underline the need for mechanisms which may secure necessary regulation, distribution and control.'

Similarly, the majority stressed the need for international control of transnational companies. It advocated a redistribution of resources available for international objectives through the United Nations and pointed to the UNDP proposals for raising resources for global redistribution, inter alia, through taxing international capital transactions or international air transport.

In line with this thinking the parliamentary majority regretted that the poorest population groups are still suffering from the structural adjustment programmes of the IMF and the World Bank, in spite of the modifications these programmes have undergone since the 1980s. The majority asked the government to argue in international fora for a development model based on our own experiences, with an active public sector and with strong redistributive policies built into the economic system. On the basis of its own past, Norway ought also to show the importance of protecting national ownership and industrial interests while the economy is being built up.

The parliamentary majority even changed the government's order of aid objectives, making the battle against poverty the first priority, instead of the promotion of peace, human rights and democracy. The four parties forming the majority regretted that the multilateral share of total Norwegian development aid had come down to 27% and recommended a restoration of the principle of approximately equal sharing between bilateral and multilateral aid. They also sought to put a brake on the government's policy of donor flexibility, insisting that the dominating category of Norwegian aid shall continue to consist of long-term, untied development grants. Regional contributions for which the countries of the region might 'compete' should only be seen as a supplement to long-term development agreements with Norway's main cooperation partners in the South.

Any government may pay lip service to general recommendations of this kind, without really changing its policies. The follow-up will depend on continued public and parliamentary alertness. But the parliamentary majority added a number of more precise recommendations. The most important ones were a renewed commitment to the target of 1% of GNP for official development aid and a call for an increase in contributions to health and education, with a view to bringing each of these sectors up to 10% of Norwegian aid within the year 2000, and increasing the education sector to 15% during the following years.

Norway

The **Reality** of Aid 1997/8

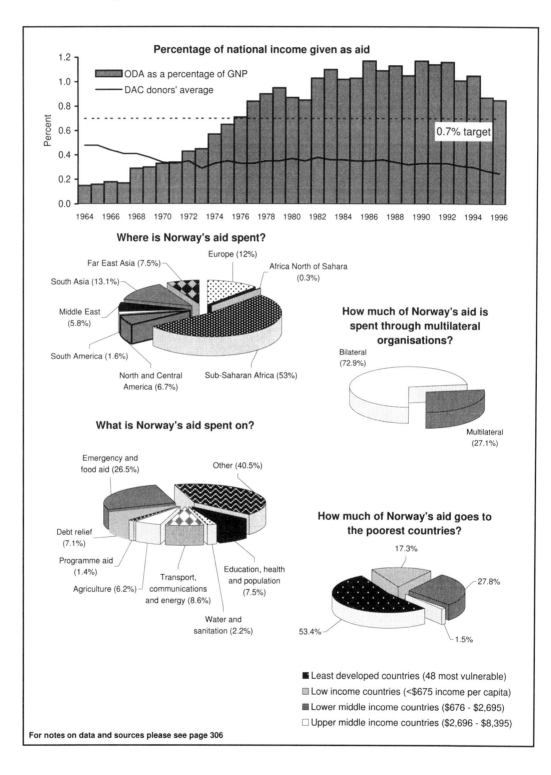

The **Reality** of Aid 1997/8

Norwegian aid at a glance

How much aid does Norway give?

Norway gave	US$ 1311m, 8473 Norwegian Krone in 1996
that was	0.85% of GNP
and	4.11% of public administration
which meant	US$ 300, 1938 Norwegian Krone per capita for 1996

Is it going up or down?

In 1996 Norwegian aid	rose by $67m up 3.1% in real terms over 1995
Norway was	less generous in 1996, dropping from 0.87% GNP to 0.85%
The outlook is	hopeful. 1% of GNP is expected by the year 2000

How does Norway compare with the other 21 donors?

Norway ranks	11 out of 21 for its volume of aid
It is	2 out of 21 in the generosity league
It gives	a higher proportion of its aid (70.7%) to Low Income Countries than 15 other donors
Private Flows	amounted to $181m, 14.5% of ODA
Total Flows	to developing countries were 1.06% of GNP and rank 4 out of 21 in the DAC

How much does Norway spend on basic health and basic education?

Norway	has not yet reported to the DAC on its basic health and basic education spending

How important are commercial interests in aid?

Norway requires	10% of its aid to be used to buy Norwegian goods

What do the public think about aid?

> In 1996, 84% of Norwegians were in favour of development aid and 12% called for increase

Norway

The budgetary follow-up

In its aid budget for 1997, the government only acted on a few of the parliamentary recommendations, thus indicating that follow-up work is continuing with a view to the 1998 budget. Total Norwegian aid for 1997 is estimated at 0.88% of GNP, approximately the same as last year. Most likely, this implies a 3% increase in real terms. Economic development, including support for structural adjustment, still gets the lion's share, with around 37% of total aid. But the administration expects social development, environment and the promotion of women to be the growing sectors in 1997, and aid to Africa is being increased from 47% to 50% of total allocations. The government managed to get its aid budget adopted in Parliament without major changes, though the three opposition parties mentioned above advocated considerable additional increases.

Launching its Medium Term Plan for 1998–2001, the government this year declared that 'in step with the possibilities to use the resources efficiently' Norwegian aid shall gradually be stepped up to 1% of GNP. No time limits were fixed. An opinion poll by Statistics Norway in 1996 showed that 84% of the population supported development aid, compared with 85% in 1986 and 1993. Thus, support is strong and stable. One half of the respondents felt that the present level of aid is reasonable, whereas 12% called for increases and 30% for reductions. The last figure represents a setback from 12% in 1986 and 26% in 1993. This may very well be a reflection of the tendency of aid administrators to complain about the lack of good governance and economic competence among our cooperation partners in the South. However, as three of the opposition parties advocate an even higher level of aid than the governing party, it is difficult to see that the authorities can avoid lifting the ceiling year by year, reaching the 1% target not later than 2001.

Multilateral increases

After Parliament's reintroduction of the 50/50 principle, it may safely be assumed that the multilateral share of Norwegian aid will be increased. But, contrary to the DAC definitions, the Norwegian aid administration has preferred to see even multi-bi funding (funds-in-trust) as multilateral financing, bringing the total present amount up to 40%. Multi-bi funding implies, not a free contribution to the multilateral body, but a tripartite agreement between the donor, the recipient and an international organisation as executing agency. It permits the donor to retain full control over the use of the allocation. Earmarked allocations of this kind, prevent the globally composed councils of international organisations from disposing of the means according to their own priorities. Given the arrogant Northern distrust of the governing abilities of the Southern majority in most world organisations, it is probably a good guess to assume that multi-bi funding will remain an important component of Norway's relations with the multilateral organisations.

In the aid budget for 1997, allocations to the World Bank group have decreased considerably, whereas the support to the development bodies of the United Nations system has grown. This is only partly the result of a deliberate political choice. The member states' assessed contributions to the financial institutions have fallen as a consequence of the latest pledging rounds. Most likely, Norway will have to rely more upon the UN system during the coming years in order to increase the multilateral share of its aid.

These predictions are based on the assumption that the minority Labour government will continue in power after the general elections in September this year. If not, the most likely outcome is a minority coalition government of the Center Party, the Christian People's Party and the Liberal Party. (The Liberals seem to be once again growing stronger in Parliament.) All these parties favour increased aid with a strong poverty orientation. They are also inclined to back the UN system more strongly. Therefore a change of government (with the Labour Party free to take more progressive stands) would rather improve the prospects for solidarity with the South. The same would probably be the case if at a later stage we should experience a broader, majority coalition between the Labour Party and one or more of the three parties with which it joined in last year's handling of the White Paper.

Social justice

Over the years, Norway has possibly rendered more aid per capita to the poorest developing countries than any other donor country. But lately there has been a marked shift towards emphasising activities like hydro power development, road construction or environment friendly technology, fields that are more interesting to Norwegian firms. However, the recent parliamentary intervention will oblige the government to give more emphasis to poverty alleviation. Parliament actually gave Norwegian aid this primary task:

> To fight against poverty and to contribute to lasting improvements in living conditions and quality of life, thereby contributing to greater social and economic development and justice nationally, regionally and globally.

Here the eradication of poverty is seen – with a global scope – as one of the preconditions for broad economic development and not the other way round. It is, however, difficult to foresee the extent to which this radical thinking will be adhered to in practice.

In the aid budget for 1997, the government states that a main emphasis will be put on the strengthening of basic social services, as a follow-up to the 20:20 initiative. In 1995, 24% of bilateral assistance was devoted to what the budget somewhat broadly identifies as social development, embracing water supply, education, science, health, social infrastructure, social welfare and culture. The intention of the government is to increase this share and to strengthen the social profile of Norway's multilateral contributions as well.

Child labour

In the international deliberations about social policies, the government of Norway has made the battle against child labour a major issue. During the Ministerial Conference of the World Trade Organisation in Singapore 9–13 December 1996, the Norwegian delegation fought alongside the US representatives to introduce this item to the agenda of the trade organisation. To most of the general public in Norway, this seemed to be in tune with traditional Nordic social thinking. Who would defend the industrial exploitation of minors under severe working conditions? But to some concerned groups, the scheme seemed problematic. The Norwegian Save the Children organisation put a case strongly against the idea, stating that trade sanctions against child labour were more likely to make matters worse for the children, driving them into prostitution and criminality as the only available alternatives. Instead, the organisation insisted, the situation of poor children should be improved by positive steps to better the social services in their countries and provide them with schooling and basic necessities. The proper mechanisms for dealing with the rights of children, it stated, were organisations like the UN, the ILO and UNESCO, not the World Trade Organisation.

This initiative brought Norway into conflict with most Third World nations. Rightly, the Norwegian goverment had wisely limited itself to calling for consideration of the issue. But why discuss this matter in the WTO if the aim was not to use trade sanctions to punish child labour? Representatives from poor countries felt that this was one more way of denying them the use of one of the few comparative advantages they have – cheap labour.

Trading in emission permits?

Programmes and projects for the protection of the environment and sustainable management of natural resources received 18% of total Norwegian aid in 1995. A considerable proportion of this assistance was used in Asia, within areas like resource surveying, administrative and legal reforms and transfer of technology. Environmental aid is supposed to increase in 1997, and a special strategy for this sector is now being worked out.

Norway, however, has its own problems in respecting the targets for reduction of CO_2 emissions established under the Climate Convention, because huge Norwegian oil and gas production is leading to a considerable increase in these emissions. This has led to a certain erosion of the reputation that Gro Harlem Brundtland and her home country had acquired for environmental reliability. The government is struggling hard to obtain international agreements about *flexible* and *cost-efficient* implementation of the international reduction targets. Norway's argument is that if it can be shown *inter alia* that Norwegian gas exports to neighbouring countries lead to less use of dirtier fuels in these countries, then the calculated reduction in total emissions should be credited to Norway, which would be permitted to exceed its own emission quota to a similar degree. It may also be cheaper to carry out environmental projects in poor than in rich countries. If Norway is financing projects that lead to reduced net emissions in the countries of the South, then these gains should in the same way be credited to the Norwegian quota.

On this basis, Norway has made agreements with Costa Rica about aid for reforestation and with Burkina Faso about the provision of solar cell panels

Norway

and improved ovens. Assuming that tree-planting and saving of firewood will permit the Southern forests to absorb more harmful emissions, Norway is asking that these gains should permit Norway to emit comparatively more CO_2 in the North. The government is negotiating a huge programme with China along similar lines. Norway's call for international approval of the selling and buying of emission quotas can probably be defended on cost-efficiency grounds. But the arrangement seems too smart to appeal to environmental NGOs in Norway. They feel that it is immoral for a minority of rich peoples in the North, who are responsible for 75% of the world's CO_2 emissions, to get away from cleaning up their own surroundings properly because they are financing environmental projects in the South – which, by the way, they ought to support anyway, for reasons of justice and responsibility.

Conflict prevention

In the course of ten years, Norwegian allocations to humanitarian relief have grown from 5% to 18% of the aid budget. Critics are concerned because this has reduced the amount that might have been available for long-term development. But, though the government has this year limited relief to 15% of the aid budget, there are no indications that its strong involvement in the field of relief will diminish in the foreseeable future.

The allocations to relief, human rights, peace and the promotion of democracy are being administered by the Foreign Ministry directly. Following up on a long tradition of Nordic involvement in UN peacekeeping, the Ministry has given a new profile to Norwegian foreign policies through its activities in these fields. The ambition of Norway is to combine immediate relief to war victims, refugees and hunger-stricken people with long-term preventive, conciliation and development strategies. Mediation and non-violent conflict solving have become parts of the foreign political agenda, as shown by Norwegian intercessions in the conflicts in the Middle East, Guatemala and other countries. In these cases, leading non-governmental organisations have done most of the footwork, establishing a 'Norwegian channel' between conflict-stricken groups abroad and the offices of mediators at the political level in the distant capital of Norway.

Preparations for immediate action in situations calling for humanitarian relief have become well organised on a long-term basis. Norway now offers packages including food aid, hospital services and personnel. Volunteers are available for immediate service to meet needs for police assistance, human rights supervision, election monitoring and similar tasks. The military are preparing for a new role in the extremely difficult area of peace building (without debiting the aid budget). In the fields of international relief, human rights promotion and peace building, Norway thinks that the United Nations has to be the leading and coordinating agency, and the government strongly supports a strengthening of the UN's resources for this work. At the same time, Norway financially supports the UNHCR and other UN agencies as operators on the ground, while relying strongly upon the contributions of Norwegian humanitarian and solidarity organisations. Norwegian People's Aid, for example, has become a leading international agency in the field of mine clearing.

Given the strong political involvement in conflict prevention and relief, there can be no doubt that these activities will continue to be a major part of Norway's aid agenda. This strengthens the case even more that there is a need for increased aid budgets to take care of long-term development.

Portugal

Gonçalo Paes Parente, OIKOS

Portuguese aid is split between different ministries and institutes. It is coordinated by the Ministry of Foreign Affairs, which also takes political responsibility for it. But development cooperation also involves the ministries of Finance, Health, Culture and Territorial Planning. The institutes responsible for the management of development cooperation are all linked, whether directly or indirectly, to the Foreign Office.

The Portuguese government's development cooperation policy is to cooperate with third countries to achieve better conditions for people in less developed countries, particularly with respect to human rights and democratic principles. In practice, this has meant a focus on governance and the legal and judicial conditions in developing countries.

Portugal has always prioritised a cooperation strategy with the African continent as well as a closer relationship with the countries of South America. This will continue into the future. Portugal gives priority to its relations with Portuguese-speaking countries in Africa (Angola, Cape Verde, Guinea-Bissau, Mozambique and São Tomé e Principe, known as the PALOP) by reinforcing language and cultural links. This is done partly through systematic support for institutional cooperation activities. Many of these are through Portuguese universities that have formal arrangements with PALOP governments and therefore are able to offer scholarships to African students wanting to study in Portugal.

In 1995, aid from Portugal fell by 25% and in 1996 there was a further fall of 15.6% in real terms. NGOs attribute this fall in part to the accession of a new government in October 1995 and to the sharp reduction in debt relief from US$130 million in 1994 to US$ 27 million in 1995.

In 1995, bilateral cooperation represented 66% of Portuguese ODA. Contributions to multilateral cooperation have increased from US$ 32 million in 1989 to US$ 92 million in 1995. Progress has therefore been made in shifting Portuguese ODA towards greater multilateral collaboration and it now accounts for a third of Portuguese aid. This is partly due to big increases in aid to the EU, which in 1995 accounted for $60 million out of the $92 million, as compared with $45 million in 1993. NGOs would like to see an increase in Portuguese contributions to the European Union, UNDP and UNICEF.

Debt relief and support for the private sector

In 1994, the Fundo para a Cooperação Económica (FCE) was created to support Portuguese enterprises interested in making investments in Africa. The financing activities of the FCE are basically centred on three fronts:

- the full utilisation of financial instruments available for projects that serve the interests of both the developing country and the investor. These take the form of FCE incentives and subsidised interest rates
- Analysis and case studies on strategic interventions required by the FCE for special projects
- Monitoring and evaluation of the activities funded by the FCE in coordination with diplomatic representatives and, in the case of investment projects, in close collaboration with the banking bodies that finance them.

Debt relief has formed a very important part of Portugal's ODA. The World Credit Tables[1] report that, although Portugal is not a major creditor, in some of the PALOP countries the proportion of official bilateral debt that is owed to Portugal is substantial.

The Portuguese government supports the solution of the accumulated debt problem through debt conversions, rescheduling and reductions under the Paris Club agreements. For Low Income Countries Portugal

Portugal

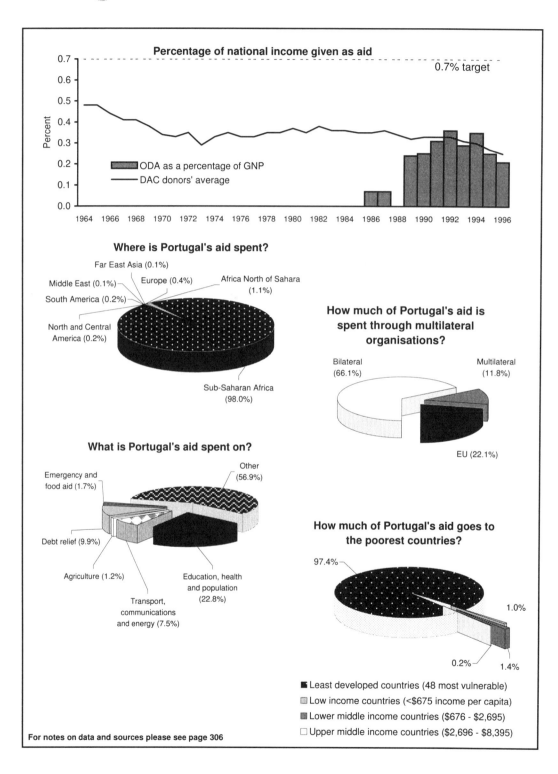

The **Reality** of Aid 1997/8

Portugal

Portuguese aid at a glance

How much aid does Portugal give?

Portugal gave	US$ 221m, in 1996
that was	0.21% of GNP
and	1.43% of public administration
which meant	US$ 22 per capita for 1996

Is it going up or down?

In 1996 Portuguese aid	fell by US$ 37m, a drop of 15.6% in real terms over 1995
Portugal was	less generous in 1996, dropping from 0.25% GNP to 0.21%

How does Portugal compare with the other 21 donors?

Portugal ranks	18 out of 21 for its volume of aid
It is	17 out of 21 in the generosity league
It gives	a higher proportion of its aid (98.4%) to Low Income Countries than any other donor
Private Flows	amounted to $35m, 13% of ODA
Total Flows	to developing countries were 0.32% of GNP and rank 16 out of 21 in the DAC

How much does Portugal spend on basic health and basic education?

Portugal reports	ODA spending of less than 1% on basic health and basic education combined

How important are commercial interests in aid?

Portugal requires	3.3% of its aid to be used to buy Portuguese goods

What do the public think about aid?

> 93% of Portuguese citizens think that development aid is important
> 32% think that the EU is in the best position to offer aid to developing countries; 69% think that the EU is in the best position to offer aid to Africa

Portugal

is reported to go beyond the 67% debt reduction that is possible under Paris Club agreements on Naples Terms. By lowering the interest rates on outstanding loans to between 2% and 3% and converting the remaining debt at a high discount rate the Portuguese claims are reduced by 80% to 90%.

Debt relief for Angola, Mozambique and Guinea-Bissau, which signed several debt rescheduling agreements in the Paris Club, comprises an especially large part of the Portuguese aid budget. The PALOP countries are eligible for debt conversion programmes from which especially Angola and Mozambique have benefited. The Counterpart funds are used to alleviate the negative social impact of Structural Adjustment Programmes and for the promotion of local investment and training.

Cooperation through NGOs

The role and activities of NGOs are of interest to the government and regular discussions are held.

The restructuring of the development cooperation agencies in 1994 merged the former *Direcção Geral de Cooperação* (Directorate General for Cooperation) and the *Instituto de Cooperação Económica* (Economic Cooperation Institute) into the *Instituto da Cooperação Portuguesa* (ICP). Within the ICP there is now a support unit for NGOs. This is limited to NGOs with the status of public utility organisations – this status is a recognition by government of the work of associations that have engaged in some type of social activity. NGOs with public utility status also get some benefits from tax relief.

Of the 40 recognised NGOs in Portugal, only eight are concerned with development cooperation and only two or three have any impact on public opinion or attempt to do development education.

NGO financing comes from four sources – the EU, the Portuguese public, UNDP and the Portuguese government. The government has provided US$ 14,705 a year to the Portuguese National NGO Platform. This consists of 44 NGOs and also organises debate and liaison within the NGO community. The Portuguese government funding is offered on the basis of co-financing. Up until this year, the Portuguese government did not have a budget to co-finance NGO activities, but a bill will be passed in the second half of 1997 under which the government will channel funds to NGOs. The basis of this funding will be a financial plan, agreed upon annually, with each Portuguese NGO applying for matching grants. It will be up to NGOs to provide a proportion of the funding ranging from 15% to 50%.

Most Portuguese NGOs, like the government, support projects in the five Portuguese speaking African countries of the PALOP.

In the first half of 1997, the Portuguese parliament was considering two bills intended to change the law governing NGO statutes and volunteers working in developing countries (known as cooperation agents). This gives an indication that efforts are being made to change the current relationship between the government and NGOs. This legislation will provide a framework of rights and duties whereas, up until now, there has been no legal status for cooperation agents.

Development education

The effort to sensitise the public and school children to the need to create solidarity between people in Portugal and in less developed countries has been able to build on a strong public interest in development issues, particularly as they relate to the PALOP. As many as 93% of Portuguese citizens think development aid is important.

During 1995 there were many public, private and NGO initiatives concerned with aid for development. The NGDO OIKOS works both with groups and associations in Portuguese society and with schools. An example is the involvement of the cultural association of *Santiago do Cacem*, which promotes exhibitions of products from developing countries and uses the radio and press to arouse public interest with the objective of making people – particularly local opinion leaders such as mayors – interested in North–South relations.

The 'Children's World' project, for which OIKOS and the Portuguese Committee for UNICEF are responsible, is bringing greater awareness of the lives of children in developing countries to Portuguese primary schools. The purpose is to create a sense of solidarity and commitment to development cooperation.

In relation to high schools, training and development activites are carried out among teachers and students along with various programmes aimed at schools themselves. These programmes aim to inform, raise awareness and motivate through games, simulations, exhibitions, meetings and conferences

Portugal's initiatives to build links/institutions that join together the Portuguese-speaking world

On 17 July 1996, Portugal together with Brazil and five Portuguese-speaking countries (Angola, Cape Verde, Guinea-Bissau, Mozambique and São Tomé e Principe) formalised the Portuguese-Speaking Countries Community (CPLP). This intergovernmental institution was created with a view to establishing relations between the seven countries in different fields.

The scope of action as laid down in the statutes is basically:

- the promotion of the language – involving 200 million people;
- political and diplomatic harmonisation; and
- cooperation between members on economic, social and cultural issues.

With the establishment of the CPLP, NGDOs should intensify their efforts *vis-à-vis* Portuguese cooperation, not only in relation to government financing, which should be larger, but also as agents, able to afford knowledge and experience that the governments must not ignore in the construction of their cooperation policies. The CPLP is a forum where Portuguese NGDOs could also increase their participation in information and education for development. Networking between NGOs in the seven CPLP members would be a good step on the way to strengthening NGO relationships.

Cooperation within this new community will undoubtedly lead to consolidation of the democratic system and will facilitate free market initiatives in each of those countries, which will prepare them for the great challenges of the contemporary world.

The CPLP has a secretariat that provides all the coordination for the project, and the general secretary is Angola's former prime minister, Mr Marcolino Moco. Since it was only created last year, the CPLP's activity is not yet very intensive and it is still too early to bear fruit.

Note
1. EURODAD, *The World Credit Tables 1996*, Brussels.

Spain

José María Vera and Marta Barceló, Intermón

The stagnation of aid

The government has committed itself repeatedly to progressing towards 0.7% and improving the quality of ODA. In late 1995 the political party in power signed the *National Agreement for Solidarity*, in which the final figure of 0.35% of GDP for development aid in 1996 was included as well as improvements in ODA orientation.

However, even apart from lack of political will, the structure of Spanish ODA is in need of an urgent and total renovation if the commitments made are to be fulfilled, and if the management of the funds is to comply with certain minimum efficiency levels and have an impact on poverty eradication.

Despite a reduction in the influence of concessional loans – aimed at encouraging exports – as a part of total ODA, commercial pressures and foreign policy strategies continue to be the two major cooperation 'conditionalities', both in the bilateral field and in Spanish participation in multilateral institutions.

On completion of its first year in office, the new government has incorporated scarcely any significant changes in ODA, apart from a greater concern about returns to Spain from aid spending, the consolidation of the Spanish Agency for International Cooperation (AECI) budgets and the initiation of a process to approve a Cooperation Law.

A decrease expected

The year 1995 saw the first ever decrease in the volume of Spanish aid as it fell to 0.24% of GNP. This decrease continued in 1996 when ODA reached 0.22% of GNP notwithstanding the political commitment made by the party in government when it was campaigning during the election. Although Agency funds and NGO grants tripled in 1995 – starting from a very low base – they were not able to compensate for the fall in concessional tied aid credits under the Development Aid Fund (FAD).

The impossibility of passing on unspent FAD funds to other aid areas, due to the budgetary structure and the variability of multilateral contributions (which have experienced a downward trend in recent years), has provoked this fall. It has been accentuated by the existing Spanish budgetary austerity, which has the aim of achieving Maastricht convergence.

The forecasts for 1997 point towards a consolidation of this budget, with an increase in multilateral contributions fed, according to government forecasts, by increased contributions to the EU and to International Financial Institutions (see Table 7).

Incoherence in financial cooperation

Despite its decrease, the FAD still accounts for more than 30% of bilateral ODA, which, added to the 15% of external debt forgiveness, makes the Minister of Economy the most important figure in the management of Spanish ODA.

The 50% fall in FAD loans is due to increased loan repayments and, fundamentally, to the difficulty in getting contracts given the limitations imposed by the Helsinki Consensus, which restricts the use of tied aid credits to low income countries and to projects that are not commercially viable. Spain has too many times turned to the use of the Helsinki exception clauses, which allow a country to claim overwhelming national interest as a reason for offering tied aid credits for projects that should be commercially viable. For example, among the list of subventions in 1995, there are projects that should be commercially viable, such as the detergent plant in China for 9000 million pesetas (11.4% of FAD appropriations for the year). Yet, in spite of this, the restrictions over countries and sectors make the use of this commercial instrument more difficult.

The FAD is the direct responsibility of the Secretariat for State for External Trade. The information available on projects is limited to their title (often not very explicit), contractor, amount and country of destination. Even this minimum information is not available for projects included in

The **Reality** of Aid 1997/8

Spain

Table 7 Percentage distribution of bilateral and multilateral ODA for 1994–7

	1994	1995	1996	1997
total ODA (million pesetas)	173.280	168.101	160.000	192.145
% of GNP	0.27	0.27	0.22	0.24
% bilateral	65.10	65.10	60.40	56.60
% multilateral	34.90	34.90	39.60	43.40
FAD as % of bilateral	70.90	70.90	34.70	36.80

Source: International Cooperation Annual Plans 94 and 95 (Achievements), information forwarded on the 5 March 1997 to the Council for Cooperation.

credit lines open to certain countries. The processes under which Spanish companies get concessional aid to support projects are totally lacking in transparency.

The fact that the FAD instrument exists for purely commercial reasons is recognised by its managers.[1] Its coordination with the rest of development policy is non-existent and the only thing that relates it to the ODA is that it complies with the financial conditions dictated by the DAC.

The administration has never evaluated a project financed by the FAD in terms of social and environmental impact and developmental soundness and although the majority of projects in recent years, as far as is known, seem innocuous, some clear cases of negative impact have been detected.[2]

Apart from debates on tied aid, summarised on occasion by the administration itself,[3] the fact that the FAD is part of the ODA is a mere accounting exercise far from the reality of Spanish cooperation.

Debt forgiveness is an increasingly important instrument, thanks to Spanish participation in the Paris Club. In 1996, debts from Burkina Faso, the Congo, Honduras and Mozambique were forgiven. This is as far as the information on this instrument goes. The type of debt, the forgiveness conditions and whether or not the debts were recoverable or classified already as uncollectible, is completely unknown information.

The commercialisation of aid also affects Spanish participation in international institutions and Agency work, especially during the last year. The importance of gaining returns to the Spanish economy and synergy with the development of Spanish economic interests abroad critically affects the management of aid.

Faced with reduced opportunities for using concessional loans, the business community and the administration are looking for new ways of making aid profitable by introducing greater flexibility in the FAD, co-financing and trust funds with multilateral banks and various technical assistance funds tied to Spanish consultancies and focused on the obtaining of further opportunities to bid for project contracts in countries in the South.

During the last year, efforts by politicians and business people in the communication media have been multiplied in order to explain to the influential public opinion that aid makes sense if it also directly benefits the Spanish economy.

An unfeasible structure

Up to ten different ministries participate in the management of Spanish ODA, albeit with the majority managing small amounts. The coordination is carried out by the Interministerial Commission for International Cooperation (CICI), an entity which in theory has high rank and functions but which in reality is limited to ratifying what different ministries present, sometimes with limited information, and to countersigning the Annual Plan for International Cooperation (PACI), which is no more than a list of unconnected actions.

Two ministries manage the greater part of ODA – over 85% in 1996. These are the Ministry of the Economy, which manages FAD loans, external debt forgiveness, contributions to the EU (in this case sharing management with Foreign Affairs) and contributions to international financial institutions. The Ministry of Foreign Affairs manages the Co-operation Agency, NGO grants and contributions to international non-financial institutions.

The lack of coordination between these two ministries is often referred to, but what it means in practice is: lack of information, different criteria and

The **Reality** of Aid 1997/8

Spain

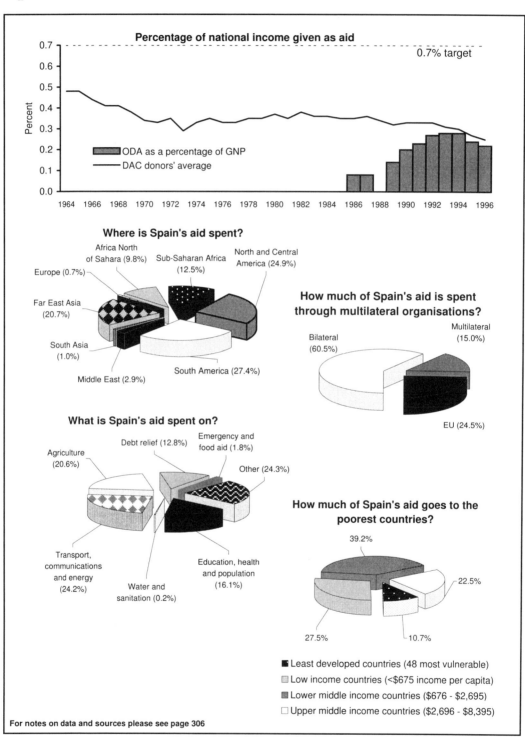

The **Reality** of Aid 1997/8

Spanish aid at a glance

How much aid does Spain give?

Spain gave	US$ 1,258m, 160,000 million peseta in 1996
that was	0.22% of GNP
and	1.45% of public administration
which meant	US$ 32 or 4,077 peseta per capita for 1996

Is it going up or down?

In 1996 Spanish aid	fell by $90m, a drop of 8.8% in real terms over 1995
Spain was	less generous in 1996, dropping from 0.24% GNP to 0.22%
The outlook is	that the budget restrictions and structure of Spanish aid have greatly reduced the feasibility of attaining 0.7% of GNP

How does Spain compare with the other 21 donors?

Spain ranks	12 out of 21 for its volume of aid
It is	16 out of 21 in the generosity league
It gives	a lower proportion of its aid (38.2%) to Low Income Countries than any other donor
Private Flows	amounted to $508m, 38% of ODA
Total Flows	to developing countries were 0.29% of GNP and rank 18 out of 21 in the DAC

How much does Spain spend on basic health and basic education?

Spain reports	1.6% of its ODA spending on basic education. It has not yet reported on basic health

How important are commercial interests in aid?

Spain required	33% of total ODA to be used to buy Spanish goods in 1993

What do the public think about aid?

66% of Spanish people think development aid is important

Spain

objectives, different geographical and sectoral priorities and corporatism and rivalry between different civil servant levels (diplomats and commercial technicians).

Following the mobilisation of the public in 1995 great hopes were resting on the proposals made to achieve quantity and quality of Spanish ODA as well as an increase in Agency and NGO funds. These have been frustrated by the impossibility of moving towards an aid management unit, which would lead to efficient management based on development and poverty eradication criteria.

Difficulties in the management of the Agency

The Agency has tripled its budget over recent years reaching almost 40,000 million pesetas in 1996 – NGO projects included. However, this increase has not been accompanied by a structural renovation.

Of the 320 people who work in the Agency, no more than 100 work directly with programmes and projects, whether in Madrid or in technical offices in southern countries. The numbers working in horizontal programmes that run across several countries at once, such as scholarship recipients or scientific collaboration, must be added to this figure. As well as being few in number, Agency staff often lack relevant skills in relation to their cooperation responsibility and many are on short-term contracts. This, plus the continuous rotation of diplomats at first and second level management without specific cooperation training, must all be taken into account.

The second factor, which is crippling the Agency, is its administrative procedures. The Agency is subject to the same planning, contracting, execution and spending justification norms as any other public entity. The lack of flexibility and adaptation make real development cooperation work difficult. As for NGOs, they also face the problem of being loaded down with bureaucracy.

No political intent has been observed on the part of the government to renovate the Agency and direct it towards its true function through stable and competent personnel, clear criteria coherent with development aims or new instruments to free up the present situation.

Lack of programming and evaluation

The problems described above are exacerbated further by the lack of annual planning. In April 1996 there was still no information on the current year's cooperation plan. Even though the government has committed itself to preparing a multi-year plan, this will be of little use if the present lack of coordination between ministries and the inadequacies in many Spanish aid instruments persist.

Apart from the evaluations of projects financed for NGOs, very few specific evaluations of Agency projects have been carried out. No FAD financed project has ever been evaluated – even though the total FAD projects would amount to roughly 1000,000 million pesetas. Neither does an established system exist to evaluate Spanish ODA.

Poverty focus

Although the terms 'eradication of poverty' and 'work with the most vulnerable groups' appear in writing in all official documents and form a part of public statements by aid directors,[4] these are in no way a priority for Spanish ODA. The reduction of a poverty criterion does not count for FAD loans, nor for a good part of Agency projects or programmes where state and institutional modernisation have joined the main list of traditional priorities: university education, technical assistance, investment in productive activities and protection of cultural and historical heritage.[5]

Social and self-help projects, are limited to NGO programmes (funded by the Agency or by regional and local government funds) and to some Agency programmes in sub-Saharan Africa. There are no indicators or no global strategy for poverty eradication that could influence overall aid.

No specific programmes have been established to comply with the commitments made by the various UN summits and in the DAC document *Shaping the 21st Century*. The gender focus is limited to those projects carried out by the NGOs and the Women's Institute (Instituto de la Mujer) that directly influence the situation of women in the South; no global gender strategy exists in the scope of the Agency as is the case with the environment.

Although quotas are paid regularly, voluntary contributions to UN agency programmes (such as UNICEF, WHO, UNDP), which were frequent in the last years of the previous government, are to be made explicitly conditional on the increased presence of Spanish civil servants in these institutions, as well as on a higher share of contracts for Spanish companies.

The 20:20 pact and aid to LDCs

The government has pointed out its commitment to the 20:20 pact on numerous occasions. In addition, it has defended it in response to a parliamentary question as well as in the Council of Development Ministers in the EU. However, the government included in the calculation of the 20:20 pact all projects carried out in the Health, Education and Sanitation sectors, including those financed by the FAD.

Intermón estimates the volume of funds allocated to basic social services, as defined by UNDP, as being roughly 10% in 1995. This percentage, greater than that of 1994, is calculated through a totalling of activities and is not a reflection of a specific strategy. No output targets have been established to measure the extent to which aid improves basic social services for poorer populations.

The geographical priorities of Spanish ODA – Latin America, North Africa and countries of commercial interest – resulted in only 14% of aid going to LDCs. This included a significant tranche of debt forgiveness for Haiti, which will not be maintained in future. If the calculation includes all aid destined for low income countries, the figure rises to 35%. This takes China and Indonesia into account as the main recipients of Spanish ODA through the FAD and demonstrates the scant regard for human rights, when export promotion is at stake.

Coherence and political will

Spanish foreign policy, like that of other Western donors, continues to be influenced by tough guidelines with reference to issues like security, trade, economy and migration. But it has some individual touches like the more intransigent stance with respect to relations and cooperation between Cuba and the EU.

Transparency in the arms trade

Some positive aspects must be underlined. In early 1997, as a result of social pressure,[6] the government unanimously approved the total ban of the production, export, use or storage of antipersonnel mines. A few weeks later, Parliament passed another motion in favour of transparency in the arms trade. This forces the government to publish reports every six months, which include the export destination, and allows for greater parliamentary control. This means that Spain will have one of the most advanced forms of control in the world in this field.

No progress has been made with reference to positive coherence with the theoretical objectives of development cooperation in commercial, agricultural, fishing or migration policy. Although the majority of these areas come under EU responsibility, the Spanish attitude in Brussels is in line with the other member states: in favour of cooperation being placed within the scope of other policies – sometimes subject to the priorities of other policies – and pushing for coherence in sectors that do not directly affect their economies.

A special mention must be made of investment policy under which all sorts of instruments are promoted – such as subsidies and export loan insurance – in favour of private Spanish investment in countries in the South. These subsidies are granted to Spanish companies with little control over questions such as repercussions in the destination country or payment of 'commissions' and bribes, and with no coordination with cooperation. Debts to particular countries are beginning to be forgiven in exchange for investment, but the debt forgiveness in exchange for funds for the environment or for social sectors has not been considered.

Movements in favour of 0.7%

In late 1995, the initiatives of the 0.7% Platform were repeated to make the case for greater quantity and quality of aid. This time the hunger strikes were replaced by various separate actions. These included a camp in Prado Street, in the centre of Madrid, and a sit-in by people from the 0.7% Platform in Madrid Cathedral as well as a march through Madrid in mid-December in which thousands of people participated.

The 0.7% movement has increased citizens' awareness and society's support for cooperation and has also aroused media interest. The most recent survey[7] indicated that 66% of the population was in favour of contributing 0.7% of GNP to cooperation. And, it is important to mention that 33% of those surveyed felt that the state should maintain aid funds even before guaranteeing the welfare of Spaniards.

The fact that the majority of town councils, including the smaller ones, and regional governments have cooperation budgets, accounting at present for 15% of bilateral ODA and channelled mainly through NGOs, is another advance achieved by the movement. These initiatives have also helped to influence the Agency budget increase and grants to NGOs. Now, the big challenge for the 0.7%

movement and the NGOs is to get a cooperation law based on solidarity passed and an aid structure established with a managing body that would allow a higher volume of development cooperation aimed at human development.

Cooperation law and the future of aid

What was known about the government draft of the Cooperation Bill at the time of writing was that it is a mixed bag. It incorporates some principles and instruments from a proposal made by the NGO National Platform. Examples are an interterritorial commission for decentralised cooperation, some new cooperation loans for development and a more advanced fiscal framework.

However, the big problems remain: dispersion in the management of instruments; a lack of Agency autonomy; maintenance of FAD separate from cooperation; and lack of initiative in the drawing up of new instruments. Although it is hoped that this Bill will be passed with the consensus of all parliamentary groups, it will be difficult to count on the consensus of civil society if the real problems of Spanish ODA are not dealt with.

The 1996 *Reality of Aid* report outlined the recommendations made by the DAC in its first peer review of Spanish ODA in 1994. In 1998, a second review will take place. Except for the reduced importance of FAD as a component of overall aid and the increased funds for the Agency, no significant advances have been made with regard to the rest of the recommendations. In some cases, such as planning capacity, the situation has worsened. NGOs and those parts of society interested in cooperation hope that the Cooperation Bill will cover these recommendations and others made from various fields, aiming at a complete renovation of development cooperation.

Notes

1. In 1995 preparation began on a bill to regulate the functioning of this fund. The FAD will be called FAEX (Aid fund for exports) and the objectives laid down will be purely commercial.
2. In 1994 a project was approved, which is being executed at present, for the construction, in Spanish shipyards, of 20 shrimp haulage ships for the Cameroon. Studies undertaken in the area have shown that the activity of these ships would have a serious environmental impact on marine resources, and a social impact on traditional fishermen.
3. Mier Durante, 'La Cooperación de España al Desarrollo: Reflexiones y propuestas', *Información Comercial Española*, no 755, July 1996.
4. *Informe sobre los objetivos y líneas generales de la política española y ayuda al desarrollo*, Conreso de los Diputados, 26 November 1992.
5. Although programmes exist in numerous sectors, one of the last events financed by the AECI was the Latin American Intergovernmental Conference on Privatisations, run by the World Bank, which took place in Chile in April 1997.
6. Over the last two years the organisations Intermón, MSF, Greenpeace and Amnesty International have carried out an intensive campaign to secure transparency in the arms trade. The first three organisations, together with five other NGOs participated in the campaign against landmines.
7. According to a survey by the Centre for Sociological Research (CIS) in November 1996.

Sweden

Svante Sandberg, Forum Syd

Swedish development policy at the crossroads

For decades, development cooperation constituted an important part of Swedish foreign policy; it was even a central issue within the overall social democratic project, the Swedish Model.

The Third World was a lead theme of party leader Olof Palme, the main architect of the Swedish Model from the 1960s and onwards. Its importance was not only for reasons of solidarity, but because, in Palme's vision, the radical political leaders of the Third World were potentially important actors in building a third political road between superpowers, between capitalism and socialism. To give those Third World leaders an alternative to the Soviet Union as a support base was therefore a strategic task in Palme's political thinking.

The changes of the 1990s

All that is now history. A lot of things have happened since the 1970s when Palme had to see Sweden's diplomatic relations with the US frozen because of his statements on Vietnam or his visit to Sandinista Nicaragua during the contra war in the 1980s.

- The end of the Cold War eliminated the ideological base for 'the third road' and Swedish active neutrality, and also gave Sweden a new geopolitical task of creating stability around the Baltic Sea.
- The assassination of Olof Palme in 1986 silenced the main person behind Sweden's active Third World policy, and gave way to more domestic policy orientated social democratic leaders, whose eventual radical inclinations were directed more towards environment and gender equality than to international issues.
- The deep economic and financial crisis that hit Sweden in the 1990s lead to considerable deconstruction of the Swedish welfare model and to rates of unemployment not seen since the early 1930s.

- Sweden's entry to the European Union had a double effect: the traditional, independent foreign policy had to be reversed and, as newcomers to the Union, most of the interest in international issues among politicians and the general public has, quite understandably, been concentrated on European issues.
- There has been an end to the social democratic hegemony in Swedish politics, especially since the Conservative Party has emerged as an equally big political force as the Social Democrats, and because the Conservative leader Mr Carl Bildt (on leave from the party to be the representative of the EU in former Yugoslavia) is now the dominant foreign policy thinker in Sweden.

A symbol of the shifts in Swedish policy is evident in the decision by the Parliament that from 1997 Sweden officially abandons its commitment to allocate 1% of its GNP to Development Cooperation. Instead, it has adopted the 0.7% level. In a few years Sweden will therefore have reduced its aid budget by 30%. The government states that the reduction is only due to the economic constraints and that the 1% principle will be re-established when the financial problems are solved. In fact, in its budget proposals for 1998 the government indicated that the economic situation is getting better, and that it is forecasting steps to start to reinstall the 1% principle from the year 2000 when the aid budget is expected to rise to 0.72% of GNP. There is some scepticism about whether this forecast is going to be fulfilled.

Rapidly decreasing support

The 1997 cut was done without major protests from within Swedish society. It rested on solid political support as it was backed up by the two main parties in Parliament – the Social Democrats and the Conservatives – as well as by the new allies of the Social Democrats, the Centre Party. Four smaller opposition parties in Parliament did join the

Sweden

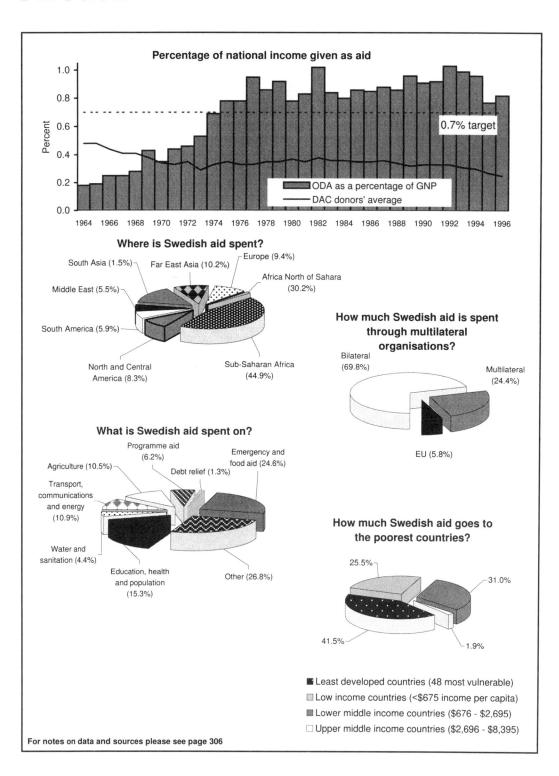

The **Reality** of Aid 1997/8

Sweden

Swedish aid at a glance

How much aid does Sweden give?

Sweden gave	US$ 1968m, 13,360 million Swedish Krona in 1996
that was	0.82% of GNP
and	2.86% of public administration
which meant	US$ 223 or 1512 Swedish Krona per capita for 1996

Is it going up or down?

In 1996 Swedish aid	rose by US$ 264m, up 7.8% in real terms over 1995
Sweden was	more generous in 1996, rising from 0.77% of GNP to 0.82%
The outlook is	for a decrease to 0.7% in 1997

How does Sweden compare with the other 21 donors?

Sweden ranks	8 out of 21 for its volume of aid
It is	4 out of 21 in the generosity league
It gives	a higher proportion of its aid (67%) to Low Income Countries than 11 other donors
Private Flows	amounted to $428m, 25% of ODA
Total Flows	to developing countries were 0.98% of GNP and rank 5 out of 21 in the DAC

How much does Sweden spend on basic health and basic education?

Sweden reports	5.7% of ODA spending on basic health and 3.6% on basic education

How important are commercial interests in aid?

Sweden requires	14.8% of its aid to be used to buy Swedish goods

What do the public think about aid?

44% of the public were in favour of the current aid level or wanted an increase in 1996

Sweden

'Percentage Campaign', which was initiated by the NGO sector in protest at the cut, but they did not give it a very high priority.

The lack of support for traditional, active Swedish Development Cooperation policy by the main political actors is one of the alarming tendencies in Sweden. It is especially alarming as the political consensus in favour of that policy was almost universal until a few years ago.

An equally alarming tendency is the rapidly decreasing support for aid among the general public. This is clearly shown in the most recent of the annual opinion surveys conducted by Sida. For decades, the proportion of the population in favour of the existing level of aid, or wanting an increase, has been between 65% in 'bad years' and up to 85% in 'good years'. A few years ago a low spot was observed when those in favour of maintaining the status quo or an increase in aid numbered less than 60% of the population. In the latest survey, published in December 1996, the proportion of people who were positive about aid was down to 44%. The part of the population that wanted to decrease or totally abolish Swedish aid was up to 42%. Although some technical changes in the survey explain part of the difference (mainly the introduction from 1996 of a 'do not know' – alternative), the shocking fact is that Sweden is now very close to a situation where the majority of the population wants to decrease aid, and that a considerable minority wants Sweden to close down completely the whole Development Cooperation programme. This would have been a totally unimaginable scenario just a few years ago! The public support differs between different aid actors: there is most confidence in the NGOs development cooperation programmes, and least in the multilateral ones. The public especially lacks confidence in the EU's programmes, which probably has more to do with the general critical public opinion of the EU than with knowledge of its aid activities. The media are a third component in this failing support for development assistance. A bastion fell when the main daily morning newspaper, the liberal *Dagens Nyheter*, which had always held a very positive position in relation to development cooperation, published a main editorial fundamentally questioning the meaning of aid during the debate on the cut in the aid budget last year.

Three scenarios

Although it still has a very extensive and fairly good development cooperation programme, above the OECD average for both quantity and quality, Sweden is now at breaking point through failing support for development cooperation. It is possible to identify three main scenarios for the future:

The complete erosion of traditional Swedish development cooperation   In this scenario, Sweden abandons the group of four small but active donor countries (Sweden, Denmark, The Netherlands and Norway), which for years have maintained a special position in the development community. It moves closer to the OECD average in terms of quantity and has a diminishing political interest in raising development issues in international fora. Sweden would then be a quiet and obedient small member state of the European Union, concentrating its foreign policy efforts exclusively towards the Baltic Sea.

A reduced traditional Swedish development policy   In this scenario, Sweden would maintain a development cooperation programme that fulfilled its basic commitments to traditional programmes and countries and left Sweden in a position above the OECD average but further and further away from the top of the OECD league table. It would take few new initiatives in development policies and, without any major engagement from either politicians or the general public, development cooperation would be an ever more silent part of a Swedish foreign policy dominated by European issues. At the moment this seems to be the most probable scenario.

A new Swedish development policy   A positive scenario could be that the current crisis has to do with the need for reform of the existing Swedish development aid policy, which was built up by the Cold War situation, and based on general political/ideological objectives, rather than goals derived from concrete development processes. In this scenario, after a process of readaptation of objectives and a series of development centred analyses, a new fresh development programme would emerge, one that was rooted in the traditional sense of international solidarity but also built on a new constituency in society for support of development cooperation. In this scenario, Sweden would return as an active, but different player in international fora, and with a modern and increasing development programme.

To support that third scenario it could be said that there are in fact signs of a new development policy being elaborated by the government, with a clearer focus on development processes rather than on more general political/ideological considerations. There is a lot of strategic thinking and policy formulation going on, both within the Ministry of Foreign Affairs and in Sida.

Government priorities

In the last year this new thinking has resulted in the production by Sida of new programmes of action in the four current high priority areas identified by the government:

- poverty reduction;
- gender equality;
- environment and sustainable development; and
- democracy and human rights.

The main areas of action in development policy identified by the government in its budget document for 1997 are:

- intensified work to reform the UN system, as a follow up to the Nordic UN Project from 1996, which led to the implementation of administrative reforms in UNICEF, WHO and UNDP. Now there are plans for new reform proposals from the Nordic countries;
- focus on the four main areas of poverty reduction, gender equality, environment and sustainable development, and democracy and human rights;
- humanitarian aid focused on prevention of conflicts and involvement in complex conflicts, mentioning the need to give ECHO special attention;
- sustainable water programmes, especially through the Sida sponsored 'Global Water Partnership';
- a new policy for Africa, to be prepared through an extensive project 'Partnership for Africa', which includes a study of the overall relations between Sweden and Africa, not only in development assistance, but also in areas like trade, investment, culture, tourism and sport. A special focus is given to the problem of aid dependency in Africa. The government's ambition is to formulate a new overall Swedish policy for its relations with Africa for the next century;
- develop a Swedish strategy for influencing the development cooperation of the EU; and
- to strengthen 'the expert group for studies on development issues', which is a new unit for evaluation and studies which has been given a wide scope of action.

A new phase for development cooperation

In the same budget document the government, or more specifically the Minister of Development Cooperation, Mr Pierre Schori, and his young think-tank, made an analysis of the international system of development cooperation, arguing that it is reaching a new phase. They identify three historical phases of development cooperation:

1. Traditional development thinking with actions based on development projects, which dominated development cooperation from the 1960s to the 1980s.
2. A reaction in the 1980s to this narrow project-based thinking, leading among other things to the need for a more macro-economic approach, through approaches such as structural adjustments, donor coordination and good governance.
3. The third phase is growing out of the globalisation process of today, which Mr Schori and his staff have chosen to see from the bright side, viewing an evolving global system, where development cooperation is turned into a system of common services within a kind of global public sector. Development cooperation, they suggest, is now evolving towards new forms of mutual relations and hopefully based on a new system of global governance where there are forms of global financing of common tasks. If successful, this would then be the last phase of development cooperation in its current form.

As part of the new policy work, the government prepared a special resolution on poverty reduction during the spring of 1997 which is to be presented to Parliament later in the year. The content of the proposal was not known at the moment of writing, but in the draft versions that have been discussed with NGOs the main theme of the government's thinking is 'growth with equity'.

Arms exports

The Swedish government is applauding all efforts to obtain more coherence in EU policies. It also

Sweden

recognises that there is a lack of coherence in Swedish policy. One area which the government does not like to mention is the role of Swedish arms exports. Partly because of its traditional neutrality, Sweden has had quite substantial armed forces and, at its service, a huge military industry. (Sweden has the seventh largest military industry in the world, quite considerable for a small country.) As the home market is small, this industry has been an active exporter, making Sweden around number 12 on the list of the worlds biggest arms exporters. A lot of hypocrisy has surrounded these exports, not least in the Palme years, with the 'Bofors scandal' in India when Swedish exporters of canons were accused of bribing the authorities in India and where the relations between Olof Palme and Rajiv Ghandi gave it a complicating context. Strict rules for arms exports have been adopted by Parliament, but it seems that there are a lot of exemptions from those rules. An embarrassing fact for the Swedish government was when the Nobel peace prize winner, Jose Ramos Horta Belao from East Timor, accused Sweden of helping the Indonesian occupying army through arms sales.

Gender

In May 1996 the Swedish Parliament established a new goal for Swedish development cooperation: 'the promotion of equality between women and men in partner countries'. The rationale for the new goal is based on two premises that gender equality is both a matter of human rights and a precondition for equitable and sustainable people-centred development. The whole of society, both women and men, and in particular leaders and opinion formers, should be engaged in promoting gender equality.

From June to September 1996, a 'gender equality experience and result-analysis exercise' was carried out within all key departments at Sida. The analysis pointed out many failures in relation to mainstreaming a gender perspective into the overall goals and strategies, but also some positive examples. Constraints and potential were identified and used in the development of a Policy and Action Programme for promoting equality between women and men in partner countries.

The main approach for promoting gender equality is to mainstream a gender perspective into policies and programmes. As a complement, inputs specifically aimed at promoting gender equality are used, for example on the empowerment of women or on the involvement of men in promoting gender equality. The development of research and tools such as gender analysis, gender sensitisation and training programmes, sex-disaggregated statistics, indicators and indices are very important.

The Beijing Platform for Action is given great importance for establishing Sida's priorities since it represents the political commitment of national governments to promote gender equality. Sida's development cooperation covers the 12 'Critical Areas of Concern' in the Platform for Action. Three areas that are highlighted in particular are gender disparities in relation to:

- human rights of women;
- equal participation in political decision-making; and
- equal participation in economic decision making and economic independence.

Experiences have shown the importance of focusing on the structural and systemic causes of gender inequalities. In Sida's efforts to reduce poverty, particular emphasis is placed on education and health.

To promote increased partnership around the Platform for Action a special initiative is being developed in four countries – Namibia, Tanzania, India and Nicaragua. Efforts are made to link institutions, organisations and individuals in Sweden and the four countries to promote mutual exchange and support on the follow-up to the Platform for Action and promotion of gender equality. Gender equality is also increasingly taken up in policy dialogue with all partners.

Sida is also giving attention to gender equality in cooperation and coordination with other actors such as the UN system, the World Bank and IMF, EU, OECD/DAC, bilateral agencies and NGOs.

As gender equality has been an overall high priority issue of the Swedish government, and the fact that Sweden has been number one on the UNDP Gender-related Development Index, sometimes gives us the notion that if there is something that Sweden especially can contribute to development processes, that should be models of changing social relations between women and men.

Switzerland

Christophe Bellmann,
Swiss Coalition of Development Organisations

Main forces

Frequently development policy considerations have been relegated to second place during 1996, particularly when they have come into conflict with Switzerland's economic interests. Discussions on the revision of law concerning what weapons and equipment should be designated as 'war material', and export risk guarantees which have favoured the promotion of Swiss exports regardless of the humanitarian consequences are there to bear witness to this. In a situation of globalisation and liberalisation of the world economy, development cooperation has tended to concentrate more on the private sector. This tendency has been very marked in 1996 with the four yearly renewal of the Framework Credit, which set the funding and objectives for economic and trade policy measures under Swiss Development Cooperation.

Outlook for aid

Switzerland has never officially set itself the target of devoting 0.7% of its GNP to ODA. Instead, in the early 1990s, the Swiss government stated its political intention to increase ODA progressively to 0.4% of GNP. This target has been maintained in principle, but the measures needed to stabilise the federal budget – which shows a structural deficit that is thought to be too high – make this target illusory for the next few years. Falling since 1994, Switzerland's ODA currently reaches only 0.32% of GNP, and financial forecasts predict 0.29% by the year 2000. This year, the Swiss Agency for Development and Cooperation (SDC) published a detailed study of the amount of money coming into the Swiss economy as a result of ODA.[1] According to this study, the CHF 1.321 million spent in ODA in 1994 brought in between CHF 1.195 and 1.351 million – a rate of return of between 90% and 102%.

Framework credits

The Swiss aid effort has a number of striking features. First of all, a dual organisation system in which the SDC based in the Federal Department of Foreign Affairs, and the Federal Office for External Economic Affairs (FOEEA) based in the Federal Department of Public Economy, are both in charge of development cooperation. They collaborate while pursuing different agendas, different approaches, and have to some extent different networks of support. Swiss ODA is based on five framework credits, which come up for renewal by Parliament approximately every four years. The five Framework Credits are for:

- technical and financial cooperation;
- humanitarian aid;
- economic and trade policy measures;
- capital participation in regional development banks; and
- cooperation with Central and Eastern Europe.

Additional credit may be granted, such as the CHF 700 million allocated for debt relief and global environment measures in 1991, or the Swiss capital participation in the Bretton Woods institutions. The last major Credit that has come up for renewal was the one for economic and trade policy measures.

Renewal of the framework credit for trade measures

For the fifth time, Switzerland has renewed its Framework Credit on economic and trade policy measures for development cooperation. CHF 960 million has been allocated for the period between 1997 and 2000. In real terms this amount is equal to the previous framework credit for 1990–6, but almost one-third will be allocated in the form of guarantees – more than under the previous credit.

Switzerland

The **Reality** of Aid 1997/8

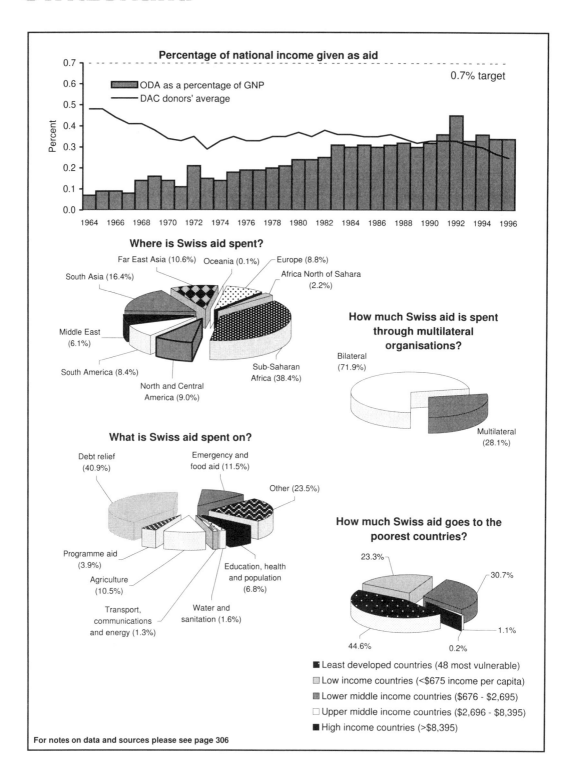

The **Reality** of Aid 1997/8

Switzerland

Swiss aid at a glance

How much aid does Switzerland give?

Switzerland gave	US$ 1021m, 1,248 million Swiss Francs in 1996
that was	0.34% of GNP
and	2.54% of public administration
which meant	US$ 144 or 177 Swiss Francs per capita for 1996

Is it going up or down?

In 1996 Swiss aid	fell by $63m, a drop of 1.6% in real terms over 1995
Switzerland was	level with 0.34% for both 1995 and 1996
The outlook is	ODA is expected to decrease to 0.29% by 2000

How does Switzerland compare with the other 21 donors?

Switzerland ranks	14 out of 21 for its volume of aid
It is	8 out of 21 in the generosity league
It gives	a higher proportion of its aid (67.9%) to Low Income Countries than 12 other donors
Private Flows	returning to Switzerland from developing countries exceeded flows from Switzerland by $345m, 32% of ODA
Total Flows	to developing countries were 0.29% of GNP and rank 18 out of 21 in the DAC

How much does Switzerland spend on basic health and basic education?

Switzerland reports	0.1% of its ODA spending on basic education and has not yet reported on basic health

How important are commercial interests in aid?

Switzerland requires	1.7% of its aid to be used to buy Swiss goods

What do the public think about aid?

67% of Swiss people think that the government is not doing enough to promote sustainable development

Switzerland

Actual disbursements will therefore be lower than had been anticipated, but, according to officials at the FOEEA, the amount disbursed will be similar to disbursements under the 1990–6 framework credit. Activities in this programme are managed by the Federal Office for External Economic Affairs, and are concerned with post-Uruguay Round compensatory measures for the Least Developed Countries (LLDCs), balance of payments assistance, debt reduction, trade promotion, STABEX, mixed credits and guarantees. The funding for this framework credit represents approximately 10% of Swiss ODA. The Parliament approved the bill in September and December 1996.

In general, Swiss NGOs regret that almost one-third of the total amount will be allocated in the form of guarantees only and not in actual payments. CHF 100 million are in the form of a *Fond d'Egalisation des Conditions*. This fund will be available to support Swiss enterprises in circumstances where competing exporters from other countries were being subsidised by their governments under mixed credit schemes to finance development projects that could be financed at market rates. In other words, the fund would have a deterrent function, trying to ensure that foreign competitors respect the Helsinki Agreement on Tied Aid Credits. This 'war chest' met strong NGO opposition as it was not considered to be part of development cooperation. Then there is a further CHF 200 million in the form of special export risk guarantees particularly adapted to developing countries. NGOs have asked that the measures adhere more closely to the principles and objectives of Swiss development cooperation, as stated in the 1976 Federal Act. In the new Framework (representing about 10% of Swiss aid), almost 50% is tied to the purchase of Swiss products, compared with only 30% in previous years. The Swiss Coalition of Development Organisations has further proposed the following direct amendments: that the links with supplies of Swiss origin should be removed; that priority should be given to the countries on which SDC is concentrated; and that collaboration with private actors, particularly those in civil society, should be supported.

New instruments

Swiss finance company for development
A new element in the fifth Framework Credit is the creation of *La Société Financière Suisse pour le Développement* (Swiss Finance Company for Development) in the form of a limited liability company, 51% of whose capital of CHF 100 million is to be raised in the private sector, with the remaining 49% coming from the Confederation. The company will be responsible for promoting private sector development in the South, in much the same way as the International Finance Corporation (IFC, World Bank Group). In particular, it will encourage private investment in regions or sectors where the private sector would not venture alone. The Swiss government's proposal could provide a constructive response to the current trend toward liberalisation, and could complement development cooperation instruments. However, in order that the *Swiss Finance Company* can truly become an institution *for Development* (as the name suggests), the Swiss NGOs want it to be tied to a clear mandate of development policy. In particular, they would like the criteria for support for particular private sector development projects to include the likely impact socially and environmentally, as well as economically. The market, in other words, the interest of the private sector in buying 51% of the share capital, will decide whether or not this new instrument will be realised.

Sale of gold reserves for solidarity fund
In February 1997, following the debate on Jewish funds in Swiss banks and the role of Switzerland during the Second World War, the Cabinet of ministers put forward the idea of a new humanitarian aid instrument, in the form of a *Fondation pour la Solidarité* (Foundation for Solidarity). To provide funds for this foundation, Switzerland has suggested selling a sixth of the state bank's gold reserves for the amount of CHF 7000 million. The interest derived from the product of the sale (between CHF 300 and 350 million annually) would go to the victims of, and preventive measures against, poverty, catastrophes, genocide and violations of human rights. Although details about the use of the *Fondation* are not yet decided, half of the funds available will be spent in Switzerland and half abroad. This proposal has still to be agreed by the Parliament and possibly the people, voting on it being planned for 1998. This is the first time that Switzerland has proposed selling part of its gold reserves. The Swiss Coalition of Development Organisations had already put forward the idea in 1983. Following this decision, it will become difficult for Switzerland to continue to oppose the sale of IMF gold, the principle of which is based on the same mechanism.

A new general system of preferences

Since March 1997 the Swiss General System of Preferences (GSP) has been renewed for ten years. The new GSP has been extended to provide for duty free entry on industrial LLDC products and for the first time, some liberalisation on agriculture. In most cases, developing countries benefit from the same advantages in terms of tariffs as the free trade partners of Switzerland. A graduation procedure for high income developing countries has been accepted, in accordance with OECD Development Assistance Committee (DAC) List (Part One) of Developing Countries.[2] The Swiss Coalition of Development Organisations has welcomed the zero-tariffs initiatives for LLDCs but regrets that market access in the agricultural sector still remains a hurdle for developing country exports. It has asked for simplified rules of origin and required additional preferences for fair-trade and environmentally sound products.

Poverty eradication

The Cabinet of ministers report on North–South relations[3] issued in April 1994 defines social justice and the fight against poverty as priorities. At the Copenhagen Summit on Social Development, Switzerland adopted the 20:20 compact in principle. The SDC takes the view that Swiss aid is already well focused on social development in comparison with other donors and, subject to the definition finally agreed internationally on which categories of spending can be included in 20:20, it is reasonably likely that Swiss ODA will already meet the standard.

SDC is in the process of defining a global strategy for social development. It has started an interdisciplinary assessment of its programmes and projects, which should be ready in June 1997, as well as a code system, which should make it possible to identify the share of aid allocated to poverty eradication. In this way it intends to achieve a better understanding of the impact of projects on the conditions of the poorest. However, concrete figures on poverty eradication and social development are still not available. The greatest problem remains the fact that, as yet, there is still no clear definition of what are understood by social development and poverty eradication. The sector codes have existed now for several years and a lot of detail is already available. NGOs consider that Switzerland should now be able to produce at least reasonable figures – even if they are not perfect – to increase interest in and accountability for poverty focus in aid spending. In addition, a clear definition of social development and poverty eradication should be established as soon as possible.

Gender In 1993 a new framework for managing gender-balanced development was issued. The policy, *Managing Gender-Balanced Development*, sets out guiding principles and lines of action. These apply equally to staff at headquarters and in the field, as well as to implementing agencies. The objective is to stimulate gender-sensitive thinking at all development cooperation levels. In the field, sectoral policies have progressively integrated gender issues. Special programmes to encourage better access to credit for women are being set up. Gender awareness training is a priority for all agency staff, including management levels. However, reliable sex disaggregated statistics have not yet been developed. SDC is working on this question. As a follow up to Beijing, an inter-departmental group has been set up to identify the measures to be taken. In addition, the Cabinet of ministers published a report in 1996 on its commitment to women within the framework of its foreign policy.

Public support

Every five years, Swiss NGOs commission opinion polls with the support of the SDC. In the most recent one (1994), over half of those polled wanted to maintain Swiss aid efforts at present levels (a 7% increase, compared with five years earlier). A quarter favoured increasing Swiss development assistance (10% less than five years earlier). Most people overestimated both public and private aid efforts. The repatriation of 'flight money' (such as the so-called *Marcos and Mobutu Funds*) deposited in Switzerland, an embargo on arms exports, higher sugar imports from the South and prohibition of toxic waste exports to developing countries are seen as major contributions to the improvement of the world economy. The promotion of peace and a reduction in the number of refugees is an important motivation for aid.

It is also generally recognised that the life style and the wasteful production methods practised by the industrialised countries must change and cannot be globalised. However, according to a different opinion poll commissioned by the Swiss

Switzerland

Coalition of Development Organisations, only 34% of the population were familiar with the concept of sustainable development.

Coherence

A coherent policy towards the South is one of the priorities stated in the North–South guidelines published by the Cabinet of ministers in 1994. Previous Reality of Aid reports have highlighted the provisions in Switzerland to ensure that development cooperation is taken into account across the range of government activity. In practice this is not always achieved.

In 1996, the Swiss NGOs criticised the fact that Pilatus PC7 and PC9 aircraft had not been affected by the revision of the law on war material, and that therefore their export could continue. These aircraft have again been used in 1996 for military purposes. The NGO Swissaid reported that they were used by the Burmese government against refugee camps partly financed by Swiss cooperation.[4]

In the case of the highly controversial Three Gorges dam in China, the Cabinet of ministers decided in December 1996 that it would, in principle, grant an export risk guarantee (ERG) to ABB and Sulzer, two Swiss companies interested in taking part in building the dam. The decision will have to be confirmed if one of these companies obtains the contract with Beijing. The case of the Three Gorges pits short-term economic and employment gains against profound social and environmental risks. NGOs argue that the building of the dam is in conflict with the fundamental principles of Swiss policy regarding development aid and that had these considerations been given proper weight, the Cabinet of ministers would not have granted the export risk guarantee. Yet, according to the federal law concerning ERG, these principles ought to have been taken into account.

Commenting on the situation, the Institut universitaire d'Etudes de developpement of Geneva drew two conclusions.[5] First, that short and medium term economic interests, including employment opportunities, took precedence over development policy criteria. Second, that in comparison with the era preceding the North–South Guidelines, public and parliamentary discussion of the issue was encouraged by policy that said that development policy had to be taken into account in reaching these decisions. As a result, there was at least no possibility of 'unintended incoherence' between conflicting policies.

A further problem associated with coherence is the lack of coordination between SDC and FOEEA. In 1994, FOEEA drew up a list of 27 concentration countries, of which only nine corresponded to those of SDC. Moreover, as part of its new Framework Credit for economic and trade policy measures, FOEEA has decided to allocate CHF 200 million to the Mediterranean region. This new orientation responds to political and economic imperatives: FOEEA wants to strengthen its links with this region because the European Union wishes to set up a free-trade area there, from which Switzerland would be excluded. For its part, SDC is setting up a 'Mediterranean section' in the Department of Foreign Affairs (DFA). But there is nothing to ensure that FOEEA and DFA will be seeking common geographical priorities and that the CHF 200 million will be spent in accordance with an overall plan and policy with respect to this region. In addition, relations between the FOEEA and SDC have deteriorated seriously this year with the debate on Swiss administrative reform. To achieve greater coherence, a merger has been proposed between the FOEEA development department and the SDC. This institutional debate is reviving tensions and preventing better coordination.

Public awareness

In September 1996, the *International Centre for Trade and Sustainable Development* was founded in Geneva. This body is responsible for promoting dialogue between Northern and Southern NGOs active in the field of sustainable development on one hand and the World Trade Organisation (WTO) on the other hand. The Centre will also facilitate access to WTO information. It does not constitute a new lobby, but an initiative that aims to improve NGO awareness in the area of trade and sustainable development. The Centre has been established by the *Swiss Coalition of Development Organisations*, the *International Union for the Conservation of Nature*, the *Consumer Unity and Trust Society* (India), the *International Institute for Sustainable Development* (Canada) and the *Fundación Futuro Latinoamericano* (Ecuador) with financial support from Denmark, The Netherlands and the Swiss Confederation, among others.

As far as education is concerned, a new foundation bearing the name of the *Foundation for*

Switzerland

> **Box 13**
> **What Swiss ODA is used for . . .**
>
> In August 1995, the governments of the Philippines and Switzerland concluded an agreement on the reduction of Philippine external debt, facilitated by the collaboration of the Swiss Coalition's Debt-for Development Unit. Under this accord, 50% of the Philippine government's outstanding commercial debt (export credit debt) to Switzerland, amounting to 42 million Swiss francs, was cancelled. The remaining 50% was converted into Philippine pesos (PhP). These PhP 455 million were then provided by the Philippine Treasury as an endowment to the Foundation for a Sustainable Society, Inc (FSSI), a Philippine NGO-managed foundation formed to manage the counterpart funds. FSSI supports sustainable productive activities of NGOs, people's organisations, cooperatives, and similar private organisations in the fields of agriculture and fisheries, and in the urban and rural small industries sector. The Foundation is in the first place a loan-granting institution, but also provides grants for activities such as technical assistance, feasibility studies and market research. It is structured as a long-term capital fund: only the interest or the return on investment and a part of the loan reflows are used to fund projects and programmes. The FSSI is exclusively managed by NGOs, the two governments being only a non-voting member of the Board (Philippines) and an observer (Switzerland) and its resources are only being allocated to civil society organisations. After a build-up phase, the Foundation started operations in April 1996. Examples of the programmes it supports are a credit line for rice trading cooperatives and guarantee funds with rural banks.

Education and Development was created in February 1997. This is intended to achieve better coordination between the various activities of NGOs and government in the field of development education. It will facilitate access to development education material and ensure that it is widely distributed to teachers. The dominant school service of the Swiss Coalition of Development Organisations will be integrated into the new Foundation. Many of the NGOs will continue their own development education activities and their work in schools, in coordination with the activities of the Foundation.

The Swiss Coalition of Development Organisations has launched a North–South Campaign for Sustainable Development. The purpose of this campaign, which will continue until the end of 1998, is to restore weight to the North–South debate and to increase ODA as well as to promote sustainable development in Switzerland. Some 21 proposals for a sustainable Switzerland have been put forward and discussions on these subjects are planned with Swiss TNCs, banks and political parties. At the beginning of 1997 the Bern Declaration, a Swiss NGO, launched an information campaign on sports shoes fabrication in Asia.

Notes

1. *Effets économique de l'aide publique au développement en Suisse* by Professors Jacques Forster IUED Geneva and Guido Pult and Milad Zarin-Nejadan, University of Neufchatel, Geneva and Neufchatel, December 1996.
2. The DAC produces a list of developing countries and territories eligible to receive ODA, referred to as Part One. Aid to countries outside this list does not count as Official Development Assistance. An additional list of countries and territories in transition is produced, referred to as Part Two. See DAC, *Development Cooperation* 1996, OECD, Paris, February 1997, pA101.
3. *Guidelines North South*, Report by the Federal Council on Switzerland's North-South Relations in the 1990s. SDC, Department of Foreign Affairs, Berne, 1994.
4. See letter from Richard Gerster, Director, Swiss Coalition, to Commission du Conseil des Etats pour la Politique de Securité, 23 April 1996.
5. *The Coherence of Policies Towards Developing Countries: The Case of Switzerland*, Jacques Forster, IUED International Workshop on Policy Coherence in Development Cooperation, April 1997.

United Kingdom

Mark Curtis, ACTIONAID

The election in May 1997 of a Labour government after 18 years of Conservative rule has opened up the possibility of significant change in the UK's aid and development policies. There are two major questions facing the new government:

- Will it reverse the trends of previous years and pursue a fundamentally different development policy (and paradigm) or simply reform with a more human face?
- Will development be a real government priority – under an empowered new Department for International Development (DFID) – or will it continue to play second or third fiddle to trade and foreign policy?

Main trends – the approach of the previous government

The new government is, to a certain extent, having to work within a framework set by the previous government. This includes changes to the Overseas Development Administration's (ODA) mission statement and changes in the aid programme to the effect that it is being reduced, redirected towards the EU and increasingly geared towards promoting the private sector.

In 1996, Ministers revised the mission statement of the ODA. Now, 'ODA's purpose is to improve the quality of life of people in poorer countries by contributing to sustainable development and reducing poverty and suffering.' To this end, ODA aims:

- to encourage sound development policies, efficient markets and good government;
- to help people achieve better education and health and to widen opportunities, particularly for women;
- to enhance productive capacity and to conserve the environment; and
- to promote international policies for sustainable development and enhance the effectiveness of multilateral development institutions.[1]

However, the changed mission does not reflect the fundamental changes in the British aid programme that result from the approach of the previous government.

Reduced

At £1900 million in 1995, UK aid to developing countries is at its lowest level since 1987 (at constant prices) and has fallen to 0.28% from 0.31% in 1994.[2] Previous government plans suggested this figure will fall to £1700 million in 1999 (constant prices).[3] Before the general election, the Permanent Secretary to the ODA intimated that the aid level will fall to around 0.25% in the next few years.[4]

Box 14 Does UK give enough?

Q: Michael Gapes MP, House of Commons Foreign Affairs Committee:

Do you think that the present level of aid which you get is high enough to meet the demands and the targets that have actually been set by Government?

A: John Vereker, Permanent Secretary, ODA:

... It is an extremely difficult question to answer, whether we are making our appropriate contribution to that, or whether the aggregate contribution to that is sufficient to secure sustainable development in poor countries. . . . Our objective view is that in sub-Saharan Africa it is undoubtedly the case that real aid levels need to rise in order to secure the level of resource transfer that is needed, in order to have a pace of sustainable development which will make a real impact on poverty.[5]

United Kingdom

Labour has reaffirmed its commitment to the 0.7% target and said that it will 'start to reverse the decline in UK aid spending';[6] Tony Blair has said that 'we will give a new priority to overseas aid'.[7] Like the previous government, however, it has been unwilling to set a timetable for reaching the target and, in reality, it is extremely unlikely that Labour will move close to the UN target.

Redirected

The Permanent Secretary at the ODA suggested in May 1996 that by 1998 more British aid will go through the EU aid programme than through Britain's bilateral programme.[8] He also predicted that bilateral aid is likely to fall by 20% in real terms from 1994/5 to 1998/9.[9] In February this year he suggested that 'for the EU share of the programme we are currently predicting a plateau of over 40% of the programme' – which would mean that aid through the EU and bilateral aid would be about the same level.[10]

This redirection of aid to the EU – whose aid programme is widely recognised as having serious deficiencies – was opposed by the previous aid minister[11] and the Foreign Affairs Committee, a parliamentary watchdog, which noted that 'we greatly regret that our bilateral programme has had to be curtailed because of increased European Community aid commitments.'[12] The Secretary of State for International Development, Clare Short, has also been very critical of this redirection of aid, noting that 'Britain's bilateral programme is one of the best and the EU's is not.' Her pledge is to 'get a better grip on how the EU money is spent' by increasing its focus on poverty.[13]

Promoting the private sector

Private financial flows from Britain to developing countries are three times larger than its aid programme and these have doubled in the last three years.[14] This trend – and the fact that Britain is the second largest DAC source of total aid and private flows – was regularly used by the previous government to deflect criticism of its falling aid budget.[15] One Minister claimed that 'it is not simply a question of what we give directly through state aid, but what is given by the private sector'.[16]

A main role of aid in recent years has been to promote the private sector in developing countries. 'Official development efforts can play a catalytic role in creating the conditions in which such a private sector can flourish', the former aid Minister noted. The role of aid is to 'promote the right enabling environment' for the private sector.[17] Aid has also been used 'to assist structural adjustment in recent years' since it 'helps recipient countries to make reforms relevant to investors'.[18]

Box 15 Tied aid (UK)

According to the previous government's figures, the percentage of bilateral aid tied to the purchase of British goods and services declined from 73% in 1991 to 54% in 1994. This still meant, however, that £557 million of British aid was tied.[19]

Findings from a report produced under the previous government showed that 'there would be marginal benefits to the UK economy from unilateral untying and somewhat larger benefits from multilateral untying'. The then government ruled out unilateral untying, however, since it 'would yield few efficiency gains for the aid programme, would bring little commercial benefit and would be unpopular with individual firms and businesses competing for aid-funded contracts'.[20]

However, the finding that untying aid would benefit the economy paves the way for significant untying under the new government. Labour has pledged to 'press for an international agreement on reducing and eliminating tied aid'.[21] As this chapter was being written, the government announced that tied bilateral aid to Africa would be scrapped.[22] This is clearly a positive move, but would affect only around 35% of all Britain's bilateral aid.[23]

This role for aid is increasing – in January 1997, Lynda Chalker launched a new initiative designed to enable British firms to work more closely with the ODA and which called for 'a more business-oriented approach to the ODA's dealings with multilateral institutions such as the World Bank'.[24] This policy also coincided with that towards international trade where previous government policy was 'to carry forward that liberalising agenda and to consolidate the role of the World Trade Organisation'.[25]

The **Reality** of Aid 1997/8

United Kingdom

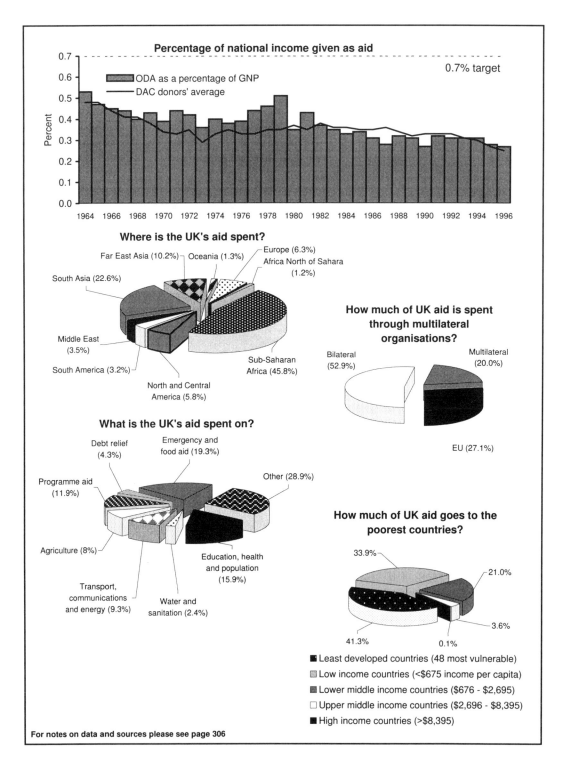

For notes on data and sources please see page 306

The **Reality** of Aid 1997/8

United Kingdom

UK aid at a glance

How much aid does the UK give?

The UK gave	US$ 3185m, £2,200 million in 1996
that was	0.27% of GNP
and	1.34% of public administration
which meant	US$ 54.4 or £38 per capita for 1996

Is it going up or down?

In 1996 UK aid	fell by $2m, a drop of 0.6% in real terms over 1995
The UK was	less generous in 1996, dropping from 0.28% to 0.27%
The outlook is	more optimistic for the period after 1998

How does the UK compare with the other 21 donors?

The UK ranks	6 out of 21 for its volume of aid
It is	15 out of 21 in the generosity league
It gives	a higher proportion of its aid (75.2%) to Low Income Countries than 17 other donors
Private Flows	amounted to $11,635m, 3.7 times ODA
Total Flows	to developing countries were 1.39% of GNP and rank 2 out of 21 in the DAC

How much does the UK spend on basic health and basic education?

The UK	has not yet reported to the DAC on its basic health and basic education spending

How important are commercial interests in aid?

The UK requires	26.6% of its aid to be used to buy UK goods

What do the public think about aid?

In 1995, 81% of the public thought that it was important to provide aid

United Kingdom

The approach of the previous government exacerbated the two major, interlinked problems with the British aid programme. The first, 'internal' problem is that British aid is not primarily focused on poverty reduction: its overall thrust remains to promote macro-economic growth, which does not necessarily reduce poverty, and to support British economic and foreign policy interests. Despite much rhetoric over the years to the effect that poverty reduction is the key aim of the aid programme, only 11% of bilateral aid went to 'basic social services' in 1995/6 – a proportion that has held constant for the previous five years.[26] Just 1% of Britain's aid went to primary education in 1994/5, the same proportion as in 1989/90.[27] There is also little evidence that Britain's poverty-focused aid currently reduces poverty, since the impact of aid is not systematically analysed.

This has led to the second, 'external' problem concerning the wider context of aid, which is that the type of development model promoted by British aid has not necessarily been in the interests of the poor. As noted above, much British aid has explicitly promoted structural adjustment, but key elements of the latter have led to increases in poverty. The promotion of the private sector and foreign investment that this policy entailed can promote development, but only under certain conditions (see earlier sections of *Reality of Aid 1997/8*). A key question is what kind of development should be promoted.

Choices for Labour

'There can be no higher moral purpose than working to eradicate poverty and promote sustainable development in the world's poorest countries' (Prime Minister, Tony Blair).[28]

Labour's pledges

The new Labour government has been outspoken in expressing many of its differences from its Conservative predecessor. One welcome change is the explicit commitment to make poverty reduction 'the key objective' of the aid programme and to shift resources towards this aim.[29] The DFID has affirmed that 'eliminating abject poverty from the world is the prime purpose of the new department'.[30] Labour has also pledged the following:

- to reverse the decline in UK aid spending (though this will not begin until year two, or more probably year three, of the new government, according to current plans);
- a commitment to the goals of of the DAC in *Shaping the 21st Century*;
- to audit all aid projects for their impact on the poor;
- to press for an international agreement on reducing and ultimately eliminating tied aid;
- to press IDA to ensure that all its programmes are geared to the reduction of poverty;
- to support an end to the dumping of EU agricultural surpluses; and
- to support an international code of conduct for transnational corporations (TNCs).[31]

It is in the views of the Secretary of State, Clare Short, that the profound differences with the previous government become most apparent. In opposition, Short noted, for example, that the ideology promoted by the previous government as well as the World Bank and the IMF is 'economically wrong and morally offensive' and this 'explains why growing numbers of people are living in abject poverty, whilst the wealth of the world has grown'.[32]

Policy options for Labour

'Whether Britain benefits from the new global trends, or becomes a victim of them, will in large part be determined by the extent to which its government develops an international strategy that is in touch with the real world' (Labour Party).[33]

Labour's new directions are welcome and, once implemented, will represent a positive way forward after the policies of the recent past. But it is unclear precisely which way development policy will go; there are major policy options facing the new government. Will its often visionary language, more critical of the current international agenda and calling for more fundamental changes – which is the Secretary of State's own position – be translated into reality? Or will more pragmatic stances, with emphasis on more mild reform, prevail? Put simply, will Labour seek to promote a new development paradigm or the current paradigm with a more human face?

The balance between these stances will determine how Labour's development policy is played out in the years to come. These dilemmas are illustrated by considering the following difficult questions:

Trade and poverty Labour is committed to a future based around global 'free trade' and has welcomed the World Trade Organisation 'as an important step towards an open international economy'.[34] The Secretary of State has called for the removal of trade barriers in Africa and the creation of 'regulatory instruments to ensure that the private sector can flourish in a way which removes obstacles from manufacturers and investors'.[35] However, there are no guarantees that a more open international economy will lead to a reduction of poverty, especially in the poorest states. Indeed, there is much evidence that the process of globalisation – which is both driving and is driven by 'free trade' – may lead to increased economic growth but also tends to concentrate wealth and increase poverty.[36] How will Labour ensure that its commitment to this agenda is compatible with eliminating poverty? How will a national government pursue progressive development policies at the same time as apparently embracing the supremacy of markets over national sovereignty?

Non-aid issues Labour acknowledges that private flows, debt and trade issues dwarf aid as the dominant forces in the future of development, and that 'aid is probably not . . . the most important instrument' in its development policy.[37] Yet the huge bulk of DFID's resources and expertise are devoted to the aid programme and the political impetus is likely to be to continue to prioritise aid policy. This will especially be the case if DFID fails to secure influence over other departments. What new ways will the government find to use Britain's resources and capacity best to promote development? Will aid policy still predominate in practice? If not, how will DFID embark on a long-term strategy of building international coalitions and forging alliances to harness non-aid resources and capacity to development?

> **Box 16 Clare Short on globalisation**
>
> 'Globalisation transforms the development debate. If the forces reshaping the world economy are ignored and the debate confined to aid flows, then we are dealing with charitable gestures, increasingly in response to disasters, while we allow mainstream policy to create growing poverty.'[38]

Commerce and human rights Labour is committed to an 'ethical' foreign policy and a development policy that promotes 'accountable government, the rule of law and strong civil society'.[39] Given that some of Britain's major trading partners and some of the world's major emerging markets cannot boast of the latter three virtues, how will government weigh commercial and human rights/development considerations?

Domestic support for international development With an overwhelming focus on domestic issues, how will DFID help build the political constituency in Britain needed to prioritise international development?

The answers to these questions will largely determine Labour's development strategy.

The Department for International Development

The creation of a new Department for International Development (DFID), headed by a Cabinet Minister and independent of the Foreign Office, offers the chance of coordinating better British development policies and of addressing this changing context. The DFID has stated that the Cabinet appointment 'brings development back into the mainstream of government decision-making'.[40] But there are risks. The DFID's success depends on adequate financing from the government budget yet some commentators have suggested that the DFID might be a softer Treasury target in spending negotiations now that it is no longer part of the Foreign Office.[41] DFID also needs staff expertise to cover areas not previously covered by the ODA.

Most important, however, is the DFID's ability to secure genuine influence within the Whitehall machine to play a, sometimes the, key role in decisions about international trade, foreign investment, debt, the environment and policy towards the World Bank. There is no guarantee that the establishment of a separate ministry will increase the government's focus on development – the risk is that its influence over the Foreign Office, of which the ODA was part, could decline. According to the Secretary of State, 'this does not mean large-scale transfers of power from other Whitehall departments to DFID' though it does mean that on issues such as trade, agriculture, the environment and debt – 'DFID has the opportunity to put its case at an early stage in the development of policy'.

United Kingdom

The **Reality** of Aid 1997/8

Table 8   Three Scenarios for the UK

Policy Areas	Scenario One: Business as usual	Scenario Two: Improved poverty focus	Scenario Three: Enhanced Development Cooperation
What happens to aid levels?	Declines	Moderate increases, focusing more on quality	Increases in quantity but mainly in quality, linked to other non-aid policies
How much focus on poverty?	Marginal	Improved	Priority
How much influence by commercial interests?	High (ATP continues, tied aid continues)	Moderate (ATP reduced, tied aid reduced)	Low (ATP disbanded, steps taken to untie all aid)
What is the role of the private sector?	Primary role in development, overtly promoted by the aid programme	Mixed policy, between promoting private sector through aid and trying to minimise social and environmental costs of private sector led development	Role of private sector more fully reshaped and harnessed to locally relevant and sustainable development
What is aid's role in the overall development co-operation effort?	Primary, increasingly acting as a catalyst for private sector-led development	Significant, geared to poverty eradication strategies	Significant, although in synergy with other policies, geared to promoting wider human development
What are the major policy issues?	Aid	Aid, debt, coherence	Foreign policy, governance, trade
What type of development is promoted?	Private sector-led with safety nets	Poverty alleviation strategy	Human development, focus on inequity as much as poverty

Three futures for aid and development

Aid and development policy generally are means not ends. The future debate on British aid should be less about the intricacies of the aid programme and more about whether the mix of interrelated policies (aid, trade, foreign policy) contributes to development in the interests of the poor. The final judgement is not whether Britain funds good aid projects but whether it promotes good development. We will increasingly need, therefore, to consider the totality of British policies that affect development.

In the current political context, there are three plausible scenarios for how aid and development policy will develop under Labour.

Business as usual   The first scenario – 'Business as usual' – will occur if, despite Labour's pledges to the contrary, the aid programme and development priorities change little from the previous government. Aid volume changes little, the aid programme remains heavily influenced by commercial interests and poorly focused on basic needs and poverty. Only minor reforms are made to debt regimes while some policies under the international trade regime (WTO), which is fully accepted, continue to increase poverty. Here, the DFID fails to transform itself sufficiently into a department capable of securing influence over wider government. Labour's pledge to curb public spending and the overwhelming political focus on domestic issues, leading to a failure to prioritise

Improved poverty focus The second scenario – 'Improved poverty focus' – will occur if Labour implements its pledges to increase aid moderately and to focus more on poverty, through, for example, implementing the 20:20 compact and reducing tied aid. Here, poverty reduction becomes the main focus of the aid programme, influence is used to reform World Bank programmes to focus more on poverty alleviation and steps are taken to reduce the social costs of private sector-led development. The DFID also exerts more influence over non-aid issues such as investment policies to help ensure that they are more closely aligned with the aims of aid and development cooperation policies.

Enhanced development cooperation The third scenario – 'Enhanced development cooperation' – will occur if Labour prioritises international development and sees an expanded and improved aid effort as part of a wider integrated development cooperation strategy. This will involve a successful DFID increasing its influence over other departments in areas such as human rights (for the Foreign Office) and trade and investment (the DTI) to ensure that developmental goals receive at least equal priority to other considerations when policy decisions are made. The UK government uses its influence to help reshape the private sector to harness its resources to promote sustainable development and seeks international and domestic allies to build constituencies to support its development agenda. Aid policy steadily becomes less important as an instrument than trade and overall foreign policy, both of which are firmly harnessed to promote human development. This becomes an overall government strategy, not simply a discrete policy area.

Conclusion

ACTIONAID urges the new government to find positive answers to the questions posed here so that next year's report – the sixth -will be the first that offers a positive overall assessment of British development policy. Given the significant challenge of moving towards scenario two – Improved Poverty Focus – some might argue for this as the most pragmatic goal. But given growing global interdependence, rising poverty and a fast-changing world, a Labour government with a long-term vision of a brighter future should take this opportunity to play an international leadership role and shift attention to the Enhanced Development Cooperation agenda. There may not be a next chance.

Notes

1. Foreign and Commonwealth Office, *Departmental Report 1996*, HMSO, London, March 1996, p 81.
2. ODA, *British Aid Statistics, 1991/92*–1995/96, GSS, London, December 1996, Table 2; OECD, *Development Cooperation*, 1996 Report, OECD, Paris, 1997, p A8.
3. FCO, *Departmental Report 1997*, HMSO, London, March 1997, p 77; and ODA press release, 26 November 1996.
4. House of Commons, Foreign Affairs Committee, *Recent Work of the Committee*, HMSO, London, 19 March 1997, p 4.
5. House of Commons, Foreign Affairs Committee, *Public Expenditure: Spending Plans of the FCO and the ODA, 1996–97 to 1998–99*, Volume II, [hereafter FAC, 1996, vol II] HMSO, London, 23 July 1996, pp 96, 99.
6. Labour Party, *A Fresh Start for Britain: Labour's Strategy for Britain in the Modern World*, undated [1996], p 20.
7. Speech at Bridgwater Hall, Manchester, 24 April 1997.
8. FAC, vol I, op cit, 1996, p xviii.
9. FAC, vol I, op cit, 1996, p xix.
10. FAC, *Recent Work of the Committee*, op cit, 1997, p 2.
11. Lynda Chalker in FAC, vol II, pp 119–20.
12. FAC, vol I, p xx.
13. Cited in Greg Neale, 'Short tells EU: get a grip on the aid budget', *Sunday Telegraph*, 18 May 1997.
14. Development Assistance Committee, *Development Cooperation*, 1996 Report, OECD, Paris, 1997, pp A21–A22, A35–A36.
15. There are at least half a dozen examples in parliamentary replies in *Hansard*. See, for example, 27 February 1997, Col 302 and 6 February 1997, Col 1763.
16. Dr Liam Fox, *Hansard*, House of Commons, 24 February 1997, Col 16. Emphasis added.
17. Lynda Chalker, speech to the Confederation of British Industry, 'The ODA's private sector initiative', 29 January 1997.
18. Lynda Chalker, 'Promoting the private sector', speech to the CBI, 23 January 1995.
19. *Hansard*, House of Commons, 14 December 1995, Col 751.
20. *Hansard*, House of Commons, 12 July 1996, Col 344.
21. Labour Party, p 20.
22. Paul Brown, 'Labour drops trade link in new promise on aid', *Guardian*, 24 June 1997.
23. Based on projected spending figures in Africa outlined by the Secretary of State (see previous note) and FCO, *Departmental Report 1997*, p 78.
24. ODA press release, 29 January 1997.
25. Lynda Chalker, *Hansard*, House of Lords, 14 January 1997, Col WA21.
26. *Hansard*, House of Commons, 10 March 1997, Cols 17–18.
27. *Hansard*, House of Lords, 5 November 1996, Cols WA51–2.
28. Blair, op cit.
29. Clare Short, speech at the School of Oriental and African Studies (SOAS), 28 May 1997.
30. DFID press release, 14 May 1997.
31. Labour Party, op cit, pp 19–22.
32. Clare Short, speech to the BOND General Assembly, 5 November 1996.
33. Labour Party, op cit, p 1.
34. Labour Party, op cit, pp 7, 22.

United Kingdom

35. Clare Short, speech at SOAS, op cit.
36. See, for example, Dharam Ghai and Cynthia Hewitt de Alcantara, 'Globalisation and social integration: patterns and processes', *Occasional paper no 2*, United Nations research Institute for Social Development, Geneva, July 1994.
37. Clare Short speech at SOAS, op cit.
38. Clare Short, speech to the Ethical Effect Conference, 11 March 1997.
39. Clare Short speech at SOAS, op cit.
40. Cited in *Financial Times*, 15 May 1997.
41. See Robert Chote, 'Short's diplomatic skills face Whitehall test', *Financial Times*, 6 May 1997.

United States

Carol Lancaster, InterAction

Overview

The future of US foreign aid continued to be an uncertain one during 1996. The US Congress slashed bilateral and multilateral aid programmes in 1996 by over $1000 million or over 15% from the 1995 level – one of the largest cuts ever made in US aid and one of the sharpest cuts of any programme in the federal budget. Both development assistance and food aid felt the squeeze.

In terms of its dollar and food aid expenditures in developing regions, these cuts contributed to the continuing decline in bilateral assistance to Africa by 17% (from $1200 million in fiscal year 1995 to $1000 million in 1996) and to Latin America and Asia (not including Egypt and Israel) by 9% and 7% respectively. Food aid for non-emergency purposes (Title III) dropped from $117 million in 1995 to $50 million in 1996, reflecting the declining interest in the programme on the part of farm groups as agricultural surpluses have diminished. These cuts meant that the United States fell to fourth place among those countries worldwide providing foreign aid.

Much of US bilateral aid is provided to better off countries, including Israel and countries of Eastern Europe and the former Soviet Union. The consequence of these cuts was to reduce further the proportion of aid to poorer countries, particularly in Africa. Also as a result of cuts, USAID was forced to reduce its work force (not counting foreign nationals and contractors) in 1996 by roughly 10% and has had to continue to close a number of its field missions around the world. A further factor leading to cuts in development aid is the rising cost of emergency relief, which is usually funded from the US bilateral aid budget.

Other bilateral aid programmes – the Inter-American Foundation and the African Development Foundation – had their budgets reduced by one-third between 1995 and 1996. Even the popular Peace Corps had its budget reduced by 10% during this period.

The cuts for multilateral aid agencies, including the World Bank, regional development banks and UN organisations like the United Nations Development Programme (UNDP), resulted in a build-up of arrears where the USA was unable to make its full contributions. This forced cutbacks in UNDP and elsewhere as US contributions diminished. Congressional cuts in the administration's request for the International Development Assistance (IDA) of the World Bank resulted in the USA being unable to fulfil its funding commitment to the organisation and led to other member states imposing limitations on the ability of US firms to compete for IDA contracts.

Foreign aid in 1997

For the fiscal year 1997, the administration sent a budget to Congress for foreign aid (including both bilateral and multilateral aid) that amounted to $12,800 million, slightly more than Congress agreed to for 1996. The Congress finally approved a budget of $12,300 million. The level of bilateral aid remained virtually the same in 1997 as in 1996 (except for a cut in the family planning programme, cushioned temporarily by unspent past obligations in the pipeline). The administration increased its bilateral aid to Asia and Latin America by 7% and 6% respectively over the 1995 level, and reduced the level to Africa by a further 5%.

In 1996, the Congress provided $700 million for the International Development Association of the World Bank – $234 million less than the administration requested – and it provided no funds at all for the African Development Bank and Fund (the AfDB soft loan window), despite administration requests for a total of $59 million for them. The budget for US foreign aid for 1997 thus maintains the drastic cuts, especially in development aid, made in 1996.

The relatively few cuts in aid in 1997 compared with the cuts of the previous year appeared to reflect several factors: a vigorous educational and advocacy campaign, organised by InterAction, on the part of non-governmental organisations on the

The **Reality** of Aid 1997/8

United States

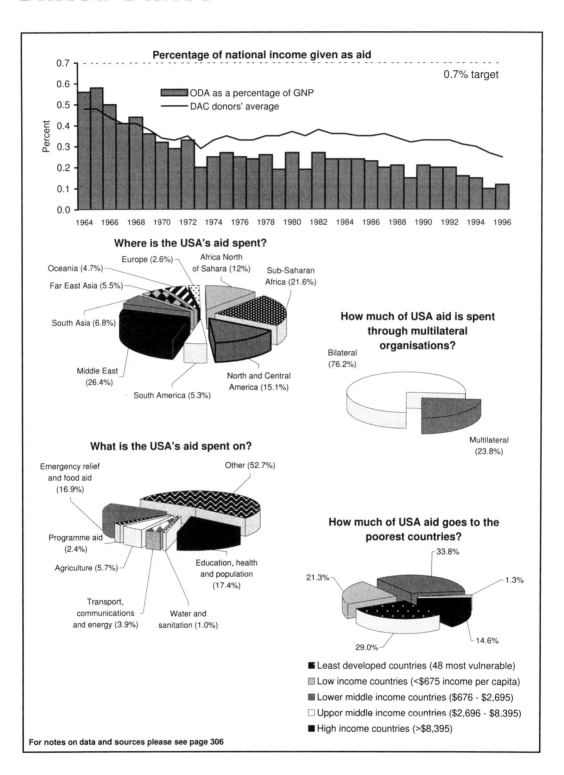

For notes on data and sources please see page 306

The **Reality** of Aid 1997/8

United States

USA aid at a glance

How much aid does the USA give?

The USA gave	US$ 9058m in 1996
that was	0.12% of GNP
and	0.65% of public administration
which meant	US$ 34 per capita for 1996

Is it going up or down?

In 1996 USA aid	rose by $1691m, up 20.6% in real terms over 1995
The USA was	more generous in 1996, rising from 0.10% to 0.12%
The outlook is	that aid as a proportion of GNP will decline

ODA rose in 1996 due to the delay in disbursing 1995 assistance to Israel until 1996. The double disbursement in 1996 gave the appearance of an increase. The level remained the same when this was not factored in.

How does the USA compare with the other 21 donors?

The USA ranks	second out of 21 for its volume of aid
It is	bottom in the generosity league (21 out of 21)
It gives	a lower proportion of its aid (50.3%) to Low Income Countries than 15 other donors
Private Flows	amounted to $36,489m, five times ODA
Total Flows	to developing countries were 0.66% of GNP and rank 11 out of 21 in the DAC

How much does the USA spend on basic health and basic education?

The USA	has not yet reported to the DAC on its basic health and basic education spending

How important are commercial interests in aid?

The USA required	29% of its ODA to be used to purchase American goods and services the last time it reported in

What do the public think about aid?

> 45% of the US public were supportive of foreign aid in 1995. A 1996 poll found that when they were told how much aid the USA gives, only 10% of respondents thought it was too much.

size of foreign aid as a proportion of the US budget (the 'Just 1%' campaign of 1995 and 1996); an effort during the latter half of 1996 on the part of the Council on Foreign Relations, the Brookings Institute and other institutes on the importance of adequate resources to support US foreign policy; and a measure of learning on the part of legislators about foreign aid and its contribution to US foreign policy and US leadership in the world.

Also important has been the succession of UN conferences – on environment, population, social development, women, shelter and food – that have energised NGOs in the United States and abroad on these issues and encouraged their activism.

The sharp Congressional cuts have provoked greater advocacy – for example, the creation of a coalition of 130 businesses and NGOs to support funding for the international affairs budget (including foreign economic aid, military assistance, investment and export promotion programmes, and the costs of diplomacy) and the creation of a 'United Nations Caucus' of NGOs to lobby in support of UN development programmes. The growth and diversity of voices (including business) in support of foreign assistance and continuing US engagement in the world has caught the attention of Congress and the administration.

NGO criticisms of the World Bank in particular were muted somewhat by the arrival of a new president – James Wolfensohn – who has reached out to non-governmental organisations for their input regarding World Bank activities and has committed the World Bank to greater participation in its project and policy development. In partnership with Southern NGOs, which have repeatedly stated the need to maintain IDA funding, NGOs are forcefully advocating full funding of IDA and payment of arrears with the US Congress while continuing to work for World Bank reform.

The continuing efforts on the part of Congress to balance the federal budget and the President's commitment to the same goal by the year 2002 suggest that significantly increased spending for foreign aid is unlikely in the near future. The White House itself has projected only minimal increases in foreign aid to the year 2002 (suggesting that, barring unexpected events, the Administration will not ask Congress for significantly increased aid monies during this time).

Another foreign aid issue during 1996 and 1997 involved the continued existence of USAID as a semi-independent agency. There were continuing efforts from powerful members of Congress (in particular, Senator Jesse Helms, the chair of the Senate Foreign Relations Committee) to merge USAID into the Department of State.

After a brief study of the issue, the administration decided in March 1997 not to merge the two agencies, but to have the administrator of USAID report exclusively to the Secretary of State (rather than to both the Secretary of State and the President) and to combine the press and some of the administrative activities of the two agencies. While the semi-independence of USAID was maintained by this decision, the details of the new relationship between the two agencies were still to be worked out at the time of writing. Meanwhile, the Senate proceeded to pass legislation transferring USAID's budget to the Department of State – in effect, a *de facto* merger of a key instrument of USAID's policies and programmes. It is, as yet, unclear whether the Senate's views will prevail and be signed into law by the President.

The broader aid debate

Foreign aid has long been a relatively controversial programme in the United States, with vocal critics and equally vocal proponents. Over the last year, however, the critics have been joined by supporters of foreign aid – for example, the Overseas Development Council – in asking to what extent US foreign aid is relevant to the post-Cold War world. The answers suggested by both critics and supporters of foreign aid are that existing programmes need to be refocused and reorganised if they are to be relevant to the new world in which we live. However, there is little agreement thus far on how aid should be refocused.

Professor Paul Kennedy of Yale University has argued that US foreign aid ought to be concentrated in 'pivotal states' – large countries (like Nigeria, Algeria or Brazil) whose economic success or failure could have major repercussions in neighbouring states or beyond. Allocation on the basis of this approach would be likely to lead to a substantial reduction or elimination of US aid to smaller states worldwide.

Professor Vernon Ruttan, in his extensive study of United States development assistance policy, argued that US bilateral aid should be managed by two government foundations – one to channel funds for humanitarian activities abroad through NGOs and another to finance scientific and technological activities of benefit to developing countries.

A third essay by the Overseas Development

United States

Council argued that US bilateral aid should be 'mainstreamed' in US foreign policy by transferring policy responsibilities and some funds for programming to the Department of State. Remaining programme funds should be managed by a separate agency, working to a large extent with NGOs in developing countries. InterAction, in its policy paper, 'American Values – National Interests', urged that development aid be focused on poverty reduction and people-centred development, with levels of aid being increased for these purposes.

Behind this debate are at least three paradigms of development that proponents of differing policy recommendations appear to hold. Among many NGOs there is, typically, a high priority put on using aid to alleviate poverty, usually through grassroots interventions. Another priority favoured by many economists and business-oriented groups emphasises the importance of appropriate economic policies to spur investment and trade and thus support the integration of developing country economies into the global economy. A third approach – popular among a number of NGOs and portions of the foreign policy establishment, emphasises the urgency of transnational problems like environmental deterioration, emerging diseases or food security and supports aid to address these issues.

As far as the US public is concerned, a recent poll by the University of Maryland found that the general public remains supportive of US engagement in the world, although it was increasingly sceptical of the US government's ability to address problems effectively, including providing foreign aid abroad. The debate on the future of US foreign aid appears likely to continue until some measure of consensus is reached on mission and organisational issues.

Aid effectiveness

Part of the debate on foreign aid involves the effectiveness of aid in promoting development abroad. A study by David Dollar and Craig Burnside for the World Bank found that foreign aid had a strong impact on growth and poverty reduction in poor countries that put good economic policies into place – but in a poor policy environment, aid had little impact on growth or infant mortality.

In fact, a number of major aid successes have been well documented. For example, there is extensive evidence that aid for family planning has played an important role in reducing the fertility rate in Kenya and elsewhere. Polio has been eradicated from the western hemisphere with the support of US aid funding. Childhood inoculations and oral rehydration therapy, both funded with foreign aid, have contributed to the dramatic decrease in childhood mortality in many countries in the world. The debate on aid effectiveness has suffered from a lack of well-documented successes even though most aid practitioners can cite numerous cases from their own experiences.

New approaches in development cooperation

At the Social Summit in Copenhagen in 1995, Vice President Gore announced that USAID would implement a New Partnerships Initiative (NPI). The Initiative included a commitment on USAID's part to raise the proportion of its work undertaken in conjunction with NGOs to 40% within five years and to expand its work to strengthen civil society, business enterprises and local governments in developing countries.[1] By 1997, there was concern among US NGOs, however, that the innovative ideas in NPI had yet to be reflected adequately in USAID programmes or in follow-up efforts to increase the work done in partnership with NGOs.

Another area where there were signs of increasing interest on the part both of the Congress and the administration involved development in Africa. Even though US aid to the countries of sub-Saharan Africa has been reduced in recent years, from $1300 million in 1996 (including food aid) to just over $1000 million in 1997, there was a proposal by several members of Congress to undertake a new initiative to promote trade and investment in Africa.

The African Growth and Opportunity Act, introduced into the House of Representatives in April 1997, would create a high level USA–Africa Trade and Economic Cooperation Forum, which would meet periodically to discuss trade and investment issues, a US–African free trade area and the creation of two equity funds (with private capital and US government guaranteed debt), one to finance equity investments and one to finance infrastructure in Africa. This initiative has been welcomed by many in Washington and by official Africans and may, if enacted, provide additional incentives for growth-enhancing policies in Africa. But it does not target the poorest people in African societies.

United States

The meeting of the Group of Seven major industrial countries in France in 1996 and Denver in June 1997 had on the agenda problems of African development. The US administration proposed its own trade and investment initiative for the region, very similar to those in the legislation introduced into the US House of Representatives. In addition, Mrs Clinton made a two-week trip showcasing US development activities in Africa in March 1997. Finally, the administration proposed to Congress in 1997 funding for a $30 million African food security initiative, part of a broader effort to allocate more resources to agriculture after several years of decline. (USAID also increased its contributions to the Consultative Group on International Agricultural Research in 1997 after cuts in funding over previous years. However, due to budgetary constraints, the Agency did not continue its support for the International Fund for Agricultural Development.)

One of the principal initiatives of the Clinton administration involving foreign aid has been pressure for management reforms at USAID. For several years, the Agency has been engaged in 're-engineering' – reforms intended to make its operations more efficient, collaborative, participatory (including enhancing the participation of its 'customers' in developing countries) and more 'results oriented'.

There have been changes in procurement processes aimed at streamlining procurement and shortening the time it takes to negotiate contracts and grants. There has been a greater emphasis placed on teamwork within USAID in designing and managing projects and programmes. There have been efforts to empower USAID's managers to make programming decisions. An Agency-wide computer management system has been developed to link all USAID's activities into a single system. These changes are still in the process of being implemented and perfected and it is as yet too soon to judge whether they will bring the benefits promised.

A key part of the administrative reforms in USAID and one that is already being replicated in other aid agencies, involves an increased emphasis on the performance of aid-financed activities – often termed a 'results orientation'. In 1993, the US Congress passed the Government Performance and Results Act, requiring all US government agencies to establish mission statements, strategic plans and performance measures and to begin reporting to Congress by the year 2000 on agency performance. USAID has produced a draft mission statement and strategic plan with four broad objectives: promoting US economic prosperity; enhancing US security; protecting the US against global dangers (for example, emerging diseases, air and water pollution, high rates of population growth in the developing world); and preventing and alleviating crises. The Agency's goals include achieving broad-based economic growth, building sustainable democracies, stabilizing world population and protecting health; managing the environment in a sustainable manner; and reducing suffering. The Agency has begun to identify desired performance indicators and 'objective, quantifiable and measurable' annual results of its activities aimed at achieving its goals.

The effort to focus on the results (rather than the expenditures) of aid activities is generally regarded as a useful change. However, there was some concern on the part of NGOs that too rigid an application of 'results' criteria could stifle the experimentation essential to achieving development success, and could distort activities toward those that could be easily measured objectively. It could impart a short-run mentality to aid programmers when real results from foreign aid investments often do not appear for years or even decades.

There were a number of smaller initiatives announced by USAID during 1996 and early 1997. One was the creation of an office of 'Emerging Markets' to support USAID's efforts in such countries as they integrated more fully into the world market. Another involved the $30 million 'Food Security' initiative for Africa mentioned earlier. It was unclear how much funding would actually be involved in these new initiatives, especially given continuing budgetary constraints. Finally, USAID committed itself to support the goals of the 'Strategies for the 21st Century' targets for poverty reduction, social development and environmental conservation to be met by 2015.

Scenarios for the future

It is clear that US foreign aid is in a period of transition. The amount of funding for foreign aid for development has been cut over the past several years and those cuts have forced shrinkage in the programmes, the staff and the field presence of USAID. At the same time, the voices in favour of a fundamental reorganisation of USAID have grown in number. Meanwhile, the Agency has been implementing wide-ranging management reforms that are still in progress, and it has announced various new policy and programme initiatives. These disparate trends do not make it easy to predict the future of US aid. What seems clear is that aid levels will not increase substantially and may be cut further by the US Congress.

Management reforms will continue to be implemented but their cost, speed of implementation and impact on productivity in the short run could become controversial. It appears likely that an emphasis on working with NGOs will continue and expand. Finally, the issue of merging USAID into the Department of State may be put aside, at least temporarily. But until there is a stronger bipartisan support for the goal of supporting development abroad, the issues that have arisen in the past are likely to resurface in the future.

Note

1. The New Partnerships Initiative (NPI) was spelled out in detail in a report entitled *NPI Resource Guide*, published in 1997.

European Union[1]

Mirjam van Reisen, Eurostep

The future of European Community development cooperation

The Development Programme of the European Community has began to focus on the question of how it may develop after the year 2000. The outcome will depend particularly on two processes: the expiry of the Edinburgh principles on the EC budget (1999) and the revision of the Lomé Convention (February 2000). In Europe, the decisions determining the outcome of these processes will be taken by the European Council, which represents the Member States. This chapter therefore focuses on the relationship between the Member States and the European Community Development Programme. Special attention will be given to financial and policy aspects.

Revision of the Lomé Convention in 2000

In the European Economic Community Treaty of 1957, provisions were made for the association of non-European countries and territories with which EEC Member States have special relations. This condition originated with a French desire to allow access for its colonies and overseas territories to the European market. In 1963, the Yaoundé I Convention was signed between six European Member States and 18 associated countries. In 1975, when the UK became a member of the EEC, the number of associated countries increased to 46, (it is now 71) and the first convention (Lomé I) was signed.[2] The cooperation with these countries was a comprehensive package that encompassed both aid and trade, and obliged the European partners to open up their markets for African, Caribbean and Pacific (ACP) country products.[3] In 1998, official negotiations will start on the future of the Lomé Convention. Prior to these, the European Commission presented a discussion document, a Green Paper on future relations between the EU and the ACP.

Gaps in the Green Paper on relations between the EU and ACP countries

The objective of the Green Paper[4] was to identify areas in the Treaty that might need to be changed and to offer proposals for consideration. The main areas identified are:

- the composition of the ACP group.
- cooperation in the area of trade;
- aid to social sectors;
- cooperation in the area of financial assistance; and
- direct assistance to private sector and to non-governmental organisations.

Unfortunately, there are some serious omissions in the Commission's analysis of how future ACP–EU relations might be improved. In general, it has not made an attempt to analyse the problems underlying the poor development performance of ACP countries.[5]

Trade The Commission's most vital argument is that the EU must harmonise its trade provisions with the rules of the World Trade Organisation (WTO). The ACP group contains a large number of LLDCs but not all ACP countries are LLDCs. There are also some LLDCs outside the ACP group. The question is whether the Lomé trade preferences should be phased out for the ACP non-LLDC countries and granted to non-ACP LLDCs. This could potentially call into question, the composition of the ACP Group.

However, many non-LLDC ACP countries are vulnerable small island or land-locked economies and dependent upon trade preferences. For instance, in the vulnerable island states of the Caribbean, production of bananas generally takes place on small farms, many of which are on

Table 9 Timetable to renegotiate EU-ACP relations

Period	Commission (CEC)	EU Member States	ACP States
Until September 1997	Consultation on the Green Paper of the Commission	Individual reflections and in consultation with other Member States on shape, form, and content of a future agreement	Consideration of general views on the future of the Lomé Convention in ACP Committee of Ambassadors (Brussels) and national/regional dialogue in ACP states
29/30 September 1997	Meeting on reports from Member States consultations in Brussels		ACP draft preliminary position on the future of Lomé
September–October 1997	DG VIII drafts EU negotiating mandate and communication on political options		
27–30 October		ACP-EU Joint Assembly in Togo	
November 1997	DGVIII publishes communication on political options		(6–7 November) ACP Council of Ministers and Heads of State Summit in Gabon map out political future of ACP/EU relations; relations ACP/third parties; ACP structure
December 1997	DGVIII negotiates draft mandate within the Commission		ACP Council considers proposals for ACP negotiating mandate
January 1998	Commission presents draft EU negotiating mandate to the Member States		ACP negotiate to establish their formal negotiating mandate
January–May 1998	EU Member States negotiate to establish formal negotiating mandate		(4–6 May) ACP Council of Ministers meets in Barbados to approve political guidelines and institutional arrangements for negotiation of successor agreement
		ACP–EU Joint Assembly	
May–September 1998	EU finalises negotiating mandate		Committee of Ambassadors prepares detailed negotiating briefs; appointment of ACP ministerial and ambassadorial spokespeople
September 1998	EU present their proposals for a future agreement to the ACP		ACP present their proposals for a future agreement to the EU
		ACP–EU Joint Assembly	
September 1998–February 2000	Negotiations take place between the EU and the ACP		
28 February 2000	Lomé IV Convention expires. For any new agreement to be implemented by 1 March 2000, there needs to be an agreement by this date		

Source: Original table from Eurostep 1997a, adapted MvR.

European Union

steep and difficult terrain. These small farmers cannot compete with multinational companies from Latin American countries. If, for instance, banana preferences for the small islands in the Caribbean were to be ruled out by the WTO it would cause mass poverty, social unrest and instability in the region.[6]

The EU has started to bring the General System of Preferences (GSP) to LLDCs outside the ACP up to the same terms as the Lomé Preferences. There are only nine LLDCs outside the ACP. The EU has cooperation agreements with most of them. Within the GSP special benefits for LLDCs have also been granted to the ANDEAN countries and to Central American countries for agricultural products. The GSP, therefore, just like the Lomé Convention, gives special benefits to LLDCs and non LLDCs and is, therefore, potentially vulnerable to the same attack of 'discrimination' as Lomé.

The question is, therefore, not so much whether other LLDCs, outside Lomé, are discriminated against, because they are not. The real question is whether the countries in the ACP, not classified as least developed, should receive these preferences.

The suggestion in the Green Paper of a reciprocal trade arrangement between the EU and the non LLDC–ACP countries does not recognise that the ACP economies are much weaker than those of the EU. It is feasible that the current arrangement can gain a WTO waiver. The EU, as the largest trading block, should, therefore do all it can within its considerable powers to ensure that important industries in the ACP continue to enjoy preferential treatment.[7]

The EU could do much more than it presently does to assist ACP countries more effectively. The Commission has recognised that a precondition for the success of any trade policy will be improvements in the internal production capacity of the Least Developed Countries. However, the Commission gives no market access, or gives only limited access, to a number of important products where ACP countries could easily increase their capacity because they are more suitable for production in ACP countries. These products include rice, sugar, manioc, beef and veal as well as bananas on a large scale. These are classified as sensitive products and they are not liberalised so as to protect EU producers. In addition, subsidised exports from the EU under the Common Agricultural Policy (CAP) distort markets in ACP countries. Local producers cannot compete against the low-priced imports from the EU.

Unfortunately, the dilemma of reconciling EU and ACP trade interests is not addressed in the analysis offered in the Green Paper.

Financial aid and debt relief The Commission emphasises efficient trade and investment policies as determinant factors in achieving high rates of exports and economic growth. However, as long as the fiscal situation of the Highly Indebted Poor Countries and other vulnerable countries is not improved it will not be possible for them to attract foreign investment, diversify production and reduce their reliance on exports of primary products. These problems require a sustainable comprehensive solution to the debt problem, which is not substantially addressed in the Green Paper.

The Commission proposes financial cooperation and increasing investment allocated to social sectors as the means to contribute to a more sustainable, longer-term development. However, financial support to social sectors does not necessarily contribute to increased expenditure in these areas. It presupposes reliable and sound governance both from the donors (so that recipient governments can plan the budget properly) and the recipient countries (to implement the budget according to stated intentions). The Green Paper does not address how this might be achieved.

Private sector and non-governmental organisations clearly have very different roles. The Green Paper does not distinguish well between them and does not indicate by which mechanisms they might be incorporated in a new Convention.

Member States differ on the future of Lomé

Member States have given preliminary reactions to the Green Paper. To show some of the fundamental differences in approaches of the Member States, the position of a few countries will be highlighted.

France and Portugal favour a position they characterise as an 'ameliorated status quo'. It advocates that the basic principles, such as the connection between aid and trade, as well as the partnership approach through political dialogue should be maintained, while conditionality should be avoided.[8]

Spain stresses that its revenues from Lomé Conventions so far have been unsatisfactory, and have not matched returns to other Member States. Spain will, therefore, propose that the process of programming the EDF and the tendering of

European Union

Table 10 Lomé preferences versus the Generalised System of Preferences

The European Scheme of Generalised Preferences defines a list of 50 least-developed countries[9] (LLDCs) that benefit from extended tariff preferences for industrial and agricultural products, beyond the General System of Preferences. These LLDCs benefit either from the Lomé Trade Regime, or from the extended GSP. The two regimes compare as follows:

Lomé Trade Regime	GSP Trade Regime
Is granted to ACP countries, includes 41 LLDCs and 29 other developing countries, including vulnerable economies such as small island states and land-locked countries. Does not include graduation.	Is granted to developing countries, includes 9 LLDCs[10] and a large number of other developing countries. Includes graduation on the basis of market share, which can affect LLDCs and other very poor states.[11]
The non-discrimination clause ensures that the preferences also apply to the other ACP countries.	Recently some distinction is made between GSP for LLDCs and non LLDCs: LLDCs have a suspension from Common Customs Tariff duties and a wider coverage of agricultural products. Special LLDC benefits are also granted to non LLDCs in the ANDEAN Community and to some Central American countries for agricultural products.[12]
Rules of origin make cumulation of the input into a products value permissable where this originates in all ACP countries and the EU. Specific rules are defined for each product or group of products.	Rule of origin permit input of a product in individual countries with further input from the EU. Some regional cumulation is allowed for the members of ASEAN, the Central American Common Market (CACM) and the Andean Community. Specific rules are defined for each product or groups of products.
Industrial products can enter without restrictions.	Gives duty free access for manufactured exports listed. Also duty free treatment in clothing and textile sector.
Tariffs on many agricultural products are reduced, or are set up for certain quantities (quotas). Quotas in 'sensitive' areas are arranged in special protocols.	Tariffs on a group of agricultural products are reduced.
The EU does not want an extension of unlimited free access in some products, it has defined as 'sensitive' products such as: rice, bananas, sugar, manioc and bovine meat (beef and veal). The EU believes that developing countries could rapidly increase exports of these products if liberalisation took place. The EU believes it should protect its own producers against competition over these products. The EU believes it can exclude a short list of products from any liberalisation package.	
Lomé trade preferences will be reviewed under the new treaty, to be negotiated in 2000. A waiver for renewed Lomé trade revisions could be obtained as there is a provision in WTO rules for non-reciprocal trade arrangements; alternatively an extension of the WTO's provisions governing special and differential treatment to cover a new agreement with the ACP could be obtained.	GSP treaties have recently been concluded with all non ACP LLDCs, with the exception of Burma. The current GSP scheme for industrial products was introduced for a four year period in January 1995, valid till 31 December 1998. The scheme for agricultural products came into force on 1 July 1996, but was only applicable on 1 January 1997 and will be valid until 30 June 1999.

European Union

contracts should be more transparent. Spain would also like the ACP countries extended with more Spanish speaking developing countries, such as Cuba, and other countries in the Caribbean, Central America and Peru, Bolivia and Ecuador.[13]

The *Nordic countries* are arguing that poverty eradication should become a strong focus of the Lomé Convention, and that other LLDCs countries outside the ACP, should be included into the ACP group.[14]

Germany emphasises the trade element of the negotiations and opts for regional liberalisation in order to move towards free trade regions. Globalisation is regarded as essential and strong privileges for ACP countries should be ended. Trade preferences should be made compatible with the WTO agreement, while the ACP's export capacity should be strengthened.[15]

Italy also has a strong focus on trade and economic cooperation, and on creating a stronger capacity for increasing capacity, with emphasis on problems at the supply side. Italy would like to see increased investment in the private sector. It advocates greater WTO compatibility in a regional approach, and cautions that specific attention to the most sensitive Mediterranean agricultural products should be given.

This brief overview illustrates that some Member States' positions are predetermined by their particular interests. This is regrettable, because the debate should aim to identify how ACP countries can best be assisted to eradicate poverty.

Composition of the ACP group

An important question is the composition of the ACP group, and particularly whether the ACP should include other poorer countries and exclude countries that are doing better. Some argue that this would help to ensure a poverty focus in the Convention. However, there are problems with this position:

- all the development programmes of the EU should have a poverty focus;
- the Lomé Convention is unique in its integration of policy areas like aid and trade. This feature should be included in other cooperation agreements as well, rather than limited to the poorest countries;

for trade to be an effective aid instrument, regional linkages are important and it would be counterproductive if some countries in certain regions were excluded from trade preferences;
- non-ACP LLDCs, or the Latin American countries, have not expressed the wish to become part of the ACP group; and
- it is properly a matter for the ACP itself to decide on the composition of its grouping. The ACP Group has taken the position that it does not want a fundamental change of the composition of the ACP.[16]

There are indications that most EU member states are beginning to accept that composition of the ACP group *per se* is not up for negotiation.

Expiry of the Edinburgh Agreement in 1999

While the Lomé Convention encompasses the original cooperation between the EC and ACP countries, assistance to other regions has increased in the past decades. The aid to these other regions in Latin America, Asia, the Mediterranean, Central and Eastern Europe, and to humanitarian assistance is funded from the general EC budget.

The budget process for the calendar year 1993 manifested great differences of opinion between the European Council and Parliament. Among other things, the Council could not agree on the provision of further funding for the former Soviet Union, Central and Eastern Europe, humanitarian aid and structural funds. Following decisions adopted by the Edinburgh Summit in December 1992, a compromise allowed an increase of funding to Latin America, Asia and the Mediterranean countries.[17] In addition, at the Summit in Cannes in 1995, the European Council agreed specific appropriations for financial cooperation with the Mediterranean and Central and Eastern Europe for the period 1995–9. These agreements will expire in 1999. The agreed figures represent ceilings of expenditure, and they are not necessarily expenditure targets, but they give a clear indication of the budgetary space agreed to by the Commission and the Member States for the period 1993–9.

European Union

The illusion of growth in disbursements from the European Community budget

Sustained underspending of EU ODA

The budgets for EC ODA have grown consistently. However, if actual disbursements are examined it appears that disbursements of EC ODA have hardly increased.

The development budget of the EC consists of an EDF part (which finances the cooperation under Lomé), and the budget lines (which are part of the regular EC budget for cooperation with other regions).

Conclusions from Table 11 are striking. First, the utilisation of the EDF is relatively positive, compared with the utilisation of the budget lines. Second, the highest under utilisation took place in 1996, with 4600 million ECU. This is partly the result of programming for National Indicative Programmes, which took place in 1996, and is also explained by the slow ratification of the EDF by the Member States. Finally, assuming that the trends of the first half of the 1990s continue, total unspent ODA in the period 1993 to 1999 would be 25,000 million ECU.

Disbursements and commitments under the EDF

The EDF represents approximately one-third of the total EC ODA budget (but about half of disbursements). It is a separate fund arranged in a separate intergovernmental agreement. The funds finance the implementation of the successive Lomé Agreements. The contributions of the Member States are divided according to a formula. They do not pay their contributions to the EDF at once. Each year an estimate is made predicting how much the Commission will need to disburse for the EDF for that year. Four times a year the Member States are requested to pay their share of the contribution to the EDF.

Disbursement of the EDF is very low. On average it takes 15 years for each fund to be utilised, while the fund is associated with treaties that cover only five-year periods. The eighth EDF,

Table 11 Financial perspectives until 1999 of external action (EC budget) and estimates of appropriations for the European Development Fund (in million ECUs)

Year	Revised financial perspectives for external action in budget lines (commitment appropriations, not actual disbursements)	Actual disbursements, budget lines and projections (1996–9)	Difference between commitment appropriations and actual disbursements	Official EDF allocation (7 and 8) for the respective periods	Annual contribution to the EDF, actual until 1997, forecasted until 1999	Difference between official EDF allocations and annnual contributions	Total unspent ODA
1993	4.120	2.118	2.002	2.300	1.610	0.690	2.692
1994	4.311	2.182	2.129	2.300	1.800	0.500	2.629
1995	4.895	2.352	2.543	2.300	1.650	0.650	3.193
1996	5.264	2.632	2.632	2.900	0.950	1.950	4.582
1997	5.622	2.811	2.811	2.900	1.560	1.340	4.151
1998	6.201	3.101	3.101	2.900	2.150	0.750	3.851
1999	6.703	3.351	3.351	2.900	2.150	0.750	4.101
Total							25.199

Source: European Commission, Preliminary Draft General Budget of the European Communities for the Financial Year 1998, SEC(97)600, May 1997: 5. Projections budget lines based on figures for past years, demonstrating that about half of the budget appropriations are used. Projections for EDF come from the Commission, on the basis of which the Member States can plan their budgets.

European Union

which financially supports the Lomé IV bis Treaty (1995–2000) was agreed at ECU 14,625,000 million in June 1995. However, the Member States' financial contributions will not be called until the seventh EDF Fund is exhausted. At present, disbursement will not be before the year 2002, long after the expiry of the Lomé IV Treaty.[18]

Disbursements and commitments under the budget Equally, actual disbursements of the budget lines are far behind the commitments. The EC budget works with two budgets, one for commitment appropriations and one for payment appropriations. Commitments are the real commitments made in a certain year, while disbursements concern the real payments implemented in a year. For the following reasons, it is more difficult to come to firm conclusions in relation to the gap between financial perspectives for the budget and actual disbursements:

- it is normal that the rate of actual commitments and payments are less than the appropriations authorised by the budget;[19] and
- for external action as a whole, the normal expenditure pattern is spread over several years. For a given commitment, about 25% is paid in the same year, 25% in the next year, 15% in the following year, and so forth. This means that as long as commitment appropriations are growing over a period, the amount of commitments will always be higher than payment needs. The higher the rate of growth of commitments, the larger the gap will be. This should be taken into account in this period where the budget of commitment appropriations grew rapidly.

Until 1997 the financial perspective and the budget for commitment appropriations were basically the same. In 1998, based on the preliminary draft budget presented by the Commission, the budget was 577 million ECU lower than the financial perspective.

Table 12 demonstrates also that the implementation rate of payments is much lower than the financial perspectives or the budget of commitment appropriations. In 1995 and 1996, the implementation rate of payments was only 80% and 83%, creating a gap of respectively ECU 786 million and ECU 745 million.

Financial profiles 1991–5 in million ECU, for EC budget, EDF, EIB–ODA and other public sector contributions

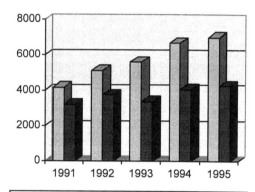

Source: Commission, May 1997, unpublished.

For almost all budget lines, the differences are very large between commitment appropriations allocated in the budget and actual disbursements, including the budget line for NGOs.

- Commitment appropriations (the amount allocated in the budget) for the programme for cooperation with Asia and Latin America (ALA) for 1995 were ECU 540 million; the actual disbursements were ECU 436 million;
- commitment appropriations for cooperation with the Mediterranean basin were ECU 534 million in 1995, while the actual disbursements were only ECU 229 million; and
- while the total commitment appropriations for budget lines on external actions was ECU 5012 million in 1995, the actual commitments were ECU 3677 million and the actual disbursements were only ECU 2352 million.

The following figures will show the differences in actual commitments and disbursements of the various budget lines. This excludes EDF and EIB funds.

The **Reality** of Aid 1997/8

European Union

Table 12 General budget: expenditure under the title of external actions in million ECUs, current prices (except 1999, prices 1998)

	Ceilings financial perspectives (CA)		Budget (CA)		Implementation (CE) Total	Budget (PA) Total	Implementation (PA) Total
		Reserve		Reserve			
1993	4120	209	4115	209	4276	2998	2580
1994	4311	212	4297	212	4483	3399	3061
1995	4895	323	4873	323	5061	4198	3412
1996	5264	326	5261	326	5524	4618	3873
1997	5622	329	5601	329	–	4827	–
1998	6201	338	5624	338	–	4886	–
1999 (1998 prices)	6703	338	–	–	–	–	–

Note: CA = commitment appropriations; PA = payment appropriations; and CE = effective utilisation.

Financial profiles from 1992 to 1995 in million ECU, for cooperation with Asian and Latin American countries

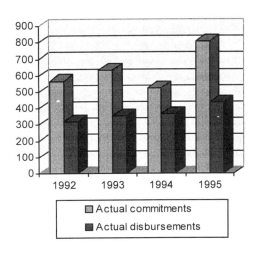

■ Actual commitments
■ Actual disbursements

Source: Commission, May 1997, unpublished.

Box 17 Conclusions of the Evaluation of the Med Programme by the Court of Auditors[20]

The fast growth of the Med programmes with insufficient human resources has led to a deficient implementation:

- basic administrative procedures of the Commission designed to avoid irregular situations failed;
- structure and procedures to oversee and monitor the programmes were inadequate and insufficient;
- serious confusion of interest developed in the implementation of the programmes and the Commission failed to put an end to them;
- excessive recourse was taken to private-treaty contracts without proper tendering;
- at all levels of the financial management there are serious shortcoming and irregularities; and
- the impact of the Med programmes, therefore, remain to be proven.

European Union

Financial profiles from 1992 to 1995 in MECU, for Cooperation with Countries of the Mediterranean basin (Med) in million ECU

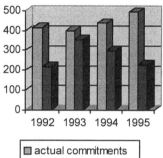

■ actual commitments
■ actual disbursements

Source: Commission, May 1997, unpublished.

Human resource constraints

In *Reality of Aid 1996*, the constraints on the implementation capacity of the Commission were highlighted. In 1997 the Court of Auditors noted severe weaknesses in the management of the programmes to all regions, and noted that 45% or more of commitments were made in December in most budget lines as a result of the working practices of the Commission.[21] Some 73% of the budget for Asia and Latin America was committed in December; more than 45% of the Mediterranean budget along with high commitments for food aid and humanitarian aid. Part of the problem is that the growth in the scope and financial resource allocations to programmes has not been matched by an adequate increase of human resources. For 1998, some extra capacity is envisaged for the departments responsible for managing PHARE, TACIS, MEDA and ECHO. These will be made available by redeployment of existing staff from within the Commission. DG VIII, the Directorate General for Development with ACP countries is among the departments that are losing staff. Yet DG VIII has a lower staff/expenditure ratio than any of the member states while it has a much broader geographical spread.

Consequently, no progress has been made to resolve constraints in specialised staff expertise on poverty, gender, population, environment, economy, participatory development and social policies in this department – constraints that have been identified by, among others, the Organisation for Economic Cooperation and Development (OECD), the European Parliament and the European Court of Auditors. This contradicts objectives expressed in resolutions adopted by the Council to increase capacity, particularly in the areas of gender, participatory development, social sectors and poverty eradication.

Table 13 EU Member State aid agencies and European Commission Staff 1991–4

Donor	Dk	Fr	Gmy	Nlds	UK	EC
HQ	5.5	3	4.2	2.7	3.1	2.1

Note: Dk = Denmark; Fr = France; Gmy = Germany; Nlds = The Netherlands; EC = EC DG VIII; HQ = HQ staff per $10 million expenditure
Source: A Cox et al, *How European Aid Works: A Comparison of Management Systems and Effectiveness*, ODI, 1997

The inadequate rate of disbursement of the EDF and the budget for external action is caused by:

• inadequate levels of staff in the European Commission as a result of staff ceilings imposed by the Member States;
• insufficient expertise in key areas of development policy in the Commission and delegations;
• bureaucratic procedures of the Commission that slow down the implementation process; and
• individual institutional capacities in ACP and other developing countries.

The 1998 budget

In May 1997 the European Commission proposed its preliminary draft general budget for the financial year 1998. This budget is based on the Financial Perspectives that had been agreed in Edinburgh in 1992. The 1998 budget is characterised by a stringent approach, intended to match the efforts of Member States to fulfill criteria of European Monetary Union.[22] The lowest growth (0.5%) has been in the agricultural budget (which is itself half the EU total budget) and in the budget lines for external actions. This means that the ceilings set by the *Financial Perspectives* have not been utilised. Only the appropriations needed to comply with the financial programming at the Cannes Summit (June 1995) for aid to Central and Eastern Europe and the Mediterranean have been met. Increases were also proposed for humanitarian and emergency assistance, programmes in the Commonwealth of Independent States and Mongolia and for the reconstruction of the former Yugoslavia.

Budget 1997, and preliminary draft budget 1998 in million ECUs (commitment appropriations)

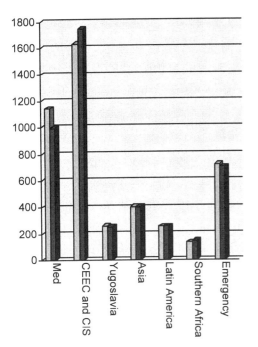

Consequently, cuts have been proposed in the budget lines for Asia and Latin America, as well as for southern Africa, even though these absorb relatively small amounts of resources. Cuts have also been proposed for, among others, the NGO budget line, decentralised cooperation and 'cooperation measures which include tropical forests'. The modest five million ECU budget line for more equitable gender relations was not cut, but neither was it increased.

The priorities expressed through these budget proposals do not reflect any sense of poverty as a main focus for external action. The Mediterranean programme and the PHARE and TACIS programmes are all at least twice as large as the programmes for Asia and Latin America. Moreover, the budget proposals do not take into consideration the severe constraints that have surfaced in the implementation of these large new programmes.

The growth of the Mediterranean programme is most ironic. As the figure on financial profiles for cooperation with Asian and Latin American countries shows, in 1994 and 1995 the actual expenditure on the MEDA programme has decreased, despite the increase in allocations for this budget line. This indicates that the budget allocations are entirely driven by ulterior political motives. The European Parliament has subsequently decided to submit the three major programmes, PHARE, TACIS and MEDA to an interim evaluation in 1997.

Equally, the humanitarian and emergency programme is disproportionately large, particularly if the 'reserve' (which is 50% of the humanitarian budget) is included as part of the general budget, which in reality is the basis on which the ECHO budget is being run. The Court of Auditors very critically assessed ECHO in 1997 and disapproved of this automatic inclusion of the reserve in the planning of ECHO disbursements as well as the general implementing capacity of ECHO.[23]

Box 18   Evaluation of ECHO by the European Court of Auditors

Main findings:

- evaluations of ECHO generally focus only on the organisations contracted by ECHO for implementing programmes;
- the functioning of ECHO itself ought to be subject to much more scrutiny by an independent evaluation unit;
- a policy document is lacking. Such a document would ensure a better coherence between Commission and Member State interventions;
- coordination and cooperation with other donors, particularly the United Nations specialised agencies, should be much improved; and
- ECHO capacity could be much improved if a separate operational office was established.

The budgetisation of the EDF

The European Parliament and the Council have budgetary authority in the European Union. However, the Parliament does not have any budgetary power over the EDF.

European Union

In 1973, the Parliament requested for the first time that the EDF be budgetised, meaning that it should be incorporated into the European Community budget.[24] The Commission, supported by Parliament, proposed a form of budgetisation, but the Council did not accept it. Since then, the Commission has included the EDF in its pre-budget proposals, and since 1977 the European Parliament has also included the EDF in the annual budget in order to maintain an overview of all the external actions of the Community, although it still does not have any control over it. Budgetisation, as proposed, would imply that the contributions from the Member States to the EDF would have to be replaced by the Community's own resources.[25]

The Commission and the Parliament have maintained the position that the European Development Fund should be 'budgetised'. This would bring the cooperation with the ACP clearly into the framework of the European Union and ensure that the Maastricht Treaty would apply. It should also lead to more coherence or consistency between different policies in the European Union. Budgetising the EDF would mean that the European Parliament could exercise two key parliamentary rights in relation to the approval of the budget and its implementation. This is a key principle of democratic parliamentary control. A provision should be included in the Treaty to guarantee long-term predicatability in terms of resources.

However, for the Member States the present arrangement with the EDF outside the budget authority of the European Parliament is advantaguous, since this gives them much greater control over EDF funding. In the Maastricht Treaty (Final Act) it was thus agreed that the EDF would continue to be financed by national contributions in accordance with existing provisions.[26]

Member State funding sources

The conclusion that the growth of payments in the Community budget has not rapidly increased also implies that the contributions by the Member States have not grown as much as is often suggested. Using the most conservative method of measuring, the underspending gap for 1995 and 1996 for the budget and the EDF is respectively ECU 1500 million and ECU 2800 million.

In most Member States these underspent funds do not re-enter national budgets on top of the next year's ODA and are, therefore, generally lost for EU development cooperation programmes.

The resources for funding the EC budget and the EDF come from different origins in most Member States. Table 14 shows that there is no uniform way in which Member States organise their contributions to the EDF and to the EC budget. More often, EDF resources come directly from Ministries of Development Cooperation – or the departments for Development Cooperation within the Ministry of Foreign Affairs. The contributions to the EC budget, on the other hand, more frequently originate from the Ministries of Finance.

Member State contributions to the EDF budget

Although the Lomé Convention, and the European Development Funds run for five years, in reality the expenditure stretches out over a period of ten to 15 years. This is the result of the complicated planning process through National Indicative Programmes (NIPs), which have to be agreed by the European Community and the recipient country. Further complication is caused by the multiplicity of instruments offered in the Convention, as well as the complexity of procedures for approval, tendering and implementation of projects.

The delay in disbursements from the EDF results in decreased annual contributions being called down from the Member States. In most countries the under utilised funds planned for particular years do not flow back into the ODA budget. In 1996/7 two countries where ODA resources were under pressure, the UK and Belgium, officially budgeted the transfer of reduced resources to the EDF in comparison with previous years based on past experience of the low disbursement rate.

Table 15 on the EDF budget underutilisation shows that, apart from Denmark and The Netherlands, unused resources allocated to or budgeted for the EC from development cooperation, from the EDF and the budget, do not remain available for development cooperation. These are transferred to the Ministries of Finance and, in some countries, small parts of these resources have in some cases been transferred to development cooperation (Belgium, Ireland), but this seems to be an exception.

The **Reality** of Aid 1997/8

European Union

Table 14   Origin of funding in Member States

	Responsibility for EDF budget	Budget line	Responsibility for EU Development Cooperation Budget	Budget line
Austria	Ministry of Finance	various	Ministry of Finance	various
Belgium	Ministry of Development Cooperation	DC*	Ministry of Finance	DC
Denmark	Development Cooperation Admin	DC	Development Coop Admin	DC
Finland	Ministry of Foreign Affairs	DC	Ministry of Finance	Var/DC
France	Ministry of Economy and Finance	DC	Ministry of Economy and Finance	DC
Germany	Ministries for Dev Cooperation (BMZ), Economy and Finance[27]	DC	Ministry of Finance	DC
Ireland	Ministry of Foreign Affairs	DC	Ministry of Finance	DC
Italy	Ministry of Finance	DC	Ministry of Finance	DC
Netherlands	Ministry of Foreign Affairs	DC	Ministry of Foreign Affairs	DC
Spain	Ministry of Public Finances and Economy	various	Ministry of Public Finances and Economy	Various
Sweden	Ministry for Foreign Affairs	DC	Ministry for Foreign Affairs	DC
UK	Department for International Development	DC	Department for International Development	DC

* DC: Development Cooperation

Prospects for the allocation of ODA to bilateral, EC and multilateral channels in EC Member States

Only five EU countries have a policy to determine the size of the development cooperation budget. At present, five countries are decreasing their aid, among which the three largest countries are France, Germany and the UK. However, during the UN General Assembly Special Session, convened to review the implementation of Agenda 21, in June 1997, Dutch Prime Minister Kok, as president of the EU, promised that EU aid would be increased, and strongly reconfirmed its commitment to the target of 0.7 % of GNP. Prime Minister Blair also announced that UK aid would be increased, but no timetables were attached. These gestures were made following a political impasse with Southern heads of states decrying the reality of aid decline as against the Rio pledge to increase aid to 0.7% of GDP.[28] There is generally no official policy on what proportions of aid should be multilateral and bilateral. In most countries, the shares of multilateral and bilateral have remained stable or the multilateral share has decreased. In the same period, the budgeted contribution to the EC has increased significantly. This suggests that EU Member States' contributions to other multilateral agencies, such as the International Financial Institutions and the UN have decreased,[29] while in reality the expenditure of the EC has hardly grown. This is, therefore, a form of hidden savings.

Towards greater consistency: from three to four Cs

The Maastricht Treaty set out three principles (called the Three Cs) underpinning development cooperation policy:

- *coherence* between different policies of the EU and the Member States in terms of supporting, or at least not undermining, the EU's development objectives;
- *complementarity* between development policies of the EU and the Member States and between the different policy instruments within the EU and Member States development policies, in order to avoid duplication; and

coordination between and within the EU and Member States; also in the recipient countries to guarantee effective operational implementation.

171

European Union

The **Reality** of Aid 1997/8

Table 15 EDF AND EC budget underutilisation

	EDF underutilisation returns to:	EC budget underutilisation returns to:	Comments
Austria	n.a.	Ministry of Finance	Austria only became member of the EC in 1995
Belgium	Ministry of Finance		In 1996 the Belgium Ministry of Development Cooperation (ABOS) succeeded in recovering one EDF – 'slice' (out of four annually). The Ministry of Finance stressed it was an exception. Consequentially the Ministry of Development Cooperation decided to budget much less than the due annual EDF recourses for 1997
Denmark	Agency of Development Cooperation		It is said that EC budget predictions are too imprecise. If the money is transferred to the next year you still have 1% of GNI, and, therefore, these resources are lost for development
Finland	n.a.	Ministry of Finance	Finland only became a member of EC in 1995. The policy of the Ministry of Finance is that redirection of resources needs the sanction of the parliament
France	Ministry of Finance		
Germany	Ministry of Economic Cooperation	Ministry of Finance	EDF underutilised funds can be used for bilateral cooperation; underutilised funds of the budget return to a special bank account, where it may be used for EC purposes or other purposes; the Ministry of Finance decides for what resources from this account will be used
Italy	Ministry of Finance		
Ireland	Ministry of Foreign Affairs, Dev Coop division	Ministry of Finance	If there is an underspend on the budget, the Ministry of Foreign Affairs must apply to the Department of Finance to redirect the funds. This may or may not happen
Netherlands	Ministry of Finance/ Ministry of Foreign Affairs		The Ministry of Development Cooperation, within the Ministry of Foreign Affairs, has an agreement that, within bands, underspending of the budget will be added to the budget of next year, without counting in the 0.8% of that year
Spain	Ministry of Finance		In 1995 the contributions to the EDF as well as to the budget were smaller than originally planned, and the amounts that were not used were returned to Public Finance and not reallocated to other development cooperation parties
Sweden	Ministry of Finance		
UK	The Department for International Development (DFID) provides for spending through the EDF and the EC budget on the basis of its own estimates of likely disbursements, rather than EC commitment figures. Underspend on EDF, when identified during the year can be transferred to other aid activities. For spending from the EC budget, aid allocations for later years are adjusted to take account of previous under or over provision		

European Union

Table 16 Policy and trends on multilateral allocations

	Decision ODA budget size	Trend	Policy of share of multilateral aid	Trend multilateral budget
Austria	not fixed: bilateral Technical Cooperation determined every 2 years at government level	unclear	not fixed	increasing because of EC membership
Belgium	in 1999 0.5% of GNP	decrease	not fixed	increased in proportional terms to 50% of ODA, policy to decrease
Denmark	1% of GNI, decided annually by Parliament	stable	fixed, around 45% of the budget	stable
Finland	raise from 0.4 to 0.7% towards 2000	increase	not fixed	increased proportionally to 43% of ODA in 1995, absolute decrease
France	not fixed	decrease	unofficially fixed between 20 and 25% of ODA	stable
Germany	not fixed, determined every year at government level	decrease	recommendation of parliament to keep ceiling of 30% for multilateral disbursements	stable in real volume, but pressure to decrease, also to decrease EDF
Ireland	0.05% annual increments until UN target is reached	increase	decrease	decreasing as % of ODA until multilateral is one third of total
Italy	not fixed	decrease/ restore	not fixed	proportional increase, absolute decrease
Netherlands	0.8% of GNP	stable	not fixed	stable, priority to maintain IDA level
Spain	not fixed	decrease	not fixed	increase
Sweden	0.7% of GNP	stable	unofficially fixed between 25 and 33% of ODA	stable
UK	not fixed: determined each year at government level	decrease	not fixed	increased as % of ODA

European Union

The **Reality** of Aid 1997/8

Table 17 Council Resolutions applying to the EC and Member States

	Resolution/Conclusion	Topic
1992	Development cooperation in the run up to 2000	coordination
	Family planning in population policies in developing countries	population
1993	Coordination of development policies	coordination
	Fight against poverty	fight against poverty
	Procedures for coordination between EC and Member States	coordination
1994	Cooperation with Developing Countries in the field of health	health
	Food Security Policy and Practices	relief and food aid
	Education and Training	education
	Fight against HIV/AIDS in the Developing Countries	health
1995	Complementarity between the development policies and actions of the Union and the Member States	complementarity
	Integrating Gender Issues in Development Cooperation	gender
1996	Gender and crisis prevention, emergency operations and rehabilitation	gender and relief
	Human and social development and European Union development	social policy
1997	Coherence of the EC's development cooperation with its other policies	coherence

The Treaty of Amsterdam (1997) set out the objective for an effective and coherent external policy and added a new principle in relation to the Common Foreign and Security Policy:

- *consistency*: the Union shall in particular ensure the consistency of its external activities as a whole in the context of its external relations, security, economic and development policies. The Council and the Commission shall be responsible for ensuring such consistency and shall cooperate to this end.[30]

Most resolutions adopted by the Council include both the European Community and the Member States. These resolutions are an instrument to move forward coordination and coherence between the different programmes of the EU, the EC and the Member States. The Council has made efforts to translate the UN World Conference on Women (Beijing 1995) and the UN World Summit on Social Development (Copenhagen 1995) into resolutions.

Council Resolution on Gender and Crisis Prevention, Emergency Operations and Rehabilitation The Council requests the European Commission and the Member States:

- to 'avoid relief operations working to the detri-

ment of long-term efforts aimed at building more equitable gender relations in society. Post-emergency rehabilitation should address the potential for positive changes supporting the reduction of gender disparities.'
- 'A gender perspective should therefore be mainstreamed into all policies and interventions dealing with crisis. . . . Special attention should be given to gender-sensitive training of staff.'

Following the adoption of this resolution, ECHO created an internal working group on gender. In this group representatives of the geographical desks and the policy and evaluation units meet about six times a year. The ECHO proposal for *Framework Partnership Agreements* with NGOs will include reference to analysis of the gender impact of proposed activities.[31]

Council Resolution on Human and Social Development and European Union Development Policy In December 1996, the Council also called on the Commission and the Member States to place Human and Social Development (HSD) at 'the very core of development cooperation'. It identifies action to:

- 'Move HSD upstream into the core of macro-economic policy design and implementation; the macro-policy dialogue with partner countries

and decisions on economic reform programmes and debt relief need to take full account; (. . .); to achieve this there is a need to involve HSD specialists as well as macro-economists in policy dialogues, design and implementation.'
- 'Secure a sufficiently high level of financial resources for HSD . . .; in this regard, the Council recalls the agreement . . . on a mutual commitment between interested developed and developing country partners to allocate, on average, 20% of ODA and 20% of the national budget, respectively, to basic social programmes.'
- 'This implies a change in donor conditionality, with greater emphasis on efforts and results in poverty reduction and HSD.'

The Council calls on the Commission to report to the Council and to the European Parliament by the end of 1998, on progress achieved in the implementation of this resolution.'[32]

A European Union development cooperation?

Has any progress been made towards a greater synthesis of development cooperation in the European Union?

In June 1997, the Development Council adopted a resolution on coherence, which is probably one of the most sensitive but crucial areas of European development policy. The resolution focuses on four specific areas where policy coherence is particularly important:

(i) peace building, conflict prevention and resolution,
(ii) food security,
(iii) fisheries, and
(iv) migration.

The resolution notes that several delegations also added the areas of agriculture, trade and the environment. The resolution calls on the Commission to enhance procedural arrangements to ensure coherence in the agreed areas.[33]

Implementation of resolutions by Member States

While the Commission needs to play an important part in strengthening coordination in European policies, whether or not this is successful ultimately depends on the implementation of these principles by Member States. A good measure for Member State commitment to create consistency at the European level is to see to what extent resolutions adopted by the Council of Ministers have resulted in implementation, and what policies exist to improve greater coordination, complementarity and coherence. An inventory among the Member States is outlined in Table 18.

There is no official reporting on progress made in Council Resolution implementation by the European Union. From this investigation the overall pattern appears to be that often the only value attached to the resolutions is in cases where they are already part of government policy. Frequently, governments attempt to influence what might be in the resolution, but do not follow up on the approved resolution. For many countries it was reported that resolutions were thought to be in coherence with policy guidelines already undertaken by that particular country. And therefore the conclusion would be that resolutions did not need implementation because they would be already part of that country's policy. It is obvious that this kind of argument is predicated on a view of the EC development cooperation as an extension of the country's priorities. Elements that contradict national views are generally dismissed as irrelevant.

Danida puts the lack of progress made in the 'three Cs' as follows:

> [b]ehind the, at times theological, discussions of these topics lie genuine differences of attitude between the Commission and the Member States and among the Member States themselves, first and foremost on the interaction between the Community development assistance and the Member State's national development programmes as regards extent, policy, geography, instruments and operation.[34]

The different positions taken by Member States concerning the future of Lomé testify to this fact.

Conclusion

In this chapter the relationship between the European Community development programme and

European Union

The **Reality** of Aid 1997/8

Table 18 Policy to implement Council resolutions

	Policy to implement Council resolutions	Policy on coordination, complementarity and coherence
Austria	statement that government wants to implement these	no policy known
Belgium	yes, particularly on food security and humanitarian aid	policy on operational coordination; coherence proposal in 1993 on agriculture
Denmark	yes, important as political signposts for EC and national cooperation programmes	yes[35]
Finland	resolutions are already part of Finnish policy	no policy
France	no	no
Germany	political statement that government intends to implement resolutions on a wide scale; no overall policy on case by case basis if relevant for Germany	political statement of intent that Three Cs are a priority; no official policy
Ireland	resolutions taken into account in formulation of policies (e.g. HSD, health, education, Horizon 2000) but there is no official statement of implementation	1996 White Paper on Foreign Policy notes importance of Three Cs. However, there is no structural framework for ensuring implementation
Italy	no	no
Netherlands	yes, Ministry reports to Dutch Parliament	yes: coherence was a priority for the Council under the Dutch presidency
Portugal	unknown	no
Spain	hardly any implementation	no
Sweden	yes, but most resolutions are already part of Swedish policy	in a strategy paper of the Ministry of Foreign Affairs the Three Cs are identified as priority in a chapter on issues of quality and efficiency
UK	where Council Resolutions specifically include Member State aid programmes the UK, having agreed the Resolution in Council, would implement it. In general, resolutions often reflect policy already being implemented in the UK programme	

the European Member States was explored in the light of the debates concerning the future of European aid. It was found that:

- Member States keep a close control over the European development programme;
- EC budgets for ODA have increased rapidly since 1990. As a result of the increased budgeted spending for the EC, ODA contributions to other multilateral institutions are being reduced;
- the European Commission does not have sufficient capacity to implement the aid programmes; hence approximately half of the budgeted funds for development cooperation are not actually spent. This amounts to approximately 3000 million ECU a year;
- underspending of EC aid leads to hidden savings in EU ODA, since most Member States do not allow the unused funds to re-enter the ODA budget on top of the next year's ODA budget. These financial resources are, therefore, lost for European real ODA spending. Meanwhile, aid from many Member States has also declined;
- Member States do not seriously engage in a process to improve EU aid. EU resolutions

concerning development aid are implemented and reported on by only a few Member States. Even fewer Member States actually have a policy to achieve greater coordination and coherence in European Union aid.
- The contribution of Member States to the debate on the future of European aid, and more particularly the future of the Lomé Convention, reflects an approach in which the different domestic interests of the Member States lead the priorities expressed regarding future cooperation with developing countries.

Notes

1. Substantial information used for this article was received from Helmuth Hartmeyer (AGEZ, Austria), Geert Jennes (NCOS, Belgium), Susanne Pedersen (MS, Denmark), Suvi Oinas (Kepa, Finland), Olivier Blamangin (CRID, France), Sheila Hoare (Concern, Ireland), Marco Zuppi (Movimondo, Italy), Birgit Dederichs-Bain (Deutsche Welthungerhilfe, Germany), Caroline Wildeman (Novib, The Netherlands), José María Vera (Intermón, Spain), Monica Lonnstrom (Forum Syd, Sweden) and Development Initiatives (UK). I thank Chris Stevens from IDS, Sussex, for his comments on the draft text. I also received comments from Member States' permanent representations and ambassadors from ACP countries. The European Commission kindly provided information. The responsibility for the content of this article is entirely the author's.
2. Technically there are 71 ACP countries, although effectively there are only 70. The Republic of South Africa acceded to the Lomé Convention during the ACP–EC Council of Ministers in Luxembourg on 24 April 1997. South Africa will not take part in trade cooperation since this will be covered by a bilateral agreement. It will not be party to cooperation on commodities (STABEX, sugar, SYSMIN) and the trade protocols. South Africa will also not use the financial resources. A bilateral framework of ECU 500 million was provided for the period 1996–9, Official Journal (OJ) of the European Community. L220, 11 August 1997.
3. The finest and most complete instrument ever, the Courier, No 155, January–February 1996. See also Louk Box, 'Lomé een voorloper die achterbleef: Landbouwhervorming als grondslag voor internationale samenwerking', ECDPM, Presentation, 26 May 1997.
4. European Commission, Green Paper on relations between the European Union and the ACP countries on the eve of the 21st century: Challenges for a new partnership, Brussels, November 1996.
5. See, for further comments, Eurostep, 'Comment on the Commission Green Paper on Relations between the EC and ACP Countries', Paper, Brussels, February 1997; M Van Reisen, '15 + 1 or 1 + 15: The Future of the European Community Development Programme', Report on the Second Seminar of the 'North–South Initiative' on 8/9 March 1997 Amsterdam, Partij van de Arbeid, March 1997: NGO EC Liaison Committee, The Future of the Lomé Convention, Common Position Statement of European NGOs, July 1997.
6. Report of MEP Fact Finding Mission Guadeloupe and the Winward Islands, 5–10 May 1997. Only 9% of the EU banana imports come from the Caribbean, and 20% from the ACP as a whole (The Economist, 31 May 1997).
7. Within WTO rules there is a provision for a waiver for non-complying agreements – an Article XXV.4 waiver for non-reciprocal trade arrangements, and an Article XXIV.10 derogation for any regional free trade agreements. It is still feasible that even the current arrangements could gain such waivers with the combined support of the EU and ACP Member States within the WTO (Eurostep, 'Partnership 2000', Eurostep's Proposals on Trade and Investment, April 1997. See also Report of MEP Fact Finding Mission Guadeloupe and the Windward Islands, 5–10 May 1997).
8. Lomé 2000: première contribution française au débat UE/ACP, 1997; Portuguese contribution, 3 June 1997, untitled.
9. The list is close to the one established by the UN (48 LLDCs). Under the EU GSP scheme Botswana and Tonga are by mistake eligible as LLDC, while Angola has wrongly been left out of the list of the industrial scheme. This situation will be corrected 'at short notice'. Letter of the Commission dated 26 June 1997.
10. These are all in Asia – Yemen, Bangladesh, Afghanistan, Bhutan, Nepal, Laos, Cambodia, Maldives, Burma. The benefits of the GSP to Burma have been temporarily withdrawn because of the practice of forced labour (Council Regulation EC no 552/97 of 24 March 1997). This includes the scheme for industrial and agricultural products.
11. This does, for instance, affect China.
12. Andean countries receive the same benefits as LLDCs in the industrial sector. For agricultural products they receive the same tariff treatment as LLDCs (duty free, with the exception of shrimps), but for a more limited list of products (letter from Commission, dated 23 July 1997). Council Regulation (EC) No 1256/96, 20 June 1996. OJ L160 vol 39, June 1996, Art 3.
13. 'Comparecencia de Villalonga en la Comisión de Cooperación del Congreso de los Deputados (Marzo 1997) Valoravión del Gobierno de las modificaciones introducidas en la Convención de Lomé por el acuerdo firmado en Mauricio el 4 Noviembre de 1995, así como el papel de la Cooperación Española en los estados ACP', Resumen, 1997.
14. Sweden, Ministry of Foreign Affairs; Finland, Department of Development Cooperation, 'Finland's views on the future of the Lomé Convention', Version II, 6 June 1996.
15. BMZ, Perspektiven der EU–AKP–Entwicklungszusammenarbeit nach dem Jahr 2000, BMZ Aktuell, Bonn, April 1997.
16. The EU has decided that it will not break relations with ASEAN over the issue of it granting membership to Burma; membership is considered as an internal matter for ASEAN. There is no reason why this rule, generally observed, that regional partners of the EC choose their own membership, should not be applied in the context of the ACP.
17. European Parliament, Directorate-General for Research, Fact sheets on the European Parliament and the Activities of the European Union, Office for Offical Publications of the European Communities, 1994.
18. In the European Commission, Financial Cooperation under the Lomé Conventions, Review of the Aid at the End of 1995, DE 88, September 1996, p 12, it was predicted that contributions would not start until 2001, at the present rate disbursement, and due to the slow process of ratification of Lomé IV bis in the member states, which is still not concluded, the Commission believes it will not be able to call on EDF 8 before 2002.
19. The figures received from the Commission on execution of the budget of payment appropriations and actual disbursements are not the same.
20. Court of Auditors, 'Special Report No 1/96 on the MED Programme', Official Journal of the European Communities, C 240, vol 39, 19 August 1996.
21. Court of Auditors, Annual Report concerning the financial year 1995 together with the institutions' replies, Official Journal of the European Communities, C 340, vol 39, 12 November 1996.

European Union

22. The 1998 European Union Budget, an analysis offered by the NGDO Liaison Committee, Aprodev, Cidse, Eurodad, Eurostep, ICSA, Solidar, Wide, May 1997; European Commission, *Preliminary Draft General Budget of the European Communities for the Financial Year 1998*, SEC(97)600, May 1997, p 29.
23. Court of Auditors, op cit, 1996; Court of Auditors, 'Special Report No 2/97 concerning humanitarian aid from the European Union between 1992 and 1995', *Official Journal of the European Communities*, DEC 125/96 final SR No 2/97, Luxembourg, 20 February 1997.
24. Resolution EP: JOCE no C 14, 27 March 1973, pp 25–6.
25. Commission des Communautés Européennes, *Rapport sur les Possibilités et les Modalités de Budgétisation du Fonds Européen de Développement*, SEC(94) 640 final. Originally, the Community's budget was based on national contibutions. In 1970 it was changed into a system of own resources, made up of custom duties, agricultural levies on imports from outside the EC and a proportion of national receipts from VAT. In 1988 a proportional sum of the Member States' GNP was added.
26. Council of the European Communities, 'Declaration on the European Development Fund, Final Act', *Treaty on European Union*, Office for Official Publications of the European Communities, 1992, p 224.
27. As Lomé included trade, originally the Ministry of Economics was in charge. It still has a key negotiating role with the EC. Later, for the development aspects, the BMZ began to play a role; lately, with increasing pressures on budgets, the Ministry of Finance has claimed an increasingly important role in improving larger and smaller parts of the budget.
28. SUNS, 17th year, 4013, 1 July 1997, p 3.
29. For instance, cuts in the aid budget of Germany for 1997 led to a drop of 7.7% in commitment appropriations for multilateral funding. These cuts will reduce funding for UNIDO, UNDP, IDA and ESAF.
30. Chapter 12, Article C.
31. *VOICE Newsletter*, vol 4, no 8, 27 May 1997, Liaison Committee of Development NGOs to the European Union, p 1.
32. Council of the European Communities, 'Declaration on the European Development Fund, Final Act', *Treaty on European Union*, Office for Official Publications of the European Communities, 1992, p 224.
33. Council of the European Union, General Secretariat, 2012th Council Meeting on Development, *Coherence of the EC's Development Cooperation with its other policies – Resolution*, Luxembourg, 5 June 1997, 8631/97.
34. Ministry of Foreign Affairs, *Strategies for Individual Organisations, Annex to the Plan of Action for Atrive Multilateralism*, Danida, Copenhagen, 1996, p 128.
35. *Strategies for Individual Organisations: The 3 Cs*, pp128–57.

The EU and Africa

Mirjam van Reisen, Eurostep

The future relationship between the EU and Africa: budget support and social investment

A pact to eradicate poverty?[1]

Traditional development projects accounted for two-thirds of expenditure under the Lomé Conventions in the 1980s, but had declined to less then 40% of all payments in 1994. Increasingly, budgetary aid or rehabilitation of existing infrastructure has replaced the traditional schemes. In Lomé III a sectoral import programme was introduced, followed by a general import programme under Lomé IV, with the aim to 'meet the needs of ACP states in financial crisis'.[2] Other instruments for programme support exist as well.

In its Green Paper on the future of Lomé, the European Commission presented the idea that budget support should by and large replace project support. Budget support seems to have particular advantages. While project support is a relatively inflexible instrument over which the recipient government has relatively little control, direct budget support can strengthen the administration and contribute to sound fiscal and policy management in the recipient country. It might also be an instrument to increase expenditure in social sectors, such as health and education.

However, budget support is also an instrument that by itself does not resolve the structural problems which cause the financial gap in the fiscal resources of the recipient country. First, it is necessary that the exchange rate is liberalised. Second, it is necessary that there is an efficient financial administrative capacity.

A lack of financial administrative capacity is often caused by a country's lack of financial means. Highly indebted poor countries have often reduced their administrations, making it difficult to keep sufficiently qualified personnel. They are often not able to exercise sufficient control over budget expenditure. The implementation of an agreed budget may, therefore, fail, and this may result in an inability to implement budget support allocated to specific sectors.

In countries with a precarious financial and administrative base, budget support requires development policies that help to create a domestic framework for sound governance, including effective financial and policy management. This means that generally for the poorest ACP countries it would seem that budget support on its own is not a good instrument and it is unlikely that expenditures in social sectors will be increased.

This raises the following three questions:

- First, is budget support possibly an effective instrument for eradicating poverty?
- Second, if budget support might be an effective instrument for poverty eradication, what supportive measures are needed to ensure that budget support can be effective?
- Third, what is required of the European Union to be able to deliver effective budget support?

The evolution of financial programme aid: clarifications of terms and definitions

Budget support is a form of financial programme aid. The main characteristic of programme aid is that it is intended to be 'policy-based lending'. Programme aid is defined as:

> all contributions made available to a recipient country for general development purposes . . . not linked to specific project activities.[3]

The original form of programme aid was food aid. Food aid has always been a very important component of European aid. In the 1970s, financial

The EU and Africa

programme aid was introduced, which took mainly the form of import support – also called 'balance of payment' support. These programmes tied the recipient government to importing specific products, from specific countries. It is clear that donors also used this kind of support to open markets for their export products.[4]

As many developing countries became increasingly heavily indebted during the 1980s, it became difficult to have access to foreign exchange for many of them. To resolve this problem, loans from the World Bank, originally only destined for projects, were made available for policy reform.[5] Generally, donors sought more flexible conditions on imports, trying to tie less aid, while introducing conditions on macro-economic policies. This was called Balance of Payment Support. Liberalisation of domestic markets and austerity programmes to reduce fiscal expenditure of recipient governments were generally central elements in the package of conditions. Increasing the flexibility of import substitution lead eventually to retroactive financing; making accounting procedures increasingly artificial.

In the late 1980s, direct support to the government budget was introduced by the United States and followed by other bilateral donors. This 'budget support' also conditioned transfers of monies to carefully specified policies and institutional reforms to be implemented by the recipient government, often in coordination with the World Bank.[6]

Balance of payment support versus budget support

Both balance of payments support and budget support are – technically – direct financial contributions to the recipient governments with the objective of reducing the government's 'financial gap'. Balance of payments support was given to reduce the gap in foreign exchange of the recipient government. Whether balance of payments support was needed was predominantly determined by the balance sheets of the recipient country's central bank. Through import substitution, such gaps in foreign exchange were rectified; and often the financial resources never reached the bank accounts of the recipient country.[7]

Such gaps evolved where there were fixed exchange rates. During structural adjustment policies, when exchange rates were liberalised, the foreign exchange gap was 'resolved', or did not exist any more in economic terms. The liberalisation of the exchange rate led to devaluations of the local currencies, which now became convertible. Devaluation implied that the quantity of the debt service would become higher than it was before. While the foreign exchange gap was resolved in this way, a gap in the budget appeared, caused by a shortage of fiscal means. Therefore, budget support was established, which is considered to be a direct contribution to the domestic budget. As a result, an analysis of government policies as a whole has become the central element for deciding whether or not budget support is given.

Conditionality leading to cuts in social sectors

With programme aid, conditionality was introduced. Conditionalities under balance of payment support focused on macro-economic aspects. The condition to liberalise the exchange rates and subsequent devaluation of the currencies led almost automatically to a decrease of fiscal means, since it increased the burden of external payments as trends in trade and capital transfers did not change. Clearly, countries with a high external debt were hit hardest. It necessitated governments making substantial cuts in their domestic budgets. In most instances, savings were made by cutting the administration itself, as well as by reducing services in the social sectors.

The potential advantage of budget support is that it can introduce conditions that help to protect social services, and generally measures that protect people living in poverty. Through budget support, more emphasis can be put directly on the fiscal expenditure of the recipient. However, it is crucial to take into account that whether or not the recipient government can actually honour these conditions will depend on the macro-economic support given to reduce the weight on external debt payments in order to sustain the entire budget.

In the following figure, the various kinds of programme aid are distinguished.

Cutting across these categories, the DAC distinguishes between *General Programme Assistance*, which does not have a specific allocation and *Sector Programme Assistance,* which is intended to benefit a specific economic or social sector, such as agriculture, health or education.

The **Reality** of Aid 1997/8

The EU and Africa

Definitions of programme aid and budgetary support

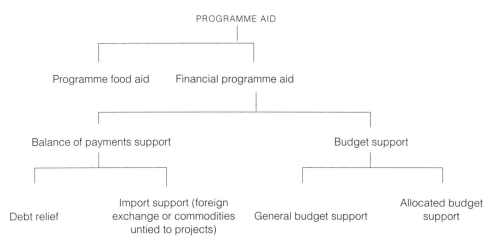

Note: *Balance of payments support* consists of contributions that are intended to be used for specific expenses in hard foreign currencies; for example, the repayments of outstanding debts or the imports of commodities; *Budget support* consists of contributions made directly to the recipient government's budget. These can be general allocations to the budget or *Sectoral Programme Assistance* contributions to specific sectors (for example, health or education). These are normally fiscal expenses in local currencies. If currencies are convertible there is no difference between Balance of Payment Support and Budget Support.

Source: Adapted from H White, 'Evaluating Programme Aid: Introduction and Synthesis', *IDS Bulletin*, vol 27, no 4, 1996, Table 1, and *DAC Principles for Effective Aid*, OECD, 1992.

Neglect of social sectors during structural adjustment

Structural adjustment policies were introduced in the early 1980s as many governments could only sustain their budgets by increasing already large external debts or drawing down natural resources at an unsustainable pace. The reform policies were based on export-led growth and included deregulation of markets, so as to integrate the developing countries into the world market. The impact of these economic reforms have had important social costs:

- rapid liberalisation resulted in a shifting of control over agricultural lands, forests and fisheries from those engaged in subsistence production to property owners. This destroyed rural livelihoods and food security;
- shift of agricultural production to non-traditional exports undermined the long-term productivity of agricultural lands and domestic food security;
- increased pressure to use natural resources and agricultural lands for economic means undermined the traditional environmentally sustainable production methods;
- intensified global competition, combined with moves to deregulate labour markets exerted downward pressure on labour standards in many industries;
- in many countries increased competition on the global market excluded small entrepreneurs from the market and reduced employment, or reduced the returns of employment measured in purchasing power;
- privatisation resulting from structural adjustment often resulted in increased costs for basic social services, which are vitally important for people living in poverty. This includes basic health care, primary education, access to clean water and fuel;
- disadvantages for women were increased, since mostly women depended on subsistence production; women in employment were in the less well paid and more vulnerable industrial

181

sectors. Women, who were usually responsible for raising their children, were the most severely affected by increasing costs for health and education, as well as diminished access to these services. Also, environmental degradation, for example reduction of firewood and fuel, as well as clean water, affected women most because they have the responsibility to collect those.[8]

A new compact between donors and recipients on social investment

During the 1990s, it became apparent that structural adjustment programmes needed to be changed so as to protect people living in poverty. The neglect of social sectors by donors and recipients as a result of many years of fiscal austerity needed to be redressed. The UN Summit on Social Development in 1995 called upon donor and recipient countries to engage in a compact to increase spending in basic social sectors. In this compact donors would commit 20% of resources and recipient governments 20% of public expenditure to basic social services. The figure of 20% was proposed as an indication of what resources would be necessary to create the desired availability of basic social services for all citizens.

The 20:20 social compact assumes that investment in social sectors can be increased by targeted support to these sectors. This would be an instrument to ensure that the macro-economic policies protect key areas for people living in poverty.

However, it could also be argued that budget support, being a macro-economic instrument, should not be allocated. If parts of the budget are allocated, while the administration does not have sufficient fiscal space to meet all its necessary domestic and external expenses, this could lead to an undesirable distortion of the country's financial base. To create more flexibility, the administration would probably have to resort to illusionary accounting. In such a situation it would not guarantee greater investment in social areas.

The 20:20 compact, therefore, should not focus strictly on input targets. The compact is valuable because it expresses the need for donor and recipient to agree on priorities in relation to the budget and the means of making that possible. The compact is also crucial because the priorities are being expressed in quantifiable or measurable contributions from both donors and recipients, expressing a need to create shared ownership in development assistance programmes. However, the 20:20 compact should also bring attention to the macro-economic policies which would enable the implementation of such a compact between donors and recipient, that has the objective to eradicate poverty.

The EU: from programme aid to budget support

Direct financial aid has been part of the various Lomé Conventions through the STABEX and SYSMIN instruments. The aim of STABEX is to promote exports by helping export stabilisation through compensation for losses caused by price or quantity fluctuations, or both. SYSMIN is a special financing facility for mining products, set up for those ACP states whose mining sectors occupy an important place in their economies and which are facing difficulties. STABEX and SYSMIN are not formally regarded as part of structural adjustment support programmes, since transfers under these instruments are, by nature, unpredictable, and, therefore, they cannot support an entire reform process. Also, contrary to Structural Adjustment Support, STABEX and SYSMIN funds are disbursed without conditionalities.[9]

Balance of Payment Support was first introduced in the third Lomé Convention. It was added to the agreed Convention because structural adjustment programmes in many ACP countries had caused sweeping cuts in government expenditure which led, among other things, to food riots and violent demonstrations. The European Community had not been involved in structural adjustment until then – partly because of disagreement between Member States. The European Community responded to the crisis by approving 'quick disbursing' aid from a special programme of ECU 600 million for import purchases for heavily indebted low income African countries.[10]

A resolution on Structural Adjustment Programmes (SAPs) adopted by the European Community in 1988 (Doc. 6453/89). It noted that:

- the mixture and pace of reforms should be suited to each country's circumstance;
- more attention should be paid to the social dimension; and
- ACP governments should have more say in planning the reforms.

In Lomé IV (1990–5) an additional fund, worth ECU 1150 million, was established to support structural adjustment.[11] This encompassed:

- sectoral investment programmes (SIPs) through direct procurement; and SIPs in the form of foreign exchange released in instalments for financing sectoral imports; and
- general import programmes (GIPs) in the form of foreign exchange released in instalments for financing general imports covering a wide range of products.

Lomé VI *bis* (1995–2000) included a structural adjustment facility worth ECU 1400 million. Direct *budget support* was introduced in the Convention, intended to alleviate domestic financial constraints. These funds could be transferred either directly to ACP states whose currencies are convertible and freely transferable, or indirectly through counterpart funds generated by the various community instruments.[12]

In 1995 the European Council adopted a new *Resolution on Structural Adjustment*.[13] The resolution applies to all European Union development cooperation policies, including those of the Member States. The Council noted:

- the inappropriate allocation of resources which, in the social sectors in particular, penalises basic services;
- that the significant reduction of public expenditure had acted to the detriment of maintaining economic and social infrastructure and, in some cases, the functioning of essential government bodies;
- that investment has stagnated or even declined;
- that imbalances influenced by trends in trade and capital transfers had not been corrected, despite efforts to cancel or reschedule debts; and
- that the real involvement of representatives of the countries concerned in defining the programmes was inadequate.[14]

With this resolution the Council asked the Commission to implement the Lomé Convention with greater emphasis on the social dimension. The Council demanded that particular emphasis should be given to supporting public finances through an approach that would prioritise social sectors. Counterpart funds should be transparently implemented in national budgets. This was, in reality, the first shift towards sectoral budget support.

Budget support instead of project support in the future Lomé Convention

The Commission's Green Paper comes to the conclusion that community instruments are most successful when they enhance sectoral approaches and support for reforms aiming to devise economic and social policies integrated into a long-term strategy. The Green Paper states:

> [t]his raises the question as to whether the EU should gradually abandon the project approach once and for all and instead try to create the right conditions for giving support in the form of direct budget aid for the states concerned and sectoral aid.[15]

According to the Green Paper, budget aid should be considered because it directly improves the fiscal situation of the recipient government. The government gets more control over budget planning and management:

> Unlike project aid, budget aid does not knock the allocation of expenditure out of kilter.[16]

Budget aid should be regarded as:

> a sign of the mature relationship between the EU and ACP countries, based on trust in which responsibility for managing resources lay with national authorities.[17]

In several EU countries, such as Italy, Belgium, The Netherlands, Denmark, the UK and Finland, budget support is getting a higher priority. Increasingly, donors such as Germany are also engaging in exchanging debt for environment or social investment, which is essentially a form of allocated budget support.[18]

Budget support is advocated over project support, or other aid instruments, by the European Commission for a number of reasons:

- budgetary aid would allow for a new and more

The EU and Africa

real 'partnership' between the EU and the ACP. A condition of this should be that there is a so-called 'new reciprocity';[19]
* the instrument of budget support is believed to be more efficient and administratively less cumbersome for donors and recipients as it will 'reduce the risks of lack of cohesion';[20]
* budget support will allow donors to attach more flexible policy conditions to the provision of aid;[21] and
* budget support allows the recipient country more flexibility by introducing ongoing programming.[22]

Evaluation of the effects of budget support

An evaluation of EC financial programme aid by the Court of Auditors in 1996 concluded that the European Commission implemented the import programmes, under the first half of the Fourth Lomé Convention, with a broad interpretation. The EC introduced a system of import programmes that were less directly linked to the physical implementation of imports. Therefore, it was, in practice, equivalent to global balance of payments support and direct budgetary aid. The Court, therefore, decided not to focus on aspects relating to imports and the generation of counterpart funds. It focused, merely, 'on the macro-economic aspects and the impact of the budgetary expenditure of the ACP States in the most deprived social categories'.[23]

What do evaluations of the structural adjustment support of the European Community programmes conclude on the desirability of EC budget support? First, the difficulty of evaluating programmes that are part of a global reform process has to be taken into account.[24] The main inputs to these programmes were not under control of the European Community. Evaluating programmes that focused on specific objectives, but did not function as independent projects also presented difficulties.[25] However, some specific lessons can be drawn.

Problems identified in relation to budget support

Clear objectives needed The Court of Auditors noted that general import programmes are pointless. They should be abandoned for direct budget support. Similarly, when use is made of establishing counterpart funds, these should be transferred to the central government's budget and included in the fiscal process.[26] Where direct budget support is employed it is easier to check the real use of aid against the primary objective of poverty eradication.[27]

Investment in social services should exceed rate of 50% The Court focused on the investigation on 11 countries. The use of counterpart funds differed enormously, ranging from 100% allocated to social sectors in Mali and Zimbabwe to 20.8% in Benin. The Court concluded that for some countries the investment did not reflect the priority given by the European Community to social sectors. The Court further noted that a rate which significantly exceeds 50% of investment of counterpart funds to social sectors in each country should be considered the minimum. Moreover, within social sectors, more priority should be given to basic social services, particularly basic health care and primary education.

The problem of substitution of funds: the need for reliable data on fiscal expenditure It is obvious that when specific funds are allocated to specific sectors this does not automatically result in increased total spending in these sectors. The government can decide to spend less of other resources in those areas (fungibility). The Court, therefore, looked at the actual budget expenditure of recipient governments. The Court experienced difficulty assembling data on the expenditure actually incurred (budgetary implementation) and looked instead at budget allocations. It appeared that allocations to social sectors as a percentage of GDP (and even as a percentage of the real budget) had increased only marginally in most countries.

In Zambia and Mali, allocations to the education sector decreased as a percentage of the total budget between 1991 and 1995. In Ghana, allocations to the health sector decreased as percentage of the total budget. On average, the spending on education increased from 3.68% of the total national budget to 3.69%. Spending on health increased, on average from 1.63 to 1.87% of the total budget. These figures are only allocation figures, in most countries actual spending would in all likelihood be even less. The figures also do not differentiate spending in primary education and basic health. The European Court of Auditors concludes:

It is apparent that, despite the support of the Community, the situation of the budget in the priority social sectors has not shown any manifest improvement for certain countries.[28]

Budget allocations for the social sectors, as a percentage of the total budget

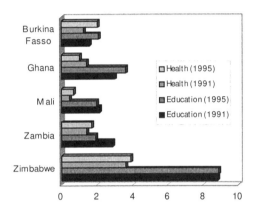

Source: Adapted from *Official Journal of the European Communities*, European Court of Auditors, Annual Report 1995, 1996, Table 12.6 (b), p 302.

Consequentially, the Court has analysed the reasons for the failure of budget support to increase domestic expenditure in social areas.

Debt The European Court of Auditors observes that servicing of foreign debt continues to be a major impediment to the effective use of budget support. It states:

> The structural adjustment loans granted by the IFIs in fact require external assistance in the form of donations which allow new loans to be contracted. The loan conditions stipulate the volume of foreign assistance that will in future be allowed to the beneficiary countries, because the own resources of the country undergoing adjustment are not sufficient to finance both the repayments of the earlier debts and budgetary expenditure.[29]

Most of the Highly Indebted Poor Country (HIPC) governments spend over one-fifth of their revenues and 15% of their total expenditure on their total debt service.

Contradictory conditionalities and lack of donor coordination The conditionalities associated with structural adjustment loans and support for social investment often demand contradictory policies in the recipient countries. The Court suggests that stronger coordination between the multilateral and bilateral donors is required to achieve coherent policy demands. The key to successful budget support is, therefore, not only the negotiation of consistent and mutually agreed priorities between donor and recipient, but also between donors themselves. A recent study on EC programme aid and management concluded along the same lines that:

> Individual donors are tending to target their own assistance on particular budget sectors for accountability reasons. A few are focusing on institutional change in budgetary processes and developing capacities and skills for this. The Commission has sought to exert some leverage on the restructuring of domestic expenditures, with mixed success. This approach is too individualistic. The main need is for a collective multi/donor/recipient agreement on priorities within an expenditure/budgetary framework for each major recipient.[30]

The European Union has an additional role to play, because a common political framework does exist which calls on the Member States and the European Union to adopt approaches that are coordinated and coherent.

The European Union policy on debt cancellation

A resolution to the debt crisis should be part of an integrated approach associated with budget support. The European Union, however, has not wanted a coordinated approach to the debt crisis. International measures relating to debt problems have hardly been discussed at European Union level. The debts of the European Union Member States are not considered to be part of the European Community development cooperation. ACP

The EU and Africa

countries have raised the issue of debt relief with European Member States and debt resulting from European Community aid offered under the Yaoundé and Lomé Conventions, but these attempts have, so far, remained unsuccessful.

The European Commission maintains that increasingly almost all aid from the European Community in the Lomé Convention has been disbursed as grants – and this aid has at least, not exacerbated the debt problem. STABEX resources were also transferred as grants, and sometimes used directly for (internal) debt relief. In an evaluation of STABEX operations to Uganda, this was found to be useful, but the problem of external debt is also recognised. The conclusion was reached that debt relief had been a successful element of the STABEX programmes, but that the relief of external debt in particular should be considered as a legitimate use of STABEX funds and the possibility of extending STABEX-based programmes of debt relief beyond the EC was raised.[31]

The Danish government instigated an investigation into the possibilities of total or partial debt relief for ACP countries in following up of the Social Summit.[32] Recently, the European Commission has been proposing some measures to address the debt owed to the European Community. Very carefully, this new policy to address debts owed to the European Community was reflected in the Green Paper on relations between the European Union and the ACP countries which stated that:

> the Community could act both as creditor and donor by developing support mechanisms and instruments to ease the burden of debt.[33]

In this proposal, the EC makes an important step forward, namely to regard the European Community not just as a donor of aid – as it has done so far, but also to consider itself as a creditor.

The intention of this proposal is further explained in the *Communication from the Commission on Support for Structural Adjustment and Debt Relief in Heavily Indebted Countries*.[34] As a creditor, the European Community holds ECU 1460 million, of which 600 million are likely to require action under the Highly Indebted Poor Countries Debt Initiative (HIPC). In the Commission's proposal it is suggested that support to heavily indebted poor ACP states would be enhanced by:

- granting additional structural adjustment support on a case-by-case basis;
- considering, on a case-by-case basis, support for reducing commercial debt; and
- strengthening support for debt management.

As a creditor, the debts to the Community come from special loans, risk capital and EIB loans. It is proposed that the Community:

- takes action to reduce the net present value of the eligible countries' debt to the Community.

Assuming that 11 ACP states participated in the initiative, the Commission estimates that the costs of the Communities' contribution to the HIPC Debt Initiative would amount to ECU 150 million, in 1996 prices. This would correspond with 5% of the total cost to be borne by multilateral creditors. For the Community, the annual costs would not exceed a few tens of millions of ECU a year on average. This would be a very small percentage of European Community aid. These figures do not include debts to European Union member states. The Commission proposes that the Community refinances outstanding debts through the provision of grants. This should particularly focus on the special loans, and should be financed by reflows.[35]

However, the European Community could go beyond the current terms on the HIPC Debt Initiative,[36] particularly since:

- more countries should be included;
- the time-frame for decisions on individual countries should be speeded up, given the track record of many countries in structural adjustment, and the size of the problems in these countries;
- the EC and the Member States' underspending of approximately ECU 3000 million per year of funds budgeted to developing countries should be allocated comprehensively to resolve the outstanding debts towards the EU, including the bilateral debts owed to the member states. (See EU chapter).

Conditionality and selectivity

The Green Paper on relations between the European Union and the ACP countries analyses how conditionality could be reformed to suit budget support. It draws on the experience of the Special Programme for Africa (SPA) and the European Union Working Group on Economic Reform in the

Context of Political Liberalisation. The points included in the Green Paper are to:

- encourage recipient countries to internalise reforms;
- apply realistic conditions which take due account of the political and administrative context;
- make a full assessment of what has been achieved in terms of sustainable development. Such an assessment should be carried out in conjunction with other donors.

This list is rather vague and no procedures for implementation are proposed. The Commission stresses that 'ownership of the programme' would be one of the greatest benefits of the financial programme approach. However, it is not clear how the recipeint governments might be consulted or included in decision-making *vis-à-vis* the application of the new conditionality, and how they can seek redress if they do not agree with a decision taken by the donors.

Coordination
The Green Paper maintains that the 'comprehensive coordinated approach' should 'also prevent any "stop and go" in aid payments'. Discontinuity in aid payments is clearly detrimental to long-term development, as has been noted by the EU Group of SPA. According to this group, discontinuity could be avoided by donor coordination prior to deciding whether or not a country is 'on track' on implementing conditions. Operational proposals offered by the group for achieving this have not been addressed in the Green Paper, despite the importance of the issue and the relevance in the context of the European Union – the largest regional grouping of aid donors.

The European Union, including the Member States, should, therefore, also play a much more coordinated role towards the international financial institutions.

The involvement of civil society and good governance
The measures that governments needed to implement during structural adjustment, increased income disparities and were extremely detrimental to people living in poverty. In general, administrations resorted to authoritarian manners of implementing these policies. As a result, civil society has by and large been excluded from participating in decision-making:

> *The hardship brought on the people by the implementation of the present Structural Adjustment Programmes made the majority of the people, including organised labour, to oppose them. This has led to the use of force by governments to suppress these protests, resulting in further alienation and in some cases, political instability.*[32]

The Lomé Convention, being an agreement between governments has also not succeeded in involving civil society and its organisations in decisions and implementation of the Convention.

Budget support presupposes a legitimate government that serves its population and implements policies that are supported by a broad consensus. It is therefore imperative that governments gain a genuine legitimacy by respecting democratic principles and human rights. Governments must seek the active involvement of the people in development and let people decide their development needs, plan and contribute to their implementation, supervise and monitor their creation. If these conditions are not fulfilled, the impact of budget support on poverty eradication will be much constrained, if not impossible. Equally, in countries in conflict, or without a government, budget support is not appropriate.

Corruption
The Green Paper does not explicitly address corruption. However, ACP governments receiving budget support must be expected to make a real effort to manage all available internal and foreign resources to contribute to the economic and social development priorities of their societies ('good governance'). Good governance must, therefore, become a major criterion for aid allocation.

To be credible in this respect, the EU must also put its own house in order. The EU countries should make corruption of foreign officials by European firms a criminal offence and, where it still exists, end tax deductibitlity for bribes. It needs to sharpen procurement and contract rules to prevent or sanction cases of corruption. Sound management cannot be put as a condition to the ACP countries, when the EU tolerates, or even indirectly encourages firms to bribe foreign officials.

The EU and Africa

Selectivity
Budget support should be based on a well-defined compact between donor and recipient government. Budget aid should only be given if the recipient government has a serious commitment to eradicate poverty and has a credible plan for achieving this goal. The government should respect democratic principles and human rights. The involvement of civil society should be a central part of such a poverty eradication plan. The general budget should reflect the priority of poverty eradication, including constrained military expenditure. Countries in conflict or without a government should also be excluded from budget support.

Administrative capacity

Capacity and expertise in the European Commision
The assumption in the Green Paper that budget support might be more efficient and administratively less cumbersome for donors and recipients is not entirely true:

- budget support needs to be carefully planned, in a coherent manner, involving the recipient government and other donors; and
- budget support needs to be carefully monitored.

This implies that the donor country needs to have the capacity and expertise to follow these processes on a continuous basis, particularly in the representations in the respective countries.[33]

Overburdening of domestic capacity
Domestic capacity should not be overburdened with different accounting requirements for various instruments and donors. Budget support should fit the budget process of the recipient country and assistance should be given to enhance the capacity of the administration to manage its finances in an efficient, transparent and accountable manners. The EU has some experience in this area.

Procedures
Procedures are required to guarantee that budget support is delivered at the right moment, and is not disbursed too late. If budget support is delivered too late, it will upset the budgetary process, which would be counterproductive. Experiences with EU financial aid have demonstrated that cumbersome EU procedures often lead to late disbursement.

Conclusions
Budget support could be an effective instrument with which to contribute to the eradication of poverty if:

- EU and ACP countries collectively agree that the eradication of poverty is a principal objective of budget support, and there is a credible plan setting out how this might be achieved; both the EU and ACP are willing to contribute resources to this end, within a single and consistent budgetary policy;
- the EU and the ACP agree on clear processes of action, including planning, decision-making procedure, time-frame of disbursements, monitoring and evaluation of progress, and criteria for aid suspension;
- governments are legitimate and respect democratic principles and human rights. Governments must seek the active involvement of the people in development and let people decide their development needs, plan and contribute to their implementation, supervise and monitor their creation.
- reliable and transparent processes on fiscal expenditure are put in place as well as measures to avoid corruption, both in the EU and in the ACP countries.

Budget support can only be an effective instrument to eradicate poverty if there are other supportive aid policies:

- the EU and the ACP must develop a coordinated and coherent positive response to the Highly Indebted Poor Countries Debt Initiative. The activities under this initiative should be speedened up. The EU and the Member States underspending of approximately ECU 3000 million per year of funds budgeted to developing countries should be allocated to comprehensively resolve the outstanding debts towards the EU, including the bilateral debts owed to the member states;
- structural adjustment policies implemented by the EU and the Member States should not contradict the objective of poverty eradication, and protect basic social services; and
- mechanisms must be developed for EU policies

The **Reality** of Aid 1997/8

The EU and Africa

- mechanisms must be developed for EU policies to avoid major contradictions in programme aid policies; coordination is required both between EU bilateral programme aid activities and EU budget support, as well as with other providers of funds, such as the IFIs.

The EU will need to improve its capacity in terms of:

- adequate expertise in the EU in order to improve the policy dialogue;
- providing continuity to allow multi-annual planning;
- tightening up procedures so as to guarantee timely disbursements of funds and avoid disruption in payments;
- establishing effective monitoring capacity, together with ACP countries, to supervise continuously the implementation of their agreed plan and to enable adjustments to be made if necessary; and
- creating transparent procedures to make a selection of countries for which budget support might be an appropriate instrument.

Notes

1. Opa Kapijimpanga (Afrodad, Zimbabwe), Simon Maxwell (Institute for Development Studies, Sussex) and Howard White (Institute of Social Studies, The Hague) gave useful suggestions for this text. The author is fully responsible for the content.
2. Commission of the European Communities, 'EU–ACP Cooperation in 1994', Special issue, *Le Courier*, July 1995.
3. Development Assistance Committee, *Development Assistance Manual*, DAC Principles for Effective Aid, OECD, Paris, 1992, p 67.
4. Samenvatting van het DAC-rapport 'Evaluation of Non-Project Assistance (NPA)', DAC, OESO, 1987, in Importsteun, Ministry of Development Cooperation Netherlands, *Evaluation*, Inspectie ter Velde, 1989, p I.
5. In recent years, regulations of import support programmes have been relaxed to allow recipient governments some more flexibility on how the aid is being used. At the same time, debt relief has grown as a means of balance of payment support, particularly in Japan.
6. *Voorlichtingsdienst Ontwikkelingssamenwerking van het Ministerie van Buitenlandse Zaken, Programma Hulp*, Ministerie van Buitenlandse Zaken, The Hague, 1997, p 4.
7. For instance, the 'fifth dimension' is assistance to support service of debts owed to the World Bank; the resources are directly paid into a fund in the World Bank.
8. See also David Reed, *Structural Adjustment, the Environment, and Sustainable Development*, Earthscan, 1996.
9. Development Researchers' Network, In collaboration with the Institute of Economic Affairs, ACCRA, Evaluation of STABEX Transfers to Ghana (1990–1991), Final Report, Rome, November 1994, p 47.
10. Commission of the European Communities, Europe Information, Development, LOMÉ IV, 1990–2000, Background, Innovations Improvements, DE 64, March 1990; according to Enzo Caputo Balance of Payment programmes implemented under Lomé III were worth 807 million ECU. Enzo Caputo, The Case of the European Union, *IDS Bulletin*, Vol 27, No 4, 1996.
11. The amount may be supplemented by a (theoretically) limited proportion of each country's indicative programme, and by other counterpart funds generated from Community instruments. Commission of the European Communities, op cit, 1990.
12. LOMÉ IV Convention, as revised by the agreement signed in Mauritius on 4 November 1995, *The Courier*, No 155, January–February 1996.
13. Council doc. 7711/95. Earlier resolution dates from May 1991 (Council doc. 6038/92).
14. This resolution applies to all developing countries undergoing structural adjustment. On the positive side, the Council resolution noted improvements in ACP countries due to structural adjustment programmes in terms of better allocation of resources and growth in income and exports. It stated that adjustment policies had limited the impact of serious macro-economic imbalances on essential public services. It noted that generally reductions of budget deficits had occurred in the countries under restructuring and inflation was controlled and exchange rates were made more compatible with economic fundamentals.
15. European Commission, Directorate General VIII Development, *Green Paper on Relations between the European Union and the ACP countries on the eve of the 21st century: Challenges for a new partnership*, Brussels, November 1996, p xv.
16. Ibid, p 73.
17. Ibid.
18. See also Mariano Valderrama on Latin America, in this volume. Compare also Cox et al, *How European Aid Works: A Comparison of Management Systems and Effectiveness*, ODI, 1997, pp 79–81.
19. European Commission, op cit, 1996, p 69. 'The move towards a partnership based on reciprocal rights and obligations and a more explicit allocation of the partner's [i.e. the ACP state's] responsibilities.'
20. Ibid. 'The use of a multiplicity of instruments which all have different purposes, procedures and methods of operation inevitably makes the EU's policy for each individual country less transparent'.
21. Ibid. 'As the situation currently stands, it is impossible to reorient or adapt policy within a reasonable space of time, but this is just what is increasingly called for. This is because economic and political circumstances can change fast, and we have to be able to react to new concerns connected with political initiatives, respond to public opinion in the ACP countries or in Europe, or give effect to the findings of evaluations in the interests of increasing the efficiency and impact of cooperation.'
22. European Commission, op cit, 1996, p 70. 'Budget arrangements which allowed multiannual programming of expenditure in tandem with greater flexibility would undoubtedly be more appropriate.'
23. Official Journal of the European Communities, Court of Auditors, Annual Report concerning the financial year 1995, Office for Official Publications of the European Communities, Luxembourg, 12 November 1996.
24. Undertaken in 1994, in Ghana, Uganda and Cote d'Ivoire, followed by Tanzania, Cameroon and Zambia. This evaluation problem is, of course, not specific to the EC, but a general problem of evaluating budget support, see White, ibid.
25. Enzo Caputo, 1996, ibid, p 62.

The EU and Africa

26. See also: Glenys Kinnock, *Opinion for the Committee on Budgetary Control*, on the Discharge of the 1995 financial year concerning title 7 of the general budget of the European communities and the EDF, Committee on Development and Cooperation, European Parliament, 25 February 1997.
27. Art. 244 (f) Lomé VI Convention.
28. Official Journal of the European Communities, 1996, ibid, p 302.
29. ibidem, p 303.
30. Cox, et. al., ibid, p 94.
31. Maxwell Stamp PLC, Evaluation of Stabex operations in Uganda, Final Report, Prepared for European Commission DG VIII, Evaluation Unit, Brussels, April 1995, p Ex Sum 7.
32. Danida, Ministry of Foreign Affairs, *Strategies for Individual Organizations*, Annex to the Plan of Action for Active Multilateralism, Copenhagen, 1997.
33. European Commission, 196, ibid, p 57.
34. Commission of the Euopean Communities, Communication from the Commission on Support for Structural Adjustment and Debt Relief in Heavily Indebted Countries – A Community Response to the HIPC Debt Initiative, Brussels, 14 March 1997, VII/175/97/EN.
35. Special loans were changed into grants in Lomé IV. Outstanding special loans to the 11 ACP countries eligible to the HIPC Debt Initiative amount to ECU 410 million (excluding loans to the private sector). These reflows are returned to the Member States, via the EIB.
36. See also Eurodad, *Comment and Analysis, The European Commission and the Highly Indebted Poor Countries (HIPC) Debt Initiative*, 10 April 1997.
37. Mr Hassan A Sumnonu, Secretary-General of the Organisation of African Trade Union Unity (OATU), in ECA, *African Charter for Popular Participation in Development and Transformation*, Arusha, 1990, p 11.
38. Transparency International, letter, 3 July 1997.
39. This is not necessarily the case. See for instance, IDS, IDR, *An Evaluation of Development Cooperation between the European Union and Ethiopia, 1976–1994*, Main Report, Sussex, Addis Ababa, June 1996.

Part III: Perspectives from the South

International cooperation in Argentina

Patricio Lorente and Hector Navarro, Association for Social Development

International cooperation in Argentina is a recent process, with the first documented supported activities being at the end of the 1960s. Then, with the interruption of democracy in the mid-1970s, there were no initiatives supported by international cooperation. The management and support of projects resumed with the reinstatement of democracy in December 1983. Many activities have been developed over the last 13 years in different areas and with varying results. Numerous projects have been directed towards the fight against poverty, which the international community has been allowed to evaluate. This has enabled it to make its support more efficient, as this report will show.

Priorities of international cooperation

The Argentine government has defined the need to optimise the use of resources from international cooperation, in both human and economic terms.

In the context of the country's development strategy, global priorities have been defined for the selection of projects, highlighting those linked to:

- improving the efficiency of the state and public administration;
- privatisation and deregulation;
- eradicating poverty;
- information and communications;
- changes in the structure of production;
- the environment and the integration of Argentina into the world market.

Of these thematic areas, emphasis has been placed on projects aimed at achieving the objectives of:

- contributing directly to the growth and expansion of productivity in different sectors of the economy;
- supporting Argentina's integration into international trade as well as into economic initiatives such as MERCOSUR[1] and the Initiative of the Americas[2] changing productive and social infrastructure by attracting external financial resources;
- accelerating the structural change of the public sector;

Table 19 Priorities and sources of international technical cooperation

Bilateral technical cooperation

Small and medium-sized enterprise	Spain, EC, Italy, Germany
State reforms	Spain, France, Italy
Environment and natural resources	Spain, Sweden, EC, Italy, Germany, Japan, Russian Federation
Energy	Spain, Sweden, EC, Italy, Japan
Tourism	Spain, Italy
Agricultural industry	Spain, EC, Italy, Japan, China, Russian Federation
Health	Sweden, Japan, China, Russian Federation
Science and technology	Spain, Sweden, EC, France, Italy, Germany, Japan, China, Russian Federation
Education	Italy
Telecommunications	Japan
Transport	Italy, Japan
Undefined Priorities	United States

Argentina

Multilateral technical cooperation	
IADB	Agriculture, cattle farming, industry, fishing, services, transport, energy, environment and natural resources, science and technology, regional integration, economic policy, housing, small and medium enterprises, university cooperation
FAO	Agriculture, environment, women and development, nutrition
UNFPA	Institutional strengthening, population policies, environment, human rights, education
UNIDO	Industrial development and promotion, small and medium enterprises, environment
UNDP	Economic growth, state management, social policies
UN Fund for Development for Women	Women and development, micro enterprises, planning, alternative energy systems
Area Education, Science and Culture	Education and culture, natural resources
UNICEF	Development and social policy, nutrition, poverty, health, infant development

- supporting programmes and policies that improve social conditions; and
- contributing to improving the environment by supporting the implementation of policies and actions designed to improve and/or maintain ecological equilibrium, in conjunction with the country's development programmes.

The Argentine context for international cooperation

During the last decade Argentina has seen a sustained increase in its poverty-stricken population (this growth was, for the period 1980–96, the largest in Latin America). Alongside this there has been a sustained increase in unemployment. Paradoxically, there has also been a marked increase in Gross Domestic Product (GDP). In Argentina's case, since 1991 with the implementation of the Conversion Plan,[3] economic reforms and state reforms, the poverty indices have increased dramatically.

Economic growth

According to analysis of the economic variables over the last five years, implementing the Conversion Plan produced a sharp fall in inflation accompanied by an upturn in GDP, which only showed negative growth during 1995 but was up four points at the end of 1996.

The balance of trade showed a positive yield of US$ 841.4 million for 1995, having been negative between 1992 and 1994 and was at US$ 259.4 million for the first ten months of 1996.

The trade balance showed a deficit of US$ 2614 million for the five-year period. This was better than for other MERCOSUR countries, yet extremely negative when compared with NAFTA and the EU. It has to be taken into account that the majority of exports from Argentina are raw materials and the majority of imports are capital goods, machines, apparatus, electrical materials, chemical products and transport materials.

Despite these economic indicators, there was no improvement in poverty indicators. On the contrary, between 1990 and 1996 there was a strong increase in poverty levels.

Characteristics of poverty

In determining the characteristics of poverty, we have used indicators linked to a person's income – the poverty line and the level of subsistence (*línea de la pobreza* and *línea de indigencia*).

The minimum income level for the poverty line is put at US$ 60 a month, while the level of subsistence is put at US$ 30 a month.

Analysis of these indicators during the period 1989–92 showed a significant increase in both, which coincided with the peak of hyperinflation in 1989, a marked decrease in 1990 and continuing high, though stable, through 1991 and 1992.

The significant increase in the poverty line for the total population of Greater Buenos Aires and the Federal Capital, measured in subsequent years, shows the increase in the number of people who are finding it impossible to meet basic subsistence needs. The number of people living below the

Argentina

poverty line grew by 10.6 points between May 1994 and May 1996. This means that in the whole of Greater Buenos Aires, the number of people with serious subsistence problems grew to over three million.

It is also useful to consider the social impact of the unequal distribution of wealth, which showed an increased gap between the richest and the poorest sectors of society: the richest 10% enjoy 36.3% of total income and the poorest, a mere 1.6% of that total.

These data illustrate that the current economic growth does not mean a more equal society; on the contrary, there is an increase in new poor (65% of the increase in poverty), contributing to the impoverished middle classes.

Characteristics of unemployment

There has been a steady increase in unemployment in Argentina during the last ten years, which is one of the principal causes of the impoverishment of the middle classes, especially for those who were barely above the poverty line threshold, as they then became part of the poor population of the country.

Between 1990 and 1996 unemployment increased 100%, from 791,000 to 2.1 million people. The main causes were crises for small and medium-sized enterprises and the rationalisation of the public sector.

Analysing the unemployment figures by gender showed higher numbers of women out of work, 22% of the total female population as opposed to 17% of the total male population. This reflects the greater difficulties Argentinean women face in finding work.

If the figures are broken down by age, they show higher unemployment among the young. In 1996, 47% of claimants were between 15 and 19 years of age, which shows the problems of finding a first job.

Underemployment and insecure employment must also be considered alongside unemployment. Underemployment, those who work fewer than 35 hours a week but who want to work more, showed an increase of 63.5% between 1991 and 1996.

Insecure employment covers informal workers in unskilled jobs. Although the members of this sector may be 'employed', they receive no social security, assistance or pension benefits, and are constantly vulnerable to falling below the subsistence level.

From these data we can conclude that the positive macro-economic growth shows no correlation with a fairer distribution of wealth or with better standards of living. A recent report by CEPAL, given out in San Pablo at the first Regional Conference on social development in April 1997, cites Argentina as the Latin American country where poverty has grown the most between 1984 and 1996. This highlights the fact that the region's economic growth between 1990 and 1996 did not alleviate the problems of poverty, given the increase in unem-ployment and the lack of new sources of work.

In summary, unemployment is the biggest challenge for the public sector and NGOs. Poverty cannot be eradicated if unemployment is not tackled and reduced effectively.

State social expenditure

Argentina is one Latin American country in which per capita social spending increased. The 1990/1 period saw an increase from US$ 548.5 to over US$ 700 in 1994/5. Taken in relation to the GDP figure, between 1891/2 and 1994/5, social spending increased from 17.1% to 18.3%.

The 1996 budget for national programmes aimed at the poor was 3,315,981,000 pesos. Of this only 61,775,000 – 1.8% – was destined for four pro-duction programmes. Two of these – the Credit and Support Programme for Small Producers of North East Argentina and the Global Credit Programme for Small and Medium-Sized Businesses have a total budget of 41,620,000 pesos for 1996. Both pro-grammes have financial support from the Inter-American Development Bank.

For the period 1995–9 the Participatory Fund for Social Investment has been established with funding from the World Bank, the national budget and provincial governments, with the aim of direct-ing some social expenditure towards the population with *necesidades básicas insatisfechas*[4] (NBI, or basic needs not satisfied) and other suburbs, through temporary employment strategies.

In spite of the increase in social spending the incapacity of the current plans to combat poverty and unemployment, in terms of efficiency and effectiveness, is still evident.

A great part of this spending is used to offer temporary employment and, though it may consti-tute valid help to the unemployed, it is ineffective given its short-term nature, the precariousness of the employment and the fact that the beneficiary quickly becomes unemployed once again. On the other hand, the difficulties of implementing pro-ductive projects aimed at the poorest groups in society through small enterprise strategies have to be recognised. Good intentions come up against the beneficiaries' lack of training and incapacity to function as a group.

Thus, social spending is excessive and inefficient, and in the majority of cases only offers a palliative, without succeeding in breaking the inter-generational circle of poverty.

Conclusions

International cooperation aimed at the needs of the extreme poor has been ineffective in achieving results beyond mere testimony, or results that are not lost over time. This applies to bilateral and multilateral projects as well as to those of the private sector. The data show that little impact has been made on the basic situation beyond some good intentions and a few projects targeted on particular population groups that have had positive results.

First, it is essential for the methodology adopted and the expected results to stipulate clearly, in each case, what the objectives are; whether the activities are aimed at the consequences of poverty (namely that they aim to improve the quality of life of those involved and relieve its most dramatic effects); or whether it is aimed at the causes influencing the social and economic conditions that generate poverty. Both types of policy are necessary but should not be confused: the methodology, activities and objectives are dissimilar and require different styles of intervention.

Second, communication between the state and organisations of civil society is needed. NGOs have specialisms, sensitivities, dynamics and technical capacities the public sector often lacks. To continue with the traditional isolation and mutual distrust between the two sectors means consigning to oblivion initiatives that could endure, be replicated or be scaled up to have more widespread impact, and could aspire to becoming permanent policies.

Third, defining priorities can no longer be postponed. In Argentina, the link between employment and quality of life is absolutely clear. As already noted, it is no coincidence that the growth in unemployment – the highest in Latin America – corresponds to a similar growth in poverty – again the highest on the continent. To work on the causes of poverty means outlining a medium-term vision that aims to act directly on its main causes: unemployment, inequality in education, and the lack of public plans for development in the medium term.

Without wishing to exclude others, we feel it necessary to direct resources from International Cooperation along the following lines:

1. Define a strategic plan for social and productive development on a national level which takes into account regional differences. In formulating this plan, International Cooperation could help by offering its knowledge and training to national and regional technical teams.
2. Reinforce the management capacity of the public sector, by training its technical teams, with the emphasis on the implementation of medium- and long-term policies.
3. Develop the capacity of municipalities as public agents for development. Municipal organisations must work on the principles of employing as their officers people with appropriate ability who take responsibility. Planning and evaluation should be a key part of their activities.
4. Reinforce, according to the existing National and Regional Strategic Plan, selected productive sectors, stressing the importance of developing small and medium-sized businesses that give the economy dynamism and provide the principal source of manual work. The Plan should contain training, credit and business programmes.
5. Support the modernisation and computerisation of the small and medium-sized business sector, in order to improve competitiveness in the global market.
6. Intervene in society's needs in extreme cases or emergencies (food, medicine, subsidised temporary work) only when the private local sector cannot possibly offer help. These actions are a good palliative and disguise the illness, but do not cure the disease of poverty and social inequality.

Notes
1. A regional arrangement for promoting trade and investment in the 'Southern Cone' countries of Latin America.
2. A debt reduction initiative.
3. The Conversion Plan is the programme for the stabilisation of the economy that has been in place since 1991. Its main features are to set a fixed exchange rate of one peso to the dollar. This has meant a decrease in inflation but an increase in recession. Most economists estimate that a market rate would value the dollar at 1.7 pesos.
4. NBI is defined by four indicators that refer to housing, sanitation and education. People who are NBI are those who live in homes where (a) they have more than three people to a room; (b) have serious housing problems such as lack of piped water (c) do not have a flushing toilet and (d) have a child of school age who is not attending school.

Western assistance to post-communist countries in Central and Eastern Europe

Krzysztof J Ners, Policy Education Centre on Assistance to Transition (PECAT), Warsaw

The context of assistance to transition

Ensuring the success of the political, social and economic transition of the post-communist countries constitutes one of the greatest challenges confronting the international community in the 1990s. Although these countries themselves carry primary responsibility for managing the transformations, Western assistance is aimed at securing the continuity of transition until it can be brought to a successful conclusion. Macro-financial and technical assistance, together with policy lending are important elements of external support. Their importance has been enhanced as a result of a relatively slow inflow of private foreign capital to Central and Eastern Europe (CEE) and the Newly Independent States (NIS). They have experienced very limited success in capitalizing on the growth of the 'emerging markets' with CEE countries and the NIS together absorbing only 15% of total capital flows to developing countries from 1990 to 1995.[1]

The concept of assistance to transition has a short history; Western support to transition dates back only to 1989.

Unfortunately, there is a lack of consistency in the way aid flows to countries in transition are reported. First, figures in the public domain on assistance to transition are usually commitments, whereas for aid to developing countries it is usually disbursements. This leads to a perception that overestimates the volume assistance to CEE countries and NIS. Also, the definitions of assistance to transition used by the G-24 Coordination Unit are broader than those used by the OECD for 'official aid' to countries in transition.

In this context, PECAT has worked out a definition that contains all forms of assistance and allows specific components to be differentiated. Thus, assistance to transition can be defined as a transfer of financial, in kind, technical know-how and skill resources[2] on a concessional or non-concessional basis, with the purpose of supporting the transition process. This definition includes transfers by official bodies as well as foreign non-profit making organisations and private foundations.

PECAT's definition includes a more diverse range of forms than could be found under the classic definition of development aid and emphasises the *purpose* of the resource transfer over the *concessional terms*.

The goal of assistance to transition The main long-term goal of assistance to transition is to enable the recipient countries to help themselves build self-sustaining market economies and viable civil societies. In the short and medium term the aim is to remove critical barriers and mobilise foreign and domestic resources and contribute to their better allocation. The transitional character of assistance to transition should be stressed.

In 1997 the issue of assistance to transition gained more attention for three main reasons:

- the fiftieth anniversary of the Harvard speech by George Marshall marking the beginning of the US plan for the postwar recovery of Western Europe, which many people compare with the current assistance to transition in CEE and the NIS;
- the process of NATO expansion eastward, with the linked debate about its costs and assistance to transition in its geopolitical context; and

Central and Eastern Europe

> **Box 19 Reconciling data on CEE and NIS**
>
> There are still major difficulties with regard to the collection and compilation of accurate data on assistance flows (see *Reality of Aid 1996*). It is unfortunate that the two international organisations collecting data (the OECD for disbursements and the G-24 Coordination Unit within the EU DG1 for commitments) have been unable to establish a comprehensive and compatible system of reporting. While the G-24 Scoreboard publishes cumulative commitments data, the OECD releases annual disbursement data. Their notions of assistance contain different components as G-24 includes export credits and investment guarantees whereas the definition of 'Official Aid' to countries in transition used by the OECD has the same concessionality level (25%) as ODA to developing countries and is supposed to meet the same standard of 'development intention'. Assistance to transition as recorded by the OECD is not supposed to include tied aid credits, although there have been exceptions for the Central Asian republics.
>
> The data corresponding to major components of assistance allocations are very limited. The CEE countries are included by the OECD in the same group as the NIS and there are practically no data about sectoral disbursements. Another weakness comes from the increasing delay in publishing information. In mid-1997 the data on disbursements for 1996 were unavailable and the updated G-24 Scoreboard to include 1996 was still not completed at the end of June 1997.

> **Box 20 Analogies with the Marshall Plan**
>
> Drawing analogies between the Marshall Plan and assistance to transition is confusing if well intentioned. At one-fifth of assistance, the grant share to the CEE countries is strikingly low, especially when compared with the Marshall Plan, which managed 88% in grant form and the remaining 12% in the form of very long-term concessional loans.
>
> Aid of $13,000 million (around $88,000 million at current prices) was supplied over three years of the Marshall Plan, compared with the $40,000 million actually disbursed to a much broader region and population of 330 million in the CEE and the NIS over the last six years. The Marshall Plan represented 2.5% of donors' GDP, against 0.04% annual average for donor countries providing assistance to transition.

- intensification of the EU accession process by ten CEE candidates in the context of the *Intergovernmental Conference* and their eventual eligibility for internal EU transfers under schemes such as a the Common Agricultural Policy.

Assistance to CEE

The cumulative *commitments* (as compared with disbursements in the paragraph above) by the G-24 countries and international financial institutions for all 13 CEE countries[3] for the period 1990–5 totalled almost US$ 92,000 million, of which one-fifth was in grant form. The total reaches over $108,000 million if debt reduction is included.[4] Since the G-24 Coordination Unit is providing data about commitments in a cumulative form, it is obvious that the overall amount has to grow over time, but a striking characteristic is the levelling-off of commitments to this group of countries over the last three to four years.

In the very first stage of transition, assistance focused on economic programmes of stabilisation, adjustment and liberalisation, as well as support to democracy building. With the evolution of transition, it is becoming clear that the crisis of the unreformed social sectors has not only human and political consequences, but also contributes to the crisis in public finances and endangers micro-economic transformation, and particularly, private sector development. The response of assistance to these new internal and external challenges of transition is gaining in importance. Thus, assistance to transition is needed beyond economic recovery.

In most developed CEE countries donors are moving away from supporting broad-based adjustment/stabilisation measures towards more finely targeted policy advice and technical assistance. The less successful countries have more difficulty attracting foreign capital and accessing international financial markets, so are more interested in lending from the IFIs.

For the ten CEE associated countries,[5] integration with the EU remains a paramount priority in their economic and foreign policies. The CEE countries are gaining increasing access to the EU markets and are transforming all areas of their political, economic and social systems so as to meet the EU entry criteria. At the same time, they benefit from EU technical and other assistance under the PHARE programme[6] and European Investment Bank (EIB) lending.

Box 21 Assistance to Bulgaria

Bulgaria, which went through a deep economic and political crisis during 1995–7, received support for the economic stabilisation and structural reform programme. During the Joint G-24/Consultative Group meeting in April 1997, bilateral support was pledged in addition to balance of payment support, of over $310 million, as well as almost US$ 50 million of targeted social and structural reform assistance. The IMF is considering Bulgaria's request for a Stand-by Arrangement and Contingency Financing Facility for a total of $688 million. The World Bank has prepared a $290 million package of assistance.

The EU is gaining importance as a donor – thanks to the activities of PHARE, EIB and the bilateral programmes of its Member States. In this way, *assistance to transition* is beginning to take on the character of *assistance to European integration*, including the emphasis on building a pan-European infrastructure. In the period 1990–4, PHARE grants totalled ECU 4200 million ($5250 million). A further ECU 6700 million was allocated for the period 1995–9.

The EIB's lending to CEE reached an all-time high of ECU 1120 million in 1995, mainly as a result of the trans-European network of road, rail and gas pipelines.

In preparing the pre-accession strategies the emphasis is on creating an appropriate legal and institutional environment for economic development and integration. In 1995, PHARE committed ECU 1150 million and is focused on two main priorities announced in the 1996 'Accession Partnership':

- institution building (up to 30%); and
- financing investment (up to 70%). Due to limited PHARE resources, the EU will be coordinating projects with the EIB, World Bank and EBRD.

It should be noted that the funds are disbursed and absorbed at a slow pace. It is understandable because the quick-disbursing macro-financial assistance provided by the IMF, the World Bank and, exceptionally, the EU, has been replaced in the first-tier countries by programme and project financing, including more 'difficult' restructuring loans and credit-lines for on-lending (generally to the private sector).

With the gap between commitments and disbursements growing and the emergence of new challenges to transition, the character of assistance is changing. At the current stage of transition, macro-financial and general technical assistance is being replaced by investment types of assistance, which are combined with assistance for structural and institutional reforms.

Although modernisation and restructuring of CEE economies need important injections of new capital, the slow disbursement of assistance to date can be attributed to problems with appropriate intermediaries in on-lending to the private sector, slower than expected progress with privatisation, problems in securing co-financing from domestic resources (an especially acute consideration for infrastructure investment), and institutional and policy impediments in absorbing loans for restructuring, especially of the social sectors. Furthermore, the fact that four-fifths of assistance is in loan form explains why many credit lines remain underutilised – the CEE countries are reluctant to increase their foreign indebtedness.

Delivery mechanisms and insufficient monitoring and evaluation

Most assistance is provided to the governments of

The **Reality** of Aid 1997/8

Central and Eastern Europe

Table 20 Official net disbursements to the CEE countries and more advanced NIS (US$ 000ms)

	1990	1991	1992	1993	1994	1995
Total DAC members	2.24	7.13	6.94	7.20	7.50	9.03
of which EU members ($ 000 millions)		4.95	5.61	4.66	4.52	7.15
(as % of DAC members)		69.50	80.70	65.70	60.50	79.10

Source: *Development Cooperation 1996 Report*, DAC OECD, Paris 1997.

the post-communist countries – particularly from the international financial institutions (IFIs) and the EU – but bilateral donors provide at least part of their assistance directly to the NGOs and community bodies. Foreign NGOs and private foundations direct their assistance mostly to the end users.

Governments, ministries and governmental agencies play an important role in the assistance process. They function as intermediaries between donors and the end users of assistance. They negotiate assistance programmes with donors and implement them. As most macro-economic assistance is conditional on the country's commitment to economic and political reform, disbursement of assistance depends on a government's capacity to formulate and implement policy. Although some progress has been observed in monitoring and evaluation (M&E) of assistance over the last two years, the situation remains diversified as some donors (Canada, the Scandinavian countries, USAID and the World Bank) have established M&E systems, while others, including the EU, are only now developing them.

Evaluation needs to demonstrate accountability for resources provided and results achieved. Disseminating evaluation concepts, skills and culture should be considered equally important, so that national public and non-government institutions can develop their own capacity to assess experiences and improve their performance.

Traditionally, evaluation requires participation of beneficiaries in the assessment and learning process. This has rarely been the case in Central and Eastern Europe. Evaluations of transition assistance carried out by donors and external consultants have been concerned mostly with accountability. Hence, and not surprisingly, 'evaluations' done by recipients unfamiliar with evaluation methodologies and culture have been driven mainly by political concerns and the curiosity of the media.

Assistance to CEE and more advanced NIS[7]

In contrast with the economic growth enjoyed by the CEE over the last few years, Russia, Belarus and the Ukraine have been unable to progress far with their macro-economic transitional reforms. This explains why assistance towards transition in the NIS countries has similar characteristics as assistance to CEE during the first stage of transition.

The OECD Development Assistance Committee (DAC) is performing a difficult role by collating information provided by donor governments and international organisations. Export credits and investment guarantees are not included, but reported as 'other flows' and unfortunately the

---

Box 22   Belarus

Belarus is a specific case as the government and democracy are ambiguous and transitional reforms delayed. Assistance to Belarus, in the current situation of collapse of democratic attempts (with Lukashenka's overwhelming victory in the referendum and resignation of the relatively reform-minded prime minister Michael Chigir), is delivered in a very 'unfriendly' environment. As a result, there is no World Bank activity there and Belarus received only 2.3% of the commitments of grant assistance through the EU TACIS programme.

OECD covers CEE and more advanced NIS jointly. Together, these groups received over $40,000 million worth of Official Development Assistance from 1990 to 1995. The fear that assistance to transition would divert resources from development aid lessened as the data started to demonstrate a

Central and Eastern Europe

rather stable volume of assistance to transition over time.[8] Disbursements for Russia and Ukraine were expected to increase and thus create a 'crowding out' effect within the group of countries receiving assistance.

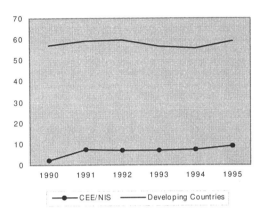

ODA disbursements to CEE/NIS and to developing countries ($ 000 millions)

Source: The OECD DAC constantly verifies its data. As a result data for the same year differ according to different issues of the DAC Development Assistance Reports.

In fact this did not occur. Disbursements to the NIS are clearly levelling-off from their peak in 1992 for Ukraine and 1993 for Russia, and there are indications that, with the continuing difficulties with macro-economic reforms, bigger disbursements cannot be expected.

Comparing donors' contributions

Germany remains by far the largest donor providing around two-fifths of bilateral assistance to CEE and the NIS. The USA is the second biggest donor. In terms of the ratio of ODA as a percentage of the donors' GNP, Austria and Germany are in the lead by a long way. These ratios have, however, decreased after the peak of 0.21% for Austria in 1991. Figures for Japan and the USA, the largest and wealthiest economies, reveal that their disbursed assistance to CEE and the NIS represents only 0.01% to 0.03% of their GNP. The assistance burden is far from being evenly shared among donors and is becoming, increasingly, the domain of a small number of donors.

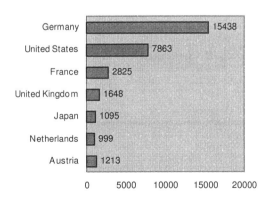

Total disbursements (1991–5) of Official Development Assistance to CEE/NIS by selected donors ($ millions)

- Germany: 15438
- United States: 7863
- France: 2825
- United Kingdom: 1648
- Japan: 1095
- Netherlands: 999
- Austria: 1213

Source: Development Assistance Committee, Development Cooperation 1996 Report, OECD, Paris, 1997.

Box 23 Bosnia and Hercegovina reconstruction plan

The World Bank, the EU and bilateral donors are preparing a $5000 million, four-year programme for rebuilding Bosnia. After the peace agreement was signed, $1800 million was spent or earmarked for emergency economic aid until the first quarter of 1997. The target for donors is to raise the assistance up to $1400 million in 1997 and $2500 million over the next two years.

An initial series of emergency projects was prepared to help initiate reconstruction efforts. To finance these projects, a $150 million trust fund was set up for Bosnia and Hercegovina, of which $25m was in grant form and $125m is to be lent on 'IDA terms'.

The World Bank and the EU are the biggest multilateral donors to the NIS. The EU's TACIS is a technical assistance programme for the NIS providing grant finance for know-how, while supporting the principle of respect for democracy, human rights and the preservation of the environment. It is an equivalent of PHARE for CEE.

The **Reality** of Aid 1997/8

Central and Eastern Europe

Table 21   Official net development aid disbursements to CEE and more advanced NIS (including contributions to multilateral organisations) 1991–5 as percentage of GNP

	1991	1992	1993	1994	1995
Austria	0.18	0.19	0.21	0.13	0.13
Canada	0.03	0.05	0.01	0.01	0.05
Denmark	0.05	0.06	0.14	0.03	0.17
France	0.04	0.03	0.05	0.05	0.05
Germany	0.15	0.17	0.13	0.13	0.19
Japan	0.00	0.01	0.01	0.01	0.00
The Netherlands	0.05	0.05	0.09	0.04	0.08
Sweden	0.02	0.14	0.02	0.05	0.05
UK	0.03	0.03	0.03	0.03	0.04
United States	0.03	0.01	0.03	0.03	0.02
Average all donors	0.04	0.04	0.04	0.04	0.04
Average donors to developing countries	0.33	0.33	0.31	0.30	0.30

Source: Development Cooperation Report 1996 and 1993.

World Bank lending per capita. Selected countries in financial year 1996 (in $)

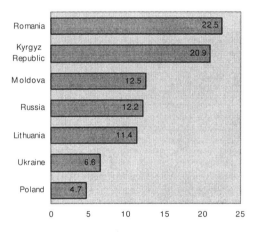

Romania	22.5
Kyrgyz Republic	20.9
Moldova	12.5
Russia	12.2
Lithuania	11.4
Ukraine	6.6
Poland	4.7

Source: World Bank Brief, Europe and Central Asia.

In 1995 TACIS committed a total of ECU 511.2 million. Over the period 1991 to 1995 TACIS committed ECU 2268.4 million, of which 35% was spent on Russia, 10.7% on Ukraine, 3.1% on Kazakstan, and 2.3% on Belarus. Multi-country programmes came to almost 30%.

The World Bank committed more than $24,000 million to CEE and all the NIS between 1990 and 1996.

Assistance provided by foreign NGOs and foundations

There are different assessments of Western foundations' assistance to CEE and the NIS. For the period between 1990 and 1995, Western foundations provided over $500 million to CEE alone, most of it in the form of 'democracy support'. There is only informal coordination of official assistance. The coordination among foreign NGOs and foundations is also limited. Furthermore, the actual size of their involvement is not systematically monitored by either the recipients, the donors themselves or independent watchdogs. There are many different initiatives, from linking cities, universities or hospitals in the West and CEE and/or the NIS, and comprehensive data on foundation contributions to CEE and NIS are not available. There is however, a consensus that George Soros is the major provider of private funding through the network of 22 local foundations and international programmes.

Assistance from foundations differs strikingly from official assistance: it is being disbursed more quickly and is less politically 'tied'. The foundations focus on sectors that are essential to democracy and poverty reduction: education, environment, human rights, local governance and support to the indigenous NGO sector. Assistance to democracy building provided by foreign NGOs and foundations is important, for matching funds for this work from within CEE/NIS are very limited.

Central and Eastern Europe

> **Box 24 Soros's funding**
>
> George Soros's national foundations' network is active in 22 CEE countries and the NIS supporting the development of democracy, civil society and educational activities. Additional parts of this network constitute the Budapest and New York Open Society Institutes, the Central European University and the International Sciences Foundation. In the period 1990–6 the total expenditure of Soros-funded activities reached $1277.6 million. If the expenditure of the New York-based Open Society Institute is deducted, some $900 million was spent in CEE and the NIS.

One of the lessons to be drawn from the experience of assistance in CEE is that although the countries of the region have made great strides towards implementing democratic systems and market economies, a democratic form of government does not by itself ensure democracy. It requires a complex web of formal and informal institutions and processes. Many of the institutions of democracy are still very immature, and some of the anti-democratic practices of the past, such as a tendency towards centralising information and decision-making, linger. It accentuates the need for assistance to build democracy, become aware of environmental and social issues, and instigate social and economic initiatives in local communities.

Poverty and assistance to transition

The economic transformations have had a devastating impact on social conditions in the region, specifically with respect to the rise in unemployment, poverty and social disintegration. Unemployment was virtually nonexistent at the beginning of transition. However, changes in economic markets and production have created a situation of grave concern to people accustomed to having a job.

The fall in incomes and emergence of poverty have been particularly difficult to bear in societies that had experienced overall income equalities.[9] Large numbers of people have found it difficult to cope with change and stress as is evident in the rise in mortality (especially among males in the 40–59 age group), and the disquieting explosion of crime, including domestic violence. The social crisis has been attributed not only to economic factors but also to the deterioration of the main 'institutions' (such as family, school, work and youth associations) charged with the socialisation of children, adolescents and young adults, as well as the loosening of administrative and police controls.

Governments have had great difficulties managing the emerging social crisis, let alone attempting to reverse it. The general response has been to increase social allocations going directly to individuals while maintaining or even decreasing revenues to social services. The movement to a market economy has been extended to include the social services of large public enterprises and the 'commercialisation' of key social services such as health, education and housing. Shrinking budgets and the lack of real reform in these sectors have often resulted in continuing inefficiencies.

The World Bank has been concerned about monitoring poverty since the beginning of the transition,[10] particularly the poverty implications of long-term structural unemployment resulting from industrial restructuring.

The adjustment lending programmes were intended to support the transition of an economy to a new, sustainable and poverty-reducing growth path, and are usually undertaken in conjunction with the IMF-supported stabilisation programmes. Adjustment programmes often call for expenditure reduction, as well as budgetary revenue increases, in order to balance fiscal deficits. They are also aimed at cutting subsidies and transfers to households.

The short-term results of structural adjustment were dramatic contractions of GDP. In this situation, the World Bank recommends targeted poverty reduction policies. Public expenditure needs to be reallocated towards the social sectors and safety nets need to be created to protect the poor and the vulnerable during adjustment. This has been an important component of the World Bank's approach in the 1990s worldwide, as well as in the post-communist countries. There is obviously a short-term contradiction because the short-term results of the adjustment measures increase the social crises in the economies undergoing radical transformations. The best-known case was the 'lost decade' of the 1980s in Latin America, when the IMF and World Bank were accused of promoting adjustment 'without a human face'. Such a criticism seems less appropriate for the World Bank's work in CEE, for it has taken a leading role since the beginning of the transition in sensitising CEE governments to the social issues.

Former recipients becoming donors

Being members of the OECD, three CEE countries, Poland, the Czech Republic and Hungary, considered offering some official development assistance to other countries (developing countries in the Czech case, and a British know-how fund type of programme in Poland to transfer Polish expertise and experiences of transition eastwards). Unfortunately, no implementation followed. Economic difficulties in the Czech Republic and Hungary, and tough budgetary measures in all three countries were responsible for the delay. Even Poland, enjoying the sixth consecutive year of fast economic growth, was unable to mobilise enough parliamentary support for the governmental assistance initiative. On the other hand, the CEE NGO sector is becoming more active in different charity initiatives targeting Polish minorities living in Lithuania and Kazakstan, and humanitarian/charity actions for Bosnia and Croatia.

These CEE countries declared they will contribute according to their ability to the reconstruction effort for Bosnia and Hercegovina.

Conclusion

The current context of assistance is marked by the phasing out of assistance from CEE countries that have significantly advanced in transition. Fewer donors are supplying assistance to them, both in the governmental sphere (such as USAID) and in the sphere of private foundations (such as the Pew and Mellon foundations).

The next stage of assistance to transition should concentrate on exploiting the lessons learned and on preparing exit strategies for these donors who consider phasing out. Strategies need to be developed to complement and/or substitute for phased out assistance by those who are continuing, and also for reallocating external resources and mobilising domestic resources to secure the sustainability of projects developed with Western assistance.

References
Development Cooperation 1996 Report, OECD, Paris, 1997
G-24 Assistance Commitments, G-24 Coordination Unit, Brussels, February 1997
G-24 Scoreboard of Assistance to CEECs, Brussels, 1996
Economic Survey of Europe 1994–1995, ECE, United Nations, New York, Geneva, 1996
Human Development Report 1997, UNDP, New York 1997
Kevin Quigley, *For Democracy's Sake: Foundations and Democracy in Central Europe*, Washington, 1997

Notes
1. *Economic Survey of Europe 1994–1995*, ECE, United Nations, New York, Geneva 1996.
2. The issue of debt rescheduling and debt relief is particularly problematic. However important these forms are in supporting the transition process, they do not constitute a 'transfer'. A clear distinction should be made between the reduction of old debt and new assistance transfers. Debt reduction is, however, very often considered by donors as a form of assistance. Recipients usually disagree, pointing out that the previous debt was created by former communist governments.
3. These countries are the Czech Republic, Poland, Hungary, the Slovak Republic, three Baltic states (Bulgaria, Romania, Albania), former Yugoslavia, Slovenia and the former Yugoslav republic of Macedonia. These commitments do not include the international programme for reconstruction of Bosnia and Hercegovina – see Box 23.
4. G-24 Scoreboard of Assistance to CEECs, Brussels, 1996.
5. These countries are Bulgaria, the Czech Republic, Estonia, Hungary, Latvia, Lithuania, Poland, Romania, Slovakia and Slovenia.
6. 'PHARE is a financial instrument of the EU's pre-accession strategy to help them bridge the gap between their political and economic systems and those of the EU.' H Van den Broek quoted by *Euroeast* No 49, November 1996.
7. According to the OECD Development Assistance Committee, these countries are Russia, Ukraine, Moldova and Belarus. More advanced NIS, similarly to CEE countries, are unavailable for concessional loans under 'IDA terms'. Other NIS are considered developing countries (Tajikistan, Albania, Armenia, Azerbaijan, Georgia, Kazakstan, Kyrgyz Republic, Turkmenistan, Uzbekistan). Their GNP per capita is below the threshold for the World Bank loan eligibility ($4715 in 1992).
8. The increase in total disbursements to CEE and the NIS in 1995 could be explained by Germany's reduction of the Polish debt, which increased Germany's disbursement to Poland in 1995 by $2500 million compared with the figures for 1993 and 1994.
9. A steep and broad decline in CEE and the NIS accompanied the move to a market economy. The average incidence of income poverty (with $4 – at 1990 purchasing power parity – a day taken as the poverty line in the UNDP's 1997 Human Development Report) increased from 4% in 1988 to 32% in 1994, or from $14 million to $119 million. In Russia alone some 60 million poor were estimated in 1993/4.
10. In June 1994 the World Bank issued a two-volume report on Poverty in Poland.

A comment on NGOs, ownership and participation in Ghana

Charles Abbey
Director, African Development Programme[1]

Government of Ghana–NGO relations

NGOs contribute to and channel a lot of donor assistance to the overall development of Ghana. The government of Ghana (GoG) has, through policies, directives, statements and activities, created and maintained a very healthy environment for NGO activities. Over 600 NGOs have been registered by the GoG and these are operating from A to Z in development.

Except for the proposed NGO Bill, which the GoG had intended to introduce and the provisions of which were vehemently opposed by the NGO community, there has not be any serious GoG–NGO conflict in Ghana. Meetings between GoG and NGOs have been held in an atmosphere of mutual respect and cooperation.

Donor–NGO relations

Ghanaian NGOs have experienced real and increasing difficulty in attracting donor recognition and funding. Often application letters to donors are not reacted to and in some instances the reactions that have been received have been 'below freezing point' and discouraging. The impression given by some donors and some international NGOs is that Ghanaian NGOs deserve little attention. This contrasts with the acknowledged need for greater participation as a prerequisite for sustainable poverty reduction.

The recent study *on Aid Effectiveness in Ghana*[2] found a number of trends relevant to NGO–donor relations:

- UNDP data show a dominance of central government as the main recipient of aid;
- the Bretton Woods Institutes have done little to encourage the government to consult with other institutions, and overall policy has been decided by a very small group of people so 'while donors and government have invested considerably in building capacity for managing aid, the approach has resulted in the creation of "tiny centres of excellence" . . . to the exclusion of all others not invited to work on donor projects';[3] and
- Although decentralisation in principle improves the scope for beneficiary participation in planning and aid management, donors appear to have difficulty dealing with this decentralised system, which they themselves supported, and sometimes call for a central coordinating point of reference.

There are some donors who are seriously working to unleash the full potential of local NGOs, realising the immense problems local NGOs have to face. For sustainability, cost effectiveness and efficiency, it is important that donors take a critical look at their funding strategies and the necessary steps to give adequate recognition and support to local NGOs to complement national government efforts. Donor funding requirements also need to be a bit more flexible, since inflexibility holds back the growth potential of some local NGOs.

Community participation

Central to every developmental activity is the participation of the target community. Some of the things that have militated against real development are donor requirements for country/community contributions that do not take due account of the economic and social status of the people. Social Watch reports that the utilisation of health facilities has been severely and negatively affected by the

Ghana

introduction of a 'cash and carry' system, which requires that payment is made before a person is attended. They report a substantial drop in hospital/clinic attendance, in some places by as much as 50%. In rural areas in particular, the policy has added to the existing economic cost of health arising from transport costs.[4]

Mobilising people to provide communal labour is not a big problem, but donor requirements on governments – such as structural adjustment and labour retrenchment – have increased unemployment rates and brought in their trail complex and serious socio-economic problems, which are acting as a disincentive to the communal spirit of the people and therefore negating the impact of real donor assistance. These requirements often spring from inadequate donor understanding of underlying issues such as traditional religious convictions, modes of social organisation, political and church structures, gender issues, use of natural resources and infrastructural questions, including education, health, employment and housing. Often it takes a deep look into the cultural practices of a particular people to discover what issues will ultimately determine whether a given development effort will bring the required transformation. Donors need to build up their understanding and also to develop more effective channels of communication with local organisations, including NGOs and CBOs so that people are properly involved in the design of projects and programmes.[5]

Aryeetey notes how donors attach insufficient attention to who initiated or participated in the design of a project, so long as it is in line with GoG objectives and officials at the top show their commitment to implement it. A project proposed by a donor consultant and accepted by a ministry does not take anywhere near enough account of the local circumstances likely to influence its outcome and the effect on the people it is supposed to benefit. The Ministry of Finance is reported to estimate that around '35% of proposals for bilateral projects are prepared with significant donor input while project design is either completely in the hands of the donor or partially controlled by the donor.'[6]

Illustrative issues

Ghana received massive donor assistance to support its programmes on basic education and reproductive health. Aid to the social sector has amounted to about a fifth of government social expenditure. Donors could take a further look at their funding strategies to improve effectiveness.

Over centralisation and regional differences

Poverty in Ghana is markedly different between the regions and between urban and rural areas. The northern part of Ghana has one rainy season while the southern part has two rainy seasons, both of which coincide with their respective major farming seasons. There are also different fishing and hunting seasons in different regions.

Understanding and taking account of these differences is critical to an effective basic education policy. During these periods, school age children are active farm hands, either supporting their parents or undertaking their own farming ventures to earn income to support themselves. A lack of consultation with the communities concerned may have the result of huge wasted effort. During these periods, some classrooms in rural areas become almost empty as pupils prefer to pursue economic activities that would provide them with money to satisfy their immediate personal and family basic needs at the expense of academic achievement. The same academic calendar operates through the country; pupils are made to sit for the same terminal examinations, with totally inadequate consideration given to local and regional environments. This is one reason why over four million semiliterate and illiterate youths roam the streets of urban Ghana as hawkers, shoe shine boys, teenage prostitutes, apprentices, thieves and drug pushers.

Social Watch cites a similar example of the effects of inequitable division of resources between urban and rural areas. Three-quarters of the poor are to be found in rural areas and women in particular are affected by poverty. Resources tend to go to urban areas. They note especially that increasing migration of young women into Accra, into a largely stagnant labour market, has aggravated the incidence of poverty among women in the city.

Youth reproductive health is another area of concern where the current donor-driven approach could be reviewed to take better account of existing resources and community participation. There are local herbs that have proved to be effective in reducing diseases that affect the reproductive health of the young. Some herbs are also effective contraceptives and it would be a welcome idea if donors could help establish centres to conduct research into and manufacture drugs and contraceptives from traditional plants and brand them with local names. With local participation in the research, manufacture and marketing of these products and with local acceptance of such drugs and contraceptives, a big push forward could be made by donors in a national effort to reduce early pregnancy, micro-nutrient deficiency and sexually transmitted diseases. The teachings and practices of churches should also be carefully considered and supported to help remove cultural and religious barriers.

Donors also need to take account of the marked differences noted at the Beijing Fourth World Conference on Women, between malnourishement of pregnant women in the north (65%) and south (45%) of the country.

Since Ghana continues to receive substantial donor assistance – US$ 653 million in 1995 or $38 per person – donors should give real attention to some of the following issues:

- structural adjustments programmes and macro-economic changes have had little significant positive impact on the man or woman in the street. Nicely written reports with statistics have not meant much to the average person. There needs to be a higher level of participation and local involvement so that strategies serve the people and recognise local differences and capacities;
- strings attached to donor assistance should not be ropes or chains to the detriment of the common people, but should be for accountability (to avoid misapplication) and to create and maintain a favourable environment for the proper engagement of civil society, including NGOs, in discussion with government and through decentralisation programmes; and
- donors should increasingly seek to identify, support and strengthen local NGOs to be active, effective and efficient channels for development assistance.

Notes

1. The ADP was founded in 1991. Its objective is to promote human development through integrated development programmes targeted at rural and peri-urban communities and community based organisations (CBOs). ADP focuses primarily on reproductive health and basic education but also gives support to self-help groups and provides humanitarian assistance mainly in the form of disaster relief. More recently, ADP has started to provide training and capacity building for CBOs.
2. E Aryeetey and A Cox, *Aid Effectiveness in Ghana: A Report of a Study Sponsored by the Overseas Development Council*, Washington DC and administered by the Overseas Development Institute, London, January 1997.
3. Ibid.
4. *Social Watch 1*, 1997, Robert Bissio (ed) Instituto del Tercer Mundo, Uruguay, 1997.
5. Aryeetey and Cox report that 'There appears to be no system for rationalising how donor support for a Ministry is capable of handling a comprehensive programme for poverty reduction to communities that deal with both economic and social items.'
6. Aryeetey and Cox, op cit.

Guatemala

Tania Palencia, ALOP

Background and history: poverty and the state in the 1970s and 1980s

The strategy governing international financial cooperation received by Guatemala began to change direction at the beginning of the 1990s. Prior experience covered virtually two decades; an experience which was largely determined by the dominant logic of the way that society worked during those years.

It was a very complex time for society as a whole. There was deepening social discontent due to the accumulation of unsatisfied demands. The bonanza of the first half of the 1970s, especially that derived from the impact of the Central American common market and the high prices of traditional export products, had introduced a cash economy to rural areas. It also generated processes of commercialisation and changed production methods that integrated communities into the market. But it did not succeed in reducing the high incidence of poverty which, during those years, affected 70% of the population.

The institutions of the Guatemalan state were almost powerless. Lasting alliances were no longer possible between the military and the business community. The corruption of military administrations was one of the direct causes of the high fiscal deficits which also fed administrative inefficiency and the concentration of services in urban areas. International loans were channelled to support large infrastructure projects such as hydroelectric or electrification schemes.

The legislative body did not function effectively or autonomously; much less so the judiciary. The state was the army. Since the counterrevolution of 1954 the state had been implementing a counter-insurgency policy in tune with postwar thinking and the international fight against communism. Through this policy all forms of protest and social organisation were perceived as 'a threat to internal security'. There had been decades of repression of rights: the right to organise, the right to free opinion and freedom of association.

In the 1970s the authoritarian and ethnocentric forms of power resembled the state in colonial times. Electoral fraud; *caciquismo* (domination by local political bosses or petty chiefs); patronage of political parties; and vote manipulation abounded and so social discontent became more generalised. When the 1976 earthquake struck there was much discussion of revolutionary ideas for bringing down the state through armed struggle.

During those years the flow of financial aid from international agencies increased appreciably, largely due to the geopolitical interest created by the revolutionary struggles. This finance was specifically directed towards alleviating poverty and attention to emergencies but it was seen as the traditional method for other countries to gain influence in Guatemala.

However, the approach of many non-governmental organisations at that time arose from seeing and experiencing the daily reality for communities in extreme poverty. These communities did not have even a minimum space in which to exercise their civic and political rights, and also lacked the guarantees to enjoy security as a citizen. The economy of survival and the absence of democratic freedoms decisively influenced this vision of aid.

Thus the activities of the majority of NGOs working in 'community development' in the last decades, replaced the lack of social investment from the state. Moreover, they stimulated forms of social organisation, such as committees for improving community associations, through which communities acquired at least a minimum knowledge of their political rights. Poverty was tackled fundamentally as a political problem.

International aid in the 1990s

At the beginning of the 1990s other national and international influences became more prominent, generating new visions and demands both from

Guatemala

external aid and NGOs. The hegemony of international finance created new patrons in the commercial relations between countries of the North and South. The United States made Latin America a priority as a labour market, more than as a source of raw materials. This led to a change in the traditional functions of the national government. The new international financial vision needed nations that liberated investment to, rather than regulated against it, 'the forces of the market'. Social investment was also included in this 'liberation'. Poverty had to fend for itself in the market, and was not a concern of the state.

In Central America international financial institutions, especially the International Monetary Fund, the World Bank and the Inter-American Development Bank, have moved away from financing large infrastructure projects in two principal directions: (a) towards strengthening political and institutional stability and relations with civil society with the aim of preventing social conflicts that would affect the stability of investment; and (b) focusing public attention on areas of extreme poverty.

Over the same time, Central America has become a region that is no longer of great international political interest. The peace processes created conditions for independent government requiring less external pressure. Eastern Europe or the countries of Africa were of more interest to NGO financial cooperation.

The criterion of 'sustainability' began to replace that of aid. The agendas of official development cooperation organisations were no longer limited to alleviating poverty but were about creating the conditions that enabled the poor to become involved in production and market processes. New areas of focus also appeared in these agenda – women, indigenous peoples, children – characterised as being high risk and often excluded socially.

Aid efficiency and impact

It can be said that international aid has moved from political affiliation to a preoccupation with ensuring a more efficient socioeconomic impact with the resources at its disposal. The change in international cooperation agencies occurred more rapidly than in national NGOs. Once again the pace and destiny of financing was governed from abroad.

On this new agenda is the professional adaptation of those directly responsible for resources. The majority of development cooperation agencies established in Guatemala are now busy increasing the administrative and strategic planning capacity of their counterparts in order to reduce the latter's levels of dependency on external aid and to boost national NGOs' self-sufficiency in looking for local funding. Monitoring and evaluating impact indicators are constant themes for discussion between NGOs and the development cooperation agencies.

Not all the NGOs established in Guatemala have acquired the negotiating capacity with their counterparts to move easily towards this approach. Many NGOs that are ready to strengthen their administrations and management capacity find no easy offers of resources to invest in these areas.

Aid coordination and dialogue

In general, there is no open forum for discussion on the allocation and volume of resources, and NGOs are not often able to speak about international cooperation on equal terms with the development cooperation agencies. Only a few NGOs have acquired this status and, among these, the majority usually represent petitions coordinated through several NGOs. In any case, their negotiating capacity tends to result more from their own efforts than from making use of non-existent mechanisms to interchange, consult and reach consensus with agencies on themes that may identify areas of priority.

Moreover, within development cooperation agencies there are still no lasting initiatives to understand and coordinate the objectives of their aid. International cooperation consortiums in Guatemala act very independently and with little communication on local and national development strategies together with NGOs. This vacuum results in the duplication of efforts, lack of knowledge of the priorities of the population itself and makes objective measurement of the impact of aid difficult.

Social investment

NGOs and international aid face a common problem: the state's inability to design policies, programmes and projects directed at promoting sustainable development has become more pronounced. Funds for social investment, especially for education, sanitation and health are used as palliatives in an emergency – a school here, a health centre there. There are no instruments to ensure that the population will be able to sustain the benefits of a project over the long-term. They do not link in to integrated community development policies.

Meanwhile, The importance of building social organisation and the strength of local power are underestimated. They tend to contract companies from the private sector to implement projects, and are willing to implement projects without involving the local population in design, use or operation. The not altogether unreasonable notion exists that NGOs attract high overheads and it is therefore more profitable to go directly to a population than to offer their labour free.

At the moment in Guatemala, there is little effort being made by NGOs or development cooperation agencies to try and influence the vision and execution of these public policies. Many NGOs come from a cultural tradition that considers the state to be an adversary and not a collaborator. Under these conditions the impact of their own resources risks being diluted in the face of state investment characterised by:

- a lack of institutional coordination when implementing the social budget;
- the lack of coherence among the public institutions themselves;
- the lack of coordination with non-governmental bodies to give investment greater impact;
- slow decentralisation of institutions; and
- poor assessment of public personnel.

Conflict resolution

The Peace Accords embrace fields of action as diverse as judicial reform, integration of displaced people into the national economy; civil participation; strengthening of local power; development of the identity and leadership of indigenous peoples; and strengthening of the participation of women in civil society. They have been virtually converted into a community and national agenda for multilateral funding, as much as for funding from international cooperation.

Almost all resources are diverted to zones affected by the internal armed conflict (Altiplano, Occidente, Noroccidente and some areas to the north of the country), where approximately 80% of the indigenous population lives. The most visible positive impact of moving financing created by the Peace Accords, independently of its origin, is that it is contributing to processes of greater social mobilisation in rural areas.

Resources received from international cooperation agencies are having an increased effect on social projects (training health promoters, stimulating the use of natural remedies, women's health, bilingual education), socioeconomic programmes (technical assistance for production, agricultural and craft credits) and civil education (human rights, civil and electoral registers, making society aware of the provisions of the Peace Accords) that almost always include strengthening community organisation.

Although the impact on the reduction of poverty is still weak, the overall effect of these resources is the empowerment of the population. Social relations in these geographic areas and the attitude of communities towards public offices (state and municipal) are changing; people have an increased capacity to make state officials publicly accountable.

Nevertheless, it is worth noting that in areas of poverty and extreme poverty in the eastern region (especially in the departments of Jalapa and El Progreso) and the south of the country (such as the department of Santa Rosa), where the population is principally *mestizo*, are being severely neglected, to the extent that planning specialists believe they already constitute the new pockets of poverty in Guatemala.

Conclusion

Resources destined for sustainable economic projects are scarce in Guatemala. This coincides with state ignorance of the growing internal market, especially in the field of food security. There are no policies, institutions or even legal provisions to strengthen small and medium-sized agricultural or craft enterprises.

This lack of security prevents people taking advantage of short-term non-governmental projects aimed at supporting production processes with financial and technical assistance. The results of these projects often disappear when the period of the programme ends. They are executed without consideration for the economic context in which the beneficiaries live.

The most successful non-governmental projects in this sense are those that integrate production, technical assistance and commercialisation.

Stimulating substantial and wide-ranging meetings in Guatemala in which different consortia of donors and different counterparts participate (and not only with their respective counterparts) would be worthwhile. They could be the beginning of an agenda for advocacy with the aim of uniting forces to tackle public policies. Even better would be the possibility of trying interconsortia forms of coordination at community level. This could also possibly lead to NGOs and cooperating agencies formulating their planning strategies *in situ*.

Haiti

Ian McFarlane, ACTIONAID Haiti and Groupe de Recherche et d'Action pour le Développement du Far West[1]

Haiti has long been seen as a symbol of struggle. It was the first state free of slavery (1791) and the first black republic (1804). Once France's richest colony, today it is the poorest country in the Western hemisphere. The struggle for democracy and against poverty continues.

A strong democratic and civil society movement developed through resistance to the regimes in the 1970s and 1980s, but 'democracy' since independence in Haiti had consisted of a seven-month interlude before the coup in September 1991. The return to democracy in 1994 and subsequent increases in aid to Haiti have raised expectations among the Haitian people that there might be an end to the struggle.

This chapter reports on the nature of development assistance since 1994. It gives an overview of donor policies at the national level and examines in detail the issues in one particular region – the Northwest – where Columbus first set foot in the 'New World' and where today poverty levels are probably the worst in the country.

The significance of development cooperation

Strategically situated one hour's flight from Miami, 70 miles from Cuba, and next to the Dominican Republic, Haiti has always been a nexus of competing interests, and aid has been a principal tool of foreign and domestic powers in playing out those interests. The pattern of disbursements of aid demonstrates the integral links between politics and aid. For example, aid was frozen after the military coups in 1987, 1988 and 1991, and aid was increased when prospects for democratic reform were established after the return of exiled President Aristide in 1994. The drastic negative effects for development brought on by the military coup from 1991–4 were exacerbated by an aid and trade embargo – GDP fell from $320 per capita in 1991 to $260 in 1994.[2] Aid has been used on numerous occasions as a lever – such as when the US Congress vetoed balance of payments support to Haiti in October 1995 in order to encourage the government to speed up privatisation.[3]

In financial terms, aid is a significant factor in Haiti. Large amounts of aid have accumulated and not been spent from the past, and new commitments are relatively high – over $2000 million for 1995–9, equivalent to $75 a person per year. The impact of this aid on poverty reduction remains to be seen. Judging from the past, if it is to be of more direct benefit to the poorest communities, aid needs to be better targeted and to be more participatory.

Haiti ranks 145 (out of 174) in the Human Development Index.[4] In a population of seven million, UNDP estimates that 3.4 million people do not have access to health services, five million do not have access to safe water, and that 2.4 million people over the age of 15 are illiterate – the poorest indicators in the Western hemisphere. Some 70% of Haitians live in rural areas where only one in four people has access to safe water (compared with approximately one in three in urban areas) and where one in six has access to basic sanitation (compared with two in five in urban areas). It is estimated that 98.5% of the rural population are below the poverty line.[5]

The management of aid

Within the government, the Ministry of Planning and External Cooperation has responsibility for coordinating aid to Haiti, although the Ministry of Finance and the Central Bank are also key in setting development priorities.

The government of Haiti's ability to manage its

own development is hampered by the complicated context in which Haiti finds itself – the UN peacekeeping mission is still in place, the army has been disbanded and a civil police force is being prepared, the state is weak (and further weakened by structural adjustment). Furthermore, on the one hand, the government lacks the capacity to absorb and manage the amounts of aid being made available, and does not have the weight to negotiate effectively with some 20 major bilateral and multilateral donors. On the other hand, there is frustration with the government's own failure to provide leadership and vision (as witnessed by extremely low turnouts at the legislative elections in April and complaints from donors). In addition, the governmental and legislative process has been seriously hindered by intense political conflict and party factionalism.

These difficulties need to be acknowledged and understood. While the government bears responsibilities, donors should be constructive and enable government to govern. Similarly, successes need to be recognised. Leadership and vision have been provided in the agrarian reform model for the Artibonite region, Haiti's most fertile area. The scheme has some weaknesses, but also some strengths, which should be replicated elsewhere – local knowledge used, land handed over to peasants including a high percentage of female-headed households, technical support provided on the ground, and credit made available. Plans for expanding the scheme to other regions are underway. Such practical, decentralised development addressing people's strategic needs and involving local, regional, national and international actors provides guidance for the future.

Development cooperation and poverty reduction

Haiti's current development agenda was initially defined by the Emergency Economic Recovery Plan (EERP), which was developed by the International Monetary Fund and the Inter-American Development Bank after the restoration to democracy in 1994. The EERP ended in the summer of 1995 and was replaced by Haiti's Letter of Intent to the IMF and the World Bank Consultative Group's framework, agreed in October 1996, and known as the Paris Plan. A key challenge for development in Haiti has always been to reach the majority rural population and the isolated regions – the *pays en dehors*. The donor programme, however, has been heavily criticised for its emphasis on the export-manufacturing sector[6] and for largely ignoring the rural poor.[7] Sectoral and programme priorities are outlined in the two tables below.

Table 22 Priorities for major donors

Donor	Focus of activities	Commitments
IDA World Bank	Policy reform, poverty alleviation and social sectors, rural development and environmental rehabilitation	390
IADB	Policy reform, agriculture, water and urban infrastructure, transport, education	715
IMF	Policy reform	165
EU	Policy reform, governance, agriculture, transport, energy, humanitarian assistance	380
UNDP	Governance, humanitarian assistance	50
France	Governance, water and urban infrastructure, humanitarian assistance	95
Canada	Governance, energy, private sector development, humanitarian assistance	75
Germany	Agriculture, water and urban infrastructure, energy	70
United States	Policy reform, governance, agriculture, health, humanitarian assistance	265
Other	Various	210
TOTAL		US$ 2415m

NB Figures include ongoing and planned commitments during 1995-7 (except IDA and IADB 1995–9).
Source: Donor estimates submitted to the World Bank, as cited in the 6 August 1996 Country Assistance Strategy.

Donors claim poverty reduction as their overall aim. To achieve that aim, some elements of the donor programme outlined above are needed (such as some civil service reform, some infrastructural development, balance of payment and technical support to key ministries such as health, education and the environment, and support to agricultural production). In ACTIONAID's view, and in that of many local organisations, however, a greater emphasis should be placed on basic social services and national productive potential than is currently the case.

Table 23 Total donor assistance to Haiti 1995-7, by sector

Sector	Amount ($000)	% (approx)
Balance of payment support	396.2	23
Governance	275.1	17
Humanitarian assistance	145.7	8
Agriculture	70.2	4
Private sector	46.2	3
Water/urban	67.5	4
Transport/ports	103.1	7
Energy	92.9	6
Education	65.1	4
Health	81.8	5
Environment	34.4	2
Emergency/recovery	371	22
Other	10.3	1
Total	1659.6	

Source: IADB Country Document 1996.

A second key point is the link between governance and poverty. Significant resources are needed to re-establish basic law and order and rehabilitate the legislative and executive arms of government. If donor spending on governance is to contribute to the reduction of poverty throughout the country, the right balance has to be achieved between technical aspects of governance and the broader issues of democracy and participation of civil society.

One way in which donors could improve their policies to meet the aims of poverty reduction for the people of Haiti would be to develop more effective ways to measure their impact. International targets have been set by the OECD, for example to reduce extreme poverty by 50% by 2015,[8] and it would be useful if the government and donors explained how those targets will be met over time.

'The Tenth Department': Haitian resources outside Haiti

In November 1994 a government ministry was established for a new 'Tenth Department', for the 1.5 million Haitians living and working abroad, mainly in the USA, Canada, Cuba, the Dominican Republic, the Bahamas and France.[9] This is a significant political and economic factor for Haiti and the 'diaspora' should be viewed creatively as potential for Haitian development. As well as their contribution in other countries, Haitians abroad, according to the World Bank, send remittances back to Haiti totalling $100 million a year. During the repressive regimes of the 1960s and 1970s many professionals left Haiti. More recently, the exodus has been increasingly driven by poverty – an estimated half a million Haitians work in the Dominican Republic or risk their lives as 'boat people' to reach the USA and the Bahamas.

Box 25 The eradication of the creole pig: aid – in whose interests?

Haiti used to have one million pigs, which served as an important source (50%) of the annual protein consumption and, in the absence of a 'banking system' a vital savings capacity for peasant families. Between 1981 and 1983, under the pretence of African swine fever spreading in Haiti (and to the USA), the USA provided funds to eradicate all creole pigs in Haiti. The USA then donated its own replacement gemelle pigs to farmers. Gemelle pigs require a concrete sty, special diet and are not well suited to the scavenging, free grazing customs in rural Haiti. The policy had devastating effects on peasant families (many of whom still remember the exact date their pigs were destroyed). Donors are now supporting the restocking of creole pigs. This is a famous episode but worth repeating as a poignant analogy for the development cooperation relationship as a whole. It begs the question of whose interests are really at heart. Should aid be continued if it means that the donor subsidises its own producers, imposes inappropriate programmes without consultation with recipients and ends up destroying local livelihoods?

A more positive and effective approach from governments like that of the USA would be to put greater emphasis on investment in human resources in Haiti rather than solely restricting immigration.

The reality of development cooperation for Haitians in the Northwest

ACTIONAID and GRAF are working in the Northwest of Haiti. This section examines some of development issues important at that level.[10] The poorest region in the country, many of the issues in the Northwest reflect those at the national level. The Northwest is a desolate and isolated region facing a major natural resource crisis. Although some UN, bilateral, government and non-governmental agencies are present, the region receives little assistance.

The Far West part of the Northwest Department is even more isolated. People survive on a subsistence basis, increasingly turning to unsustainable sources of income such as charcoal production and unrestricted goat herding. Long periods of drought have left nutritional and health levels at crisis point, with 350,000 people affected. The few health and education centres that exist are understaffed and lack essential materials. Infrastructure is poor, and travel to and within the region extremely difficult. The region has a strong tradition of civil society and resistance.

Food aid

'We have been receiving food aid for 30 years, and I am still hungry' (peasant woman in Bombardopolis).

Large amounts of food aid have been supplied to the Northwest, mainly in the form of US grain, some through food for work programmes. Local community groups recognise the need for food inputs in times of crisis such as the famine of 1997. However, they point out that this type of aid causes tensions in the recipient communities, undermines local production and fails to provide appropriate nutritional needs. They would prefer other products such as rice, vegetables, meat and oil. More importantly, groups want to solve their problems of water and isolation, as well as access to markets, off-farm activities, land reform and access to savings and credit in order to prepare for, and manage, crises.

Environmental degradation

With the exception of the attempts at agrarian reform, few resources are put into environmental concerns at the national or regional level – yet these are at the root of many of Haiti's problems. Only 2% of the donor programme is for the environment and to date, according to the World Bank, the majority of projects have been limited in scope and impact.[11]

Each year the equivalent of 6000 hectares is lost though erosion. Forest cover has been destroyed in over 97% of Haitian territory, and at the current rate only the pine forest area in the south-eastern part of the country will remain forested in 2008.

In the Northwest, in May 1997, three consecutive harvests had been lost. In desperation, and fully aware of the environmental consequences, more communities were turning to charcoal burning and goats. It was said that people were even burning roots and shrubs because so few trees were left. The Northwest, one of nine departments in Haiti, provides 40% of the charcoal for the capital Port-au-Prince.

A Ministry of Environment has been created in Haiti with donor support, and at the micro-level some projects deal with replanting, nurseries, irrigation and wells, but only a substantial environmental plan at the national level and integrated development programmes at the local level can revert the situation.

Can aid work?

One of the striking features of the Northwest (and Haiti as a whole) is the strength of civil society. A range of local groups, having survived difficult political periods, have emerged and engage in self-help initiatives. These groups include women's and mixed groups, as well as local, regional and national branches of peasant associations, and sector specific organisations (such as the Jean Marie Vincent Foundation on literacy, established in Jean Rabel). On the whole, community organisations maintain close links with local government structures (CASECs or Community Councils).[12]

Two key success indicators in aid projects have been identified by these local groups – participation and projects that enhance productive assets. In rural Haiti there are numerous success stories of local-level training and micro-projects in literacy, livestock, environment, credit and marketing.

At the level of large-scale aid, the example quoted above from agrarian reform in Artibonite demonstrates that it is possible for government, the international community and local groups to work in synergy. Too often in the past, the links between the micro and the macro have not been established, not least because of the tendency of agencies to remain in Port-au-Prince.

Recommendations

For the Northwest:
1. The Northwest has been described as a 'permanent disaster', with recurring drought and famine. Appropriate and rapid action is required in times of crisis in consultation with local groups. Equally important, however, is the need for effective disaster preparedness and mitigation, and for emergency interventions to be placed in a long-term strategy to strengthen food security at the community level.
2. The platform established by the government to provide a coordination mechanism between state, donors and civil society towards the emergency response in the Northwest could be extended and improved to ensure coordination for longer term development needs. These needs could be addressed through gender sensitive integrated development programmes, building on local expertise and, to enhance people's productive assets; savings and credit schemes; health and education rehabilitation; land reform and access to markets.
3. Building on a proper analysis of the region's needs, and through a consultative mechanism, priorities should be decided for the long-term integration of the region in terms of physical infrastructure – roads, water and electricity supply – and in terms of integrating a regional development strategy into a national plan.

At the national level:
1. The current levels of international assistance should be maintained in the foreseeable future to ensure that gains for sustainable democracy are not lost.
2. Donor spending should be better targeted towards poverty reduction for the benefit of the poorest in Haiti, especially in rural areas. As a minimum, as agreed at the World Summit for Social Development in 1995, donors should aim to allocate 20% of their aid to basic social services (including primary health care, basic education, water and sanitation) and donors and the government should develop a timetable for reaching the OECD target of reducing the number of people in extreme poverty by 50% by 2015.
3. Aid should reinforce national and local government structures when these are essential to ensure aid reaches the poorest, and should involve effective local consultation with civil society. Donors could consider support for enabling the provisions for local government as set out in the 1987 constitution. Aid should not act in parallel to government where this undermines the state.
4. A greater effort should be made, and resources allocated, to ensure donors and government are transparent in their development programmes. The involvement of community groups in the design, implementation and evaluation of programmes will make aid more effective and lead to a more sustainable democracy.

Notes
1. This chapter has been written by Ian McFarlane, ACTIONAID in close consultation with ACTIONAID colleagues and ACTIONAID's partner in Haiti, Groupe de Recherche et d'Action pour le développement du Far West (GRAF). The consultation included discussion with local community groups, national and international NGOs, government and donors. A full list of interviews and documentation is available.
2. Country Document, InterAmerican Development Bank, 1996.
3. See Mark Weisbrot, *Negotiation or Imposition*, Roots, 1997.
4. UNDP, *Human Development Report* 1996, OUP, New York.
5. F Stewart, *Adjustment and Poverty 1995*, quoted in Reinert and Voss, *Development in Practice*, February 1997.
6. See for example L McGowan, *Democracy undermined, economic justice denied*, Development Gap, February 1997.
7. Reinert and Voss, *op cit.*
8. OECD Development Assistance Committee, *Shaping the 21st Century*, OECD, Paris, 1996.
9. Bulletin from the Haitian Ministry for Haitians living abroad, 1996.
10. More detailed information is available from a pilot study and consultations facilitated by GRAF and ACTIONAID.
11. World Bank, *Country Assistance Strategy*, August 1996.
12. The 1987 constitution made the government of Haiti more accountable at the local level.

Breaking new ground in donor coordination in India

Binu S Thomas[1]

India has warned that declining aid levels could force developing countries to turn their backs on market-led development and return to state-run economies. Speaking at the United Nations last year, India's Permanent Representative to the UN Prakash Shah said that falling aid levels could 'discourage developing countries that have in the recent past undertaken major programmes for economic liberalisation and market reforms from pursuing them and might even force them to retreat into managed economies.'[2]

India is the fourth largest aid recipient in the world. But like most of its neighbours in South Asia, it has in recent years been discriminated against by official donors in terms of aid flows in relation to other low income economies. India has suffered a 5.9% per annum real decline in aid over the decade 1985–95.[3] This situation could dramatically worsen if the threats to graduate India from ODA assistance – of which it is by far the single largest recipient – materialise. India sees ODA as being critical to sustain levels of public investment in social and infrastructure sectors.

Globally, ODA now accounts for only one-quarter of net flows to developing countries. While private flows to developing countries jumped from US$ 48,500 million in 1990 to an estimated US$ 234,000 million in 1996, official development finance declined in real terms from US$ 86,100 million to an estimated US$ 71,800 million during this period. But private flows have again gone to a handful of countries. In 1996, India received a little over US$ 6000 million in private capital flows – foreign direct investment and portfolio investment – or less than 2.5% of all private flows to developing countries.[4]

Changes in the nature of ODA could herald further reduction in aid to India. In recent years ODA that has traditionally been used to fund long-term development and poverty alleviation – on which India has a strong case – is now being increasingly directed towards refugee assistance, debt relief and peacekeeping. For instance, the British government's spending on humanitarian relief rose from £129 million in 1990/1 to £350 million in 1994/5 while its contribution to international peacekeeping went up by more than eight times in the five years to 1996.[5] Multilateral aid, which has tended to favour low-income countries like India, is also under pressure in an era of dwindling ODA. In 1995, 65% of aid from multilateral sources went to low-income countries, compared with only 46% for bilaterals.[6]

With donor commitments to multilateral assistance falling (although disbursements based on past commitments still show an increase in several cases), the outlook for countries such as India – given their high dependence on multilateral assistance – appears bleak. In 1970, only 12% of aid to India came from multilateral sources; today the figure is over 60%. In neighbouring Nepal, the share of multilateral assistance has risen from 34.6% in 1975/6 to 59% in 1994/6.[7] Similar trends are visible elsewhere in the subcontinent.

Ironically, none of the reasons for favouring multilateral assistance over bilateral modes of funding have really changed. Recipients of aid still find it convenient to deal with a few international bodies rather than a large number of donors, each with different policies and procedures. Because of their size, these international organisations can carry out larger and more specialised programmes, for which small donors may lack the funds or the know-how and finally multilateral aid is convenient as individual donors do not have to invest in selection, implementation and supervision of programmes and projects.[8]

The Development Assistance Committee of the OECD also sees great merit in the donor countries extending 'coordinated support' to developing countries; of donors achieving 'policy coherence';

and of improving monitoring and evaluation.[9] All this would, if anything, suggest a greater rather than a lesser role for multilateral institutions in official development assistance.

This is not to suggest that multilateral donors do not need to get their act together. 'There is a need for greater coordination at the multilateral level to prevent overlapping and duplication,' says Professor M A Oommen of the Institute of Social Studies, New Delhi, who recently completed a EU-sponsored study of aid to India.[10]

The following analysis attempts to examine whether multilateral and bilateral donors in India have taken steps towards greater coordination and policy coherence, as envisaged by the OECD, and with what result.

In March 1997, five UN agencies in India came together for the first time in a collaborative manner to support a community based primary education programme. UNESCO, UNICEF, UNDP, the ILO and the UNFPA committed US$ 20 million towards a programme aimed at girl children and improving teacher performance in disadvantaged rural and urban schools in 160 blocks in eight states of India.

The five-agencies initiative reflects 'a new spirit of coordination among UN agencies in India,' said a UN press release. Through this interagency initiative the five participating UN agencies have harmonised their respective funding cycles to 1997–2001 in the area of primary education, thereby providing greater synergy to their development efforts.

The framework for interagency collaboration among UN bodies in India was set out in January 1997 when the UN system in India released a UN System Position Statement. This was an alternative to the Country Strategy Note that the UN had asked aid recipient countries to prepare and which India did not consider appropriate to produce. The position note identified nine priority areas for the UN system in India. These are population stabilisation, gender equality, health of women and children, HIV/AIDS, primary education, food security and nutrition, water, employment and sanitation.

Representative of the views of the 19 UN agencies working in India, the common position statement seeks to develop a common understanding of development problems and 'as much as possible' develop joint strategies for implementation. 'The primary objective of interagency cooperation is to increase the impact of development assistance. . . . The activities of most of the UN agencies cut across social sectors. Therefore, pooling together resources will maximise return on investments.'[11]

Interestingly, the UN system in India appears to have taken the initiative to foster greater interagency cooperation even before it was done internationally. The UN General Assembly Resolution 50/120 adopted in 1996 requests all UN Resident Representatives in full consultation with national governments, to facilitate a coherent, coordinated and integrated United Nations follow-up to the international conferences at the field level.

At the global level, a UN System Conferences Action Plan (UNSCAP) was set up by the Administrative Committee on Coordination (ACC) in October 1995 for the joint and integrated follow-up to the conferences. Within the UNSCAP, three interagency task forces were established dealing with Employment and Sustainable Livelihoods (chaired by the ILO), Basic Social Services for All (chaired by UNFPA) and Enabling Environment for Social and Economic Development (chaired by the World Bank). In April 1996, the ACC also decided to establish an Interagency Committee on Women and Gender Equality chaired by the Special Adviser to the Secretary General on Gender Issues.

However, in India the first steps were taken by the UNDP Resident Representative at the end of 1994, when four UN interagency working groups (IAWGs) were constituted dealing with gender and development, population and development, HIV/AIDS and primary education. Two more IAWGs dealing with food security and nutrition, and water and sanitation were constituted in April 1996. The work of the IAWGs is monitored by the heads of the participating agencies at the regular interagency meetings and facilitated and monitored by the UN Resident Coordinator and the UN Interagency Support Unit, which was established in 1995. It is still unclear how the IAWGs will feed into the global follow-up to the UN conferences.

The primary education IAWG has only six UN agencies represented on it, while gender and development with 15 has the largest representation. Each working group has a lead UN agency, which takes responsibility for developing a common agenda (The one on gender is led by UNICEF and UNIFEM jointly.) Primary education is the only IAWG without a lead agency, apparently because members, most notably UNICEF and UNESCO, could not agree on who should lead.

The government of India, aware that it would not be easy for UN agencies to work together in practice, has signed up only for a US$ 900,000 preparatory phase of the US$ 20 million UN System Primary Education initiative when the management structure, financial disbursement modalities, state action plans, monitoring and evaluation arrangements and so on would be finalised. It will be a real test for the UN system in India whether it can turn cooperation on paper into joint implementation at the field level. 'The US$ 20 million commitment made by the five agencies is an expression of faith. This is the best chance for the UN system to show it can work together and deliver at low cost,' says Bhaskar Bhattacharji, Assistant Resident Representative, UNDP, in New Delhi.[12]

Some other notable events that have taken place under the banner of the IAWGs so far include:

- In October 1996 the IAWG on Food Security and Nutrition, which consists of about a dozen UN agencies and is led by the FAO, had an exchange of views with a member of the Planning Commission, Government of India on the Ninth Five Year Plan as it relates to Food Security and Nutrition.
- A Subgroup on Monitoring Indicators set up by the IAWG on Population and Development is working on establishing a common set of economic, social and population indicators that could be used by the government of India, the UN system and others to monitor India's progress towards achieving the recommendations of recent UN Conferences.
- The IAWG on Water and Sanitation made a submission to the formulation of the Ninth Five Year Plan at the request of the Ministry of Rural Areas and Employment.
- The IAWG on Gender and Development has set up an advocacy subgroup which has facilitated four meetings of women activists in India and constituted a think-tank of six prominent Indian women to take forward the recommendations of the regional meetings and lobby the Planning Commission on Gender Sensitising the Ninth Five Year Plan.

In September 1996, an effort was made by UNDP to widen donor coordination beyond the UN system, to include bilateral donors in India as well. A number of Multi-Bi Sectoral Coordination Groups were established, each facilitated by a multilateral, bilateral, or, in some cases, even by a large NGO. As of March 1997, 14 of the 18 sectoral coordination groups had met at least once. The groups and the names of the facilitation agencies are:

- Agriculture (facilitated by FAO)
- Drug Control (UNDCP)
- Education (European Commission)
- Environment (USAID and UNDP)
- Employment and Income Generation (ILO)
- Forestry (Society For Promotion of Wasteland Development)
- Gender (UNIFEM)
- Good Governance (Ford Foundation and UNDP)
- HIV/AIDS (UNAIDS)
- Industry and Private Sector Development (UNIDO)
- Infrastructure (World Bank)
- Micro-Enterprise Development (AusAID)
- Nutrition (USAID)
- Population (UNFPA)
- Power (Japanese Embassy)
- Cooperation with NGOs (UNDP)
- Water and Sanitation (UNDP/WB Water and Sanitation Programme).

It is too early to say to what extent this new spirit of coordination and cooperation will yield results. While external pressures such as falling aid levels are bound to work in favour of greater donor coordination, internal pressures that militate against it remain strong. These include one-upmanship behaviour of bilateral and multilateral donors, with each seeing the other as being less effective than themselves; competition to attract more of a shrinking aid cake; and, ironically, the problem of spending existing resources. The UNDP programme in India, for instance, underspent almost 30% of its fourth country programme (1990–7) allocation.

Prior to the UN's recent effort at fostering multilateral–bilateral coordination and cooperation, the only worthwhile effort in India has been in the area of gender. For many years, an interagency WID group comprising multilaterals, bilateral and international NGOs has been meeting about ten times a year in New Delhi. The WID group, which has a good track record on donor coordination, played a major role in facilitating Indian NGO participation in the Beijing process. Several donors pooled their resources and had to do a significant amount of lobbying within their own institutions to find agreement on certain common policies and procedures acceptable to all contributing donors.[13]

Unfortunately, no attempt was made to evaluate donor cooperation and coordination following Beijing, which could have provided valuable learning for the UN's latest efforts on what does and does not work in the area of inter-donor collaboration. The IAWG on gender continues to

India

benefit from its link with the larger WID effort. Both Canada's CIDA and The Netherlands' embassy have made financial contributions to the advocacy efforts being mounted by the IAWG. There are also, thanks to the efforts of the WID group, 'gender focal points' in many agencies. Bilaterals such as the Japanese, who were not previously involved, have since Beijing, started showing greater interest.[14] The IAWG briefs members of the larger WID group on its activities to ensure both work in a cooperative mode.

Changes in the government of India's policies in certain areas are also pressuring donors both to revisit their development strategies and to cooperate and coordinate more with each other. In the area of primary education, the government has formulated guidelines for its ambitious District Primary Education Programme (DPEP), to which all donors interested in funding primary education in the country have to adhere.

In the past, India rarely depended on external funding on a large scale to promote primary education. Traditionally, externally funded projects focusing on selected aspects of primary education operated in different states. In 1983, when the British ODA commenced Phase 1 of the Andhra Pradesh Primary Education Project (APPEP), it focused exclusively on civil works and on teacher training. Later, other components were added. However, it is no longer possible to have projects that support only particular components. Donors funding DPEP have been forced to take a comprehensive view of education. They have also to adhere to guidelines such as limiting the construction component to 24% and management to 6%. In other words, 70% of funding has to be on programme running costs (equipment such as blackboards and books as well as salaries) directly.

The DPEP, which is operational in over 100 districts, selected on the basis of their low ranking in terms of female literacy, is an important effort to invert the planning pyramid. India's attempts at decentralised planning have shown that there exists limited scope for local initiatives in district planning. This is because crucial allocation decisions are taken at the national or state level. The DPEP attempts to alter the pattern of resource decisions, favouring local initiatives at the district level. Against the normal process of schemes being formulated at the central level and executed at the local level, under DPEP, guidelines are prepared at the national level and plans are developed at the local level.[15]

The DPEP approach is also important because, in India, the focus of primary education needs to be shifted from access to improving achievement levels. In India, 95% of the rural population has access to a primary school within a walking distance of one kilometre, but the achievement levels remain abysmally low. Locally developed and owned strategies hold the key to improving achievement levels and to keeping children in school. At present, nearly one in two children drop out before they reach their fifth year in school. Innovations such as the use of *bridge languages* (languages that bridge the gap that exists between tribal dialects and the standard Hindi dialect, so that the learner feels that the language used in the classroom is only an extension of what is used at home and not radically different), tailoring programmes to suit the more socially backward scheduled castes and scheduled tribes, incentive schemes and so on, have been made possible through the DPEP.[16]

The DPEP is an important example of aid supporting locally-owned strategies. It has found support from the World Bank, the EU, UNICEF and British ODA. The 'DPEP has broken new paths in international cooperation, in that it belongs to the new genre of development cooperation, which emphasises sustainability, equity, local ownership and execution and is supportive of national policies in the education sector.'[17]

Under the DPEP, twice every year a Joint Supervision Mission (JSM) (comprising up to six or seven experts identified by the government of India and donor representatives) visits each state – where different donors could be financing the programme in different districts – to review progress. Donors negotiate with the government of India as to who will head the mission. This usually operates on a rotational basis. A common progress report is then prepared. Donors are finding the JSM idea quite a good one. 'The Joint Supervision Mission has been very useful for exploring common agendas between the ODA, other donors, the state government and the central government,' says Anthony Davison, head of the ODA Field Management Office in New Delhi.[18] The ODA has committed a sum of £86 million (about US$ 135 million) over a seven-year period to supporting DPEP in ten districts of Andhra Pradesh and West Bengal.

As the donors fund different districts and each has a fairly holistic funding programme involving both the hardware and software aspects, there are not too many demands on them to cooperate with each other at the operational level. This, says the ODA's Davison, is unlike co-financing ventures such as the Nepal Primary Education Project where the

India

Asian Development Bank provides the hardware and the ODA the software. This obliges both parties to work closely together because if the school buildings are not complete, the educational inputs cannot start.

Even so, donors have had to work together to harmonise their policies and procedures to suit the requirements of state governments, which cannot, for instance, have different tendering procedures to suit different donors supporting the DPEP in a particular state. There have been quite a few changes in ODA norms to suit DPEP guidelines, with more to follow. The ODA has agreed to use World Bank bid documents for tendering. It has been asked by the government of India to replace Limited National Competitive Bidding for expenditures in the range of UK£ 75,000–250,000 (US$ 120,000–400,000) with open competitive bidding.

The World Bank has shown flexibility by dropping its demand that state governments resort to international bidding for procuring vehicles. Some wrinkles, however, still require ironing out. Seeking telephone and fax quotations, for instance, is quite acceptable to the ODA, but is not acceptable to the World Bank. The ODA has also been trying to get the government of India to agree to a process of concurrent evaluation rather than just a mid-term review. 'There are certain global guidelines on impact evaluation which we are obliged to follow,' says Davison.

International NGOs operating in India, many of which are recipients of Official Development Assistance in their home countries, have also been trying to work out areas of cooperation and coordinated action. Last February, some 21 NGO and bilateral donors met in Bangalore in a meeting hosted by the Bangalore-based Donor Agency Network to discuss issues of common concern. Three issues that received special attention were donor collaboration; transparency, accountability and code of conduct for donors; and dependency syndrome, withdrawal and sustainability. ACTIONAID India, through its Donor Partnership Unit in New Delhi, has also been working to bring about greater cooperation and coordination between multilaterals, bilaterals and international NGOs operating in India.

Overall, the last couple of years have seen some important initiatives being undertaken by multilaterals and bilaterals in India towards improving donor cooperation and coordination. Some of this has been prompted by the fast changing external aid situation and others by changes in the government of India's policies. Even so, there is still far too little interagency dialogue taking place on a regular basis to move things along at a rapid pace.

Even in the DPEP, where the government of India's policies have pressured donors to enter into a dialogue, there is not enough interagency dialogue happening. 'There used to be World Bank and EU coordination meetings to explore common systems until some 18 months ago. But these have since dropped off,' says Davison.

The first steps towards improving the effectiveness of external assistance to India has been taken through the IAWGs, the Multi–Bi Sectoral Coordination Groups, Joint Supervision Missions of the DPEP and so on. But how far and how fast these initiatives will result in improving the impact of aid will depend on efforts of individual agencies to translate coordination and cooperation from mere words into deeds. In an era of shrinking aid budgets, India has perhaps as much of a stake in ensuring the success of the new interagency initiatives as the donors themselves.

Notes

1. The author is Coordinator, Policy & Advocacy Unit, ACTIONAID India. The views expressed in this chapter are not necessarily those of ACTIONAID India.
2. 'Aid Cuts to Thwart Third World Reform Says India', *Deccan Herald*, 6 July 1996.
3. Development Assistance Committee Report (OECD), 1996.
4. Data from OECD Press Release SG/COM/NEWS (97)56 and 'Global Development Finance' published by the World Bank and reported in article 'World Bank Concern Over Fall in ODA to Poor Countries', *Business Line*, 24 March 1997.
5. Speech of Clare Short MP as Shadow Minister for Overseas Development of the UK to BOND General Assembly, 5 November 1996.
6. From the chapter 'The Changing Face of Aid' in *The World Debt Tables, 1997*, World Bank.
7. Chandra Prasad Bhattarai, *Foreign Aid in Nepal: A Brief Analysis*, ACTIONAID Nepal, July 1996.
8. Max van den Berg and Bram van Ojik, *Rarer than Rubies: Reflections on Development Cooperation*, Novib, The Hague, 1996.
9. DAC, *Shaping the 21st Century: The Contribution of Development Cooperation*, OECD, May 1996.
10. Interviewed by the author.
11. United Nations Position Statement – India, January 1997.
12. Interviewed by the author.
13. Author's interview with Rita Sarin, Programme Officer, Embassy of Sweden, New Delhi.
14. Author's interview with Ayami Noritake, Programme Officer, UNIFEM, New Delhi.
15. N V Varghese, Decentralisation of Educational Planning and the District Primary Education Programme, NIEPA, New Delhi, 1996.
16. Author's interview with N V Varghese, National Institute of Educational Planning and Administration. New Delhi.
17. Department of Education, *DPEP Guidelines*, Ministry of Human Resource Development, New Delhi. May 1995.
18. Interviewed by the author.

International cooperation with Latin America

Mariano Valderrama, CEPES, Peru

The new leadership of Japan and the European Union

From the latest available OECD statistics, bilateral aid to Latin America in the period 1994/5 represented 12% of the world total. The countries that contributed the major volume of foreign aid to Latin America were, in order of importance, Japan, the USA, Germany, France and Spain.

From this, the following tendencies can be highlighted: first, the decline of North American help, which in 1984/5 represented a little more than 50% of the external cooperation to this region, but which more recently has not reached even 20%. On the other hand, Japanese assistance has increased fivefold between 1984/5 and 1994/5 to become the most important contributing nation.

Furthermore, European Union member nations provided more than 50% of external aid to Latin America, highlighting the new presence of Spain (which is the third highest European country by the volume of its cooperation). This presence is consistent with the increase of Hispanic investment in the region and the implicit role assumed by Spain in European Union relations with Latin America.

Japanese aid tends to be given in the form of equipment, professional assistance and loans. The Japanese give more money for infrastructure and avoid involvement in subjects such as democratisation. Nevertheless, Japan's influence over Latin American governments is growing.

These trends to some extent reflect the decline in global resources available for international development cooperation, which has resulted in reduced foreign aid for Latin America. The aid tends to be concentrated on certain regions and countries: Central America (Honduras, Guatemala, Nicaragua, El Salvador), the Andean region (Bolivia, Peru) and the Caribbean (Haiti). Within these same areas, there tend to be certain areas of priority where aid is directed, mostly according to levels of poverty.

Countries with higher economic status, like Argentina, Costa Rica, Chile, Venezuela and Uruguay, do not apply for technical cooperation, but concessional loans and private finance for these countries have increased notably.[1]

New forms of cooperation: debt conversion and funds

Some traditional forms of assistance, such as food aid, have tended to disappear from the region and new forms have been introduced, such as programmes to reduce and convert debt into social development or natural resource protection funds. Over the period from the end of the 1980s through the first half of the 1990s, debt conversion allowed the generation of US$ 850 million for environmental protection projects in 23 countries. The largest number of conversions took place in Costa Rica.

The Initiative of the Americas launched by President Bush in 1990 proposed a reduction in the commercial debt of the countries that joined the Brady Plan and subscribed to an agreement with the US government. A percentage of the principal is to be remitted and the interest to be paid in 'local currency', which would then be assigned to fiscal funds for environmental protection and sustainable development. In 1992, Chile and the USA agreed to reduce US$ 15.7 million of debt from a total of US$ 39.3 million. Chile financed environmental protection projects to pay interest on the US$ 23 million. Bolivia reduced its debt of US$ 300 million to the USA by promising to invest US$ 2 million in a programme of environmental conservation and sustainable development. Peru is implementing a similar agreement. Spain has begun discussions about the possibility of starting reduction operations or debt conversion with Latin America, although there are many obstacles to overcome (see box below on debt swaps).

> **Box 26   Debt swaps**
>
> Although the operations of exchanging debt for development or social investment do not reach a significant amount in terms of total volume of debt and percentage of total cooperation, they are generating very interesting mechanisms of development. Various countries have agreed on debt conversion operations in Latin America: Germany, Canada, the USA, The Netherlands and Switzerland, to name a few.
>
> For the celebration of the 700th anniversary of the Helvetian Confederation, the Swiss government decided to remit US$ 700 million of bilateral and commercial debt. In exchange, beneficiary countries were committed to use their resources in local currency for development funds. In Latin America this has occurred in Nicaragua, Honduras, Peru, Bolivia and Ecuador. In the case of Peru, the Swiss debt conversion originated the formation of a *Contravalor* Fund, which allows financing of local development projects organised by community associations, NGOs and local government. There are various other operations to convert debt.
>
> In conjunction with the Peruvian government, Germany has converted a debt of 30 million deutschmarks to establish an Environmental Protection Fund. At the moment an agreement is being established to convert an initial DM 50 million into local currency (valued at DM 20 million) for social development projects. There have been similar agreements with Finland (114 million Finnish Markkaas) and Canada (C$ 25 million) and negotiations to reduce and convert debt are being held with USAID. An interesting example is the agreement between the Episcopal Conference of Ecuador and the Government of Ecuador where US$ 28 million of debt (bought at 15% of the value from funds donated by support organisations) was converted and US$ 10 million was directed to a programme that allowed large-scale access to land by peasants through a credit fund of US$ 6 million. Some 350 peasant organisations (approximately 12,200 families) became beneficiaries by being able to buy 422 million hectares of land. The same group in Ecuador became the beneficiary of a debt conversion with Belgium to a value of nearly US$ 3 million, which enabled more than 80 'community funds' to be created to increase production levels and promote employment diversification in the Bolivar region.
>
> Government of Mexico records report a swap of US$ 23 million in 1988/9. This funded the activities of the Development, Promotion and Assistance Fund which was created through the initiative of the Archdiocese of Mexico after the Mexican earthquake to implement projects in popular housing, employment and education – projects which continue to operate. UNICEF has carried out 18 debt exchange operations to finance projects oriented to childhood in eight countries, including Bolivia, Jamaica and Peru.

Civil society and private sector as protagonists: Do they really play this role in international cooperation?

The participation of civil society in cooperation is widely talked of by development cooperation institutions. But, in practice, the management of development cooperation, whether by multilateral organisations like the Inter-American Development Bank (IADB), the World Bank or the European Union, or by the principal donors and their Southern counterparts, is the responsibility of bureaucratic leaders.

The private sector is benefiting from but not acting in the processes of development cooperation. Moreover, organisations like the Multilateral Investment Fund of the IADB, created to promote private initiatives in Latin America, do not include representatives from the private sector as participants in their process of decision making. Decisions are made by the members who represent the principal contributors (Japan, the USA and Spain) who actually act under the pressure of Councils of Representatives of the associated governments.

The process of increased participation of civil society results in proclamations. But it is not practised by the principal donors. In the case of economically lighter weight countries, such as The Netherlands, Switzerland or Canada, and in the

Latin America

various projects of the United States Agency for International Development (USAID), for example, if they find an open door they will try to encourage regional bodies and sectors of civil society to participate by formulating and implementing development initiatives.[2]

One of the problems of development cooperation is the high level of centralisation. A great effort is being made to develop programmes for poverty reduction in remote areas, but the decisions are concentrated in the capital cities. There are some exceptions. In Bolivia, for example, a Law of Popular Participation was approved, which makes it possible to manage the country's budget and resources for development cooperation in a decentralised way, with more participation from the local government and population. In Spain, the increasing participation of Spanish communities and autonomous parliaments and the distribution of a significant part of development assistance through NGOs has contributed to more decentralised project management.

One of the most active forms of participation of civil society in development cooperation tasks is that of NGOs, which historically have received support from, and have maintained an interchange with, the private development agencies of the North. There are more than 20,000 NGOs in Latin America and they manage an amount equivalent to a quarter of the total bilateral ODA. There are countries such as The Hetherlands, Switzerland and Spain in which the percentage of resources directed towards NGOs is larger. At present, many multilateral and bilateral organisations are developing projects through NGOs, but in these cases, they generally take a more instrumental role, acting as contractors or providers of services.

Among NGOs, one can distinguish those that work within a development concept and have connections with popular organisations from those new institutions that act like consultants or contractors of the state to implement projects – often in social or emergency programmes set up to compensate for the social costs of economic adjustment. The NGOs that work more closely with popular organisations have, with them, developed a series of initiatives, not only in areas like agricultural development, health, education or micro-businesses but have also contributed to social democracy, supporting the empowerment of local governments, the defence of human rights and the ability of people to form basic organisations.

Notes

1. Direct net foreign investment in Latin America (including bonus payments and capital investments), increased from 23,900 million dollars in 1989 to 90,300 million dollars in 1995.
2. Traditionally, projects were negotiated within bilateral commissions and their execution was the responsibility of public institutions, sometimes in agreement with a technical mission from the donor country. Now, in various cases, bilateral commissions define some basic features of cooperation; and for the specific features and the execution of the projects, the participation of diverse institutions is convened (such as decentralised public entities, universities, NGOs and consulting companies).

Internal management in relation to Uganda's external debt

V E Edoku, African Forum and Network on Debt and Development (AFRODAD) and Uganda Debt Network (UDN)

The African Forum and Network on Debt and Development (AFRODAD) in conjunction with the Uganda Debt Network (UDN) have a common strategy and programme to undertake research on key debt issues in the region. The research activities are intended to provide information and data required for dialogue, lobbying and advocacy on debt issues at national, regional and international levels. The Uganda Debt Network is an NGO that was formed to bring together civil society, organisations, institutions, individuals and other interested groups who are concerned about Uganda's debt burden and how it is hampering economic, social and human development. It was also formed to facilitate dialogue between policy planners, decision makers and implementers of government policy and the general public about Uganda's debt management and its impact on economic and social development. This research, which was commissioned by the two NGOs, focuses in particular on internal management of external loan resources as a factor in the Uganda debt crisis.

Summary of main points

1. It is observed that Uganda's debt burden is not sustainable as the country is not able to meet its external debt obligations in full now and for the foreseeable future without major debt relief. The country is faced with payments constraints of two kinds: inadequate local currency funds and inadequate foreign exchange reserves.
2. The country therefore adopted a debt strategy which places emphasis on debt relief and assistance to augment immediate debt repayment capacity based on tight financial and economic reforms supported mainly by World Bank and IMF funding. The strategy has been largely successful and Uganda has benefited from debt relief from multilateral and bilateral donors and creditors. The latest achievement is the debt relief package approved by the World Bank in April 1997 under the HIPC Debt Initiative. The package, which will reduce Uganda's debt by US$ 338 million in net present value (NPV) terms by April 1998, is expected to enable Uganda to exit from the debt rescheduling process it has been on since 1981.
3. In spite of the above successes, the more important consideration is to increase export earnings and future repayment capacity which satisfies the World Bank and IMF definition of debt sustainability. This specifies that external debt is sustainable when 'a country is able to meet its current and future external debt obligations in full, without recourse to relief or rescheduling of debts or accumulation of arrears, and without unduly compromising economic growth'. Therefore, the debt strategy that places more emphasis on macro-level issues and short-term external debt reduction measures should now change to increasing or expanding the domestic capacity to service the loans in the medium and long term on a sustainable basis.
4. In pursuit of this policy, Uganda should consolidate its borrowing strategy, strengthen its loans negotiations machinery and develop appropriate guiding principles for contracting new debt. Debt sustainability and concessionality considerations should be strictly adhered to, ceilings on how much Uganda can borrow externally as fixed from time to time should be

Uganda

observed as well as debt sustainability indicators. It is also important to ensure that the foreign capital borrowed is absorbed efficiently and that the amount of debt that can be serviced without risking external payments problems is carefully determined and linked to repayment capacity. This would primarily mean acceptability of the projects funded from external resources on the basis of their quality, viability, expected benefits and capacity to repay the loans.
5. It is noted that the current institutional arrangements and functional linkages that would ensure efficient aid and debt management, are not well coordinated. The arrangements and units are numerous, complicated and need to be streamlined. To avoid contracting loans with bad and complex terms, which make them extremely difficult to manage, there is a need to ensure that the various work units are well equipped, trained and professional in their work. Although some steps have already been taken to improve the situation, there is still much to be done, not only in the areas of policy, borrowing strategy and loan negotiations, but also in external debt, project monitoring and evaluation and tracking project implementation.
6. The study therefore proposes a simplified and improved debt and project coordination structure involving the creation of four committees, two at technical and operational level and the other two at policy and executive level with linkages to the line ministries/end users and to the creditors/donors. A new proposal is the involvement of the private sector and civil society through representation on some of the committees so that their contributions and concerns at all stages of the loan/project phases are not missed.
7. There is a clear need for improving the institutional and functional arrangements to address problems of external public and publicly guaranteed loans. Further research and capacity building is required to improve on internal debt management systems and practices.

Macroeconomic framework

Overview of the economy and development objectives and policies

The focus of Uganda's development objective is rapid improvement of the living standards of the population through accelerated economic growth and human resource development, combined with social justice. The Government Policy Framework Paper (PFP) 1995/6–1997/8 identifies three main strategies by which this can be achieved, namely:

- by exploiting the high potential for growth in agriculture, industry and tourism;
- by maintaining favourable macroeconomic policies and forces; and
- by achieving and maintaining political stability and peace.

To this may be added improved public-sector management, promotion of private sector development, financial sector reforms and protection of the environment. The underlying objective is to achieve a structural transformation of the economy and society from its present low levels of production of a largely subsistence nature to a commercial, industrial and technologically developed and monetised economy with widespread and equitably distributed economic and social benefits. Much has been done towards the realisation of these objectives but the performance is beset by a number of problems including the non-gearing of external resources to achieve these stated objectives.

Recent economic performance Uganda's economy is dependent on agriculture. Both the monetary and non-monetary agriculture contributes over 45% of GDP, 80% of export earnings and it employs 80% of the labour force. Coffee alone contributes over 50% of total exports. During the 1960s, the economy grew at approximately 5% per annum, but during the 1970s to early 1980s the economy performed poorly due to political instability and turmoil. Since 1986, there has been a sharp improvement following formulation and implementation of policies and programmes geared towards structural adjustment and an average economic growth of over 6% in real terms has since been achieved.

External sector performance Present economic growth is mainly based on external transfers, constituting 12.3% of aggregate investment in 1995/6. Total public and private investment is 11% of GDP. This large inflow of aid is mainly for investment, of which some 4% is for private investment. The effect of the inflow of foreign aid is an improvement in the country's balance of payments (BOP) position, which recorded an overall surplus of US$ 130 million in 1994/5, equivalent to 2.5% of GDP.

In addition, non-coffee export performance has been improving since 1986. The projection for non-traditional exports in 1995/6 is US$ 180 million. This has increased foreign reserves to an equivalent of over four months of imports of goods and services. This is still inadequate for sustainable growth, which requires that the inflow of foreign exchange from exports continues to increase markedly. This requirement is not easily achievable. The main reason is that Uganda is a high-cost country because of several factors, which, among others, include:

- the fact that the country is land-locked and very far away from the sea;
- very high taxes on petroleum products, resulting in high transport and marketing costs;
- many inefficiencies in the production and distribution of goods and services;
- inadequate road network, government effort to improve on it notwithstanding; and
- highly priced utilities and, in particular, the intermittent power supply which entails a real cost to producers.

The net result is that increases in earnings from exports (both traditional and non-traditional) are low and do not match the increases in imports. Hence, the deficit on Uganda's balance of visible trade.

The net result is that increases in earnings from exports (both traditional and non-traditional) are low and do not match the increases in imports. Hence the deficit on Uganda's balance of visible trade.

On the capital account, however, major inflows of donor assistance, both BOP support and project aid, have created a surplus which has compensated to some degree for the deficit on the current account. But this situation cannot guarantee sustainable economic growth. Obligations arising from principal maturities on an ever increasing stock of debt have resulted in rising outflows. In addition, export earnings are inadequate, imports are high and the size and composition of external debt is unmanageable.

The above situation calls for a deliberate strategy to utilise external resources to invest in resource-based industries, which would cut down imports and make industries competitive, to invest in export-oriented industries with a view to increasing export earnings, to rationalise and utilise external resources in a more productive, effective and efficient manner to enhance domestic capacity and capability to produce competitively for exports.

Overview of external debt burden

Uganda has a total of about 300 loans from about 80 creditors, excluding private sector external debt.

Uganda's debt stock is now US$ 3500 million, up from US$ 3000 million in 1993/4 and US$ 3400 million in 1994/5. This represents a per capita debt of US$ 176 against a per capita income of only $274. The debt stock is inclusive of arrears, most of which is to non-Paris Club governments and commercial creditors.

About three-quarters of the debt is multilateral, owed to IMF, IDA and AfDB groups. Less than a quarter is bilateral, owed equally between Paris Club and non-Paris Club members. Private, non-syndicated debt (other loan category) is only 2.4%.

Most of the loans (80%) are at interest rates ranging between 0% and 4.99%, followed by interest rates of 5% to 9.99%, which constitute 4.9%. A small portion of the loans (2.3%) is at interest rates of more than 10% which is high and comparable to some of the variable interest rates.

As a result of Uganda's debt and adjustment strategies, donors have provided funds for multilateral debt service and the commercial debt buyback of 1993 reduced scheduled service and arrears. In addition, Uganda has benefited from debt forgiveness and other exceptional financing such as rescheduling. The projected debt service and interest payments is now as follows:

Table 24 Debt service and interest payments

Year	Debt servicing (US$ millions)	Interest payments (US$ millions)
1997	176.9	46.6
1998	190	48.5
1999	192.6	47.4
2000	198.8	44.7
2001	183.4	42.7

These amounts show that the debt burden has not been overcome and will not be reducing in the near future.

Total debt service (maturities include IMF) as a percentage of export of goods and services was projected as 23% and at 1.57% of GDP in 1995/6,

Uganda

down from 43% and 2.8% respectively in 1993/4 and from 26% and 2% respectively in 1994/5. Since 1991/2, Uganda's debt and debt service ratios have been falling due to a boom in coffee exports and due to high international coffee prices in 1994/5 and a rise in the dollar value of GDP due to appreciation of the shilling.

The most significant ratios are the total debt stock to exports ratio (602% in 1996/7), which is a measure of the debt overhang, and the debt service to export of goods and services ratio (25% in 1996/7), which is a measure of liquidity. They are significant because they are a key measure of debt sustainability as defined by the World Bank/IMF and therefore they distinguish one country's debt severity situation from an other.

The overall picture is that despite the fact that the economy has recorded positive growth in the last decade, Uganda's external sector performance is not strong and the country is highly indebted.

Factors contributing to Uganda's debt management problems

Uganda's debt strategy

An important part of the debt strategy has been, and will continue to be, to seek assistance to augment immediate payment capacity. This is mainly through debt relief, which can free foreign exchange resources to increase reserves and free local currency for other budgetary expenditures. The achievement under this strategy has been phenomenal, although insufficient. Uganda has benefited from and is continuing to seek debt relief measures and disbursements that can enhance its immediate foreign exchange payment capacity and budget. The latest achievement is the debt relief package approved by the World Bank under the HIPC Debt Initiative. The World Bank agreed to support a package of debt relief that will reduce Uganda's debt by US$ 338 million in NPV terms, of which US$ 160 million will be provided by the World Bank itself by April 1998. The details now being worked out are expected to enable Uganda to exit from the debt rescheduling process.

It is noted that when measuring debt servicing capacity, a World Bank model that projects BOP flows and links them to activities of key sectors of the economy is used. With details of economic sectors, credit sources and types and the terms of borrowing, the model can project interest and principal payments and relate them to projections of exports, GDP, government revenue and future access to external finance. However, these broad macroeconomic level analyses and projections are not necessarily linked to individual project performances. This is an issue of concern that has a direct effect on loan repayment problems and is the subject matter of this study.

The primary objective should be to increase export earnings and future debt repayment capacity. In this connection, it is crucial that external borrowing leads to an increase in productive capacity. Not only must there be an expansion of goods and services for domestic needs, but also of exports to finance, among other needs, future interest and amortisation payments of foreign debt. In other words, investment must be made only if investment returns exceed the cost of capital. For this reason, the terms of new borrowing must be assessed to ensure that the returns are such that the country is able to make debt service payments when due. This is an important consideration, which should be part of the overall debt strategy.

The strategy as it is now places more concerns with external debt reduction measures than with increasing or expanding the domestic capacity to service the loans. Reduction of debt stock, scheduled debt service and arrears through commercial debt buy-back, provision of funds for multilateral debt service, debt cancellations and now through the HIPC Initiative are some of the external measures that have been achieved.

Debt sustainability considerations

According to the World Bank and IMF, external debt is sustainable when 'a country is able to meet its current and future external debt obligations in full, without recourse to relief or rescheduling of debts or the accumulation of arrears, and without unduly compromising economic growth'. A country attains this situation when the following criteria for debt sustainability assessments have been satisfied:

- its ratio of net present value of debt to exports is between 200% and 250% (the debt overhang ratio); and
- its debt service to exports of goods and services ratio is between 20% to 25% (the liquidity ratio).

Many highly indebted poor countries will not be able

to achieve these ratios in the near future. In the case of Uganda, recent projections show that unless major debt relief is received now, a sustainable debt overhang ratio as defined is achievable only after the year 2006, while a sustainable liquidity ratio is achievable after 2001.

It should be noted that these debt sustainability considerations are based on macro-level analysis. There is a need to link macro-level analysis and projects to expected individual project performances and realities. Equally important and related is the question of proper allocation of loan resources between productive and service sectors. In other words, there is a case for broadening the criteria for assessment of debt sustainability beyond macro-level analyses and projections.

Sectoral allocation of external debt

The best debt database cannot produce debt data differentiated by economic sectors. Sector differentiation was not comprehensive with most of the loans lumped under the Economic Services sector. An attempt was therefore made to obtain information that assigned names to the loans with a view to identifying the sectors to which they belonged. This set of information was used to construct loan balances by sector as shown in Table 25 below.

It is clear from Table 25 that most of the loans are for the economic/financial sector (45.6%). This covers loans contracted for BOP support, economic recovery programme, structural adjustment programme and Enhanced Structural Adjustment Facility. The agricultural sector is the second largest recipient of loans (12.5%). Most of this is for rehabilitation and restructuring of the sector including coffee and cotton marketing rehabilitation. In the social services sector (10.7%), most of the loans went to health (4.2%) followed by defence (3%) and education (2.6%). Directly productive and social sectors had a smaller share relative to the economic/financial sector.

A review of outstanding loans due to parastatal enterprises reveals the same pattern. Most of the government guaranteed borrowing for lending-on (56.3%) is for utilities/infrastructure, of which Uganda Railways Corporation gets 18.6%, National Water and Sewerage Corporation 11.7%, Uganda Electricity Board 11.5% and Uganda Posts and Telecommunications 11.3%. Loans to PEs in the industrial sector constitute 36% of which the sugar industries receive 18.8%, steel and metal 4.2%, textiles 3.9% and agro-industries 3.5%. All these are mainly import substitution industries. Export-oriented loans are for hotels (3.4%), tea (1.4%) and marketing boards (0.9%).

Table 25 Loan balances by economic sector as at 30 June 1995

Sector	Amount (US$ 000)	%
Agriculture	427103	12.5
Mining and quarrying	6468	0.2
Manufacturing	197845	5.8
Energy (electricity/water)	148373	4.4
Construction (stadium, building equipment, Namuwongo housing project)	20660	0.6
Trade (wholesale/retail)	74910	2.2
Tourism (hotels and restaurants)	16960	0.5
Transport/communication (road/telecom)	375482	11.0
Social services (of which):	366429	10.7
general services	*32476*	*0.9*
education	*88140*	*2.6*
health	*141632*	*4.2*
defence	*104181*	*3.0*
Economic/financial (SAP, BOP support, ESAF, economic recovery programme credits, budget support)	1558510	45.6
Unidentified loans (rescheduled)	222967	6.5
GRAND TOTAL	3415706	100.0

Source: Compiled by the researcher from various sources.

Financial institutions obtained 6.8% of the loans, mainly for lending-on and a big percentage of them became non-performing and have had to be repaid directly through the budget, thus putting more pressure on the budget.

Sectoral allocation of loans is a broad indication of the government's priorities in the economic and financial reforms, the result of which is the positive economic growth being experienced. The success of the reforms in the last decade is used as a strong argument in support of more debt relief for Uganda. The study has found no evidence of efforts to secure debt relief on the basis of specific projects. Therefore, as already noted, growth that is dependent on general external transfers is not sustainable over the long term. As a guiding

Uganda

principle for sectoral allocation and utilisation of external loan resources, Uganda should aim to fund its budget and economic growth more from domestically generated revenues – hence the need to ensure that external loans are project specific.

Looked at from the expenditure point of view, the debt burden is a hindrance not only to economic but also to social development. More than twice as much government recurrent expenditure goes on debt repayment than on education and health combined. This situation has, however, now changed with the implementation of the Universal Primary Education (UPE) Programme and the public expenditure focus on benefiting other priority sectors like primary health care, rural feeder roads and agricultural extension services as part of the Poverty Eradication Programme.

Complexity and coordination

The borrowing process is very elaborate and there is no proper coordination. The line ministry/beneficiary agent identifies a project and sends a proposal to the MPED, which examines it for conformity with current objectives, policies and the Public Investment Plan (PIP). If approved by the Development Committee of the MPED it is forwarded to the Ministry of Finance (MOF), External Aid Coordination Department for sourcing for external finance. Once a lender has been identified, the loan proposal is sent to the Macroeconomic Policy Analysis Department for debt sustainability analysis, after which the loan is sent for legislative approval before the MOF is authorised to sign a loan agreement with the lender. Before signing, a legal opinion from the Attorney General is obtained. Copies of the signed loan agreement are sent to BOU and the Treasury for recording of the loan and its terms. Except through perhaps their representatives in Parliament, civil society has apparently no role in this process, even though the loans contracted are for the benefit of the country at large.

The system needs to be streamlined. Professionalism is required in loan contracting to avoid bad and complex terms, which make the loans extremely difficult to manage, for example, multi-tranche loans where each tranche has different repayment terms.

It is important to note here that the capacity of projects to contribute to loan repayments is not specifically focused and that there is no deliberate attempt to develop expertise in this area and to link it to the external borrowing strategy and loan negotiations machinery. This is a serious weakness, which should be addressed.

Steps are being taken to improve the institutional arrangements for debt strategy development and loan negotiations, monitoring and servicing. They do not, however, include proper involvement of civil society. The External Debt Strategy Committee held a workshop to enhance coordination, but civil society did not participate. A Donor Liaison Committee meets quarterly in Kampala, but there is no participation of civil society in that either.

External debt monitoring

The study shows that monitoring external debt is quite complicated and involves numerous tasks. Tracking project implementation by end users and/or project coordinators as part of the monitoring process is necessary for measuring the contributions of the projects to economic growth and loan repayments. There is at present no establishment in government to coordinate this function. The Department of Monitoring and Evaluation previously established in the MPED is not functioning. The PMU in the MOF is concentrating on debt verification and subsidy reduction and has limited capacity for monitoring and assessing returns to projects. This is an all round serious weakness, which should be addressed immediately.

More importantly, and to emphasise, monitoring should include analysis of returns on investments financed from loan resources; analysis of loans for given end users in terms of debt service capabilities; ascertaining the philosophy behind allocation of loans to specific sectors/projects; and an assessment of end users' contributions to economic growth. These are very important aspects but they are not receiving the desired attention in the management of debt. Much attention is given to debt sustainability in the macro sense. Attention should focus on the micro aspects.

Institutional arrangements and capacity building

Debt operations and management functions are diverse and involve multiple players. The effectiveness of debt operations therefore depends on the efficiency of internal management systems and good coordination at all levels. Presently, coordination of external debt management is not explicit.

Although the responsibilities of each entity are well-defined in broad terms, a needs assessment conducted in 1996 identified gaps in the current debt management performance and developed performance indicators for the various debt management functions. One of the gaps is ineffective coordination at the executive and management levels for the various types of debt. This includes development of skills, computerisation, provision of attractive remuneration and other physical needs.

There are complex linkages between those who initiate loan proposals and approve projects for financing; those who source for funds; those who formulate debt strategy and policies and carry out debt sustainability analysis; those who perform the debt recording function and make payments; those who monitor the debt and those who implement the projects. This arrangement presently lacks effective and adequate coordination between line ministries and parastatal bodies; the lenders; the MPED, BOU, the MOF, the private sector and the legislature. Therefore, for effective leadership and coordination, focusing on debt and aid policy, debt and development strategy and capacity building for debt and aid management, a series of committees should be created, activated, strengthened and coordinated. The starting point is the line ministries or PEs who are the beneficiaries and end users of the loans and would have direct contact with the various committees and indirect contact with the lenders on operational and technical issues.

The highest level is the parliament, which grants legislative approval for external loan agreements to be signed by the MOF. This would be a big improvement on the now much needed coordination in Debt and Aid Management. The Secretariats of the various technical coordination units would need to be well staffed, trained, equipped and motivated for a befitting output. It is strongly recommended that this arrangement (documented in detail by AFRODAD and the UDN) be approved and operationalised as soon as possible.

Gender equity in education in Zimbabwe

Munhamo Chisvo
Zimbabwe Women's Resource Centre and Network

Gender equity in education

Donors and governments place special emphasis on basic education. Donors' rationale for targeting support to basic education is both economic and social.[1]

The economic rationale is that education is basic to development, and societies' investments in education, at every level, pay off in higher productivity and greater wealth, holding other things (such as technologies) constant. The issue of gender in basic education is critical because women and girls are active producers in any economy in the world. As women are often involved in low productivity informal-sector activities, an investment in their education may result in significant returns in areas otherwise exerting a negative effect on overall economic growth. At the same time, because education is a resource for future development, failure of a society to provide basic education to one-half of the labour force will result in a failure of these workers to be able to take advantage of investments in higher levels of training and skills development later.

The social rationale is equity. If education is a benefit of development, then it must be made equally available to all citizens regardless of sex, and other such factors. Basic education is often a requirement for access to additional training or other resources, hence those who are denied access at basic levels tend to fall further behind, thus eventually increasing inequity in the long-run. Investments in education for women will both improve infant (and family) health and may reduce fertility. The implications of these demographic trends could be highly important.[2]

Turning to tertiary education, the rationale for supporting vocational training is that it reduces production bottlenecks that result from missing skill levels in societies. In addition, when unemployment is a problem, as in Zimbabwe, special vocational training can help workers prepare themselves for employment in areas where other skills are required. Further, as women and girls are frequently employed in low-income, low productivity occupations, skills training improves their productivity or enables them to switch out of these occupations and into other employment. The growing number of female-headed households, especially in rural areas, also means that more women are sole supporters of their families.

Vocational training may provide them with the additional skills they need to provide adequately for themselves and their children. In some instances, some areas may suffer shortages of male labour due, for example, to out-migration, and may fill these gaps by training women to take up labour roles formerly filled by men.

Donor funded programmes in education largely fall under the following broad categories, some of which are intertwined:

- gender equity in education;
- general support to disadvantaged areas and groups;
- capacity building (planning, management and supervision);
- AIDS;
- information/research;
- curriculum development and teaching materials;
- special needs education;
- Zimbabwe Foundation for Education with Production (ZIMFEP);
- scholarships;
- teacher training, technical, vocational and university education; and
- other programmes.

Donor programmes to support gender equity in education

Until recently, gender equity was not an explicit objective of donor assistance programmes in education, nor was it articulated in education policy by the Zimbabwe government. The concept of gender equity in education has, however, been gathering momentum over the past three years, spearheaded by efforts by UNICEF, which have concentrated on highlighting the plight of the girl child. UNICEF's initiatives have been in the form of research and awareness campaigns that focus mainly on sensitising policy makers, educationalists, parents and the general public to the plight of the girl child through organising and funding workshops and seminars and producing reading materials (such as *Mwanasikana*) collaboratively with the Ministry of Education.

These efforts have culminated in initiatives to revise the curriculum and learning materials, especially to eliminate gender stereotyping in the standard textbooks by working closely with publishers and printers of textbooks for primary and secondary education. UNICEF, with financial support from the Canadian International Development Agency (CIDA), and its own technical support has helped the Ministry of Education (MOE) produce and distribute materials (books) containing appropriate role models to all primary schools in the country. A total of 160,000 copies of such books, entitled *There is Room at the Top* (Books 1 and 2), have so far been targeted at children of both sexes in the 4–7 age group. The research for these books, edited by the Curriculum Development Unit in the MOE, was carried out by the Zimbabwe Women Writers group and they have been distributed to schools countrywide. Book 3 of the series is also almost complete and another 80,000 copies are scheduled for distribution in the near future.

They are also developing primary school readers that feature Zimbabwean women in non-stereotypical, non-traditional jobs. These should not only provide children with much needed reading material, but should, in addition, excite their minds and widen their horizons with regard to career choice, generally raise their aspirations in life and help them to realise that, regardless of their sex and social background, it is still possible to achieve their chosen goals in life.

The efforts by UNICEF and CIDA are commendable but deal with only part of the complex problem of gender disparities in the education sector – a problem of great concern to the government. A study of dropout rates of pupils from primary school carried out by the Policy Planning Division of the MOE in 1986 revealed that, of the pupils who enrolled into Grade 1 between 1980 and 1986 and graduated from Grade 7 between 1986 and 1992, the completion rate for girls was consistently lower than for boys. The study also revealed that the major causes of girls' lower completion rates are cultural influences on parents' preference for the education of male over female children, heavy domestic work demands on girls, early marriages and teenage pregnancies. Other studies have indicated that girls' participation and performance are much lower than those for boys at secondary school level than at primary level as reflected in the table below.

Table 26   Completion rates: Grade 1 to Form VI, 1992

	Completion rates		
Level of education	Boys	Girls	Total
% of Grade 1 enrolment reaching Grade 7	74.5	73.1	73.8
% of Grade 7 enrolment reaching Form I	73.3	64.4	68.9
% of Form I enrolment reaching Form IV	73	63.5	68.5
% of Form IV enrolment reaching Form V	6.6	4.9	5.9

Source: Ministry of Education, 1995.

The net effect of these dropouts is female under-representation in all significant sectors of the nation's productive activities. It is not surprising therefore, that in the modern formal employment sector, women still constitute an insignificant proportion of senior personnel. Black women professionals, for example, constitute only about 7% of the skilled and semi-skilled labour force and about 12–16% of the total workforce in the formal employment sector according to a Sida, Zimbabwe study in 1990. On the other hand, women contribute over 70% of the labour on farms, 62% of the labour in livestock care, 81% of the labour in fuel gathering and 96% of the labour in domestic tasks. Overall, women contribute 80% of the labour required for all basic rural tasks.[3] In Zimbabwe's circumstances, these disparities represent a significant wastage of human resource potential and national productivity. The role women can play in the nation's productive activities has never been fully realised.

Literacy

The government has realised the importance of education in human resource development and attitude change and has thus put in place policies and practices (with the assistance of donors) aimed at addressing the plight of girls and women in education. These include the Adult Literacy Programme in which the majority (over 80%) of participants are women. The 1993 Central Statistical Office district household survey revealed that adult literacy rates (those who are able to read and write) in the age group 20–60 years was 79%, up from about 50% in 1980.[4] The rate for women had risen from 47% to 73% and for men from about 63% before independence to 88% in 1993.[5]

A new literacy strategy drawn up in 1989/90 and also assisted by donors emphasises functional education such as peasant education, primary health care, environment, workers, population, family life and cooperative education. This strategy has been crucial in making the beneficiaries, women in particular, function better in the working environment as well as being socially better placed for the good of their health and that of the population around them.

The relative success of the literacy campaign was complemented by formal education, which was declared a birthright in post-independence Zimbabwe. School enrolment at all levels increased dramatically. Although there was an imbalance in primary school enrolments in 1980 in favour of boys, by 1989 equity in primary schools had been restored. During that decade there was an 88% increase in the number of schools with a 161% increase in male pupils and 195% increase in female pupils. An imbalance, however, still remains in the secondary school system, which tends to be dominated by boys. In 1995, male pupils constituted 54% and 60% of pupils enrolled at 'O' and 'A' level respectively.

Enrolment in tertiary education also increased but not so much for female students. Gains have been made in agricultural colleges, where one-third of the students are female.[6] Yet by 1995, female students at university accounted for only 21% of total enrolment, down from 25% in 1985.[7] The university intake by faculty for male students is way above that for female students. The highest rates in 1995 were in arts (35% women) and medicine (34%).

The 1995 intake for technical colleges by field of study shows a worse picture with the highest female enrolment in electrical engineering at 14%.

Teacher education in Zimbabwe used to be dominated by women up to 1980, but no longer. In 1995, 50% of primary school teachers were men. The involvement of women in both technical and university education has been slowly rising, but men currently dominate all areas of tertiary education.

These trends confirm the need for comprehensive approaches to gender inequities integrating short-term and long-term measures. In the long run, approaches might take the form of changes in curriculum, attitudes and obstacles related to policy and legislation. In the short run, resources need to be made available for removing resource constraints affecting enrolment of the girl child. This can be achieved through scholarship programmes earmarked for women and girls. So far, donor programmes tend to focus on the long-term measures rather than the short-term measures, which require huge financial commitments.

At the same time, donor initiatives taken so far to promote awareness of the need to invest in the girl child or to open up career opportunities available to girls may have a limited impact for a number of reasons. First, the success of role model readers distributed to schools depends on the attitude of the teachers responsible, especially if they are not integrated into the standard curriculum and may compete with the latter for time. Perhaps this programme could have targeted specifically women teachers to enhance the possibilities for success.

Second, the impact of the approach is also dependent on the attitude and resources of the parents. Unless the attitudes of the parents change and they are better equipped financially to be able to send a girl to school, the scope for eliminating gender inequalities may remain limited.

Donor programmes in support of gender equity, in addition to being new, also tend to be confined to activities at lower levels of education, yet the greater disparities are found at tertiary levels of education. Similar initiatives targeted at tertiary education could also constitute important direct, short-term intervention measures.

To complement donor efforts to eliminate gender inequities in education, the government has made a deliberate effort to promote deserving women to managerial positions, especially within the MOE, even if they may have less experience (in terms of years of service) than their male counterparts. However, comparatively few women apply for promotion to administrative/managerial positions. A change in attitude and confidence still has to be instilled in potential women educationalists through training.

To address some of the above concerns, the government with support from Sida, has embarked on a comprehensive two- to three-year programme of Gender Equity in Education. This programme has greater scope and a higher budget than earlier initiatives and is the first of its type in terms of magnitude, comprehensiveness and focus. The objective is to eliminate differences in the dropout rates between boys and girls and to improve girls' participation and achievement in primary and secondary schools by the year 2000, thereby promoting equal opportunity in education. This project, which will be run by the MOE, has a number of planned outputs including:

- *scholarships* for a total of 170 commercial farm children;
- *staff training* in gender issues and sensitisation, including the training of a national team of trainers;
- *career guidance* for girls between Form I and Form VI, including the production of a career guidance manual for use by officers and teachers;
- *research, evaluation and monitoring* of the gender equity project; and
- *information generation* on gender issues.

This programme, though one of the few to provide scholarships for girls, has its limitations. One of these is that there are too few scholarships compared with the demand.

In addition to this donor programme, there are a variety of other programmes that are not specifically targeted at gender issues, but nevertheless impact upon women and girls and could be refocused to address gender issues directly. These programmes include the Strengthening of the Planning Capacity, Curriculum Development and Textbooks, Special Needs Education and Buildings. It will be necessary to highlight in brief some of them here.

Other donor programmes in education

General support to disadvantaged areas and groups

This category is primarily one of building or construction programmes. However, it also covers scholarship programmes targeted at the disadvantaged sectors of the population.

Additional facilities for primary schools in rural areas Building projects are one effort donors are making to support disadvantaged areas and population groups. In 1994, Sida embarked on a project designed to assist government efforts to fund universal access to education. The objective was to build and furnish schools and teachers' houses in disadvantaged areas on a self-help basis. The project was implemented by the Ministry of Local Government, Rural and Urban Development. By June 1993, 1080 teachers' houses and 1100 classroom blocks, equipped with latrines and running water, had been built or were under construction. By June 1995, disbursements of up to SEK 129 million (about US$ 18 million) had been made, including the financing of staff houses for education officers in rural areas.

Given the high enrolment rates for girls in primary education, this programme may have benefited them in much the same way as it has benefited the boys. Investment in primary schools should be increased since benefits from such an investment are likely to reach girls more than they would in secondary and tertiary level education.

Teachers' houses at secondary schools in rural areas Following independence in 1980, the government opened new rural secondary schools at a much faster pace than it provided additional houses for teachers. To facilitate the recruitment of qualified teachers, accommodation had to be provided and donors such as Sida and the European Union (EU) funded a teachers' housing programme alongside the government's school construction programme. By June 1995, the teachers' housing programme sponsored by Sida had drawn a cumulative total expenditure of SEK 71.1 million (about US$ 10 million) from the time it was launched in 1981.

Zimbabwe

No element of gender targeting was incorporated into this programme. Yet, giving first preference to female teachers would have provided them with an incentive to teach in rural areas, providing role models for girls in rural areas who are more prone to sex discrimination practices than their urban counterparts.

Education for children in commercial farming areas About 150,000 school age children live in the large commercial farming areas. Many of these children have been denied access to education, either by inadequate schooling facilities or by poverty. A programme initiated by the Ministry of Education has been under way to upgrade and expand existing school facilities in the large commercial farming areas and to establish additional ones. Sida agreed to support the programme as well as provide scholarships, initially to 90 farm children, with a girl:boy ratio of 7:3. Under this programme, commercial farmers who agree to set aside part of their land for a primary school are given assistance equivalent to US$ 50,000 per school to enable them, together with the school's committee, to build the school on the farm. Total disbursements by Sida so far total SEK 9.8 million (about US$ 1.4 million). Girls were targeted in this programme following the realisation that they do not have the same access to education as boys,[8] with illiteracy more than twice as high among female farm workers than male and severely limited employment opportunities for women on commercial farms. However, there are relatively few scholarships in this programme compared with the target population in the commercial farming areas. Perhaps this is an area where other donors could come in.

Rehabilitation and completion of school buildings Under this programme, donors have been providing support for the completion of schools, or their rehabilitation following natural disasters (often in the form of storm damage). This programme has been supported by Sida following a pilot project in 1990/1. The programme offers direct support to disadvantaged schools, the school community provides labour and other inputs while the parent teacher associations are accountable to the Ministry for the assistance received. Total disbursements so far have accumulated to SEK 14 million (about US$ 2 million).

School sanitation Government efforts to create good sanitation and health conditions in rural schools have been augmented by donors, including the EU and Sida. Although this programme and the one for rehabilitation of schools are not specifically gender-targeted, culturally appropriate school facilities, especially in terms of sanitation or boundary walls can encourage parents to send their daughters to school. Provision of sanitary facilities in Bangladeshi schools, for example, had a positive influence on community, teacher and student attitudes towards school and addressed an important parent objection to girls' attendance.[9] Similarly, a survey of 2000 Pakistani parents reported that they did not mind the absence of desks and chairs in girls' schools, but two-thirds criticised the absence of latrines.[10]

Textbooks, teaching materials and curriculum One of the biggest constraints on Zimbabwe's education system has been the unavailability of textbooks in schools. This affects the girl child more, for she often receives less teacher time, less instructional support at home and elsewhere, and the non-scholarly demands on her time often necessitate more frequent absences from school.

One of the major impediments to effective distribution of books has been lack of transport. While the situation improved slightly with the procurement of trucks in 1986 and 1990 for distribution to district level, Sida agreed to finance the purchase of 55 pickups during 1991/2 and 1992/3 for distribution to school level. Cumulative disbursements under this activity totalled SEK 21.9 million by mid-1995 (about US$ 3 million).

This alone, however, did not solve the problem. There has been a shortage of paper for textbooks in Zimbabwe and many schools are unable to finance an adequate supply of books. The Ministry therefore proposed a programme whereby Sida financed the import of paper paid for by publishers in local currency, thereby enabling the Ministry to provide the needy schools with books. Some funds were also directly transferred to the Ministry for the purchase of textbooks. Cumulative disbursements by June 1995 reached SEK 14.2 million (about US$ 2 million).

Much of the debate on textbooks and teaching materials has focused more on the need to develop curriculum that ensures gender-neutral instruction and less on just making textbooks available to the pupils in their present state. The focus is rightly on stereotypes, which dampen girls' aspirations and therefore discourage attendance and achievement and result in decisions to enter low-paid traditional female employment. Hence, the conclusion is that educational programmes would yield larger benefits for girls if these issues were addressed.

Relative to other investment options, the cost-effectiveness of revamping textbooks to raise female educational attainment and achievement is questionable, especially in the short-term and more so in countries where a female's status is low, where textbooks of any kind are in short supply and where there is a vast array of other factors influencing female educational attainment and achievement. In the short-term, simply improving the quality of education for all children by putting books into the hands of children and teaching materials into the hands of teachers may accomplish much more.

Second, abundant research shows that children with textbooks learn more than those without books and that children with higher levels of learning achievement stay in school longer.

Finally, improving the overall quality of education first may be the most productive short-term investment option to attract and retain girls in schools.[11] Investments in subsidising girls to attend low quality schools or establishing alternative low quality educational programmes are unlikely to attract or retain girls.

Programmes to support teacher training, technical and vocational colleges and universities

Various donors and NGOs fund a number of specific projects in tertiary education. In this section, a brief commentary will be given on projects funded by donors and the extent to which they specifically address the pronounced gender inequalities at higher levels of Zimbabwe's education system. The following table presents an inventory of some of the donor funded projects in the Ministry of Higher Education showing some of the activities under each project as of March 1996.

The Higher Education Ministry has a general policy that emphasises promotion of women and achieving a gender balance in tertiary education. However, this policy is neither explicitly stated in policy documents or project documents, nor strictly pursued during project implementation. Rarely do

Table 27 Inventory of donor funded projects with the Ministry of Higher Education

Project name/donor	Description	Typical project activities
EU/Lomé IV 96.3	Faculty of Vet Science, UZ	Construction Equipment Scholarships
Japan 24.0	Chemical Science, UZ	Construction Consumables Equipment maintenance
Denmark 2.2	Clothing Design Centre, Danbiko	Construction Staff training Curriculum development Organisation development Institutional cooperation
French Aid FN58000	Chinhoyi Technical Teachers' College Hillside Teachers' College, French Department	Technical equipment Teaching aids Training materials Staff development Technical cooperation Staff development Scholarships Books Photocopying facilities Teaching aids
Chinese Aid	UZ and Harare Polytechnic	Technical cooperation Civil engineering equipment
UNFPA	Population Education in Teachers' Colleges	Institutionalisation of population education
UNICEF	Teacher Education Primary	Teacher training assistance AIDS education
GTZ	National, Vocational Training and Development	Expertise transfer Staff development Equipment Consumables MIS
CIDA	Zim Canada General Training Facility	Human resource development

the donor projects seek to change the status quo with regard to the participation of women in tertiary learning. In cases where women have benefited the more, for example in staff development as discussed in the next section, this has been by default and not as a result of a deliberate policy to target them, as would be expected in a sector where women's participation is severely marginalised.

This may not be surprising in a sector where the decision-making process has been dominated by men, where historically few women occupied top posts and where either gender training has been absent or the issue of gender is only beginning to be appreciated.

Conclusion and recommendations

Strategies to deal with fundamental problems facing women are yet to be incorporated explicitly into aid development programmes in Zimbabwe. The lack of focus on women, and hence the apparent failure of aid to reach women adequately, in both health and education programmes, typifies what could be happening in other sectors of the economy. Part of this could go to show the extent of the need for training local programme officers in government on gender issues so that, together with donors, they can successfully integrate gender issues into their development programmes.

While gender training is about to be launched in basic education, its absence in health and higher education is particularly striking. The absence of gender training in the two health manpower development programmes under the Family Health Project is a cause for great concern in a sector where women should naturally be the major beneficiaries, yet their participation in sector management continues to be low and many sector programmes fail to reach them adequately. The absence of gender training in the Higher Education Ministry is another major issue given the extremely low participation rates for women in tertiary education.

Many of the aid development programmes in both health and education lack gender sensitivity and this can be traced back to the programme planning stage. Gender training would be an important strategy to ensure that aid programmes equally (or adequately) reach women and reduce ill health and poverty. Gender equity programme cycles of two to three years, similar to the one envisaged in the Sida-initiated Gender Equity in Education Programme in the Ministry of Education, could do for a start in higher education and health.

Government and donor priority in tertiary education has historically been given to providing the necessary infrastructure for training by upgrading facilities. Yet, although noble, very little of this effort by either the government or donors has reached and benefited females. This is because of their low involvement in technical and vocational training apart from teacher training.

Now, priority should rightly shift to the achievement of gender balance in tertiary education. Donors in particular can play a lead role because they have the ability to influence government through the manner in which they allocate and disburse their development assistance. As an example, donors could insist on explicit policy statements on the issue of gender equality before they disburse their aid. This could be complemented by gender training targeted at policy and project planners and implementors within the Higher Education Ministry.

Government also could take the lead in producing a White Paper for education explicitly spelling out (among other things) its position on the issue of gender, what strategies it proposes to employ to tackle gender inequalities in the lower and higher education system both in the short and long run, and what it envisages the role of donors to be in the process.

Strengthening the planning capacity

Donors also need to shift fundamentally from piecemeal to comprehensive programmes that address structural causes of gender imbalances and poverty. More effort must be put into building an infrastructure that will in the long-run institutionalise and sustain donor programmes in health and education. Nutrition, for example, needs to be viewed as a long-term investment of between 10–15 years or more.

The experience with the nutrition programmes has shown that the advocacy role of donors should not be confined to promoting only the activities of the agency. This occurs when the donor does not share the country's perception of the nutrition problem (for example, the case of iron deficiency anaemia) and the strategy to address those problems or when there are donor biases that are at odds with the government's plans.

Another area of concern in nutrition programmes is the clear lack of emphasis by donors on one of the most important, although indirect, solutions to the nutrition problem. Women often face serious constraints regarding access to and control over factors of production, such as land, labour, capital and technology. At present, donors tend to shun programmes aimed at empowering women economically. For example, the government's land resettlement programme, which, if streamlined or improved upon, could be an effective programme for increasing women's access to and ownership of land and their subsequent control over production. This could be one way of augmenting and sustaining existing donor initiatives to improve nutrition. Support for the land reform programme, however, would perhaps entail greater donor commitment and longer programme cycles than the usual two to five years.

As highlighted earlier, women could also have more control over the productive resources currently available through greater participation in decision-making within the home. However, donors (like the recipient government) tend to shun programmes directly intended to promote greater participation of women in decision-making and in fundamentally reforming power structures in the home and community. Yet these could have a significant impact on welfare variables such as child and adult nutrition.

Donors need to match their capital investments to the recurrent budgets of government. When donors supply capital goods, they should make provision for their maintenance if the donor-aided programmes are to be sustainable. Many of the health programmes do have a direct positive impact on the health of women and children, but sector policy papers are critical in directing donor assistance to the government's priority areas. However, the process of preparing sector policy papers may involve severe intra-government conflicts since various line ministries have different vested interests. Donors, therefore, will have to take notice of this, and accommodate these complexities in their decision-making processes as well. Improving female education should not end up by being just a topic of national policy concern, but should be integrated into education development plans to ensure adequate planning, monitoring, evaluation and financial support from both the government and the donor community.

Donors or central government should not seek to replace or override local NGOs in the decentralisation process but, instead, should work, strengthen and share with them to the greatest benefit of the poor and women. Ongoing local projects on girls' and women's education should be used as vital sources of information on the determinants of female participation and attainment, and on administratively feasible approaches. A systematic evaluation of their performance will greatly improve governments' and donors' capability to design and implement effective programmes.

Donors and government should also explore other options, such as those for lowering the opportunity costs for girls' education. These include the establishment of day-care centres, modifying home technologies, adopting flexible school schedules and intensifying provision for safety nets (such as morning or evening school), which are options that require fewer resources.

Donors and the government should start paying more attention to providing for the education and skills needs of the growing informal sector. There are seven times as many women employed in the informal sector as in the formal sector.[12] The majority of women, therefore, are largely left out by donor and government education programmes targeted at the formal sector.

The provision of skills training to the informal sector could be extended without significant additional costs, for existing infrastructure (technical and vocational training colleges) could be used. Most donors have been supporting the strengthening of these infrastructure by providing for their construction, equipment and skills transfer. This assistance can now be fully exploited by expanding or refocusing the scope of the training programmes to cater for the larger informal sector where women and girls, the vulnerable, are concentrated.

Some donors, including the German Technical Cooperation in Zimbabwe (GTZ) have already (but just) started in initiatives (for example, using Masvingo Technical College) to extend training to informal-sector entrepreneurs although, so far, on a reactionary demand-driven basis (trainees need to come forward and request training). More attention should now be paid to proactive measures to create the demand for training in the informal sector. For example, girls and women in the informal sector often do not hear about training opportunities because these are announced in places or through media to which they do not typically have access or familiarity.[13] Also, location and timing of training opportunities can either encourage or discourage female involvement. Because recruits to training are often more mature girls or women, they often have other major family or household responsibilities. Even low-paid self-employment may be difficult to give up.

Some compensation (or payment) may be necessary during training to free them for initial participation and thus enable them to get an opportunity to learn and appreciate the importance

Zimbabwe

of training. They need to become able and willing to invest their own resources (time and finance) into their further training.

The great challenge of gender-aware development planning is to put women into the picture without censoring or excluding men. Effective empowerment of women involves social change that both women and men should initiate. It is impractical to expect sustainable structural changes in the social conditions of women if men have not been involved in the process from the start.

Developing an effective approach towards improving female education requires setting goals, identifying target groups by examining current patterns of female enrolment by geographic, demographic and income groups, determining which barriers are key to specific settings of sub-populations, developing sustainable, cost-effective strategies, determining the level of investment necessary to attain specific goals and ensuring financial support, monitoring programmes and evaluating their outcomes.

Finally, no discussion centred on strategies to promote women's health and education is complete without addressing directly the role poverty plays in undermining efforts to improve them. Absolute poverty is a condition of many children, particularly those on commercial farms and those in female headed households. Simply lowering the costs of education or raising its benefits will probably do little to rescue such children.[14] Their survival depends on the education of their parents and on their parents' ability to support them. But often, income needs prevent women from participating in the myriad of literacy, family planning, health and nutrition, and skill training programmes that aim to improve their living standards. Attracting women to these programmes sometimes demands efforts even greater than those required to attract their daughters to school. It requires an immediate opportunity to increase their incomes. Donors and the government could play a pivotal role in this by having a budget for women in all development programmes. Having already launched a successful poverty assessment study, Zimbabwe could take a lead role in this mainstreaming of women towards alleviating poverty.

Notes

1. In Zimbabwe, education falls under two ministries, Education and Higher Education, in order to separate the activities in primary and secondary (lower-level) education from those in higher (tertiary level) education. Donors support programmes within both ministries.
2. Mary B Anderson, 'A Manual for Integrating the Gender Factor into Basic Education and Vocational Training Projects', *The Gender Manual Series*, submitted to the United States Agency for International Development, AID/WID, Washington DC, February 1986.
3. Ministry of Education, *Project Documents: 1995–97*, project document prepared for Sida, Harare, October 1995, p 9.
4. Ministry of Health and Child Welfare, *Women's Health in Zimbabwe: A Path to Development*, MOHCW contribution to Beijing Conference and WHO Global Commission on Women's Health, October 1994. See also Government of Zimbabwe, *Social Dimensions of Adjustment: Progress Report and Action Plan*, Report prepared for the Consultative Group Meeting, Paris, 12–14 December 1993.
5. René Loewensen and Munhamo Chisvo, 'Transforming Social Development: The Experience of Zimbabwe', *UNICEF Report*, Harare, July 1994.
6. Ministry of Health and Child Welfare, *Women's Health in Zimbabwe: A Path to Development*, MOHCW contribution to Beijing Conference and WHO Global Commission on Women's Health, October 1994, p 21.
7. Ministry of Education, *Project Documents: 1995–97*, Project document prepared for Sida, Harare, October 1995.
8. Martin Nyagura and Anna C Mupawaenda, *A Study of Factors Affecting the Education of Women and Girls in Commercial Farming Areas of Zimbabwe*, Harare, January 1994.
9. World Bank, *Staff Appraisal Report: Bangladesh Secondary Primary Education Project*, Washington DC, 25 February 1985.
10. Robert Culbertson et al, *Primary Education in Pakistan*, Development Associates, Washington DC, 1986.
11. Rosemary Bellew and Elizabeth M King, 'Promoting Girls and Women's Education', *Policy Research and External Affairs Working Paper Series: Education and Employment*, World Bank, Population and Human Resources Department, Washington DC, No 715, July 1991.
12. M A McPherson, 'Micro and Small Scale Enterprises in Zimbabwe: Results of a Country Wide Survey', *GEMINI Report*, No 25, Bethesda, DAI/GEMINI Publication Series, 1991.
13. Mary B Anderson, 'A Manual for Integrating the Gender Factor into Basic Education and Vocational Training Projects, *The Gender Manual Series*, submitted to the United States Agency for International Development, AID/WID, Washington DC, February 1986.
14. Rosemary Bellew and Elizabeth M King, 'Promoting Girls and Women's Education', *Policy Research and External Affairs Working Paper Series: Education and Employment*, World Bank, Population and Human Resources Department, Washington DC, No 715, July 1991.

Part IV: Aid Trends, Facts and Figures

World aid at a glance

How much aid do the 21 OECD donors give?

The donors gave	US$ 55,114 million in 1996
that was	0.25% of their total GNP
and	1.71% of their combined government expenditure
which meant	US$ 67.85 per person

At one quarter of 1% of their GNP, DAC donors reached a record, 30-year low for aid as a percentage of GNP

Is it going up or down?

In 1996 aid	fell by US$ 3768 million, a real terms decline of 4.2%
11 donors	were less generous, reducing the proportion of their GNP that they give in development assistance
private Flows	amounted to US$ 234,000 million, an increase of US$ 80 million over 1995, and 4.2 times the volume of ODA. This is a record high, exceeding, in real terms, the previous peak of 1981

How much of their development assistance do OECD donors report spent on basic health and basic education?

9 out of 21	donors do not report at all on their spending on basic health and basic education
the average	for the 12 donors who do report, is that they spend 1.2% of total ODA on basic education and 1.8% on basic health

How much goes to the poorest countries?

58% of OECD aid	went to countries where the average income was less than $2 a day in 1994/5, compared with 63% in the previous year

How much OECD aid is tied to purchases from the donor country?

On average 22% of DAC is actually given on the condition it is used to purchase goods and services from the donor country

World aid in 1995 and 1996

ODA as a percentage of GNP in 1996

Elsewhere in *The Reality of Aid*, NGOs argue that the eradication of poverty is an international public good and a moral imperative. There are many ways in which governments and people can make a contribution to eradicating poverty, but one is through resources. Aid is an international resource capable of being targeted on poverty. Taking aid as a percentage of GNP enables a like-with-like comparison to be made between individual country efforts to make a contribution to the eradication of poverty.

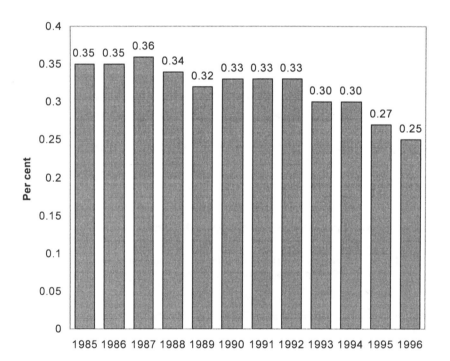

The **Reality** of Aid 1997/8

World aid in 1995 and 1996

ODA volume

Poverty eradication is affordable. It has been calculated by UNDP that around $80,000 million a year is needed to provide global basic social services (basic education, health and nutrition, reproductive health and family planning and low-cost water supply and sanitation) and to close the gap between the current income of poor people and a minimum income at which they would no longer be in extreme poverty. Out of their combined GNP of US$ 22,062,000 million, donors only managed to find US$ 55,100 million, a quarter of 1%.

ODA as a percentage of central government expenditure

Many opinion polls have shown that the public and often politicians hugely overestimate the proportion of public expenditure that is used for official development assistance. In 1995, aid as a percentage of central government expenditure fell to its lowest level since 1980 – 1.71%.

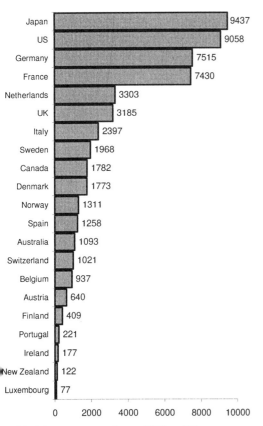

ODA in current prices, US$ millions

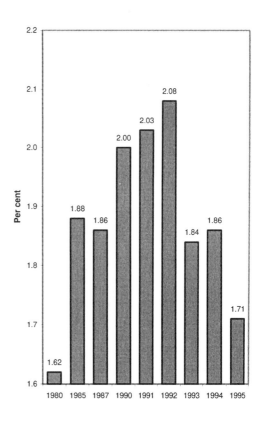

The **Reality** of Aid 1997/8

World aid in 1995 and 1996

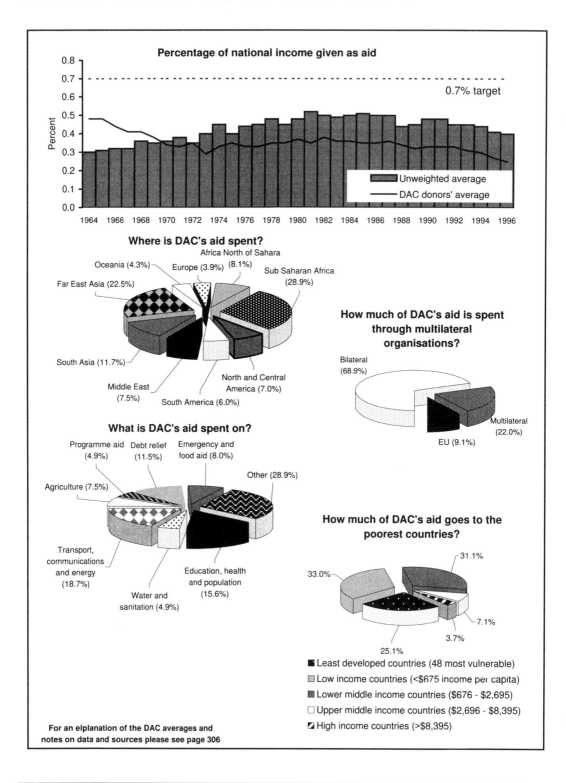

246

Trends in aid and development cooperation

Tony German and Judith Randel
Development Initiatives

Since the start of the decade, governments have been struggling to adapt to post-cold war instability and the globalisation of finance, trade, energy, employment, migration and the environment.

A series of UN summits has underlined the importance of both national action and international cooperation on poverty and social development, gender, population and environmental degradation.

Last year's *Reality of Aid* noted that political will was needed if official agencies were to make the transition from being concerned largely with aid administration to a broader development cooperation approach.

This chapter examines recent trends in aid, development cooperation and government policy to see how far OECD governments have prioritised poverty and taken significant steps to promote sustainable development.

Some encouraging words are being spoken. At the policy level there seems to be a clearer focus on poverty. And there is some evidence – for instance in the UK and Switzerland – that issues such as human rights and coherence are at least being discussed more openly, even if they have insufficient weight to prevail against donors' political and commercial interests.

But donor assertions about wanting to be the developing countries' active partners in efforts to eradicate poverty would have sounded more credible had they not coincided with the failure of most DAC members to live up to their recent commitments on aid volume. To date, there is little evidence of donor rhetoric being translated into changed aid spending patterns or a different approach to external trade. Donors may wish for the ends – but they show little sign of providing their share of the means.

Aid volume

Donors' performance inconsistent with commitment to ending absolute poverty

'Eradicating absolute poverty is eminently affordable'.[1] This is the conclusion of the 1997 Human Development Report. The cost of achieving global access to basic social services – basic education, basic health and nutrition, reproductive health and family planning, low-cost water supply and sanitation – and transfers to alleviate income poverty would amount to US$ 80,000 million – way below the UN target for aid and less than half of 1% of global income.

NGO reports in *Reality of Aid 1997* and the aid figures for 1995 and 1996 confirm a failure to find remotely adequate resources to fund commitments to end absolute poverty. Despite improved rhetoric, it is difficult to take the notion of partnership at face value when most donors are failing so abjectly to live up to the targets they have set for themselves.

In 1995, DAC aid amounted to $58,800 million or 0.27% of GNP, which at the time was the lowest level ever recorded.[2] The real terms cut in aid on the previous year was 9%.

In 1996, aid fell yet again to $55,100 million[3] or by 4.2% in real terms, reaching another new low at 0.25% of GNP.

Since the Earth summit in 1992, when developed countries reaffirmed their commitment to the UN 0.7% GNP aid target, aid has fallen by almost 17% in real terms.[4]

The world's largest donor, Japan, has announced cuts in its aid from 1998 onwards and has abandoned its forward commitments to aid

The **Reality** of Aid 1997/8

Trends in aid and development

Table 28 Real terms changes in ODA 1995 and 1996

Year	ODA US$ actual	ODA US$ real terms	Real terms fall over last year	ODA % GNP
1995	58.9	58.9	9.0%	0.27
1996	55.1	56.4	4.2%	0.25

Source: OECD Press Release, 18 June 1997.

volume over a five-year period. The USA, Germany and France – the second, third and fourth largest donors – all expect their aid to decline in 1997. These four donors account for 60% of global ODA. Most NGO reports predict either stagnation or further falls; there is no sign of an end to the decline in aid volume (see Table 31 on The Outlook for Aid for a country by country breakdown).

Reality of Aid NGOs point out that donors justify aid cuts in terms of the continued need to reduce budget deficits. In the EU, NGOs like NCOS in Belgium and KePa in Finland refer specifically to pressure to meet the EMU criteria laid down at Maastricht – ironically, the same agreement incorporated the Campaign against Poverty in the Developing Countries into EU legislation for the first time.[5]

Waning generosity Politicians often attempt to explain away aid cuts on the basis that they are temporarily necessary until domestic economies are in better shape. But Canadian NGOs point out that no plans have been announced to restore or even stabilise their aid budget – though new spending is planned on universities and defence. Cuts affecting US aid in 1996 were some of the sharpest in the federal budget. NCOS in Belgium says that development cooperation came off badly in relation to other departments in the 1997 spending round.

Among the four countries that have consistently exceeded the UN target, there seems to be continued political commitment on aid volume, with Denmark sticking to its fixed percentage target; NGOs in Norway reporting efforts to restore aid to 1% of GNP, while Sweden and The Netherlands have fixed their aid budgets at 0.7% and 0.8% respectively for the coming years. But, with the possible exception of the UK, the view among NGOs is that G7 donors have no real political commitment to the UN target, despite their public positions.[6]

Other resources for development cooperation

Figures for 1996 show that private flows to developing countries rose by $80,000 million to $234,000 million. Having been three-quarters the size of aid in 1988, private flows are now four times larger than ODA. But, as Reality of Aid has consistently argued, these flows remain overwhelmingly concentrated in the fast growing economies of Asia and Latin America, and are not focused on social development or human capital. Direct investment in Far East Asia from DAC countries in 1995 totalled US$ 18,700 million, compared with just $1000 million in sub-Saharan Africa.

Donors also exhibit markedly different balances between private and official resources to developing countries, ranging from Sweden where private flows are a quarter of Swedish ODA to the USA where private flows are nearly five times ODA.

Trends in the distribution of aid

Aid spending in poorest countries declines to just half of ODA

Over 3000 million people live in Low Income Countries with per capita incomes below $675 a year. In 1990, those Low Income Countries received 62% of DAC ODA. By 1994, these countries' share of aid had slipped to 53%. In 1995, low income countries received barely half (51%) of total ODA.[7] A smaller share of a smaller cake.

Record falls in aid for sub-Saharan Africa

Reality of Aid has reported a consistent decline in the priority given by donors to poorer African countries since 1991.

In 1995, bilateral aid fell by $1530 million in real terms, a 14% drop on the 1994 figure. The multilateral fall was even worse, down 22%, or $1660 million. Aid to 35 countries in sub-Saharan Africa has declined. This compares with increases in 13 countries and no change in two. In 1995, 17 out of 21 donors cut their bilateral aid to sub-Saharan Africa. The cuts amount to more than the entire national outputs of all 16 million people living in Malawi, Guinea Bissau and Sierra Leone.

Allocations to other regions Only two regions avoided a real terms fall. Aid to the Americas rose by slightly less than 1% and to CEEC/NIS it went up 10% in real terms.

By contrast, as ACTIONAID India points out, allocations to South Asia have declined by $2300 million in real terms, with the bulk of the cuts falling on populous, poor countries – India, Pakistan and Bangladesh. Most of these cuts are in multilateral aid.

Both actual allocations and the share of aid going to North Africa have gone down, with reductions to every country in the region. Aid to Egypt fell by a quarter (more than $500 million) mainly as a result of the massive decline in support from Italy, which fell from $616 million at its peak in 1994 to a mere $22.5 million in 1995.

Allocations to individual recipients Shifts in aid between countries reflect both recipient need and donor political interest. The rise in aid to Rwanda over the last year illustrates the former and the appearance of Palau as the sixth largest recipient of US aid the latter.[8]

The new focus on Vietnam and South Africa evident among donors in 1994 continued in 1995. In addition, Ethiopia has moved into the top 15 recipients for Finland, Italy and the UK. Aid to Palestine has increased markedly; it is now in the top 15 for Norway, Spain and Switzerland. Haiti moves into the top 15 for Canada, Portugal and Spain.

Burma's military government is among Japan's top 15 aid recipients; Japan gives three-quarters of global ODA to Burma.

Concentration and post-aid relationships

While several donors are talking about concentrating resources on fewer recipients, there appears to be no initiative to coordinate such concentration – even within the EU.

Italy aims to concentrate on 32 recipient countries – down from 101. As a result, in some countries NGOs are the only form of Italian cooperation left – a trend that is becoming more widespread with the growth of decentralised cooperation and shrinking aid budgets combined with increased concentration.

As donors choose to concentrate on a smaller number of countries, and as some developing countries cease to be eligible for ODA, new issues have arisen. Should a revised Lomé Convention include poorer countries currently outside the African Caribbean and Pacific (ACP) group? Should it exclude richer ACP states? And who should make this decision – the EU or the ACP? In Canada, new questions are being debated about maintaining constructive and supportive relationships with recipients when aid is no longer appropriate.

Aid spending on poverty

It has been argued in previous *Reality of Aid* reports that all sorts of expenditure are capable of reducing poverty if they take as their starting point the needs and capacities of people in poverty and poorer countries. However, some types of expenditure are, *a priori*, more likely to have a positive impact on poor people than others. Among these are basic health and basic education – precisely, as NGO reports make clear, the things on which taxpayers in donor countries believe their aid should be spent.

Despite a consensus on the importance of investment in human capital and education, spending remains pitiful by any measure.

For the past two years the DAC has been reporting spending on basic education and health as subsets of overall health and education spending. The average percentage among the 12 donors who managed to report on basic health was 1.8% of their ODA and 1.2% on basic education.

Taking primary education as a percentage of total education expenditure since 1993, in only two countries (Norway and Sweden) does it exceed 30% for any one year, though The Netherlands manages an average, creditable in the circumstances, of 23% over the period compared with the DAC average of 13%. An analysis of developing country budgets in 1992/3 showed an average of 42% being spent on primary education in ten African and 12 Latin American countries and 39% in six Asian countries.[9]

NGOs are positive about some specific steps being taken in individual countries, but so far the changes they report do not suggest that the bulk of aid spending is directed towards the optimum strategies for poverty reduction.

The fact remains that stated expenditures on

Trends in aid and development

Table 29 Bilateral ODA commitments by sector, 1995

Sectors	All developing countries		LLDCs	
Social infrastructure – general	5026.3	11.92%	711.8	9.42%
Education	3056.1	7.25%	487.9	6.46%
Health	1883.8	4.47%	444.7	5.89%
Water supply and sanitation	2408.7	5.71%	288.8	3.82%
Economic infrastructure – general	797.6	1.89%	42.1	0.56%
Energy	5436.4	12.89%	320.8	4.25%
Transport and communications	5790.2	13.73%	541.4	7.17%
Agriculture	2754.9	6.77%	622.8	8.24%
Industry, mining, commerce	819.9	1.94%	115.7	1.53%
Trade and tourism	1026.4	2.43%	254.3	3.37%
Multisector	3961.1	9.39%	512.9	6.79%
Programme assistance	1978.2	4.69%	542	7.17%
Food aid	1510.8	3.58%	795	10.52%
Action relating to debt	2399.4	5.69%	881.7	11.67%
Emergency assistance	2963.6	7.03%	975.6	12.91%
Unallocated	266.8	0.63%	17.9	0.24%
TOTAL	42180.2	100.00%	7555.4	100.00%

Source: Geographical Distribution of Financial Flows to Aid Recipients 1991–1995, OECD, Paris, 1997.

critical areas for poverty eradication and basic social services show gross underfunding. Bilateral aid commitments to education, health and water/sanitation amounted to US$ 7400 million in 1995, 17% of the total.

Last year Reality of Aid noted the declining share of aid to agriculture. In 1995, this trend sharpened dramatically with bilateral commitments to agriculture falling from 8.6% to 6.7% of the total. In LLDCs, the trend is even more marked. The average spend on agriculture in LLDCs in 1993/4 was 11%. In 1995 it had fallen to 8.2%.

Bilateral versus multilateral?

The proportion of aid spent multilaterally for the DAC as a whole remains fairly constant at around 30%. But the general scrutiny being applied to development cooperation, combined with shrinking global aid, means donors are paying more attention to the relative merits of different multilateral channels and tend to focus more on domestic returns from multilateral spending. In Spain, for example, voluntary contributions to UN agency programmes (such as UNICEF, WHO, UNDP) are to be made explicitly conditional on the increased presence of Spanish civil servants in these institutions as well as on a higher share of contracts for Spanish companies.

Contributions to the UN represented only 5.5% of multilateral aid in 1995 as opposed to 14% in 1993. Multilaterals are having to compete more for resources. Credits to UNDP, WFP and UNFPA were halved in one year and those to UNICEF reduced to a fifth of their previous level. A couple of countries intend to increase multilateral spending. In Norway, multilateral allocations are perceived as having more potential for sustainable development and Parliament has recommended that the principle of an equal sharing between bilateral and multilateral aid should be restored. This would require a major shift from the current 27%. In Italy, the increasing share of multilateral aid (now around 90%) is seen as a way of securing an improved international reputation for Italian aid (still suffering from a legacy of bilateral mismanagement).

Most countries show no inclination to increase multilateral spending. Rather, the trends are towards bringing multilateral allocations more into line with national priorities – sometimes development priorities, sometimes business interests. Belgium, for instance, plans to halve the number of multilateral organisations it supports – currently 57 – and bring them more into line with its own sectoral and geographical priorities.

The Reality of Aid 1997/8
Trends in aid and development

A lack of transparency in multilateral disbursements is evident between the EU and its member states. Underspending against commitments year on year results in many member states clawing back allocations charged against EC development cooperation in their budgets, but never spent. This money does not, on the whole, re-enter a development cooperation budget, either bilaterally or multilaterally. The implications and the startling scale of this are explored in the chapter on the EU.

Commercial interests in aid

Increased openness in the debate about development cooperation is reflected in more transparent discussion about the legitimate place of business interests in aid, both in terms of direct returns to the donor country from aid and the role that business can be expected to play in contributing to sustainable development.

In France, the government has long argued that commercial returns from the aid budget are part of the price of public support for the (relatively large) development cooperation expenditure. In Germany too, aid expenditure is increasingly legitimised in terms of jobs created in the donor country. The Danish minister for Development Cooperation has taken a similar view, arguing that popular support for maintaining development aid at 1% of GNP is possible, because broad layers of Danish society, including private companies, take part in development work. This view may be part of the reason why several countries are examining in greater detail the returns from their aid programmes.

An example is Switzerland's[10] study, which found that for every franc of Swiss aid, between 90 cents and Sfr 1.02 was spent in Switzerland even though 71% of Swiss aid is untied.

In a number of countries there are initiatives underway to try to harness the capacity of the private sector in the interests of sustainable development. Denmark has looked strategically at the role of companies (and others) in enabling it to deliver its aid programme and sees a need to maintain this capacity – perceived both as an obligation and in Danida's own interest. A new initiative in Switzerland has been the formation of a foundation, half funded from market sources, to promote private-sector involvement in developing countries.

At the G7 meeting in 1996 the USA proposed action to stimulate trade and investment in Africa based on its own African Growth and Opportunity Act, introduced in April 1997. This would create a high level US–Africa Trade and Economic Cooperation Forum to discuss trade and investment issues, a US–African free trade area and the creation of two equity funds (with private capital and US government guaranteed debt), one to finance equity investments and one to finance infrastructure in Africa.

Aid tying

Aid tying is seen as one of the tests of the clout of the business lobby. Various countries, including Ireland, The Netherlands, the UK and, most recently, Belgium have made serious but unsuccessful attempts to achieve multilateral untying.

The political difficulty donors face in trying to reduce tied aid is illustrated in Belgium where the Secretary of State for Development Cooperation announced his intention to abolish tying. However, under pressure from the business lobby to increase the tying of multilateral aid, the Minister for Finance and Foreign Trade has promised to promote a 'more Belgian reflex' in dealings with multilaterals.

Previous *Reality of Aid* reports noted the anti-competitive nature of aid tying and the consequent overpricing of goods and services bought with aid money. In 1994 (the most recent figures available) there was a marginal decrease in tied aid from 24% to 22% of total ODA. On an estimate of overpricing of 15%, this means US$ 1900 million lost from the global aid budget.

While a minority of countries block multilateral untying, NGOs report that OECD disciplines on tied aid credits help ensure that aid is not used to subsidise projects that could be financed commercially. In Spain, the Helsinki Agreement on tied aid credits is reported to have had an impact on the degree to which aid can be used as a commercial instrument.

In Denmark, consultants' fees for overhead costs triggered a conflict with Danida, which then experimented by opening 16 contracts to international competition. The result was lower prices. Even Danish bids dropped in price and, according to the minister's review of the situation, Danida would have had to pay 10% more if the 16 projects in the market test had not been put up for international tender.

In 1996, the UK ODA (now reincarnated as the Department for International Development, DFID) released a report showing that aid tying distorted the UK economy, harmed exporters and discouraged efficiency. Even so, ministers declined to

Trends in aid and development

make a unilateral gesture on untying because the aid budget had to be seen to be helping UK industry. Ironically, ODA's study showed that UK exporters had much to gain from multilateral untying.

A major review of Australian aid,[11] noting the UK experience, has recommended modest unilateral steps to reduce tying. This review is explicit about self-interest in aid: 'Commercial and diplomatic benefits may well flow from aid projects, but although these can be welcomed as an additional benefit, they should play no part in project planning.'

Public attitudes

The belief that popular support for development cooperation depends on domestic returns and jobs created at home is contradicted by findings from Canada. Research released by CIDA shows that public support for aid is mainly philanthropic. The evidence suggests that arguments for aid based on returns to the Canadian economy were received with cynicism – and were perceived negatively because they were out of line with what people saw as the altruism on which aid should be based. This supports a consistent trend seen in opinion polls over time: the public thinks aid should be about helping people in real need.

The media continue to play an important role in forming public attitudes to aid and development and in informing the public, particularly on humanitarian situations. The Netherlands' public has shown a real interest in the increased focus of Dutch aid on sustainable human development. But NGOs in Sweden and Belgium note in their reports the corrosive impact of the media on public support for aid. Sometimes, as in Belgium, this has taken the form of rehashing old aid scandals and taking a 'miserabalistic' view of development cooperation. Many NGOs can attest to the frequent requests from journalists for stories that focus on aid misuse. In Sweden, the main daily morning newspaper, the liberal *Dagens Nyheter*, symbolised the Swedish media's shift in attitude when its editorial page changed from being broadly supportive of aid to being much more questioning.

Public support for development cooperation remains generally strong. In the EU an average of 67% of people support development cooperation, 87% of them think it is important. In Japan, the largest aid donor in volume terms, the figures for 1995 and 1996 are virtually identical: 80% of the population thinks that aid should stay at the present level or be increased.

For decades, the proportion of Swedes in favour of the existing level of aid or wanting it increased has been between 65% in 'bad years' and up to 85% in 'good years'. But currently, there is little support for traditional, active Swedish development cooperation policy by the main political actors. In the latest survey, published in December 1996, the proportion of people who were positive about aid was down to 44%.

The problem with polls framed around attitudes to existing aid levels is the public's general tendency to overestimate greatly the proportion of public expenditure that goes to development assistance. A 1996 poll in the United States found that the median response to a request to estimate aid as a percentage of national income, overestimated by close to a hundred times the true value. This year NGOs in Australia and Switzerland report the same phenomenon.

While public altruism and commitment to humanitarian interventions remain generally robust, polls show that knowledge about aid and development cooperation is very limited and that the public is sceptical about information on aid.

Significantly, mobilisation of public support for development cooperation is becoming a strategic issue for aid ministries. A focus on results and effective aid and importance of transparency are highlighted in a number of countries.

In Australia AusAID and the NGO coalition ACFOA are to plan longer-term cooperative work on public attitudes; in Austria, the administration has strengthened its own efforts to inform the public about aid activities and create a positive image for development cooperation. In Canada, the NGO coalition is promoting the notion of global citizenship. In Japan, the Ministry of Foreign Affairs is expanding its information activity to win support for the aid programme and in Spain the government has organised campaigns to promote public support, as well as financing activities by NGOs.

In Sweden, the government has responded to the decline in support by stating the need for intensified work on development education and information and by increasing its allocation for information activities by over 37%. Relative to other donors, Sweden's past investments in information and education have been high. In many countries the resources and priority given to building an informed constituency are minimal.

Trends in aid and development

Table 30 Official aid spending on public information and development education per head of population

	Year	US$
Australia	1996	0.08
Austria	1997	0.75
Belgium	1996	0.31
Canada	1995/6	0.06
Denmark	1997	0.24
Finland	1997	0.17
Germany	1997	0.05
Ireland	1996	0.50
Japan	1997	0.01
Netherlands	1997	1.10
Norway	1996	1.26
Spain	1995	0.16
Sweden	1997	1.69
Switzerland	1996	0.48
UK	1995/6	0.03
USA	1996	0.01

Source: Reality of Aid Questionnaires.

Globalisation: The integration of development and foreign policy

Over the past five years, many DAC donor governments have undertaken reviews, either of foreign policy as a whole, or of development cooperation policy. Statements such as *Canada in the World* or the Dutch, *A World of Conflict* have clearly underlined the need for a more integrated approach to global challenges and for ideas of sustainable development to have more influence on government policy.

In the last 18 months, this approach seems to have been having an impact on both the structures and policies of several DAC donors.

France, for example, has attached the development minister to the Foreign Ministry and has established an Interministerial Committee for Aid to Development to improve coordination.

In Belgium, where there are currently separate departments of Foreign Affairs and Development Cooperation, the non-Cabinet State Secretary for Development Cooperation has suggested that Belgium should follow the Dutch and Danish examples and establish a single ministry, integrating foreign affairs and development. This would, he argues, result in a more coherent approach to issues such as conflict resolution.

In the United States, while USAID has managed to retain its semi-independent status, some functions have been merged with those of the State Department, and the USAID administrator now reports exclusively to the Secretary of State, and not to the President as well.

In Italy, concern over instability in former Yugoslavia and the Mediterranean, and upheavals affecting traditional partner countries, have led to a major rethink on development cooperation. Italian ODA will now be seen in its broader geopolitical context, with a new focus on political, economic and social stability.

Stronger focus on poverty as an objective of donor policy

Past *Reality of Aid* reports have noted NGO concerns that the integration of foreign policy could lead to a weakening of attention to poverty. But NGO comments in this year's report suggest that this is not happening.

Novib reports that following a foreign policy review in 1996, Dutch aid policy has shown a remarkable shift towards basic social services. If the Norwegian government follow their Parliament's recommendations, then aid from Norway will also have its poverty orientation strengthened.

CID in New Zealand points out that, whereas poverty reduction was only implicit in NZODA's guiding principles from 1992 to 1995, it is now explicit. KePa reports that, while framing development policy in the broad context of Finland's external relations, poverty has prime place. The new UK Secretary of State has talked of focusing ruthlessly on poverty.

ACFOA's report refers to the major review of Australian aid dated April 1997, which recommends 'One Clear Objective'. The report is refreshingly explicit:

> At present, the managers of the aid program struggle to satisfy multiple objectives driven by a combination of humanitarian, foreign policy and commercial interests. The intrusion of short-term commercial and foreign policy imperatives has hampered AusAID's capacity to be an effective development agency. It would be naïve to suggest that foreign policy will not play a role in determining which countries receive

Trends in aid and development

Australian aid. However, when deciding the most appropriate aid activities for particular countries, the single guiding principle must be the pursuit of poverty reduction through sustainable development.[12]

In its chapter on Canada, the CCIC underlines the crucial link between clarity on aid objectives and public and political support for aid. Over-high expectations of the roles and possible impact of development cooperation leave it vulnerable to perceptions of failure.

Consequences of integrating development and foreign policy

These moves to dovetail development and foreign policies can have both positive and negative consequences for development cooperation. Positive, if they result in development considerations being 'mainstreamed' and seen as central concerns of government. Negative, if development priorities cannot hold their own at the cabinet table and always end up losing out to trade or political objectives.

Canada provides a good example of both. NGOs welcome the foreign minister's leadership on landmines, human rights in Nigeria and Burma and on the issue of child labour. But they are dismayed by the Cabinet decision to amend certain aspects of environmental legislation by edict in order to facilitate the export of CANDU reactors to China.

Attention to coherence

NGO reports this year suggest that one consequence of the increasing integration of external policies is that the issue of coherence is more firmly on donors' agenda. As yet, it is difficult to find instances of development priorities having significantly influenced foreign policy – but at least the issue of coherence is under discussion and becoming harder to avoid.

The incoming UK government has signalled the importance it attaches to development cooperation by establishing a new Department for International Development, headed by a Cabinet level Secretary of State and separated from the Foreign Office. In addition, the incoming Foreign Secretary has said that he will make human rights a key part of the foreign affairs agenda.

In addition to the priority given to coherence in the Maastricht Treaty, the EU Development Council passed a resolution on coherence of EU development cooperation with other EU policy in 1997. During both the Irish and Dutch EU presidencies, coherence was a key issue, with both NGOs and government taking on the coherence of EU policy in relation to specific commodities.

At EU level, it has been possible to achieve changes in favour of developing countries and a number of *Reality of Aid* reports highlight work around fisheries, chocolate and beef. However, as the EU chapter points out, whether or not this is successful depends ultimately on the implementation by Member States and, to date, a greater focus on coherence at policy level seems to be having little impact on national practice. Belgian and Swiss NGOs quote arms sales to Kenya and Burma as examples. Forum Syd also points out that while the Swedish government is keen to address coherence in EU policy, there seem to be a lot of exceptions to the strict rules on arms exports adopted by the Swedish Parliament.

Nonetheless, it seems clear that the increased focus on aid and external relations is leading to more open discussions about the uses of aid and is providing more opportunity for the legitimacy of competing claims on aid resources to be openly weighed.

The Swiss Coalition highlights the gap between its government's 1994 North–South guidelines (which said that development cooperation must be taken into account across the range of government policy) and the decision in principle to grant export risk guarantees to Swiss companies bidding on the Three Gorges Dam project in China. The Swiss Coalition goes on to point out that while short-term domestic interests prevailed over development policy in the Three Gorges case, at least the balance between competing interests was aired publicly and there was 'no possibility of unintended incoherence'.[13]

Poverty reduction and aid implementation

As Table 35 on mainstreaming attention to poverty reduction shows, many NGOs in this year's *Reality of Aid* report fairly positively on some donors' intentions to increase the attention paid to poverty and to the priorities outlined at the Social Summit and in the DAC's *Shaping the 21st Century*.

But even at the level of objectives this is not universal, especially among the largest donors. Japan, France and the USA together disbursed US$ 26,000 million (47% of total ODA) in 1996. Looking

Trends in aid and development

at the USA, only the fifth of five USAID objectives focuses on interests other than those of the USA itself – and the word poverty is not mentioned.

While Japan allocates some aid for basic human needs as a 'safety net' for the poor, the Japanese basically regard aid as a promoter of growth through industrialisation and expansion of exports of industrial goods. In France, sustainable development and the reduction of poverty have been reaffirmed as 'priority objectives', but it is almost impossible to find any logic linking the distribution of French aid with these objectives. The majority of donors will need to make a great effort to translate policy statements into effective implementation.

NGO reports and Table 39 on Political Responsibility and Management of Development Cooperation mention some specific actions countries have taken to improve aid management. Italy's adoption of the project cycle approach and the major steps taken in The Netherlands to decentralise its aid administration are examples of positive initiatives that could make a significant impact on donors' effectiveness. Another positive example is the DAC review of aid from a developing country perspective currently under way in Mali.

Taken together, NGO comments on policy changes suggest a new determination to address poverty. But policy without implementation will not benefit the poor. As the sections on aid spending illustrate, so far there have not been significant shifts in resources towards the right sectors – and most aid agencies cannot be said to be embarking on the wholesale reorientations of their work that are necessary. The comments of the Simons Committee, discussed in the Australian chapter, sum up very effectively the sense that emerges from several NGO reports. It mentions the need to

> reorientate the aid programme to focus squarely on development outcomes. Unequivocal priority must be given to activities which maximise the development benefits and have the greatest long-term impact on poverty.

The comment that AusAID has not been 'good at consistently translating policies into strategies and program activities' can be applied to most aid administrations. 'An effective aid programme does not engage in activities because they will have *some* impact on poverty, it selects activities which maximise the impact on poverty.'

A key problem highlighted by several NGOs is that so much aid is not handled by departments that, at least in principle, are equipped and directed to deliver effective aid. In Austria, the Ministry of Foreign Affairs, which coordinates development policy, is responsible for less than one-fifth of ODA. German NGOs also argue strongly that development cooperation would be improved if BMZ were responsible for more than the 70% of German aid it currently controls.

The lack of appropriate staff and skills with which to implement poverty-oriented aid is highlighted in the European Union, where council resolutions on gender, social policies and poverty are contradicted by the failure to build human resources in these sectors.

New focus on flexibility: trend away from focus on countries towards sectors

Many *Reality of Aid* reports this year reflect a new emphasis on aid resources being used more 'flexibly'. Donors are less prepared to keep giving to traditional recipients – and say they want to be able to react quickly to changing situations. This implies a stronger tendency for allocations to reflect donor policy priorities.

NGOs are concerned that this flexibility genuinely serves the interests of developing countries and is not another opportunity for misuse of aid – or for the inconsistent application of principles.

In Finland, NGOs are concerned that the considerable resources being allocated for flexible use might not always be applied in ways that are entirely consistent with the long-term development of recipient states.

German NGOs point out that, in the past, failure to meet clear policy conditions on aid did not preclude the provision of ODA in circumstances where their strict application would interfere with German interests. Raising flexibility to the level of a policy runs the risk of legitimising such misuse of aid.

In The Netherlands, flexibility is inherent in the new government approach based on themes and sectors, rather than countries. In the new budget there will be no predictions about how much money will be spent in each country or region. The scale of aid to a particular country depends on the extent to which it is believed possible to achieve Dutch policy aims in that country. NGOs are full of praise for the policy aims, but wary of the complex and untransparent procedures surrounding this way of allocating aid resources.

In Norway, there has been an attempt to put a brake on the government's policy of donor flexibility in favour of long-term, untied development grants as being most consistent with achieving sustainable development.

Parallel with the emphasis on flexibility, some donors, such as Denmark and the EU, are moving away from project aid towards sectoral and budgetary support. Sector programme assistance consists of support to specific sectors of the budget in a developing country. It is intended to be integrated into the recipient country's sector policy and coordinated with support from other donors.

This year the Irish government will examine the feasibility of programme aid to specific sectors of the recipient country's budget. Such Sectoral Investment Programmes (SIPs) will focus particularly on education and health. MS in Denmark and Concern in Ireland suggest that this approach will make it even more difficult to assess benefits to the poor. Concern argues that since programme aid is more distant from the individual beneficiary, Irish Aid will have to ensure that mechanisms exist for tracing the link between SIPs and poverty alleviation.

Gender slowly becoming mainstreamed in policy, much less in practice

Policies and mandates on gender are now universal among DAC donors. Historically, donors have distinguished between WID specific activities – discrete projects and programmes designed to benefit women – and WID integrated activities, where attention to the impact on women is integrated into the overall project. Increasingly, integrating gender concerns, and looking at the differential impact of activity on men and women, has been seen as the more promising strategy. There are, however, very different approaches ranging from donors who see gender as integral to sustainable human development and those who see gender equality as a strategic objective in its own right. DAC members have signed up to the agreed goal of making gender equality an overall strategic objective, but only Denmark, Finland, the Netherlands, Norway and Sweden have adopted gender equality as a strategy. Similarly, in the EU, despite a Council resolution on gender and development cooperation in 1996, implementation is reported to be patchy.

In Australia, gender is referred to at all levels in policy documents and is acknowledged as having been mainstreamed. However, there are large gaps between the policy statements and actual implementation. Similarly, in Canada, CIDA's Performance Review Division looked at WID and gender equity and, while final conclusions are awaited, initial findings suggest there was little observable improvement between 1992 and 1995.

In Denmark and Finland, by contrast, gender is integral to development cooperation. In Denmark, the overall aim of policy is gender-specific poverty reduction. In the Netherlands, in line with the general departitioning of aid, gender has been moved out of its separate unit and into social development, with a policy to integrate with other sectors. In Sweden, gender is both mainstreamed and specific: the policy is to ensure that the aid programme as a whole and policy dialogue in particular contain inputs that both promote gender equality and mainstream gender issues.

Germany and Switzerland, like Belgium, take the view that gender should be incorporated as a trans-sectoral theme and they pay serious attention at the policy level to the promotion of women and gender-aware approaches to development.

In France, gender issues fill a particularly significant gap between the good intentions proclaimed by the government and the reality. In 1994, the DAC Aid Review recommended attention to gender but little progress has been made. France has been largely content to put into place some isolated projects, but a gender dimension has not been integrated into practice.

Engendering the peace process

Gender in relation to conflict and peacebuilding has become a much more prominent issue. In 1996, the EU passed a resolution on Gender, Crisis Prevention, Emergency Operations and Rehabilitation as a result of which the European Community Humanitarian Office (ECHO) created an internal working group on gender. In future, framework partnership agreements with NGOs will refer to analysis of gender impact. In its 1997 *Guidelines on Conflict, Peace and Development Cooperation*, the DAC drew attention to the special role women can play as bridging partners in dialogue, peace negotiations, reconstruction and rehabilitation strategies.[14]

Trends in aid and development

In Canada, gender equity policies are supposed to inform humanitarian aid. In Australia, a parliamentary committee is looking at the rights of refugee women and gender considerations are included in humanitarian relief. In The Netherlands, there are several initiatives around gender, conflict and rehabilitation of war victims as well as the promotion of the active involvement of women in peace building and rehabilitation, including various small projects aimed at promoting women in local peace negotiations.

Some progress on measurement – but too much preoccupation with detail and not enough on inputs

An important aspect of donors' focus on *Shaping the 21st Century* over the last year has been attention to impact. Collectively and individually, donors are trying to measure assistance to poverty in a way that did not happen five years ago. The new statistical reporting system in New Zealand (FMIS) and attempts in Canada and Switzerland to measure allocations to different priorities are examples at the national level. At the international level, the joint World Bank, UN and OECD seminar on Indicators of Development Progress held in May 1997, which brought statisticians from the UN and other international bodies together with donor and recipient governments to develop a common system of indicators for progress, is a major step forward.

NGOs make some important comments on measurement. The Swiss Coalition says it is high time that data collected over several years (even if not perfect) were published to stimulate public interest in poverty eradication and to increase accountability. This ties in with points made in earlier *Reality of Aid* reports – that too much preoccupation with methodology of measurement can prevent even broad comparisons being made. The best should not be allowed to become the enemy of the good. The CCIC points to the danger of establishing standards of proof for aid that are unachievable and not applied to other aspects of public expenditure.

A common concern of NGOs is that donors should not include humanitarian assistance in their definitions of basic human need, for social summit definitions are really about long-term development needs.

In their reports, NGOs are expressing a wish to measure both the impact of aid interventions and allocations to different priorities. Both are seen as important because, without major allocations by donors to basic needs and social sectors, the desired impact on poverty is unlikely to happen by 2015.

Notes

1. UNDP, *Human Development Report*, 1997, p 112.
2. Since records began in 1950.
3. ODA is provided both as grants and as loans. To qualify as ODA, a loan must have a grant element of at least 25%. The grant element measures the concessionality of a loan. A grant element is nil for a loan carrying an interest rate of 10% (as this is assumed to be the market rate); it is 100% for a grant and if the interest rate is subsidised, it lies between the two. Out of the 21 donors, 16 give more than 90% of their bilateral ODA as grants. Of the remaining five, Japan and Spain stand out with grant shares of 37% and 50% respectively. The DAC has set standards that require the grant element of ODA loans to each LLDC to average 86% over three years. In 1994/5 every donor exceeded 95% and only three were below 99%.
4. Aid has declined in real terms from $67,900 million to $56,400 million, a fall of 16.93% (1995 prices).
5. Maastricht Treaty, article 130u.
6. The UK government came to power in May 1997 retaining the UN target, but having dropped an earlier commitment to reach 0.7% GNP within five years.
7. The implications of this fall are hard to read since the statistical reason is a large increase in the share of unallocated ODA.
8. Palau, east of Indonesia, with 16,000 inhabitants, became a Free Associated State in late 1994, agreeing to limited sovereignty and granting the USA access to military bases for 50 years. US development assistance to Palau was US$ 191 million in 1994 and $132 million in 1995 (OECD, *Geographical Distribution of Financial Flows to Aid Recipients 1991–1995*, OECD, Paris, 1997).
9. Paul Bennell and Dominic Furlong, 'Has Jomtien Made any Difference? Trends in Donor Funding for Education and Basic Education since the Late 1980s', *IDS Working Paper 51*, March 1997.
10. *Effets économiques de l'aide publique au développement en Suisse*, SDC, Berne, December 1996.
11. *One Clear Objective, Poverty Reduction through Sustainable Development*, Report of the Committee of Review, April 1997, AusAID, Canberra, 1997.
12. Ibid.
13. See Jacques Forster, 'The Coherence of Policies Towards Developing Countries: The Case of Switzerland', Paper presented to the EADI International Workshop on Policy Coherence in Development Cooperation, IUED, Geneva, April 1997.
14. OECD, DAC, Guidelines on Conflict, Peace and Development Cooperation, agreed at the High Level Meeting of the DAC, May 1997.

The outlook for aid

The outlook for aid

Official development assistance, or aid, is the one global resource capable of being targeted on the eradication of poverty. In 1992, at the Earth Summit in Rio, many heads of state committed themselves and their countries to giving 0.7% of their national income in aid for sustainable development. In 1994, at the World Summit for Social Development, heads of state committed themselves to the goal of eradicating poverty and reaffirmed their commitment to 0.7%. In 1996, all DAC donors signed up to the goals identified in *Shaping the 21st Century*. The first of these is a reduction, by one half of the proportion of people living in extreme poverty by the year 2015.

Since 1992, aid as a whole has fallen by 17% and, in 1996, at 0.25%, total DAC aid reached its lowest level since records began in 1950. The average effort made by donors (the unweighted average) was 0.4% of GNP. Some countries, allowing their performance to slip with little apparent concern for commitments made, blame domestic fiscal circumstances. Others, particularly the Nordic countries, have taken their commitments responsibly and have exceeded the target. The key question is, how can senior politicians/governments make statements about these targets and fail to meet them so consistently and so grossly with apparent impunity.

Table 31 The outlook for aid

Country	ODA as % of GNP in 1996	Target for aid	Most recent affirmation of the target	% Change in real terms 1995–6	Outlook
Australia	0.29	0.7	Minister for Foreign Affairs, Hon Alexander Downer, in 1996/7 budget paper	–15.1	Very poor. In March 1997 the team undertaking the major Review of Australian Aid reported its view that the 0.7% target was no longer credible and should be replaced by an achievable three- to five-year target
Austria	0.28	0.7	By Austrian government on signing Maastricht Treaty when joining EU	–14.0	No realistic prospect of any increase. Austrian aid is projected to decline to 0.27% of GNP in 1997, rise slightly in 1998 but return to 0.27% in 1999
Belgium	0.35	0.7	Secretary of State for Development Cooperation in *Kleur Bekennen*, a major government statement on ODA in October 1996	9–6.4	In 1995, it was one of the few countries to show an increase, reaching 0.38% of GNP. The current Secretary of State is expected to be able to stabilise Belgian aid at over 0.3% of GNP. He has even set an interim target of 0.5% by 1999
Canada	0.31	0.7	Government statement by Minister of Foreign Affairs in February 1995	–15.4	Remains bleak. Unless ODA is increased, the projection for the year 2000 is 0.25%. Government has always stated a commitment to 0.7% when fiscal situation allows it. Canada now has one of the healthiest fiscal situations in the OECD

The **Reality** of Aid 1997/8

The outlook for aid

Denmark	1.04	1.0	By Danish government in state budget, 1997	10.5	Target for aid remains at 1% of GNP with a further 0.5% for environment and emergencies
Finland	0.34	0.7	By Cabinet in September 1996	9.3	Target has been affirmed as a long-term goal. Government's short-term aim is to reach 0.4% by 2000
France	0.48	0.7	By President Mitterand at the Rio Summit in 1992 and reaffirmed many times during the first half of the 1990s	−11.3	Has an 'underdeveloping' budget of cooperation. Aid will decline to 0.5% of GNP in 1997 and, although France is keen to keep its position as a large donor, it seems as if the government has abandoned its 0.7% target
Germany	0.32	0.7	By Chancellor Kohl at the World Summit on Social Development in 1995	3.8	Target of 0.7% is probably further away than ever. Aid has been declining for the last few years, from 0.4% in 1991 to a projected 0.3% for 1996; in 1997 it is projected to drop below this level. Some sources talk about 0.29% or 0.28%
Ireland	0.3	0.7	In June 1996 the new government committed itself to an interim target of 0.45% of GNP by 2002	14.5	Aid is continuing to rise in real terms but has yet to meet the 0.05% annual increase to which the government committed itself
Italy	0.2	0.7	The target was confirmed at the NGO Forum on the World Food Summit in 1996	33.9	ODA was virtually halved in 1995. Its aid has thus passed from 0.42% of GDP in 1989 – its highest point – to 0.14% in 1995. The 0.7% target does not represent a real commitment in the Italian political agenda
Japan	0.2	0.7	By Japanese Delegation to the Earth Summit in 1992	−24.7	From 1998 the government will cease to have a medium-term goal for ODA, which will be cut by 100m yen (10%). The government still recognises 0.7% as a long-term goal but there is pressure on ODA because of the budget deficit
Luxembourg	0.41	0.7		21.6	
Netherlands	0.83	0.8	By Dutch parliament in November 1996	6.2	Devotes a fixed percentage of its income to 'pure' aid to developing countries. A new (lower) norm of 0.8% of GNP has been set and reaffirmed for 1997

The outlook for aid

Country	ODA as % of GNP in 1996	Target for Aid	Most recent affirmation of the target	% Change in real terms	Outlook
New Zealand	0.21	0.7	By NZ officials at Habitat II in 1996, but only the words 'striving to fulfil' were endorsed	−7.3	Continues to support the target and is making increases of approximately 0.01% per year
Norway	0.85	1.0	Parliament made a renewed commitment to the target of 1% of GNP for ODA in 1996	3.1	Aid is expected to increase to 0.88% of GNP in 1997 and to reach 1% of GNP by the year 2001
Portugal	0.21	0.7	By prime minister at the Earth Summit in 1992	−15.6	The government is more interested in the comparison with the DAC average than the 0.7% target
Spain	0.22	0.7	By prime minister in early 1996 election campaign and in October statements to the press by the Secretary of State for International Cooperation and Latin America	−8.6	New Secretary of State for Cooperation has questioned the prospect of reaching 0.7% before the year 2000. Budget restrictions and the structure of Spanish aid greatly reduce the feasibility of achieving the target
Sweden	0.82	1.0	Government and parliament are constantly reaffirming their aim to restore ODA to its 1% level as soon as the financial situation permits	7.6	Government expects ODA to be 0.7% of GNP for 1997, 1998 and 1999 with a small increase to 0.72 for year 2000. Sida is more optimistic – with 0.75% for 1999 and 0.78% for 2000
Switzerland	0.34	0.4	In 1996, the government confirmed its aim to increase ODA to 0.4% of GNP, but did not set a timetable	−1.6	Federal Council has never set itself target of reaching 0.7%, stating only 0.4%. However, this target remains as a principle with the budgetary stabilisation measures making it illusory until at least 2000
UK	0.27	0.7	The new Secretary of State, 28 May 1997	−0.8	A two-year freeze on public expenditure will keep aid to its planned levels. Secretary of State has announced her intention to seek an increase at the end of the two years
USA	0.12	None	The USA has never committed itself to the target	20.6	Prospects are that aid as a proportion of GNP will decline further in the future

Leadership on public and political opinion

Previous *Reality of Aid* reports have noted that while the OECD public remain broadly as supportive as ever of the need to eradicate poverty, public support for aid is more elastic. It fluctuates from time to time in different countries, particularly when policy-makers and opinion formers focus on the need to cut budget deficits or to talk down aid effectiveness. If the strong humanitarian commitment of the public is to be broadened into a deeper awareness of interdependence and the need for development cooperation, political leadership at the highest levels will need to be found. The table below reports on the current state of public opinion and leadership on development issues.

Table 32 Leadership on public and political opinion

Country	Levels of public support shown in most recent polls	Leadership for public opinion on development cooperation
Australia	An April 1996 survey carried out by Frank Small & Associates found that some 60% of Australians wanted aid to remain at the same level or to increase. Also, based on a survey of 1028 adults in 1993, Garth Luke (*Australian Attitudes to Overseas Aid*, April 1997) found that Australians have a high level of awareness of poverty but little understanding of its causes and little hope of any change. They have a low level of confidence in both government and NGO aid programmes and tend to overestimate the amount of official aid	ACFOA, NGOs, the churches and to some extent the media take the lead. Joint Committee on Foreign Affairs, Defence and Trade held a parliamentary seminar on aid in July 1996 as a means of encouraging public debate on the aid programme and to feed into the preparations for the Review of the Australian Aid Programme. NGOs have stated that more resources need to go towards building public understanding on development. A seminar is being planned by AusAID and ACFOA to commence planning longer-term cooperative work on public attitudes to aid
Austria	No recent polls. There is public support, but political support is traditionally low	Foreign Ministry, Standing Subcommittee in Parliament and the NGO coalition AGEZ take the leadership role promoting aid. The aid administration takes responsibility for wider issues such as trade and environment. The administration strengthened its own efforts to inform the public about its activities and to create a positive image of development cooperation in a broad sense
Belgium	The Belgian public has the least confidence in development cooperation in Europe, but nonetheless 51% is in favour of more Belgian official aid, 72% think it is important but one out of every two Belgians doubts the accuracy of information provided on development aid	NGOs are the forerunners in conveying a positive image of the South and development cooperation, while Belgian television and a Flemish newspaper have launched a series of old official aid scandals and have conveyed a largely 'miserabalistic' and sceptical view of the South and development cooperation. ABOS publications are meant to reach a broader public, but are not well known

Leadership on public and political opinion

The **Reality** of Aid 1997/8

Country	Levels of public support shown in most recent polls	Leadership for public opinion on development cooperation
Canada	Polls in November 1995 and December 1996 indicate a downward trend of those in favour of long-term aid over humanitarian relief (74% in 1991 to 49% in 1995). A focus study released by CIDA in September 1996 indicated that people would rather focus on the philanthropic side of aid over the returns for Canada	A CCIC Taskforce on Building Public Support for Sustainable Human Development recommended a series of actions in 1996 for the NGO community to coalesce to promote notions of 'global citizenship' in all their public messages. This was in response to diminishing public space for discussion of international issues. The first week in February is International Development Week, but because aid cuts have now eliminated funding for direct NGO participation, CIDA produces generic material for use during this week
Denmark		Politicians, NGOs and media researchers lead the field in bringing awareness of international issues to the public
Finland	A March 1997 opinion survey conducted by Mori for UNFPA sampled 1004 Finns on their views of priorities in Finnish development assistance. The highest percentage favoured health care (69%), then education (58%), emergency aid (55%), children's living conditions (49%), the environment (40%), AIDS/HIV prevention (36%), family planning (32%), country infrastructure (28%), agriculture (25%) and 1% replied spontaneously that aid should not be given at all	Ostensibly, the Department for Development Cooperation in the Foreign Ministry is responsible for promoting information and support for ODA. With the deep cuts in ODA in early 1992, though, emphasis on lobbying and information has been increasingly the province of NGOs, which, with churches, politicians, the media and industry, are the main players
France		NGOs are the driving force for public awareness of development issues. The government states that it and its people have an interest in providing aid (commercial, employment, geopolitical and military). It has seen development education as the non-governmental sector's responsibility, but a combined awareness raising campaign is now planned for 1997
Germany	Recent surveys among the population show that 28% regard poverty as the third most important global problem after hunger/malnutrition and the environment	The aid administration is interested in both wider questions of interdependence and those of a short-term domestic interest to Germany
Ireland	No recent poll	The development community as a whole, including NGOs and solidarity groups promote international issues. NGO-led initiatives with

The **Reality** of Aid 1997/8

Leadership on public and political opinion

		social sectors have strengthened commitment to development issues by youth, trade union and women's movements. The government funds development education through an independent and representative body – the National Council for Development Education
Japan	In October 1996, 32.9% of the population felt aid programmes should be expanded; 46.9% that they should remain at the current level; 12.9% that they should be reduced; 1.8% that they should be terminated and 5.6% said they did not know	Ministry of Foreign Affairs is expanding its information activities to win support for its aid programmes, but the media is more active in reporting development issues
Netherlands	No recent poll	Debate very much led by academics and NGOs. Churches and labour unions also take part. The media also support the debate with many newspaper editors specialising in development issues. The aid administration has a public policy aimed at public support for development cooperation and there is a permanent budget for development education channelled through a national commission (NCDO) which is free to divide the funds among NGOs. Two magazines are distributed, one in schools, the other, free
New Zealand	no recent poll	NGOs and government lead the field. Minister's Advisory Committee in 1995 recommended the government fund an ongoing programme of public awareness and development education in partnership with NGOs and requested NZ$ 500,000. The minister said he would allocate a modest amount for carefully targeted development education activities through NGOs and NZ$ 140,000 was included in the 1996/7 budget. The minister was concerned to increase public awareness of New Zealand's place in the world at large
Norway	An opinion poll by Statistics Norway in 1996 showed that 84% of the population were in favour of development aid, compared with 85% in 1986 and 1993. Thus, support is strong and stable. Half the respondents felt the present level of aid was reasonable; 12% called for increases and 30% for reductions. The last figures show a setback from 12% in 1986 and 26% in 1993	NGOs, church groups, a few minority political parties and youth groups within the parties play a leading role. The government mainly promotes public support through its contributions to the information activities of the NGOs

263

Leadership on public and political opinion

Country	Levels of public support shown in most recent polls	Leadership for public opinion on development cooperation
Portugal	Public support is high: 93% think development aid is important, 69% that the EU is in the best position to deliver it to Africa and 71% that it can help solve the problems of poverty	There are many NGO initiatives to build public awareness and solidarity and to work with schools to create informed commitment to sustainable development
Spain	A CIS survey in November 1996 found that two out of three favour 0.7% of GNP going to developing countries; 32.7% feel the state should help less developed countries continually through development cooperation projects and development aid; and 62.4% feel it should guarantee the well-being of Spaniards before helping other countries	NGOs and the 0.7% platform lead the arena. Politicians and members of the business community also show interest and play a role. The government has organised two campaigns to promote public support and has financed many others via NGOs
Sweden	Sida carries out a survey annually. In 1996, 44% favoured increasing/maintaining level of aid – compared with 85% in 1975; and 42% were in favour of diminishing/abolishing aid – compared with only 15% in 1975	Most visible leads in promoting aid are NGOs and churches. The strong downward trend in support for development aid indicates a lessening commitment by politicians. However, the government has stated the need to intensify work on development education and information and the 1997 budget has increased its allocation to information activities through Sida by over 37% from MSEK 24 in 1996 to MSEK 33. Combined with government funds to NGOs for information work (for 1995) the figure is estimated around MSEK 100
Switzerland	The Swiss Coalition of Development Organisations has commissioned an opinion poll on sustainable development. Only 34% knew what this was, 20% had never heard of the concept and 67% consider the state is not doing enough to promote it. Some 64% consider that companies' efforts are insufficient, but 50% consider their own behaviour is sufficiently ecological	NGOs take the lead in promoting aid
United Kingdom	No new poll since September 1995 survey found that 81% agreed that it was important to provide aid. Support for development NGOs tested by Gallup in January 1997 found 70% of the public giving donations, 31% doing so regularly, with 70% buying goods	The incoming government has replaced ODA – the Foreign Office department responsible for aid administration – with DFID, a department of development cooperation with an independent cabinet seat and an explicit intention to increase public awareness. These steps, with the appointment of a high profile Secretary of State who is talking of the need to mobilise political will both domestically and within the

Leadership on public and political opinion

	benefiting development NGOs	DAC, suggest a new leadership on development issues. With the Foreign Secretary also stressing a more ethical approach to foreign affairs, NGOs are hopeful that development is becoming a genuine priority for government. Only time will show whether this new will is swamped by domestic interests
USA	A July 1996 survey, *An Emerging Consensus: A study of American Public Attitudes on America's Role in the World*, reported that when Americans are asked to set their preferred level of investment in international efforts, the majority usually sets a level the same as or higher than actual levels. When respondents were asked how much out of every $1000 of the US economy goes to foreign aid, the median estimate was $100, while the actual figure is between $1 and $1.50. Only 10% thought that this amount was too much	USAID is active in promoting public and political support for its programmes, but has acted virtually alone in recent years. Senior policy-makers occasionally mention the importance of sustainable development, but tend to pay it little attention in their planning or policies. Much attention paid to international interdependence and globalisation, but that does not usually generate concern for poverty alleviation or aid-funded economic development. In addition to administration officials responsible for development programmes, the NGOs are the principle leaders in promoting an understanding of development cooperation. Currently, political elites show little interest in development issues

Spending on public information and development education

Creating the conditions conducive to generating adequate resources for development is the first of the joint responsibilities of developed and developing countries outlined by DAC donors in their set of development goals in *Shaping the 21st Century*. Informed public and political attitudes to development cooperation and the role it plays in eradicating poverty and creating global human secutiry are critical conditions for achieving adequate resources and coherent policies for sustainable development .

Reality of Aid NGOs have monitored government (and in some cases voluntary) spending on public relations, public information and development education. There is not a single classification, so these figures should not be used for inter-country comparisons.

Table 33 Spending on public information and development education in US$ millions

Country	Year – most recent for which figures are available	Spending per capita on public information, PR and development education (US$)	Total government funds for public information and development education	Total voluntary funds for public information and development education	Government funds spent via NGOs
Australia	1996	0.08	1.49	n/a	0.754
Austria	1997	0.75	6.10	3.78	4.73
Belgium	1996	0.31	3.10	n/a	0.012
Canada	1995/6	0.06	1.68	n/a	n/a
Denmark	1997	0.24	7.24	n/a	3.54
Finland	1997	0.17	0.87	n/a	n/a
France	1996	n/a	negligible	18.60	negligible
Germany	1997	0.05	4.31	n/a	2.79
Ireland	1996	0.50	1.81	3.20	n/a
Japan	1997	0.01	1.20	29.60	n/a
Netherlands	1997	1.10	17.10	n/a	11.9
New Zealand	1996/7	n/a	n/a	n/a	0.1
Norway	1996	1.26	5.50	n/a	n/a
Spain	1995	0.16	6.20	23.50	1.5
Sweden	1997	1.69	14.90	n/a	10.4
Switzerland	1996	0.48	3.40	n/a	1.05
UK	1995/6	0.03	2.00	n/a	1.13
USA	1996	0.01	3.90	n/a	0.75

Source: NGO Reality of Aid questionnaires.

Measuring aid for poverty eradication

Aid and poverty eradication

Opinion polls show that the public want aid spent on the poorest people and on basic needs. But until recently few comparable figures were available to show how much aid donors were investing in these areas. Out of 21 donors, 12 are now producing figures for the DAC on basic health and education. As the table shows, the amounts being spent are pitifully small – but at least we can now see how much donors are allocating to these priorities.

The DAC has now established clear goals for progress by the year 2015. These targets for impact on poverty will only be met with the help of aid allocated to social development. So it is important for donors to do two things.

First, they need to focus aid resources onto activities that will give the best possible prospects of sustainable poverty reduction – in other words, they need to mainstream attention to poverty. Second, they need to agree on comparable measures of aid towards poverty reduction – and on interim targets that will show just how energetically donors are working in partnership with recipient governments towards the long-term goals.

The charts below document the degree of attention to poverty reduction and social development and the current measures used nationally and internationally to account for aid to direct poverty reduction.

Table 34 Current measures of aid for basic needs or direct poverty reduction as a percentage of total ODA

Country	Basic education 1994	Basic health 1994	Water and sanitation 1994	Progress towards improvements in measurement of aid for poverty reduction	Most recent government estimate of aid to basic needs/poverty reduction	Definition used for basic needs/ poverty reduction
Australia	1.9	4.5	3.2	The Aid Review has made a number of recommendations aimed at improving the effectiveness of the aid programme to maximise impact on poverty. A new poverty reduction framework is recommended. Analytical capacity also to be increased for better measurement of economic and distributional impact of project proposals.		The use of the term basic needs has been avoided and no definition attempted

The Reality of Aid 1997/8
Measuring aid for poverty eradication

Country	Basic education 1994	Basic health 1994	Water and sanitation 1994	Progress towards improvements in measurement of aid for poverty reduction	Most recent government estimate of aid to basic needs/poverty reduction	Definition used for basic needs/ poverty reduction
Austria	Not yet reported	Not yet reported	0.5	No progress	No direct classification	No aid classified as 'direct poverty reduction' or 'basic needs'; thus no definition is available
Belgium	0.2	1.5	2.1	No tangible targets or measurements of aid to poverty reduction. Secretary of State thinks all development cooperation should aim to reduce poverty	Survival Fund Budget for 1997 is BEF 650m, over two-thirds of which is spent via UN agencies	No definition
Canada	Not yet reported	0.2	0.9	For first time 1997/8 expenditure plan provided a comprehensive set of numbers in respect of CIDA's performance on basic needs. CIDA has improved reporting so that it can calculate the % of the programme allocated to each of six priorities, all of which should address poverty reduction. 1995 policy on poverty reduction suggests there will be an evaluation of the policy within five years	27.8% of total ODA was spent on basic human needs in 1995/6 (excluding BHNs programming through Canada's contributions to the World Bank and IMF)	CIDA definition of basic human needs includes food aid, emergencies and humanitarian assistance. If these were excluded in 1995/6 estimate for BHNs would be approximately 14%. A CIDA policy statement on basic needs was released in May 1997
Denmark	1.1	0.2	2.2	The evaluation of poverty reduction completed in 1996 includes detailed recommendations for monitoring progress on achieving poverty reduction objectives	More than 20% to basic social services	No definition as such but the evaluation gives a long list of closely related causes of poverty

The **Reality** of Aid 1997/8

Measuring aid for poverty eradication

Finland	1.4	5.4	7.3		Not calculated in such terms	Not defined in detail but is identified with a range of priorities designed to achieve 'practical results'
France	Not yet reported	not yet reported	3.2	No progress	No estimate	No specific definition
Germany	2.9	1.6	7.5	Government has commissioned major study, Criteria for the Assessment of Poverty Oriented Programmes, on criteria for (self-help oriented) poverty reduction, including indirect and structural forms of poverty reduction. At time of writing it had not yet been published	14.2% of ODA is planned to be spent on direct poverty reduction in 1997, of which basic needs will be 50.7%	Vague definitions of 'self-help oriented poverty reduction' and 'basic needs' included in the BMZ policy document and a full list of self-help oriented poverty came into public domain for first time last year
Ireland	0	0	6.7	It is hoped that changes to the accounting system will help provide a clearer picture by the end of 1997	No specific figures available	Department of Foreign Affairs is working on identifying which parts of the programme can be considered human development priorities. Defined at the 20:20 Oslo meeting in April 1996, these include maintenance transfers and subsidies to the poor; agricultural extension and support for small-scale (including women) farmers; credit, marketing and technical support for small-scale production; employment opportunities; support for shelter and public transport

The **Reality** of Aid 1997/8

Measuring aid for poverty eradication

Country	Basic education 1994	Basic health 1994	Water and sanitation 1994	Progress towards improvements in measurement of aid for poverty reduction	Most recent government estimate of aid to basic needs/poverty reduction	Definition used for basic needs/ poverty reduction
Italy	Not yet reported	1	0.7	Administration is preparing a new marker system to reflect the poverty reduction initiative	No government estimate	Current marker system has no definition of direct poverty reduction or basic needs
Japan	Not yet reported	Not yet reported	9.5	Interest in DAC goals in *Shaping the 21st Century* is a positive development in prioritising attention to measurement of aid for poverty reduction	In 1995, 36.3% of ODA was allocated to the basic human needs sectors	Basic human needs defined as the sum of aid allocated to social infrastructure (education, health, water), agriculture, food aid and emergency relief. NGOs criticise this as too broad
Netherlands	1.5	0.7	2.7	Has taken initiatives to improve international systems of measurement and accountability for social development assistance	1995: 18.4% 1996: 19.45% 1997: 20.31%	Basic social services were defined and calculated in 1997 and include contributions to multilateral agencies and some emergency expenditure
New Zealand	0.1	0.7	0.5	A new information system that will improve statistical reporting capabilities is being installed and a social impact specialist has been appointed to the Evaluation Unit in the Development Cooperation Division	1.03% of bilateral commitments or 1.43% of sector allocatable commitments	OECD classifications of reporting are used, which means any sectors that come under the classification of basic social services: basic education, pre-primary and primary school, literacy, basic health and water and sanitation

The **Reality** of Aid 1997/8

Measuring aid for poverty eradication

Norway	Not yet reported	Not yet reported	2.2	Parliamentary calls for increased health and education spending to bring each up to 10% of ODA by the year 2000	In 1996, 23.9% of bilateral aid was spent on social development	Broad government definition of social development embracing water supply, education science, health, social infrastructure, social welfare and culture
Spain	1.6	Not yet reported	0.2	There is no indicator to register the achievement of these objectives	19.42% of ODA to basic social needs	No classification exists, but Secretary of State for Relations with Parliament has said it will contain activities not included in the UNDP definitions with regard to 20:20
Sweden	3.6	5.7	4.4	Sida's 1995/6 annual report showed expenditure on basic education of US$28.9m and on water and sanitation of $20.2m	In 1995/6, 31% of disbursements to social sector	In reports from the government there are no classifications of direct poverty reduction or basic needs
Switzerland	0.1	Not yet reported	1.6	SDC has sponsored interdisciplinary study to measure ODA spent on basic needs/direct poverty reduction and will evaluate effect on poverty eradication. To be published end June 1997	No estimate available	Classification codes have been in existence for two years. Major problems remain with defining poverty eradication – this is still a subject of discussion within SDC
United Kingdom	Not yet reported	Not yet reported	2.4	Government has measured aid against its objectives using its policy indicator marking system since 1993	11% of bilateral aid goes to basic social services	'Direct assistance to poor people' is defined in the policy indicator marker system and 13.6% of bilateral aid (excluding emergencies) was allocated under this category in 1995/6

Measuring aid for poverty eradication

Country	Basic education 1994	Basic health 1994	Water and sanitation 1994	Progress towards improvements in measurement of aid for poverty reduction	Most recent government estimate of aid to basic needs/poverty reduction	Definition used for basic needs/ poverty reduction
United States	Not yet reported	Not yet reported	1.0	USAID does not classify its spending in this way	In 1993/4, 30% of bilateral aid was estimated to be used for the social sector	Social sector programmes were defined as education, health, family planning, including planning in public administration, water supply and sanitation

Source: DAC Report 1996 Table 27 and NGO questionnaires.
* Data for government estimates of aid to basic needs/poverty reduction taken from NGO questionnaires.

Mainstreaming poverty eradication

Table 35 At a glance on mainstreaming attention to poverty reduction

Country	Progress towards mainstreaming poverty eradication as the goal of all aid	Recent trends in aid for social development and commitments to 20:20
Australia	The government-commissioned review of Australian Aid reported under the title of 'One Clear Objective: Poverty Reduction through Sustainable Development'. It recommended that the single, clear objective of Australian aid should be to assist developing countries reduce poverty through sustainable economic and social development. It suggested a more strategic approach where unequivocal priority must be given to activities that maximise the developmental benefits and have the greatest long-term impact on poverty	No mention of 20:20 compact, but there has been an improvement in the past year with more emphasis on education and health and a higher percentage of the aid programme going to social and administrative infrastructure. Assistance for social development is seen more as an investment in future development. Education (particularly for women and girls) is recognised as 'development's most basic building block and a vital contributing factor to the alleviation of poverty'
Austria	No progress to improve measurement and evaluation. No aid specifically classified for or targeted to direct poverty reduction or basic needs. Claimed poverty reduction is mainstreamed as goal for all aid, but statistics do not support this	No explicit progress can be observed regarding the commitment to 20:20. What priority is given to social issues is seen as an investment in future development
Belgium	The current Secretary of State thinks that as a basic rule all development cooperation should aim to reduce poverty. However, Belgian Survival Fund, established in 1983 is the the only resource directly targeted on the poorest. It is seriously under-funded and under-spent	New policy stresses micro-level sectoral concentration on health, education, agriculture and 'the social economy' – local socio-economic initiatives based on cooperation rather than profit-seeking, such as informal savings and health insurance. 20:20 compact to be included as a condition in every bilateral agreement between Belgium and a developing country
Canada	The 1995 CIDA Policy on Poverty Reduction applies to all CIDA programmes. The degree to which this has been implemented is difficult to determine. Poverty profiles and reduction strategies are to be integrated into country and regional policy frameworks. All programming is to be made consistent with the goal of poverty reduction and all non-poverty programming is to be assessed for its impact on the poor. CIDA is using a threefold classification: targeted poverty programmes working directly with the poor; poverty-focused programmes that benefit a disproportionately larger number of poor than non-poor and policy interventions that impact the environment for poverty reduction	Minister for Foreign Affairs committed Canada to 20:20 at the Copenhagen Summit and officials from CIDA participated in the Oslo follow-up meeting in 1996 and support the resulting policy statement. It has been pointed out that the agreement reached at Oslo gave the initiative to developing countries to request a 20:20 compact from a donor and, as yet, no country has made this request of Canada. However, the May 1997 CIDA policy statement on Basic Human Needs sets out suggested measures for carrying out the commitments: (a) supporting countries that wish to establish a partnership; (b) encouraging participation of government, non-government and private sector in carrying out the commitments; (c) encouraging participation of international organisations to implement 20:20; (d) accounting for the mobilisation of resources to achieve 25% to basic human needs and in support of 20:20

Mainstreaming poverty eradication

Country	Progress towards mainstreaming poverty eradication as the goal of all aid	Recent trends in aid for social development and commitments to 20:20
Denmark	Danida has placed poverty reduction firmly on the top of the Danish development cooperation agenda. In response to a request from parliament to pay more attention to operationalising the poverty reduction strategy, an evaluation was prepared. There is a three-legged poverty reduction approach to (a) sustainable and socially balanced economic growth; (b) development of the social sector, including the promotion of education and health services as prerequisites to the development of human resources; and (c) promoting popular participation and development of a society based on the rule of law and good governance. Is an implicit message that Danish development assistance will make every effort to contribute to poverty reduction	Denmark's commitment to allocate 20% of ODA to basic social services has resulted in over 20% of ODA going to basic social services. Aid to social development is seen very much as an investment in the future. The evaluation of poverty reduction in Danish aid moves away from perceiving poverty as primarily about lack of income, focusing instead on inability to cater for basic needs, lack of opportunity to exploit human resources, isolation, lack of status and power and a high degree of vulnerability
Finland	Poverty alleviation has been the main policy focus of government ODA since 1993 as opposed to a formal classification of direct poverty reduction. Present policy continues with this, concentrating more specifically on the status of disabled people and the participation of women in social and economic activities	Social development highlighted as means and end of poverty reduction. No decisions made on 20:20 compact or on aiming for a 20% goal; neither is mentioned in the 1996 Decision-in-Principle. According to the government's new ODA profile, aid to social development will be increasingly emphasised, perceiving it as an investment in future development
France	No formal classification, but government aims to reduce poverty. There has been no real progress towards mainstreaming poverty eradication into the overall goal of aid. A 1996 study found that poverty alleviation is not listed as a practical priority by any aid institution; it has not been incorporated into the programming or evaluation; it is not the subject of any special strategy or policy statement; it does not appear as a development concept, as the subject of statistical analysis, or as a criterion for allocating aid.	
Germany	Poverty reduction is a key objective, with education and protecting natural resources. The feminisation of poverty is a key issue for analysis but needs to be reflected more in projects. There has been no further progress to mainstream poverty reduction as the overall goal of aid – the trend appears to be quite the opposite, partly evidenced in decreasing aid allocations to Africa. Still no specific criteria for targeting or for participation in the poverty programmes	The 20:20 compact was accepted by Germany in principle at the World Summit for Social Development. However, projected spending on basic education and health show decreases in 1996 and 1997. 20:20 has been integrated as a political goal in some agreements with Southern governments, but there has been no clear political signal that it will be properly implemented

The Reality of Aid 1997/8
Mainstreaming poverty eradication

Ireland	The first priority of Irish Aid is to provide assistance to poorer developing countries and to meet basic needs, particularly of more disadvantaged sections of the population. While poverty alleviation and basic needs are prioritised in Irish Aid it is recognised that there is a need for a stronger poverty focus in the initial analysis so that it is a central aspect of implementation and can be identified in evaluation and monitoring. Some progress has been made in this direction by the strengthening of the Evaluation and Audit unit through additional sectoral experts	Ireland supports the 20: 20 compact with country programmes and reviews for the next three years placing increased emphasis on social sector investment and basic needs. For example, Zambia's three-year country plan is committed to allocating at least two-thirds of the total budget to basic needs. Through the Resolution on Human and Social Development adopted by the EU Development Council under the Irish presidency, it is hoped that the development cooperation of EU member states will be more focused in addressing basic needs as investments for the future. The DCD uses the broader concept of Human Development Priorities in calculating the proportion of Irish aid directed towards poverty reduction
Italy	The government has paid increasing attention to poverty reduction in recent years. The poverty-reduction-oriented aid strategy works through human development and creating a social network, which is seen as a crucial condition for development. At present, the administration is preparing a new system to reflect the poverty reduction objective; and the ministry has suggested criteria for evaluating initiatives that support human development	There is no government commitment to 20:20. However, social development is becoming increasingly visible in Italian ODA and the director of the aid administration talks of social development as a change of culture for Italian ODA
Japan	For Japan, the mainstay of development cooperation is to bring about growth through supporting the economic infrastructure. Japan played a key role in preparing and setting the goals for *Shaping the 21st Century*, which put poverty reduction at the heart of aid	At the World Summit on Social Development, the prime minister said that Japan had already met the 20:20 compact terms by providing more than one-third of ODA to the social sectors, and would continue to do so as it expected to expand social sector aid. No mention was made of raising the compact in Japan's dialogue with recipients. The distribution to social infrastructure increased from 23% in FY 1994 to 26% in 1995
Nether-lands	All Dutch aid is supposed to be directed to poverty reduction but specific targets are set for basic needs and OECD targets on reduction of absolute poverty, access to basic education and reduction of infant mortality are reiterated. Poverty eradication is the overriding goal and the fact that quantitative targets of 20% of aid to basic social services, 4% of aid budget to reproductive health care and at least 0.25% of GNP to Least Developed Countries indicate progress at the policy level	The 20:20 compact has been incorporated into the Dutch ODA budget with a level of 20.31% expected to be achieved in 1997. A large part of the Dutch ODA geared to poverty reduction falls under the wide-ranging theme of social development. The explanatory memorandum indicates that access to basic education and health form part of fundamental human rights. Also stated is that investment in basic human needs is required as fundamental to both personal and country development

Mainstreaming poverty eradication

Country	Progress towards mainstreaming poverty eradication as the goal of all aid	Recent trends in aid for social development and commitments to 20:20
New Zealand	Poverty reduction is now part of the Principle Purpose of NZ ODA and it is stated as a primary focus under the guiding principles of NZ ODA	Has not committed itself to the 20:20 compact. While supporting the idea in principle, the ministry believes it does not readily apply to its main area of interest in the Pacific. There is an increasingly explicit emphasis on social development in the policy framework, particularly through education and training, which accounts for 34% of all ODA. A social impact specialist has been appointed to the Evaluation Unit in the Development Cooperation Division working on criteria for evaluating impact
Norway	Aid is not specifically classified as direct poverty reduction or basic needs, but there has been progress in mainstreaming poverty into the main aid principles. Parliament has played an active role. It has changed the order of the government's objectives to put poverty reduction at the top and has also urged an international role for Norway in promoting poverty reduction and economic models that favour equity based on the Nordic experience	There is a clear commitment to the 20:20 compact. The emphasis in aid to social development is that it is seen as both an investment in the future and a handout
Portugal	Aid is not focused strongly on poverty reduction, except in so far as the countries concerned are among the poorest in the world	Debt reduction and governance issues are given far greater priority than social development
Spain	There has been little progress in this area, although the consolidation of the budget destined for NGOs must be seen as progress of some sort. There is no indicator to register the achievement of poverty reduction objectives so it is impossible to measure progress	The government supports the 20:20 compact but no policy has been made explicitly relating to it, nor have any objectives been set. Spain supported the 20:20 compact in the EU Council of Ministers and believes it has fulfilled the goal in Spain. However, all cooperation expenditure in the health sector, and the purifying and supply of water has been included in the calculation
Sweden	Poverty reduction is one of four main areas in Swedish ODA. A special resolution on it was prepared during Spring 1997 for presentation to parliament later in the year. There is no classification of direct poverty reduction or basic needs, but Sida claims that 31% of their disbursements went to the social sector. Of this, 44% went to education with 40% allocated to primary education. Another high budget area is natural resources (14%), within which there are sectors of high social priority, for example water and sanitation (18%	The government has never been happy with 20:20 compact and acted against it at Copenhagen Summit, the official reason being that it is difficult to calculate reliably what is spent on social development. There is no mention of it in government plans and no efforts are being made to identify allocations to social sectors within the 20:20 definitions

Mainstreaming poverty eradication

Switzerland	of natural resources sector) and rural development (14% of sector). Proportion of NGO assistance dedicated to social sector is 47% Despite classification codes having existed for two years, there is still a problem with defining poverty eradication. The SDC has sponsored an interdisciplinary study to measure the amount of ODA spent on basic needs/direct poverty reduction and evaluates the effect of Swiss cooperation on poverty eradication. This will be published at the end of June 1997. Switzerland is currently setting up a strategy for a social development policy and in the long-term wants to be more involved in the international debate	Has made a commitment to 20:20 compact, but the problems of a definition prevent a true evaluation. SDC estimates that if an international definition is arrived at, then Switzerland will have met the target, as its ODA is very much focused on social development in comparison with other donors
United Kingdom	Poverty reduction is supposed to be the overarching goal of UK aid but the statistics suggest that in 1995/6 'Direct assistance to poor people', excluding emergency aid, represented 13.6% of total bilateral expenditure. The incoming administration has emphasised poverty reduction very heavily in speeches and has actively endorsed the OECD targets in *Shaping the 21st Century*	The UK has not made a commitment to 20:20. Social development, particularly reproductive health and basic education, had increased in institutional importance in British aid before the May 1997 election. The focus of the new Department for International Development on poverty and human development is expected to increase attention to social development approaches
USA	Statements of administration a central goal of US aid. However, there is no specific effort to define or implement this goal *per se*. Much of what USAID does is, however, directed towards this end	Government position at World Summit on Social Development was not to support the 20:20 compact because of concerns that it would establish false targets. Some, in Congress and in the US public, see aid for social development as equivalent to domestic welfare programmes. Others, especially in the development community and administration, view social development abroad as an investment in the future of the USA as well as people in the recipient countries

Source: NGO Reality of Aid questionnaires.

Approaches to gender

Approaches to gender in development cooperation

For many years many donors have, at policy level, recognised the importance of taking gender into account in strategies to achieve sustainable human development and poverty reduction. Here *Reality of Aid* looks at progress towards the objectives. The majority of donors refer to gender in key policy statements – variously treating it as one of several priorities or a cross-sectoral issue. Many donors have taken concrete steps – producing guidelines, offering training, undertaking reviews. But to date, gender still seems to be an item to be ticked off a checklist, rather than a matter of reflex – something which has become inherent in the thinking of aid personnel. As a result, aid spending priorities and implementation practice have a long way to go if they are to be consistent with the rhetoric.

Table 36 Approaches to gender in development cooperation

Country	Status of gender policy and way that it is incorporated into aid strategies	Steps taken to meet commitments made at Beijing	Progress towards the DAC goal of gender equality as an overall strategic objective	Expertise and resources for gender
Australia	*Gender and Development: Australia's Aid Commitment*, Policy Statement announced by Hon Alexander Downer, Minister for Foreign Affairs, March 1997. Part of the strategy for implementation is the incorporation of a system of WID markers. Gender has been mainstreamed but critics argue that it has neither been consistent nor systematic with large gaps between rhetoric and reality	The new policy is intended to indicate a commitment to actions that will meet women's immediate needs, in accordance with the Platform of Action. At this stage there is no way of measuring impact or outcomes	Gender equality is not specifically stated as an overall strategic objective for the Australian Aid Programme	Training programmes have been carried out at all staffing levels, but there is still a lack of corporate commitment to gender issues and consolidation of training is minimal. The Women in Development Fund has been abolished. Gender considerations are included in the criteria for all AusAID programmes. Within AusAID gender issues are the responsibility of the director of the Social Sector and Gender Section, with two dedicated staff
Austria	Gender is claimed as an aim of the overall aid strategy	The government has employed a gender in development consultant	There is little progress as yet	A gender in development consultant has been employed as part of the commitment towards gender
Belgium	New policy proposals incorporate gender as a trans-sectoral theme, with access and involve-	*Kleur Bekennen*, the new policy statement, does not refer to the Beijing	*Kleur Bekennen* rarely addresses the issue of gender inequality and the	Bilateral financing of projects with a gender component remains very limited. Capacity on gender issues con-

Approaches to gender

The Reality of Aid 1997/8

	ment of women guaranteed through a selection of priority sectors: improved access of girls and women to education, health and family planning; improved access of women to income generating activities; fight against violence against women; local capacity building	conference at all	feminisation of poverty. But it identifies gender equality as one of seven criteria for testing the developmental value of aid programmes	sists of a two person unit but has achieved an extension of its advisory role and much more influence in project planning. Contributions to UNIFEM and UNFPA have increased
Canada	One of six programming priorities. CIDA has in place a Gender Equity and Women in Development Policy. CIDA undertakes both integrative and women-specific actions, the mechanisms for implementation include consultations with women, support for women's organisations, partnerships and policy dialogue with other governments, multilateral institutions and capacity development and institutional strengthening	There has been no structured government action relating specifically to the commitments of the Beijing Platform of Action. Government response is to be found in its individual initiatives in a number of policy areas. Canadian women's NGOs are monitoring government action across a broad spectrum of policy areas	In 1996 CIDA's Performance Review Division undertook a performance review of the WID and gender equity (GE) policy and priority. Final conclusions have yet to be published but the conclusions of one study are not very positive, saying that there has been 'little observable improvement from 1992 to 1995 in the WID/GE knowledge, attitudes, systems and practices of the Agency'. CIDA staff gave the Agency a considerably higher rating for developing women specific projects rather than integrative ones	Despite a strong training programme since mid-1980s in WID and gender, a recent study found that 'large percentages of staff say they do not have the skills that they need to integrate WID and gender into programmes and projects. ... These findings indicate that there is a WID/GE skills crisis in CIDA. This crisis stems from the failure of the WID/ GE training programme in the 1990s'. By 1995, 35% of staff lacked gender training compared with 25% in 1992; those who took training did so more than five years ago

Approaches to gender

Country	Status of gender policy and way that it is incorporated into aid strategies	Steps taken to meet commitments made at Beijing	Progress towards the DAC goal of gender equality as an overall strategic objective	Expertise and resources for gender
Denmark	Danida's WID policy was first formulated in 1987 and revised in 1993. The overall aim of Danish development policy is gender specific poverty reduction – meaning that any work for poverty reduction has to be based on the different roles and needs of men and women	The Ministry of Foreign Affairs has published recommendations for follow-up on the programme of action. This includes a detailed breakdown of follow-up against individual recommendations in the Programme for Action	The Ministry of Foreign Affairs reports that efforts will be made to implement the DAC Gender Action Plan and Denmark will continue its active participation in the DAC expert group on WID	Danida has a special department for International Gender Equality and WID consisting of a head of department and one gender adviser. The Ministry of Foreign Affairs also has one WID adviser in the Technical Advisory Services. Four Danish embassies have a WID adviser
Finland	Gender is emphasised as an integral part of development cooperation policy and has long been a part of Finnish ODA perspectives. The present profile stresses promotion of the status of women and young girls in various contexts	There is a commitment to implement the Beijing programme 'in all contexts'. In February 1997 a national action plan was drawn up in line with the Beijing commitments by the Ministry of Social Affairs and Health, which includes a chapter on development	Gender is taken up as a strategic objective in development cooperation, but the current government policy profile only refers to the position of women in relation to other strategic priorities. There has been no recent evaluation of how gender issues are taken up and implemented	The trend is to incorporate gender in all aspects of development work rather than in isolation. The DDC has in the past had a coordinator working specifically on women in development. The present post deals with gender and cultural issues, as gender matters are meant to be taken up by all key sections of the DDC
France	France is still working on how to incorporate gender into aid strategy. There is no mainstreaming of attention to gender and a lack of high level commitment	No commitments at this stage	The DAC recommendations have had little impact on aid policy apart from a few isolated projects aimed at women	Minimal resources have been channelled into WID or gender issues. There is one full-time post for WID in the Ministry for Cooperation and some field based WID staff. There is little attention to gender in planning or evaluation
Germany	Gender is one of the five cross sectoral issues in German Aid. The promotion of women is given high priority in the existing	The lead ministry on Beijing was not BMZ but the Ministry for Families and Elderly People, Women and Adoles-	While a legal framework for gender equality has been laid down in many areas, the implemen-	$40m allocated over the next five years for social and legal counselling of women in developing countries – a reallocation of funds rather than a new

Approaches to gender

	policies on poverty eradication and in many declarations and has been an issue since 1988. The gender aspect and necessity of gender specific analyses in planning and design is stressed. There is also a shift in emphasis from WID to gender aware development	cents. Implementation is disappointing, with follow-up reintegrated to the Ministry for Families. A number of commitments were made, including a national follow-up conference and a (yet to take place) public awareness campaign on issues such as participation, equality and partnership	tation, or putting fine words into practice, is a problem	budget line. A list of gender projects has been presented, with one pilot project geared to Southern NGOs. A council of gender experts is to be set up for this pilot programme under the leadership of GTZ. A gender expert employed by the BMZ will manage the programme
Ireland	Irish aid encourages mainstreaming of gender. WID specific projects are supported in Ethiopia, Tanzania and South Africa. A gender guidelines document was adopted by the Department of Foreign Affairs in 1996 and some progress has been made in implementing these	In December 1996 the Department of Equality and Law reform launched the government's National Plan on Implementation of the Beijing Platform for Action. New and additional resources are required to ensure that aspirations are matched by effective implementation	The 1996 White Paper on Foreign Policy states that gender has become a significant focus of the Irish Aid Programme, both bilateral and multilateral. Beijing was a catalyst for this focus and also the Irish presidency of the EU initiated a discussion on the impact of conflicts on gender	Three of the six priority countries have a local gender expert as advisers to the programme. The Evaluation and Audit Unit has three sectoral experts – Health, Education and Economics. Country planning exercises in Uganda and Tanzania involved a gender expert in each three-year plan
Italy	Has introduced administrative measures to empower women: gender analysis and gender planning in project cycle. Human development programmes have taken initiatives on the role of displaced women in the context of emergencies and economic recovery in conflict areas	The government prepared for the conference on the basis of an interministerial activity, which produced technical and political inputs for the Special Government Office for Equal Opportunities	Has a poor record in implementing this overall strategic objective because of paralysis in the administrative machine	

Approaches to gender

Country	Status of gender policy and way that it is incorporated into aid strategies	Steps taken to meet commitments made at Beijing	Progress towards the DAC goal of gender equality as an overall strategic objective	Expertise and resources for gender
Japan	The government WID (GAD is not used) policy focuses on three priority areas – education: closing gender gaps in education by 2005; health: reducing maternal mortality to 200 per 100,000 by 2010 and infant mortality to 35 per 1000 by 2015; economic and social participation. Despite an increase in WID projects it is difficult to say how well gender is incorporated into the aid strategy	Government announced its 'WID Initiative' at Beijing and stated 'full consideration will be given to the active participation of women in development and to securing of benefits for women from development'	There is no mention on how Japan is meeting these objectives, although the government cites all the discussions at DAC	A WID steering committee was set up in 1989 and both JICA and OECF have WID divisions
Netherlands	Until recently gender formed a separate part of aid administration. Now it is part of social development with a policy to integrate into other categories. A strategy memorandum is to be published soon, its main points being to safeguard reproductive rights, increase political participation and combat violence against women. Policy for peace and stability has many initiatives involving women in peace and gender-oriented activities	The Platform of Action is being used to develop the priorities of reproductive rights, political participation and violence against women	Gender equality has been adopted as a strategic objective. This will be reviewed alongside a target for 1998 which says that 50% of expenditure in the bilateral programme should be spent in sectors that benefit the position of women	The budget for Women in Developing Countries Programme is 44 million guilders. UNIFEM will receive 6.6 million guilders in 1997. In the Dutch embassies, where one-third of the ODA budget will be spent, gender specialists are employed
New Zealand	Annual review of WID Action Plan shows increasing integration of WID into NZODA. A key strategy is 'Activities that enhance the role and position of women and	The Minister's Advisory Committee on External Aid and Development conducted a review set within the context of the outcomes of	A key strategy of NZODA is to undertake activities that enhance the role and position of women and increase their equitable	The aim is to have 50% of the NZODA programme WID integrated by 1997. There is also support for NGOs on a 3:1 funding basis up to a maximum of NZ$ 50,000

Approaches to gender

	increase their equitable participation in and benefits from development efforts'. At the last review it showed that 30% of the programme components able to be measured were WID integrated and a further 33% classified as partly WID integrated	the three recent UN conferences and steps are being taken to meet the recommendations from the review	participation and benefit from development efforts. This falls short of the DAC recommendation that addresses equality
Norway	The MFA has recently approved a strategy for gender equality with emphasis on integrating gender perspectives wherever possible in all bilateral and multilateral aid	A follow up programme has been elaborated	Gender impact is being systematically stressed in dealings with international and other NGOs seeking financial support. In education policies, focus is now on girls and women. Practical effects of these efforts are still difficult to assess	According to NORAD, NK 1418m within the total aid programmes were contributing to the promotion of women, or 16.7% of the budget. 763m were defined as 'women related', 452m as 'women directed' and 202m as 'women specific'. The bilateral part was 967m and multilateral part 451m. NORAD has two women advisors and a gender course is obligatory for all staff
Spain	No defined strategy exists for the introduction of the gender perspective in cooperation projects. Objectives are set each year and gender is one of the objectives but with no specific policy for its application, thus there is no means of measuring achievement	No specific measure has been taken up to meet these commitments	No specific measures have been taken to follow these recommendations, though there is a desire to introduce gender as a cross-sectoral policy. The DAC principles are the basis of a policy but this is a long-term aim and the necessary structure has yet to be created to implement any specific policy	No specific gender skilled personnel but there is one person within AECI who is in charge of pushing for the introduction of a gender policy. Some specifically women targeted projects have been carried out, which in 1995 amounted to approximately 0.9% of bilateral ODA

Approaches to gender

Country	Status of gender policy and way that it is incorporated into aid strategies	Steps taken to meet commitments made at Beijing	Progress towards the DAC goal of gender equality as an overall strategic objective	Expertise and resources for gender
Sweden	In May 1996 a new goal for Swedish aid was established: 'the promotion of equality between women and men in partner countries'. The main approach is to mainstream gender alongside specific inputs to promote gender equality. Gender issues are increasingly taken up in policy dialogue	Sida's development cooperation covers the 12 critical areas outlined in the Platform for Action, the three highlighted ones being human rights, political and economic decision-making and economic independence. A special initiative is being developed in four countries to link with Sweden to promote mutual follow-up	Gender equality is a specific goal of Swedish ODA. It is seen both as a matter of human rights and a precondition for equitable and sustainable development. Sweden plays an active part in promoting gender equality through international fora including the DAC	A Gender Equality Experience and Result Analysis Exercise was carried out in 1996 with all key departments in Sida. Some 57% of all Sida staff are women. Sida has a very competent central gender equality unit as part of its policy department, and gender experts in all its different departments
Switzerland	Gender questions seem to be well-established and well-defended in Swiss positions presented at international conferences. Since 1993 SDC has been practising a balanced men-women development policy based on three principles of making sure that projects/programmes (a) do not have a negative effect on women and children in developing countries; (b) benefit women at least as much as men; and (c) provide more support and resources to women who are responsible for family and children. The approach is interdisciplinary at institutional and operational level	An interdepartmental group has been set up to identify the measures to be undertaken under the direction of the Office for Equality between men and women. A Cabinet of Ministers report on women in relation to the Swiss framework of foreign policy was issued in November 1996	Switzerland clearly recognises gender questions as a matter of priority in the context of its development cooperation programme	A special unit of two women employees has been formed within SDC and recently strengthened. It is supported by a 12-member cross-sectoral internal advisory working group. In practical terms, policies containing a gender dimension have progressively been introduced in the field. Several programmes now have a national gender advisor (Indonesia, Mali, Niger, Pakistan, Nepal, Mozambique, Madagascar); gender strategies are being prepared in Asia and Latin America. Gender awareness training is a priority for all SDC staff, including management. SDC is compiling sex-disaggregated statistics

The Reality of Aid 1997/8

Approaches to gender

UK	Strong commitment from minister and senior civil servants in ODA. Building human capacity through improved education and health, particularly for women, is one of ODA's four departmental aims. Social Development Department has produced guidelines on preparing monitoring and evaluating projects for their impact on women. A PIM exists for looking at this, though ODA states that its policy does not focus on women's needs in isolation, but seeks greater gender equity through also working with men	Department of Education and Employment took lead but ODA played central role, particularly in consulting NGOs. It has produced a briefing 'One year on from Beijing' outlining achievements since the conference. This includes rolling out the Platform for Action to other parts of ODA, pushing the EU Development Council to accept a resolution on gender issues in EU programming as well as specific bilateral programmes amounting to £2.4m	Have been working through DAC/OECD expert group on Women in Development on coordinating and strengthening the commitment to gender activities among member states	Social Development Department is seen as the 'guardian' of gender policy and implementation. It acknowledges this and is employing a number of mechanisms, including working with NGOs, to mainstream gender throughout ODA
USA	Foreign aid programme recognises the importance of investing in women to achieve sustainable development. In 1973 Congress passed the 'Percy Amendment', which directed foreign aid efforts to focus on integrating women into the economies of developing nations. In a review of it in 1993, it was concluded that progress had been slow. As a result, a new Gender Plan of Action was announced in 1996 'to ensure the integration of gender considerations in [USAID] programmes' and to 'foster the institutional changes needed to support women in development'	Clinton administration established an 'InterAgency Council' to coordinate implementation of the Platform of Action and announced eight commitments at Beijing. These were followed through with many federal agencies carrying out additional activities. The Council's activities are to be extended beyond the year 2000 and it will promote and monitor implementation of the Platform in domestic and international policy and programmes	USAID has not made gender equality a major strategic objective of its aid, but it has undertaken a number of initiatives in the area of promoting women in development	A senior WID policy adviser has been appointed in USAID's Bureau of Policy Planning Coordination to reinforce the integration of gender issues into USAID policies across sectors. There is a WID fellows programme, career incentives and other initiatives aimed at building WID expertise in USAID. Much of the expertise is currently in the WID Office, which seeks to ensure that gender is considered a variable in project design, implementation and evaluation

Source: NGO Reality of Aid questionnaires.

Humanitarian relief

Humanitarian relief, conflict and emergencies

During the early 1990s the volume and proportion of ODA allocated to humanitarian assistance increased dramatically alongside the number of humanitarian emergencies. Bilateral emergency aid from all DAC members combined totalled 7.5% of bilateral ODA in 1995, compared with 8.4% in 1994. Complex emergencies have demanded complex responses from donor countries, often leading to new relationships and a more pressing need for coherence between foreign, defence and development policy. Old distinctions between relief, development and rehabilitation do not hold up in the field and here *Reality of Aid* documents the extent to which systems and funding are adapting to recognise that. One of the sharpest examples of the need for coherence between defence, foreign and development policy is over the issue of landmines – produced, exported and used by the same countries which at the same time fund demining operations through their aid programmes. In this chart the progress that has been made towards signing a universal treaty banning anti-personnel landmines by December 1997 is documented.

Table 37 Humanitarian relief, conflict and emergencies

Country and % bilateral ODA to emergencies in 1995	Announced ban on anti-personnel landmine exports	Signed June 1997 Brussels statement on banning anti-personnel landmines by December 1997	Recent trends in government approaches to long-term conflict and rehabilitation	Approach to coherence between aid, foreign policy and export policy in areas prone to conflict
Australia 3.88%	Yes	No	No real change in government's approach to long-term conflict in developing countries and no special rehabilitation programme as such. All funds managed by the Humanitarian Relief (HUR) section of AusAID. The basis for decision on the allocations of emergency aid is set out in a statement of guiding principles which were agreed and adopted in 1994. Each year, notional allocations for NGOs are set for each region/country and negotiated with NGOs, which may then make submissions for funds. Allocations are often made through the World Food Programme as the government feels it has more influence within multilateral organisations and a greater degree of accountability	Interdepartmental committees meet to ensure proper coordination and policy coherence, but some problems are apparent. For example, the government attempted to provide mediation assistance between the Papua New Guinea government and the Bougainville Revolutionary Army. Assistance is also ready for a Restoration Programme to address priority health, education and infrastructure needs. At the same time Australia's Defence Cooperation Programme provides training and other help to the PNGDF. Recent developments in PNG have brought adverse publicity to Australia's role and the conflict between military and aid arrangements

The **Reality** of Aid 1997/8

Humanitarian relief

Austria 20.54%	Yes	Yes	
Belgium 3.1%	Yes	Yes	Secretary of State has raised conflict prevention to one of the three major objectives for development cooperation and the 1997 budget contains two new lines for this purpose. Conflict prevention is seen as strengthening the societal base and implies field diplomacy, and restoring confidence in civil society and, in areas where peace has been restored, quick support to rehabilitation efforts including disarmament and mine clearance, education and employment, rehabilitation of the administration and judiciary and prosecution of war criminals. In stable societies, conflict prevention is interpreted as respect for human rights and democratisation	The goal of conflict prevention is frustrated by activities of other ministries including the availability of export credit guarantees for arms exports and the construction of an arms plant in Kenya. The transfer of authority for banning arms exports to the level of the Flemish and Francophone communities has been particularly harmful to coherence. Furthermore, the Ministry of Foreign Affairs considers diplomacy to be its exclusive competence. Coherence and coordination have been easier to achieve within an EU framework
Canada 11.91%	Yes	Yes	Proactive in approach. Initiated and signed treaty for worldwide ban of anti-personnel mines, to be concluded in December 1997. In October 1996 a special Canadian Peacebuilding Initiative was created with an allocation of $10m to be administered by CIDA under the International Humanitarian Assistance window. Substantial resources have been directed towards peacekeeping and peacebuilding activities in relation to Rwanda/Zaire, Haiti and Guatemala. Department of National Defence has created Disaster Assistance Response Team with 180 personnel ready to be deployed quickly to provide medical care, potable water, engineering services and effective, reliable communication. Reservations have been expressed on this unit's likely lack of sensitivity to local culture and and minimal capacity for continuity associated with short-term missions. Basic Human Needs and Women in Development and Gender Equity Policies are intended to give policy direction to the allocation of funds by IHA	Department of Foreign Affairs and International Trade take the lead in developing policy with respect to areas of conflict, but it does so in close collaboration with the Department of National Defence, CIDA and other appropriate ministries. There is also both formal and informal consultation with NGOs active in the area of concern. Existing policy on the export of military equipment preventing export to parties engaged in civil or interstate conflict has been called upon to be strengthened. It has been proposed that all military commodity transfers be subject to an 'impact assessment review'

287

Humanitarian relief

Country and % bilateral ODA to emergencies in 1995	Announced ban on anti-personnel landmine exports	Signed June 1997 Brussels statement agreeing to negotiate and sign agreement banning anti-personnel landmines by December 1997	Recent trends in government approaches to long-term conflict and rehabilitation	Approach to coherence between aid, foreign policy and export policy in areas prone to conflict
Denmark 7.93%	Yes	Yes		
Finland 10.45%	No	No	Specific changes in practical approaches to long-term conflict are hard to detect. On the other hand, the government has increasingly emphasised the need to focus on preventive measures, rehabilitation and long-term solutions in the context of humanitarian assistance, as well as in its overall foreign policy outlook. An evaluation of Finland's humanitarian assistance, published in 1996, proposed a more proactive rather than reactive approach. Countries facing post-conflict rehabilitation are included in the government's categories of development cooperation partners. Finland is also contributing ODA to rehabilitation in several countries, including Bosnia. Again, there are as yet no precise and coordinated approaches to rehabilitation	The government stresses using humanitarian aid to respond to crises 'with due consideration to our foreign policy objectives'. The evaluation published in 1996 recommends the drawing up of a statement of purpose to give better definition to the relationship between humanitarian relief and other areas of foreign policy. This has yet to be made
France 2.15%	Yes	Yes		
Germany 9.12%	Yes	Yes	The government – especially the BMZ and Foreign Ministry – emphasise increasingly the importance of conflict prevention and humanitarian aid. Substantial funds are made available. In 1996, NGOs welcomed the introduction of a new budget title for the BMZ which integrates emergency, food and refugee aid. It is hoped that this will lead to a	The political framework conditions introduced by the BMZ in 1991, take recipients' military expenditure into consideration, among other things. However, they are not consistently implemented in the aid programme, let alone in other areas of foreign policy like arms exports and trade. The DAC review of German aid

The Reality of Aid 1997/8

Humanitarian relief

			more consistent approach in linking short-term and long-term aid	supports NGO concerns in this regard: 'However, these framework conditions do not seem to be applied with equal force in the policy dialogue with recipients when it comes to the respect for human rights and development-oriented government actions. Nor are they directly applicable to trade and foreign policy relations'
Ireland 9.09%	Yes	Yes	The 1996 White Paper on Foreign Policy states that the government will place renewed emphasis on prevention of violent conflict and improved national response to humanitarian crises. There has been a substantial increase to the Emergency Humanitarian Assistance Fund. In 1994 the Human Rights and Democratisation budget line was established. In early 1996 the government introduced a unilateral ban on anti-personnel mines. A basic commitment to the resolution on linking relief, rehabilitation and development. Since 1995 the government has had a specific budget line for rehabilitation. In 1997 allocations under this line are estimated at IR£ 4m. The growing importance of this line saw the appointment of a rehabilitation adviser to the Evaluations and Audit Unit	During Ireland's presidency of the EU, the Development Council adopted a resolution on anti-personnel landmines to improve coordination of landmine programmes such as mine clearance, victim rehabilitation and mine awareness activities. A Joint Action by the European Council put in place a common moratorium on the export of all anti personnel mines
Italy 10.92%	Yes	Yes		
Japan 0.58%	Yes	No	It is hard to say what Japan's policy on conflict is. Aid is provided for rehabilitation in Cambodia, Bosnia and the Middle East. In 1996 the government set up a new programme for support of rehabilitation and development. There are no figures as yet	Japan bans all arms exports to all countries (its violation is subject to criminal punishment). Also the ODA Charter adopted in 1992 states that Japan will give full attention to trends in recipients' military expenditures and production of weapons of mass destruction
Luxembourg 16.28%	Yes	Yes		

289

Humanitarian relief

Country and % bilateral ODA to emergencies in 1995	Announced ban on anti-personnel landmine exports	Signed June 1997 Brussels statement agreeing to ban anti-personnel landmines by December 1997	Recent trends in government approaches to long-term conflict and rehabilitation	Approach to coherence between aid, foreign policy and export policy in areas prone to conflict
Netherlands 15.59%	Yes	Yes	A new department has been established to promote efficiency and democratisation and to end human rights violations. Much effort has been made to prevent conflicts by integrating foreign and development policies. There are two budget categories: one is human rights, conflict management, democratisation and good governance, the other is humanitarian aid. The policy for peace and stability has three major pillars: (1) conflict prevention (2) crisis management (3) rehabilitation. There is, however, no special funding window for rehabilitation. The major part of humanitarian aid is channelled through agencies like the Red Cross and UNHCR	Peace and stability are major issues in Dutch aid policy. Coherence between foreign policies, economic, defence and aid policies are considered as a prerequisite to intervene in conflict situations. In the Council of Ministers a special meeting between the Ministers of Foreign Affairs, Defence and Development Cooperation is held to streamline the Dutch policy with regard to peace and stability. This meeting is called the REIA (Council for European and International Affairs)
New Zealand 2.06%	Yes	Yes	Bilateral programmes do not operate in countries, other than Bougainville in which conflict is an issue. NZODA has a fund for responding to emergencies and it is principally kept for cyclones in the Pacific, though grants are made in response to other emergencies throughout the year. When the cyclone season is over funds are made available for rehabilitation programmes through NGOs and UN agencies. No new processes have been established and relief and rehabilitation is only really considered in the context of activities funded through other agencies as New Zealand has little direct involvement	Not really an issue
Norway 20.29%	Yes	Yes	It is a high priority field but there are no new policies. Strong emphasis is put on efforts to give emergency aid a lasting rehabilitation and development impact	Humanitarian relief is closely integrated in foreign policy. Norway has practically no arms exports to areas prone to conflict (Turkey has until recently been an exception)

Humanitarian relief

Portugal 2.23%	Yes	Yes	
Spain 2.45%	No	Yes	No change in government policy. Spain does not take the lead in response to conflicts but will join a position adopted by other countries, mainly in the EU. No new rehabilitation funds exist	In relation to the influence of foreign policy and export policy, in general terms there has been no progress. As regards arms exports, progress has been made in early 1997 concerning anti-personnel mines. Parliament passed a total ban on production, export, use or warehousing of such. Shortly after, Parliament passed another ruling in favour of greater transparency in the trading of arms
Sweden 22.71%	Yes	Yes	In the budget reduction for 1997 allocations for humanitarian relief were cut. In its documents the government underlines the need for both conflict prevention and rehabilitation rather than merely concentrating on disaster relief	The government is promoting coherence in EU policies and recognises incoherence in Swedish policies, but does not like to mention the role of Swedish arms exports. Sweden in the twelfth largest arms exporter in the world and although strict rules have been adopted by Parliament, exceptions apparently occur. Sweden has been accused of helping Indonesian occupation of East Timor through arms sales
Switzerland 12.45%	Yes	Yes	In parallel with the debate at the OECD task force on conflict resolution, a discussion group has been set up within the Department of Foreign Affairs whose task it is to oversee the prevention of conflicts and coordinate aid instruments (coordination between emergency aid and long-term cooperation). When Switzerland wishes to intervene in a conflict, this group is in charge of establishing a consistent approach at the outset between all parties involved. The government has not taken any concrete measure or established any new funding windows to respond to the needs for rehabilitation	The problem of coherence continues, despite the debates on the discussion group. The debates on the revision of law on arms export in particular have focused attention onto coherence in Swiss policy. NGOs report that Pilatus aircraft were exported to Burma where they are used against refugee camps partly funded by Swiss Development Cooperation. The export risk guarantee to the Three Gorges Project in China highlights the unresolved issue of coherence

The **Reality** of Aid 1997/8

Humanitarian relief

Country and % bilateral ODA to emergencies in 1995	Announced ban on anti-personnel landmine exports	Signed June 1997 Brussels statement agreeing to ban anti-personnel landmines by December 1997	Recent trends in government approaches to long-term conflict and rehabilitation	Approach to coherence between aid, foreign policy and export policy in areas prone to conflict
United Kingdom 10.9%	Yes	Yes	There are changes in government approach to focus increasingly on defusing conflict, tackling the underlying causes and reconciliation. A new Conflict Policy Unit has been established with a seed corn budget and guidance for agencies seeking to support conflict reduction activities. While there have been attempts to create new windows for rehabilitation funding via the EU, the situation in the UK is ambiguous. The new DFID guidelines provide a useful framework to encourage better humanitarian projects and better coordination in emergency situations. A key area for change is enhancing DFID's responsiveness to requests for support in the area of rehabilitation	DFID does not take the lead on overall response to conflict – this is the responsibility of the Foreign Office. DFID does, however, lead on the humanitarian response to conflict. The UK signed the Brussels Statement (see left hand column) on landmines – an improvement on its previous position. The incoming Foreign Secretary announced in May 1997 that British foreign policy would include greater emphasis on human rights and, as one of the four largest arms exporters in the World, Britain had particular responsibility to ensure that the arms trade was properly regulated and arms sales criteria tightened
USA 14.05%	Yes	No	There has been heightened attention to the issue of civil conflict in developing countries in the policy statement of US officials. USAID has also established an 'Office of Transition Initiatives'; to develop and offer programmes of rapid recovery from civil conflicts (involving demining, demobilisation, the establishment of political institutions). This programme has expanded in recent years. There are no specific programmes to engage women in rehabilitation although their role is not ignored	President designated USAID administrator to take lead in disaster relief. Where civil conflict involves broader political issues (as it usually does), the National Security Council often decides the US response and involves Department of Defense, Department of State and USAID. USAID rarely comments on or is knowledgeable about arms exports. It lies outside its formal responsibilities. It has, however, taken a position against the export of landmines generally within the administration and has had some influence on thinking there

Source: NGO Questionnaires, DAC Report 1996, Table 14, Mines Action Canada. The position of other OECD members and permanent members of the security council is as follows: Countries that have not announced a ban on anti-personnel landmine exports or signed June 1997 Brussels statement affirming the objective to negotiate and sign an agreement banning anti-personnel landmines by December 1997: China, Greece, Hungary, Republic of Korea, Poland, Russia, Turkey. Countries that have announced a ban on anti-personnel landmine exports but not signed the Brussels statement: Iceland. Countries that have signed the Brussels statement but not announced a ban: Czech Republic. Countries that have announced a ban on antipersonnel landmine exports or signed June 1997 Brussels statement affirming the objective to negotiate and sign an agreement banning anti-personnel landmines by December 1997: Mexico.

Trends in ODA through NGOs

Table 38 Trends in ODA through NGOs (US$m)

Country	Most recent year figures available	Total ODA spent through NGOs	Bilateral ODA spent through NGOs	ODA grants to NGOs for their own work	NGO income from voluntary sources	Trends in NGO–government relations
Australia	1995	85.9	76.3	9.6	129.8	Following an NGO effectiveness review by AusAID in 1994/5, an NGO reform package was introduced which included more rigorous accreditation processes for all Australian NGOs applying for AusAID funding. NGOs are concerned that the government is attempting to reduce the number and type of NGOs able to participate actively in the development cooperation programme. Some NGO funding windows have also been closed and small grants schemes for NGOs reduced, but the NGO matching grant scheme has been increased by 17% in real terms
Austria	1995				46.5	NGOs have historically had a major role in delivering Austrian aid because of the principle of subsidiarity, which requires the government to deliver its programme via the smallest possible unit. Now the government is developing its own programmes, often with the support of NGOs, but there is concern about direct links with Southern NGOs which call the role of Northern NGOs into question, particularly because the quality of their work is not publicly discussed or seen. Most NGOs do not get any public funding and, even in the recession year of 1996 managed to increase their voluntary funding. There is also frustration with relationships with the EU, and its failure to take account of the unique nature of Austrian NGOs
Belgium	1995/6	76.1	76.1	n/a	102.5	NGO share of ABOS budget has increased since 1994, in line with the declining spending capacity of ABOS itself. A further increase to 17% of budget is expected in 1997 but is not expected to rise after that. The Secretary of State has presented a co-financing reform, which will be operational from 1998. It aims to shift thousands of single NGO projects towards more consistent five-year programmes and offers incentives for professionalism, scaling up, cooperation between NGOs and evaluation

Trends in ODA through NGOs

Country	Year	Total ODA through NGOs	Bilateral ODA through NGOs	ODA grants to NGOs	NGO voluntary income	Trends in NGO–government relations
Canada	1995/6	191.1	70.2	120.9	287.2	The most important development in government/voluntary sector relationship over past year was November 1996 ministerial approval of an agency-wide policy framework on role of voluntary sector in international development cooperation. NGOs had hoped for more emphasis on role rather than the relationship. A respect for diverse roles of the sector, accountability, participation, dialogue and simplification were the set of principles stated. It has an important section on the role of NGOs in strengthening and amplifying the voice of civil society. Implementation is vague, though CIDA does commit itself to reporting on actions and strategies. Cuts of 7.2% in 1997/8 were allocated across the board for each NGO apart from one. A further 8% cut is expected for 1998/9
Denmark	1996	142.5	n/a	n/a	n/a	No new trends
Finland	1996	27.2	n/a	n/a	16.1	The situation has improved following the reverse in ODA cuts and the state's recommitment to the 0.7% limit
France	1994	46.7	n/a	n/a	345.5	
Germany	1996		456.61*			The BMZ has tried to keep its promise of annual increases of 10% in the co-financing budget for non-denominational NGOs and it is expected that, despite general cuts, this will be maintained in 1998. The possible transfer of administration/management to the GTZ, the executing agency for German aid, is under discussion and, from an NGO perspective, would entail a number of problems, as in some respects NGOs and GTZ can be seen as competitors
Ireland	1996		20.85		24.9	The revision of the NGO co-financing scheme resulted in an increase in aid to Irish NGOs, particularly larger ones in a block grant scheme. The government is committed to maintain current level of 12% of ODA support to NGOs. Key issues are economy and efficiency in carrying out projects, with particular emphasis on effectiveness in addressing poverty in a sustainable manner
Japan	1995			6.6	100.442**	Opportunities of dialogue between NGOs and the Ministry of Foreign Affairs is increasing. Meetings held four times a year. Government has also started to contract NGOs for implementation of bilateral aid projects and evaluation
Netherlands	1995	331.5			254.2	57 million guilders of emergency aid will be channelled through both national and international NGOs. As agreed in 1996 the four co-financing organisations

The Reality of Aid

Trends in ODA through NGOs

New Zealand	1996	7.8	5.2	2.6	25.5	(Bilance, Icco, Novib and Hivos) will be allocated 9.5% of funds for genuine aid in 1997, an increase of almost 40m guilders
						Funding for NGOs has risen markedly in real terms since 1990/1 and increased by 14% between 1995/6 and 1996/7. Proportion of NZODA devoted to NGO programmes has doubled since 1990. The number of NGO programmes has grown and NGOs are currently discussing new involvement in part of the bilateral programme. A new block grant system was introduced in 1994/5
Norway	1996	306	306			A major part of the funds channelled via NGOs consists of emergency spending contracted out to Norwegian NGOs. There is no indication that the role of NGOs in Norwegian development aid will diminish. NORAD has sharpened its preconditions concerning the organisations' administrative, managerial and professional competence. It has also increased its claims for economic and budgetary control
Portugal	1995		3.48			Bill to be passed in second half of 1997 to enable the government to channel funds to NGOs under a co-financing programme. Legislation is being developed to change the law governing NGO statues and volunteers working in developing countries
Spain	1995	86.2	5.4	80.8	137.1	Difficulties exist with the NGO National Platform such as a lack of flexibility and excessive bureaucracy. There is a need for evolution towards global grants and to leave the present system of individual project by project grants. ODA is also allocated to NGOs from regional governments and councils – over US$ 110m in 1996
Sweden	1994/5	329		214.8	114.5	In reduced budget for 1997 the government explicitly stated that the NGO support should not decrease but maintain its previous level. After a main evaluation on NGO support and a few sectoral studies, Sida is preparing for reorientation of the rules for relations with NGOs
Switzerland	1995	137.4	87.2	50.2	185	Despite budget cuts in ODA, government support and collaboration with NGOs does not seem to be affected. From 1996 to 1998 ODA spent through NGOs is predicted to increase by 3%. No new requirements on NGOs' evaluation processes have been set out, but for several years SDC has been asking NGOs to concentrate their intervention on programmes and not to finance too many small projects at any one time

The Reality of Aid 1997/8

Trends in ODA through NGOs

Country	Year	Total ODA through NGOs	Bilateral ODA through NGOs	ODA grants to NGOs	NGO voluntary income	Trends in NGO–government relations
United Kingdom	1995/6	281.7	184.8	96.9	569.2	The key trend is that the amount channelled via Joint Funding Scheme has remained level. The long-awaited NGO strategy will probably now be subsumed within the forthcoming White Paper. Much more attention is being paid to monitoring and evaluation than before. Logical frameworks are required for each project
United States	1995		715.9		4800	In 1996, 34% of development assistance funds (about 30% of ODA) were programmed through NGOs. USAID has introduced a New Partnerships Initiative (NPI) and Strategic Partnerships to involve NGOs more in implementation. NPI aims to strengthen linkages between NGOs, the private sector and organisations of governance. Strategic Partnerships is a programme in which NGOs would be responsible for implementing the USAID programme in countries where there is no USAID mission. The increasing orientation of the USAID programme on results has led to concern that evaluation will focus too much on short-term quantifiable indicators, over longer-term qualitative interventions

Source: NGO Reality of Aid questionnaires.
* These data from the BMZ budget comprise DM 296m to Church NGOs, DM 231m to political foundations, DM 32m to nondenominational NGOs, and DM 128m to NGOs supporting the building of social structures.
** 1994.

Managing development cooperation

Political responsibility and management of development cooperation

Table 39 The political responsibility for OECD aid

Country	Political responsibility	Staffing and management
Australia	The Minister for Foreign Affairs, the Hon Alexander Downer, holds direct responsibility for the aid programme, with a parliamentary secretary, Mr Andrew Thompson MP, providing advice to him. The Secretary for the Department of Foreign Affairs is Mr Phillip Flood (former head of AusAID) and the Director General of AusAID is Mr Trevor Kanaley	In 1996 AusAID employed 595 staff including 58 overseas and 94 in-state offices. The aid programme is managed by AusAID, an administratively autonomous agency within the Department of Foreign Affairs and Trade. AusAID works closely with the department and with other relevant government bodies. AusAID is headed by a director general who is also a member of the senior executive of the Department of Foreign Affairs and Trade. AusAID has three divisions each headed by a deputy director general: Asia, Africa and Community Programmes Division; Pacific and International Programmes Division; Corporate Development and Support Division
Austria	Prime responsibility lies with the Ministry of Foreign Affairs but it administers only 19% of ODA. The Ministry of Finance has responsibility for multilateral financial aid and tied aid loans	There is no institutionalised dialogue on development cooperation within government both between and within relevant ministries. Responsibility for policy coordination rests at the highest possible level, with the foreign minister
Belgium	Non-cabinet State Secretary for Development Cooperation responsible for 60–70% of ODA who reports direct to the prime minister. Ministry of Finance controls 25% of ODA. The bulk of the rest is split between Foreign Affairs, Foreign Trade and NDD, the Belgian official export credit guarantee agency. The current Secretary of State has recently argued the case for a single administration for international cooperation, implying an integration of the current departments for Foreign Affairs and Development Cooperation	As of early 1997, ABOS had around 325 aid staff and the Ministry of Finance, 11. Of these 11, seven deal with financial and economic issues. Academic staff on ABOS are largely technicians such as medical doctors and engineers. It employs virtually no economists or social development advisers. The lack of professional development staff is a significant problem

The **Reality** of Aid 1997/8

Managing development cooperation

Country	Political responsibility	Staffing and management
Canada	The Minister of Foreign Affairs and International Trade maintains overall responsibility for foreign policy including aid. He works with a Minister for International Cooperation and La Francophonie (a Cabinet post) who is responsible for the Canadian International Development Agencies. The Minister of Finance is responsible for relations with the World Bank, the IMF and debt policy	Figures set out in Cida's 1997/8 expenditure plan indicate a decline in its administration budget of 2% for 1997/8 and a further 2.8% in 1998/9. When the (non-ODA) Countries in Transition Programme is excluded, the budget will decline by 1.9% in 1997/8 and by 2.8% in 1998/9. By 1998/9 this budget will have declined by 19.3% since 1994/5. By comparison, the budget allocation for the voluntary sector will have declined by 37% over the same period. There are an estimated 1126 full-time equivalent staff in CIDA in 1997/8. This level of staffing is the same as it was in 1993/4, despite significant cuts to the budget. The staffing breakdown of technical expertise shows a significant bias towards economics, sociology and statistics (30), engineering (32) and physical sciences (15)
Denmark	Minister for Development Affairs has full ministerial status within the Danish foreign ministry and is responsible for all aid	Staffing levels have remained fairly constant from 1995 to date with just over 460 employees. However, the cost per full-time member of staff increased 10% from 1995 to 1997 with a total cost of DKK 182m in 1995 to DKK 199m in 1997. No figures exist for technical breakdown of expertise
Finland	Mr Pekka Haavisto is Minister for Environment and Development and holds the portfolio for development cooperation, even though the department responsible for this remains the Foreign Ministry. The Department for Development Cooperation of the Finnish Foreign Ministry (UM Kehitysyhteistyoosasto) is the new name for the more familiar FINNIDA. For the moment the change is in name only and has not been accompanied by restructuring	Staffing levels of those dealing with development cooperation have decreased from 104 in 1995 to 85 in 1996
France	Aid management and procedures remain complex and opaque. There has been some improvement with the appointment of a development cooperation minister within the Ministry of Foreign Affairs. Several ministries are involved in managing French aid. Apart from the Ministry of Cooperation, there is the Ministry of Economy and Finance, which handles contributions to	Of those staff within the various ministries dealing with overseas aid, the percentage breakdown is as follows: Ministry for Cooperation 11.49% Treasury 48.68% Ministry for Overseas 10.19% Foreign Affairs 7.68%

298

The **Reality** of Aid 1997/8
Managing development cooperation

	international organisations, debt funding and cancellation, concessional loans and grants for programme aid in support of structural adjustment. Others include the Ministry of Research, the Caisse française de Développement, and the Education, Defence, Agriculture and Overseas Ministries. The president retains final responsibility for foreign affairs including aid	CFD 6.68% Ministry of Research 5.74% Others 3.46%
Germany	The Minister for Economic Cooperation – a cabinet post – is responsible for aid and handles about 70% of the ODA budget. The Ministries of Foreign Affairs and of the Economy are also involved as well as the Lander. The aid management system is complex and it has been recommended (by the DAC among others) that the BMZ should be given enlarged scope in both policy-making and field activities. This has not happened	Staffing levels for the BMZ are planned at 530 for 1997
Ireland	Minister of State within the Department of Foreign Affairs is responsible for aid	Total number of staff in the Development Cooperation Division is 58 of which 43 are concerned with bilateral, 8 with multilateral (others 7). Diplomatic staff in Irish aid offices amount to 6 personnel and there are 67 Irish Aid staff working under contract on projects. This makes a total staffing of 125. There is one health adviser, one education adviser, one rehabilitation specialist and one evaluation specialist
Italy	ODA is managed by the DGCS (Directorate General for Development Cooperation) within the Ministry of Foreign Affairs. Multilateral aid is managed by the Treasury	In 1995, DGCS had a staff of 557 compared with 569 in 1994. It has multidisciplinary expertise, but lacks administrative officers and economists. This contrasts with the growing importance of administrative procedures and financial and macro-economic initiatives
Japan	ODA is managed by four ministries: Foreign Affairs, International Trade and Industry, Finance, and Economic Planning	In 1995, the number of aid administration staff was 1936 with JICA employing 1184, OECF 333 and MoFA 419

Managing development cooperation

Country	Political responsibility	Staffing and management
Netherlands	Development cooperation is integrated in the Ministry of Foreign Affairs (MFA). The Minister for Foreign Affairs, the Minister for Development Cooperation and a state secretary take political responsibility for development cooperation. Before the review of foreign policy, which was officially changed in September 1996, there was one department responsible for development cooperation. Now, most policy sections within the MFA work for both the foreign and development ministers. The extent of the emphasis on development cooperation varies with each theme and region	At the top of the restructured ministry are the ministers for Foreign Affairs and Development Cooperation and a state secretary. Immediately below them is a secretary general who is the most senior civil servant in the organisation. One step below this are four directors-general: (1) Regional Policy (2) Political Affairs (3) International Cooperation and (4) European Cooperation. These four take charge for three departments – bilateral, multilateral and policy. There are five bilateral departments – one for each region (Europe, North Africa and the Middle East, sub-Saharan Africa, Asia and Oceania and the Western Hemisphere). There are 11 policy theme departments and three multilateral departments. Also, with the bilateral programme restructured, around 100 members of staff have been deployed to various embassies. Within the embassies there are specialist staff members for women, environment and human rights
New Zealand	The Associate Minister of Foreign Affairs is responsible for NZODA, but the Minister of Foreign Affairs retains control over major policy direction and involvement in Pacific Island aspects of NZODA. This is a new division of responsibility. Aid is managed by the Development Cooperation Division of the Ministry of Foreign Affairs and Trade in conjunction with diplomatic posts overseas	There are 55 members of staff within the Development Cooperation Division. This department is responsible for distributing all of NZODA. There are two streams within this division. Diplomats are rostered into positions for up to two years whereas other staff are permanently employed in this division. There are no precise figures for technical specialists, though various specialists work in the evaluation unit – Environmental, Human Resources and Education, WID, two development economists, Small Business Development and Social Impact

The **Reality** of Aid 1997/8

Managing development cooperation

Norway	Cabinet Minister for Development Aid directly responsible for multilateral and multi-bi aid. NORAD manages bilateral aid under the supervision of the minister. However, the Minister for Foreign Affairs has increased his influence on aid matters through the growth of both bilateral and multilateral allocations to relief, human rights, peace and democracy, for which he is directly responsible. The Foreign Ministry now has three ministers – one for Foreign Affairs, one for Trade, one for Development Aid	In the Foreign Ministry there are 99 aid-related staff responsible for NOK 4641m within the 1997 aid budget. NORAD has a staff of 200 responsible for NOK 4190m for 1997
Portugal	Portuguese aid is split between different ministries and institutes, coordinated by the Ministry of Foreign Affairs, which takes political responsibility for development cooperation. Main ministries involved are Finance, Health, Culture and Territorial Planning	
Spain	The management of ODA is characterised by the duality existing between the Ministry of Economy and the Ministry of Foreign Affairs. In 1996 MFA was responsible for 28.3% of ODA, Ministry of Economy (now incorporating trade and tourism) 57.8%, regional corporations 10% and other ministries 3.9%	With regard to management of bilateral aid, between external and central services about 336 people are employed to manage an annual budet of $257m. This is for technical, scientific, cultural and NGO cooperation projects and programmes. For total bilateral aid (the previous plus cooperation undertaken by regional government, councils and the FAD) the number of people involved rises to 410 managing funds of around $715m
Sweden	Mr Pierre Schori, deputy minister of Foreign Affairs is minister for Development Cooperation and Refugees. In the Ministry there is a section on Development Cooperation and the Regional Desks. Traditionally, within the Swedish government system, Sida is quite independent of the ministry. However, the main policy decisions on Development Cooperation are taken by the Ministry	Since 1995 the five different government agencies for Development Cooperation were reorganised into the new Sida. In December 1996, Sida employed 650, 57% of whom were women
Switzerland	In 1995, Swiss Development and Cooperation was responsible for 79% of ODA, and the Federal Office for External Economic Affairs for 10.7%, other departments 9%, cantons and communes 1.6%	In 1995, SDC employed 353 people and FOEEA 28. There is no breakdown of technical expertise as such, but there is a clear tendency to reduce the number of experts working in the field and to replace them with local experts. Ten years ago around 350 experts in social and economic development were working in the field, now SDC has only around 50 in the field

Managing development cooperation

Country	Political responsibility	Staffing and management
United Kingdom	The incoming Labour administration has replaced the former Overseas Development Administration (part of the Foreign and Commonwealth Office) with a Department for International Development, headed by a Cabinet minister. The new government's pledge to pursue a coherent programme of action on debt, trade, the IFIs and human rights means a much broader remit for DFID. Precise allocation of responsibility between DFID and the new Foreign Office, the Department of Trade and Industry, the Department of the Environment and the Treasury were still being clarified at the time of writing	ODA employed 1077 permanent staff plus a large number on fixed-term contracts both overseas and in the UK. There has been a programme of decentralisation of aid management to developing countries. Of the 139 professional advisers employed by ODA, 33 were economists; 33 in health and population, social development and education combined; 26 in natural resources/environment and 15 in engineering
United States	USAID is responsible for the management of most US bilateral aid. The administrator of USAID has in the past reported both to the President and the Secretary of State. Recent changes now require the administrator to report solely to the Secretary of State, likely constraining the independence of USAID. The Senate has proposed that budget authority for USAID be transferred to the Department of State, a move that would severely reduce the ability of USAID to plan and manage its programme. The Department of State does not at this time have any significant development expertise of its own	USAID has 7687 personnel. Of these, 2485 are employed by USAID, 1696 based in the USA and 789 in the field. It also has 2016 consultants or project staff ('non-direct hire') in Washington and 3186 in the field

Glossary

20:20	A compact which states that 20% of ODA and 20% of central government expenditure in developing countries should be devoted to basic social services: health, family planning, education, nutrition, water and sanitation	DAC	Development Assistance Committee of the OECD – a group of 20 donor countries plus the EU which monitors aid flows and consults on ways of improving the quality and effectiveness of aid
ABOS	Algemeen Bestuur voor Ontwikkelingssamenwerking (Belgian Ministry for Development Cooperation)	Danida	Danish International Development Assistance, Ministry of Foreign Affairs
ACP	The African, Caribbean and Pacific states, currently 70 in number, parties to the Lomé Convention of the EU	DCD	Development Cooperation Division of the DAC
		EBRD	European Bank for Reconstruction and Development
ADB/AsDB	Asian Development Bank	EC	European Commission
ADP	African Development Programme	ECHO	European Community Humanitarian Office
AECI	Spanish Agency for International Cooperation	ECU	European Currency Unit
AfDB	African Development Bank	EDF	European Fund for Development, the main financing mechanism for EU aid under the Lomé Convention
AFRODAD	African Forum and Network on Debt and Development		
AIDS	acquired immune deficiency syndrome	EIB	European Investment Bank
		EMU	economic and monetary union
ALA	Asia and Latin America	ERG	export risk guarantee
ASEAN	Association of South East Asian Nations	ESAF	Enhanced Structural Adjustment Facility
AusAID	Australian Agency for International Development	EU	European Union
		FAO	Food and Agriculture Organisation (of the UN)
BHN	basic human need	FDI	foreign direct investment
BMZ	Ministry for Economic Cooperation and Development (Germany)	FINNIDA	Finnish Ministry of Foreign Affairs
		FMIS	new statistical information reporting system in New Zealand
BOP	balance of payments		
BOU	Bank of Uganda	FY	financial year
CACM	Central American Common Market	G7	The group of seven main industrial countries
CAP	Common Agricultural Policy (of the EU)	G-24	Group of 24 developed nations meeting to coordinate assistance to Central and Eastern Europe
CBO	community based organisation		
CEC	Commission of the European Community	GATT	General Agreement on Tariffs and Trade
CEE	Central and Eastern Europe		
CEEC	Central and Eastern European countries	GDP	Gross Domestic Product – the total value of a country's output per year
CFA	African financial community franc	GEF	Global Environment Facility
CFSP	Common Foreign and Security Policy	GNI	Gross National Income
		GNP	Gross National Product – GDP plus income from economic activity overseas
CGGP	Commonwealth Good Governance Programme		
CIDA	Canadian International Development Agency	GSP	Generalised System of Preferences
CPLP	Portuguese-Speaking Countries Community	HIPC	Highly Indebted Poor Country debt initiative

Glossary

HIV	human immunodeficiency virus	OECF	Overseas Economic Cooperation Fund (Japan)
HPI	human poverty index		
HSD	Human and Social Development	PHARE	Poland/Hungary Assistance for the Reconstruction of the Economy (now extended to whole of Eastern Europe)
IADB	Inter-American Development Bank		
IDA	International Development Assistance – the part of the World Bank that offers loans at very concessional rates to poor countries		
		real terms	A figure adjusted to take account of exchange rates and inflation, allowing a 'real' comparison over time
IFAD	International Fund for Agriculture and Development		
		SADC	Southern African Development Coordination
IFC	International Finance Corporation		
IFI	international financial institution	SAP	Structural Adjustment Programme
ILO	International Labour Organisation (part of the UN)	SDC	Swiss Agency for Development and Cooperation
IMF	International Monetary Fund	Sida	Swedish official aid agency
JICA	Japan International Cooperation Agency	SILIC	severely indebted low income country
LIC	Low-Income Country	SME	small- and medium-sized enterprise
LLDC	Least Developed Country – UN list of 47 poor and vulnerable countries	SPA	Special Programme for Africa
		SSA	sub-Saharan Africa
LMIC	Lower Middle Income Country. Between $676 and $2695 per capita income	TNC	transnational corporation
		UN	United Nations
		UNDP	United Nations Development Programme
MAI	Multilateral Agreement on Investment	UNESCO	United Nations Educational, Scientific, and Cultural Organisation
Med	Mediterranean Basin		
MEP	Member of the European Parliament	UNFPA	UN Fund for Population Activities
		UNGASS	UN General Assembly Special Session
MERCOSUR	A regional arrangement for promoting trade and investment in the 'Southern Cone' countries of Latin America	UNHCR	United Nations High Commissioner for Refugees
		UNICEF	UN Children's Fund
NGDO	Non-Governmental Development Organisation	UNIDO	United Nations Industrial Development Organisation
NGO	non-governmental organisation	UNIFEM	United Nations Development Fund for Women
NIS	Newly Independent States – refers to the countries of former USSR		
		UNSCAP	UN System Conferences Action Plan
NORAD	Norwegian official aid agency		
NPV	net present value	Uruguay Round	Last round of multilateral trade negotiations under the GATT
NZODA	New Zealand's Overseas Development Assistance Programme		
		USAID	United States Agency for International Development
OATU	Organisation of African Trade Union Unity	WFP	World Food Programme
		WHO	World Health Organisation
ODA	Official Development Assistance – official aid, of which at least 25% is a grant, with the promotion of economic development or welfare as the main objective	WID	Women in Development
		WSSD	World Summit on Social Development held in Copenhagen in March 1995
OECD	Organisation for Economic Cooperation and Development	WTO	World Trade Organisation

Exchange rates

Annual average US dollar exchange rates for DAC countries

DAC countries	Currency	1994	1995	1996
Australia	Dollars	1.3691	1.3496	1.2769
Austria	Schillings	11.4190	10.082	10.5788
Belgium	Francs	33.4650	29.4972	30.9755
Canada	Dollars	1.3659	1.3728	1.3638
Denmark	Kroner	6.3597	5.6038	5.7982
Finland	Markkaa	5.2233	4.3666	4.5923
France	Francs	5.5521	4.9908	5.1158
Germany	Deutschmark	1.6218	1.4338	1.5047
Ireland	Punt	0.6697	0.6245	0.6254
Italy	Lire	1612.7000	1629.0	1543.0442
Japan	Yen	102.2300	94.07	108.8170
Luxembourg	Francs	33.4650	29.4972	30.9755
Netherlands	Guilder	1.8197	1.6050	1.6861
New Zealand	Dollars	1.6871	1.5240	1.4536
Norway	Kroner	7.0565	6.3372	6.4574
Portugal	Escudos	166.0400	149.93	154.2134
Spain	Pesetas	133.9600	124.69	126.6909
Sweden	Kroner	7.7157	7.1336	6.7071
Switzerland	Francs	1.3671	1.1823	1.2361
United Kingdom	Pounds Sterling	0.6533	0.6336	0.6408
CEC	ECU	0.8402	0.7652	0.7878

Source: OECD

Notes on Country At a Glance data

How much aid does country x give?

Country x gave
US$ source: OECD DAC Press release 18 June 1997;
national currency source: *Reality of Aid* questionnaires from each participating agency;
percentage of GNP source: OECD DAC Press release 18 June 1997 (1996);
percentage of public expenditure source: OECD National Accounts 1960–95 and DAC Report 1996, Table 14 (1995). This figure is a calculation of ODA as a % of 'government final consumption' and should give a fair comparison across different countries;
per capita is a calculation of total ODA divided by total population. ODA volume (1996) from OECD DAC press release 18 June 1997 and population from DAC Report 1996, Table 48.

Is it going up or down?
Source for 1996 volume compared with 1995: OECD DAC press release, 18 June 1997. The figures are in current prices, that is they have not been adjusted for inflation and exchanges rates. The percentage change is in real terms, namely taking inflation and exchange rates into account. Sources for 1996 percentage compared with 1995 outlook: OECD DAC press release, 18 June 1997 and *Reality of Aid* questionnaires.

How does country x compare with the other 21 donors?
Source for ranking for volume and GNP: OECD DAC press release 18 June 1997 (1996 figures);
source for low income countries (LICs) (1995 figures): OECD DAC Report 1996, Table 42;
source for private flows: OECD DAC Report 1996, Table 13; and
source for total flows (1995 figures): OECD DAC Report 1996, Table 13.

How much does country x spend on basic health and basic education?
Source: OECD DAC Report 1996, Table 27 (1994 figures).

How important are commercial interests in aid?
Source for fully tied aid as a percentage of total ODA: OECD DAC Report, Table 31 (1994 figures).

What does the public think about aid?
Source: Reality of Aid Questionnaires

DAC averages explained
Donors frequently refer to the DAC average when discussing their aid as a percentage of GNP. Fifteen out of 21 donors can claim to have exceeded the DAC average in 1996. But this figure does not really give a true picture of the generosity of DAC donors. This is because the average is arrived at by adding the GNP of all DAC donors and dividing this by donors' combined ODA. This produces a weighted average – which tends to be skewed downwards by the poor aid/GNP ratios of large donors such as the USA and Japan.

NGOs believe that an unweighted average (a simple average of the GNP percentage of all donors) produces a fairer picture of donors' relative generosity. Recently, the DAC has been quoting this figure – which it refers to as average country effort – more widely. Using this test of performance, only six donors exceed average performance.

For the sake of consistency, Country at a Glance charts show the (weighted) DAC average. The World Aid at a Glance charts show the (weighted) DAC average as a line, but also plots the (unweighted) average country effort, showing the discrepancy between the two figures.

For more information on any of these data please contact: Development Initiatives, Old Westbrook Farm, Evercreech, Somerset, BA4 6DS, UK. Tel + 44 (0) 1749 831141. Fax + 44 (0) 1749 831467 and e-mail: devinit@gn.apc.org